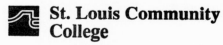

THE END OF CINEMA
AS WE KNOW IT

EDITED BY JON LEWIS

THE END OF CINEMA
AS WE KNOW IT

American Film in the Nineties

New York University Press • *New York*

NEW YORK UNIVERSITY PRESS
New York and London

© 2001 by New York University

Library of Congress Cataloging-in-Publication Data
The End of cinema as we know it : American film in the nineties /
edited by Jon Lewis.
p.   cm.
Includes bibliographical references and index.
ISBN 0-8147-5160-1 (alk. paper) — ISBN 0-8147-5161-X (pbk. : alk. paper)
1. Motion pictures—United States—History. 2. Motion picture industry—
United States—History.   I. Lewis, Jon, 1955–
PN1993.5.U6 E53 2001
791.43'0973—dc21   2001003695

New York University Press books are printed on acid-free paper,
and their binding materials are chosen for strength and durability.

Manufactured in the United States of America

10 9 8 7 6 5 4 3 2 1

For Martha and the boys, Guy and Adam

Contents

The End of Cinema As We Know It and I Feel ...

An Introduction to a Book on Nineties American Film

Jon Lewis

ALMOST HALF A century ago, Jean-Luc Godard famously remarked, "I await the end of cinema with optimism." Lots of us have been waiting ever since for this prophecy to finally come true.

Nineties cinema was destined to be important even if it wasn't any good. History is sometimes driven by chronology. Events happen because the calendar turns a rare and significant page. The nineties featured two such significant calendar events. First there was the celebration of film's centenary. Surveys and retrospectives, reruns and retreads of old products and product lines were mounted in anticipation and celebration of the motion picture's one-hundred-year anniversary. The centenary brought proof positive, if such proof was still necessary, that movies were the dominant art form and format of the twentieth century. Scholars and journalists alike encouraged a reexamination of the classical American cinema, the auteur renaissance, the so-called new Hollywood with an eye on each moment's importance to "the American century." The studios viewed the centenary as an occasion for nostalgia and self-congratulation, two sentiments they have always found easy to muster.

From mid-decade on, the celebration of film's past gave way to the inevitable countdown to the millennium. Films staging the end of the world proved to be exciting, profitable, and fun. Toying for an hour or two with some sort of revelation and rapture reflected and refracted a culture that awaited the end of this or that with irony if not optimism. The millennium (on and off screen) promised a sort of cosmic spring-cleaning. Cinema loomed as a possible casualty. But nobody seemed all that worried. It wasn't like there'd be nothing for us to watch in the movies' absence.

The way films were made and exhibited changed significantly at century's end. The vast twenty-first-century entertainment market-place now features all sorts of new audiovisual products and new ways to consume them (over and over again). Films, some of which are not exactly "films," can now be projected on screens in significantly re-vamped theaters, in homes on big, highly resolved TVs with multi-channel and multispeaker home entertainment setups, on little screens in minivans and on home computers, or on private, personal viewers we can strap on like those telephones travel agents use. But with all this new gear, and all sorts of new product, will we necessarily get different, better movies? Or might we someday in the not so distant future look back on the '90s with nostalgia and wonder how things might have been different, if . . . ? This book assumes the historic importance of nineties American cinema and endeavors to examine the key films and filmmakers, the corporate players and industry trends, film styles, and audiovisual technologies . . . cinema as we once knew it before the dust of the twentieth century had fully and finally settled.

SOME QUICK OBSERVATIONS ON THE NINETIES

The movie business in the nineties was characterized by an increasing concentration of industrial power among a select group of multina-tional players. Relevant here are four big mergers—Time and Warner Communications, Paramount Communications and Viacom, the Dis-ney Corporation and Capital Cities/ABC, and Time Warner and Turner Broadcasting (a deal complicated further by an end-of-the-century merger-in-principle with America Online). To this growing conglomer-ation and vertical and horizontal integration, we can add some signifi-cant inter-industry developments: strategic alliances between Internet companies, telephone carriers, cable television outfits, and what were once upon a time just film studios.

Nineties Hollywood was dominated by five companies that con-trolled the industry more completely than the old studio trusts ever did. This conglomeration was accompanied by growing internationaliza-tion. As the importance of foreign markets increased, Japanese, French,

Australian, Canadian, and Italian companies, at one time or another during the decade, took control of a major "American" film studio. By decade's end the term "American film" had become relative, perhaps even obsolete.

New technologies radically changed production, distribution and exhibition. *Forrest Gump* (1994), one of the biggest hits of the decade, ably exploited computer-generated imagery, so much so it made possible, even inevitable, a future cinema in which location shooting and live production might become obsolete. More and more multiplexes were equipped with one or another variant of digital, Dolby sound. The result was not only higher-quality film exhibition but an increasing production emphasis on action-based sound effects (*whammies*, producer Joel Silver calls them), pop music packages, and MTV video and recording company tie-ins.

Exhibition technologies impacted significantly on motion picture production. Much of what we saw on screen—*The Rock* (1996), for example, or better yet *The Matrix* (1999)—was made to suit and exploit the new sound and image capabilities of the modern movie house.

But despite these improvements, there are plenty of indications that "going to the movies" may be on its way out. A vast array of sophisticated home box office delivery systems and exhibition software and hardware became available in the nineties: hardline cables carrying digital signals, advanced home-TV satellite dishes, the perfect and convenient and cheap DVD, big TV screens and home entertainment components. Proposed tie-ins with tele-computer home information systems in development (and much in the financial news) at decade's end promised to destabilize the theatrical filmgoing experience even further. We can now envision a not so distant future in which we will never have to leave our houses to see a movie. The rare movie we will leave our houses to see will be exhibited in dramatically new formats (like today's IMAX) or at new and different sorts of venues (with five-star restaurants, with theme park attractions in the lobby).

What made certain films and filmmakers important in the nineties had less to do with relative quality than with success in the marketplace, a success complicated and multiplied exponentially by merchandising, global distribution, ancillary formats, and the multitude of delivery and exhibition systems. The important films were those that seemed to use filmmaking technology best, films that declared in their very form and format their status as contemporary, new, or different.

With each big film the ante was upped with regard to special effects, (pseudo-) realism, even gross-outs. Film production resembled nothing so much as a high-stakes poker game, a game in which all the players bet heavy on the audience's continued desire to see and hear bigger and louder movies. It was a strategy that carried with it the promise of astronomical profits and paydays. But as every good card player and every savvy industry player knows, it was also a strategy that required lots of cash on hand. Only players with enough money to safely play in such a high-stakes game had any chance of walking away from the table a winner.

THE END OF CINEMA AS WE KNOW IT

Just as the 1990s came to a close, I wrote to some friends and colleagues who I think write persuasively on contemporary film and I asked them to take one quick shot at the decade past.

The thirty-four essays that comprise this book are their responses. I insisted on brief essays, but that was about all I did to determine things in advance. So, while this anthology does not necessarily present a comprehensive tour through the decade, it does offer an indication of what films, what events, what stories, what signs of a future with or without cinema most interested film scholars at the end of the 1990s.

The first part, "Movies, Money, and History," includes Thomas Elsaesser's "The Blockbuster: Everything Connects, but Not Everything Goes," my essay, "Those Who Disagree Can Kiss Jack Valenti's Ass," Jan-Christopher Horak's "The Hollywood History Business," and Murray Pomerance's "The Man Who Wanted to Go Back." These essays examine the ways film history (its unfolding, its preservation, and its retelling) has become inextricably tied to corporate matters. The ways films were made, released, and screened, policed and censored, preserved and restored in the nineties—how film history was made and remembered—bear out that, in the final analysis, in Hollywood, it's always about the money.

"Things American (Sort Of)," the second section, speaks to the increasingly misleading term "American film." Few films these days are made in Hollywood. And while most of the studios maintain corporate offices in Los Angeles, the financing, production, distribution, and exhibition of so-called American films have become so complex and international these days that geographic borders seem quite beside the point. The three essays in this part—Charlie Keil's "'American' Cinema in the 1990s and Beyond: Whose Country's Filmmaking Is It Anyway?" Justin Wyatt's "Marketing Marginalized Cultures: *The Wedding Banquet*, Cultural Identities, and Independent Cinema of the 1990s," and Hilary Radner's "Hollywood Redux: *All about My Mother* and *Gladiator*"— focus on how American cinema in the nineties, in terms of investment as well as on-screen content, was a global affair.

With the decade only just ending as work on this project began, the task of identifying certain films as somehow the most important, the most indicative of what lay ahead was very much the stuff of educated guesswork. Time will tell whether the contributors to part 3 have chosen films that spoke specifically and only to a certain place and time or if they have identified films that will emerge as classics of a certain style or type of filmmaking that took root in the United States in the last years of the twentieth century. In part 3, "Four Key Films," Pat Mellencamp, Henry A. Giroux and Imre Szeman, Eric S. Mallin, Frank P. Tomasulo, and Krin Gabbard provide the following short list: *The Matrix, Fight Club* (1999), *The Blair Witch Project* (1999), and *Saving Private Ryan* (1998). What does such a list of important if not good, of indicative if not classic, films tell us about the nineties? What does the list tell us about American cinema as we once knew it, about a new American "cinema" that threatened to emerge at century's end?

It is axiomatic that nineties films—commercial nineties films, at least—were apolitical. A commitment to political correctness at the studios and at the MPAA led to a watering down of content. This was less a political than an economic strategy, as inoffensive films can be marketed to the largest possible audience. The five essays in part 4, "Pictures and Politics," do little to refute the notion that, with regard to content, nineties American film went soft politically. Instead, these essays reveal the different ways politics on and in films became an issue. In "The Confusions of Warren Beatty," Dana Polan examines the complex politics of celebrity. Thomas Doherty, in his essay, "Movie Star Presidents," focuses on the representation of politics on screen. Like Polan, Doherty examines how politics in the nineties became the stuff of cinematic spectacle, subsumed, confused, and conflated with celebrity images. Maureen Turim's essay, "The Fantasy Image: Fixed and Moving," discusses the official, federal political reaction to on-screen images, their alleged connection to and liability for the off-screen, on-the-street behavior of impressionable, violent-movie, computer-game–addicted youth. Ralph E. Rodriguez and Chon A. Noriega discuss films that fashion themselves as political, films targeted at niche markets inclined to consume politically liberal insights into the lives of peoples of color in North America. What both Rodriguez and Noriega argue is that even the best political intentions are thwarted by concessions to genre, conventional storytelling, and narrow and naïve attempts to rework time-worn ethnic stereotypes.

R. L. Rutsky's "Being Keanu," David R. Shumway's "Woody Allen, 'the Artist,' and 'the Little Girl,'" Marita Sturken's "*Affliction*: When Paranoid Male Narratives Fail," and Alexandra Juhasz's "The Phallus UnFetished: The End of Masculinity As We Know It in Late-1990s 'Feminist' Cinema" all take aim at one of the decade's most talked about topics, the apparent crisis of masculinity in nineties culture. Rutsky and Shumway focus on two very different male celebrities: the transcendentally handsome and inscrutable star Keanu Reeves and the consistently newsworthy New York Jewish comic actor, writer, and director Woody Allen. Sturken sets her sights on a single indicative film, *Affliction* (1997). The film, like the Russell Banks novel on which it is based, focuses on a fruitless battle between an abusive father and an underachieving son—two all too familiar nineties men bound by blood and despair. In "The Phallus UnFetished," Juhasz closes the chapter by examining two very popular and different films: *Fight Club* and *South Park: Bigger, Longer and Uncut* (1999). That these two films represent "male trouble" in the nineties in some interesting or important way dauntingly satisfies the essence of the essay's subtitle: it's "the end of masculinity as we know it."

Cinema is of course a visual medium, and as such it has from its start been engaged in setting the standards of physical beauty, even perfection. In part 6, "Bodies at Rest and in Motion," Elizabeth Young and Jerry Mosher examine another sort of cinematic body: the deformed, reformed, or just fat. In the body of the female monster in the 1935 film *Bride of Frankenstein* (brought back to life again in two very different nineties films, *Frankenhooker*, 1990, and *Gods and Monsters*, 1998), Young finds a deft game with gender and homosociality. Mosher examines the ways certain nineties films depict and exploit images of fat people. Because overweight bodies are so unusual in obsessively fit Hollywood, fat has become an easy way of identifying film characters as outsiders, as objects of rejection, humor, or if they're lucky, pity and sympathy.

Much was made in the nineties of a supposed indie revolution. After all, a handful of independently produced and released titles did well at the Academy Awards and at the box office. Some of the decade's most memorable movies (*The Blair Witch Project* and *Being John Malkovich*, 1999, come immediately to mind here) were made and distributed by so-called independents. But economic analysis hardly bears out such optimism about an emerging alternative American cinema. The nineties saw a decline in the number of indie distributors and the purchase of premier indie outlets by conglomerate studios. The four contributors to part 7, titled "Independents," take a long hard look at the alternative scene at the end of the century. Their accounts are, collectively, hardly upbeat. In his Independent Feature Project (Independent Spirit Award) speech, writer-producer James Schamus rants about the impossibility of independence in the contemporary marketplace. Robert Sklar shares Schamus's frustration as he too contends that the 1990s indie scene was far too closely tied economically and formally to traditional studio product lines. Sklar finds independence only at the far margins of Hollywood, in, for example, the intentionally offensive *oeuvre* of Harmony Korine. To find the independent spirit, Kathleen McHugh and Murray Smith venture even further from the studio mainstream. McHugh's discussion of Cheryl Dunye's *The Watermelon Woman* (1996) and Smith's examination of Wayne Wang's adaptation of Paul Auster's *Smoke* (1995) and *Blue in the Face* (1995) suggest that independence is rooted not in production budgets or in distribution strategies but in a certain way of making movies, a production grammar that was once dubbed a new American cinema.

The essays in part 8, "Not Films Exactly," focus on works even further from the mainstream, even further from the traditional setting of the movie theater. Chuck Kleinhans's "Pamela Anderson on the Slippery Slope" examines the decade's most talked about "film"—the home video of celebrities Pamela Anderson and Tommy Lee's honeymoon vacation. The distribution and exhibition (transmission, downloading) of the honeymoon tape, Kleinhans maintains, promise all sorts of problems and products for the future—films that aren't really films made available instantaneously to anyone with a modem and an Internet connection. Hamid Naficy focuses on the only other amateur video to attain as much nationwide interest: the beating of Rodney King by several officers from the LAPD. Naficy takes a provocative look at this much-seen artifact, arguing in part that the video operated in terms of familiar, fictional cinematic images of people of color in American cities today. In "Live Video," Laura U. Marks ventures to the museum to find films that aren't exactly films. An offshoot of performance art and performance video, "live video" is the stuff of mixing and matching new technologies to provide an expressive and inexpensive alternative to Hollywood-style filmmaking.

The contributors to part 9, "Endgames," take the collection's title seriously. Christopher Sharrett, Heather Hendershot, Paul Arthur, and Wheeler Winston Dixon spell out the end of cinema in terms of postmodern irony, cynicism, and exhaustion; religious fundamentalism and fanaticism made widely accessible by clever entrepreneurship and media savvy; the doomsday formulas in disaster-genre pictures and the cinematic stagings of Armageddon in popular Hollywood films; and finally the decline (into oblivion) of what we once used to call film culture.

At the risk of complicating matters here at the start, perhaps this is not the end of cinema but rather a transitional period from one new American cinema to another. Perhaps what we are seeing are only new material conditions under which film history will persist. American film has always had a tendency toward repetition (of styles, stars, genres). Even such significant technological developments as the advent of sound, color, and the introduction of TV have only revealed the flexibility and resilience of the industry and the medium it produces.

The basic corporate structure that makes and delivers American films is stronger than ever. If there is to be an end of cinema, I am sure it is something these few companies have planned for and are now engineering. Maybe optimism isn't the right term here . . . Godard was just being clever anyway. So long as there is so much money at stake and at risk, we can all relax. Even if films will soon no longer exactly be films, even if cinema is once and for all (in some specific, narrow way) really dead, it's not like there will be nothing for us to pay for and watch in the future. The likes of Time Warner and Disney will see to that.

PART I

MOVIES, MONEY, AND HISTORY

I

The Blockbuster

Everything Connects, but Not Everything Goes

Thomas Elsaesser

EVERYTHING CONNECTS

About two-thirds of the way into *Jurassic Park* (1992), there is a scene where Hamond and Sattler talk in the Jurassic Park restaurant about the nature of illusion and reality. The scene begins, however, with the camera exploring the adjacent gift shop. It is a slightly eerie moment, because it is as if the movie was at this point turning round and looking at us, but in the future tense. Set within a theme and adventure park, which exists only as a fiction, the film invites us to imitate the visitors in the fiction. Insofar as this fiction of a fiction will produce "real memorabilia," the film is itself an advertisement for the games, gadgets, and toys that one can buy after seeing the movie. It therefore does not come as a surprise to learn that six months before the release of the film, Amblin Films issued a *Jurassic Park* style book for advertisers and merchandisers, which alone cost $500,000 to produce.

In today's media world—to paraphrase E. M.Forster—everything connects. A feature film, a theme park, a toy store, and a computer game have a lot in common: they feed off each other as they play off each other. When one considers that *The Lion King* (1994) took $80 million at the box office, but made $220 million as a videocassette, one can understand why commentators have argued that a film today is merely a billboard stretched out in time, designed to showcase tomorrow's classics in the video stores and the television reruns. *Jurassic Park* may make the intermedia connections more explicit than most, insofar as it mimics the links within its own fiction, but it also shows that if everything connects, this does not mean that anything goes.

Big, loud, and expensive: Spielberg's perfect blockbuster, *Jurassic Park* (Universal, 1992).

And yet, since the 1980s, it was precisely as if anything did go and the sky was the limit. The New Hollywood staged such an extraordinary comeback from its premature burial and put on such a permanent revolution of the eternally same, that one has to ask, was it the charisma of the directors that did the trick? Or was it the new generation of stars, with their talent agents and deal makers? Was it the synergies with the music business, the new technologies of sound design, of special effects and digital imaging devices? To most observers, the answer to why the contemporary Hollywood cinema climbed back to popularity all over the world was simple: money. However, as one tries to understand the ebb and flow of all this cash, it also seems that money is very nearly that which blinds one's insights, and not merely because it catches one in an economic or even technological determinism. The energies that feed the system, the aggregates of power that circulate, the creative manias, cunning strategies, and ingenuity that animate the makers, as well as the fictions and fantasies that stir and attract audiences, may find in the exchange of money their most convenient and probably most banal materialisation. But the conglomerates being put together by the software firms, the music industries, the creative agencies, and broadcast television companies are on the brink of realizing—in both senses of the word: becoming aware of, and translating into action—not only economic clout but also political might. DreamWorks, the name that Spielberg, David Geffen, and Jerry Katzenberg have chosen for their new studio, is brilliantly and nonchalantly candid: the manufacture of dreams that "work" (i.e., "function," but also "do their job").

In order to explore what this job is, I want to look at some of the more internal or micro-links that alongside the macro-level synergies hold today's media culture together. If the macro-level comprises the profit-oriented connections, the micro-level encompasses the pleasure-oriented connections. At the macro-level, it is possible to distinguish further between the "horizontal" links, where everything connects in the world of entertainment and leisure (advertising, consumption, fashion, toys, as well as other aspects of popular or everyday culture), and the "vertical" ones, where everything connects at the level of business, industry, technology, and finance. More broadly speaking, the macro-level points to the relations that exist between the film industry and other forms of modern capitalist business practice, where the strategies of the multinationals do not differ all that much, whether they produce/sell cars or movies, silicon chips or television programs, computer software or stars, soft drinks and junk food or sounds and images.

The micro-level, on the other hand, is at first glance more mystifying, but not altogether mysterious: why do we go to the movies, rather than watch individual films? The micro-levels of pleasure highlight, among other things, the fact that as scholars we may have much at stake in the distinction between "film-as-text" and "film-as-event," but as audiences we evidently have quite pragmatically resolved one of the central but rarely asked questions of film studies, which is not whether a film is "art" or "entertainment," but whether films are "products" or "services."

PRODUCT DEFINITION: IS A FILM A COMMODITY OR A SERVICE?

The industry talk of money and profits, of merchandising and franchising, of tie-ins and spin-offs, of secondary markets and residual exploitation rights at once disguises and underlines what lies at the heart not only of contemporary Hollywood, but of the American film industry ever since its beginning: the struggle to define a product, to decide what it actually is that it is in the business of. The history of Hollywood could be written as the successive moves to install and define the *commodity "film,"* while at the same time extending and refining the *service "cinema."* As to the first, it has not always been as self-evident as it now seems that a strip of celluloid, a can of film, or "two hours spent in the dark" can be a commodity. As to the second point, the cinema had to oust and/or compete with other providers of the same service, whether we call it mass entertainment or performing arts, leisure activity or popular spectacle.

A commodity is something whose value to the consumer is both material and immaterial, something that both enhances the self and can be used to communicate or signify to others. A car, for instance, is a perfect commodity: its material value is as an individualized means of mass transport, but its immaterial value is that of a status symbol, and as a status symbol—say, a BMW—it enhances the self-(image) of the owner and signifies something to others (such as "irresponsible, unmarried thirty-something showing off"). These self-images and the meanings attached to them by the culture at large, however, are not fixed and eternal. They can change over time and are always embedded in history and ideology. In the 1970s, for instance, BMWs in Germany were known as Baader-Meinhof Wagen (after the names of the two leading members of a German terrorist group), because they were the preferred getaway cars during the group's frequent shoot-outs and bank robberies.

A film, on the other hand, was once quite difficult to define as a commodity, not only because what distinguishes the cinema from an automobile is the peculiar and remarkable convergence of money and culture, of commerce and art. It has also been difficult because a film essentially commodifies an experience, which by its nature is highly subjective and context-dependent. "Film," too, is material *and* immaterial, but in a combination that would seem to cut across the distinction between commodity and service, unless one defines the cinema as a "service supported by commodities." Going to the movies involves all kinds of things other than watching a film. It presupposes the simultaneous coexistence of two systems. One, we can now say, is concerned with turning an experience into a commodity: the film as it lives in the collective mind as an event. The other is concerned with providing a service: the theater, the comfortable seats, the ice cream and soft drinks, as they provide the pleasant atmosphere of simulated luxury for time out with friend or lover. Going to the movies is an activity in which the film is only one of the elements, and maybe sometimes not even the most crucial or memorable one. The cinema, once one looks at it as both an industry and a culture, is really these two systems sitting on top of each other, loosely connected, or rather connected in ways intriguingly intertwined. One is the system that links a space and a site to bodies endowed with perception via a certain set of expected and anticipated pleasures or gratifications. The other system is that which connects writers, directors, producers, cinematographers, actors, and moneymen around an activity called making a film. That the two systems have very little to do with each other is indicated by the fact that some filmmakers can make films that never get shown in cinemas, and some films do not get made until they are already sold to the cinemas. When one thinks of how many films get shown at festivals like Cannes or Berlin and how few of them end up getting general release, one cannot but conclude that the system is wasteful and doesn't work. It just does not seem to "connect" in a meaningful, rational way to audiences.

The structure of desire that the movies work on is a well-known one: we enjoy the cinema as legitimized voyeurism, accessing the lives of others, but we also apprehend the films as a mirror of the self. If this is a notoriously complex theoretical issue, it nonetheless also comes down to some simpler points, one of which is the importance of repetition, of doubling, which we can picture as a movement of enfolding or mise-en-abîme. The same as different: genre cinema and the norms of

story construction involve the self in remembered pleasure and anticipated memory, both of which lock the spectator into a kind of repetition
compulsion that ties the cinema experience to recollection and expectation. These shifting structures of temporality and the moment, of place
and space not only constitute key aspects of human subjectivity, they
generate a subjectivity (in the form of "desire" or "fantasy") that can be
attached to objects and products. This is what we understand by "commodity fetishism," because what defines the commodity in this context
is precisely the ability of an object to attract and fix a desire or a fantasy.
When buying a movie ticket, we are effectively taking out a contract, by
which in exchange for our money, we are guaranteed (temporary access
to) a normative, quality-controlled product. Conversely, our part of the
deal is to be prepared to pay: not for the product itself and not even for
the commodified experience it represents, but simply for the possibility
that such a transubstantiation of experience into commodity might
"take place." Neither the term "product" nor "service," neither the idea
of "consumption" nor the concept of "leisure" quite capture the nature
of this act of faith.

THE BLOCKBUSTER: HOLDING IT ALL TOGETHER

On the face of it, it is the blockbuster in its contemporary form that combines (in the most exemplary but also the most efficient form) the two
systems (film-as-production/cinema-as-experience), the two levels
(macro-level of capitalism/micro-level of desire), and the two aggre-
gate states of the cinema experience (commodity/service). When, on a
Friday night, we go to the movies, what do we want to see? Nine times
out of ten it will be the big movie, which has announced itself like a
weather front weeks before, by the turbulence it creates in the news
media, the novelty shops, and the department stores. In short, we want
to see the movie that promises to be an event. This movie may have
many different titles, but essentially it has one generic name: it's called
a blockbuster. What characterizes a blockbuster? First, a big subject and
a big budget (world war, disaster, end of the planet, monster from the
deep, holocaust, death battle in the galaxy). Second, a young male hero,
usually with lots of firepower, or secret knowledge, or an impossibly
difficult mission. The big movie is necessarily based on traditional stories, sometimes against the background of historical events, more often

a combination of fantasy or sci-fi, with the well-known archetypal heroes from Western mythology on parade. In one sense, this makes blockbusters the natural, that is, technologically more evolved, extension of fairy tales. In another sense, these spectacle "experiences," these "media events," are also miracles, and not at all natural. Above all, they are miracles of engineering and industrial organization. They are put together like supertankers, aircraft carriers or skyscrapers, office blocks, shopping malls. They resemble military campaigns, and that's one of the main reasons they cost so much to make.

It is a notorious fact that the cost of moviemaking has spiraled to astronomical heights. Today, the sort of movie that premieres under the conditions just described costs between $80 and $120 million to make, with some like *Titanic* (1997) consuming as much as $200 million. That's enough to build 4,000 homes, provide uncontaminated drinking water for 600,000 people for one year, or rewire the telephone system of an entire city the size of Rome. In fact, the only other kind of product that costs as much—and on the scale of basic human necessities is as frivolous as a movie—is an assault helicopter, a set of intercontinental missiles in a submarine, or an atomic test on the Muraroa Atoll in the Pacific. And at this level, the Hollywood story has much in common with the arms race. What Hollywood has done is to have continually raised the stakes: by making filmmaking ever more costly and extravagant, it has made sure that the number of competitors has become smaller and smaller. Of course, I am exaggerating. But the high cost of moviemaking is rather like the membership fees to country clubs and golf courses: it is designed to keep out the undesirables, the upstarts. It is designed to keep most of the world's countries from being able to afford a film industry. And it keeps most of the world's independent filmmakers from getting their films into the cinemas. Once upon a time, European nations could afford a film industry. Today, with the possible exception of France, none can: not Italy, not Spain, not Britain, not Germany. Once upon a time, second-run cinemas and art houses would show independent productions. Now, not even the multiplexes keep one screen out of their fifteen for the art crowd, unless it happens to be for a movie that has garnered a prize at Cannes, Venice, Berlin, or Rotterdam.

Via its stranglehold on exhibition outlets, the American film industry has achieved the extraordinary feat of being able to open the same film in thousands of theaters on the same Friday night, and within the same month all over the globe. Why should such a feat be desirable in the first place? The answer, of course, lies in the shifting economics of international box office earnings. While Hollywood in the 1940s and 1950s could recover its production costs in the huge U.S. home market alone, so that export earnings were pure profit, over the last ten to fifteen years, the foreign markets have accounted for more than 50 percent of the U.S. film industry's total earnings, making economies of scale in the advertising and marketing of a big-budget picture not only desirable but essential.

Not unconnected with the changes in exhibition is a third development by which such tactics of synergy—the new name for vertical integration—have revived the fortunes of New Hollywood. Synergies not only occurred through the new management practices in the production sector (fewer, but more expensive, one-offs and prototypes) and the control of cinema exhibition via the hegemony in distribution. Synergy also affected the management of the software libraries, meaning the exploitation of film and TV rights via cable stations, or the "dumping" practices on foreign (TV-) markets, such as the repackaging of repeats on TV-Gold. The explosive growth of TV channels has proved the importance of owning these libraries: even if a studio was bankrupt, as MGM was, even if all its physical assets had been sold or dispersed, it was still a gold mine because of the rights to old content. Hence Tino Balio's assertion: "If you're a big corporation you can *never not* make money with movies." This contrasts with the conclusion drawn by James Schamus (producer and screenwriter of *The Ice Storm*, 1997): "If you are an independent production company, then you can *never* make money with movies, even if they are successful at the box office and with critics." Why this difference?

The answer lies in the fact that the new integration/synergy model can be seen as a sort of pinball machine. The principle behind it would be something like this: you launch with great force the little steel ball, shoot it to the top, and then you watch it bounce off the different contacts, pass through the different gates, and whenever it touches a contact, your winning figures go up. The media entertainment business is such a pinball machine: the challenge is to "own" not only the steel ball, but also as many of the contacts as possible because the same "ball" gets you ever higher scores, that is, profits. The contact points are the cinema screens and video stores, theme parks and toy shops, restaurant chains and video arcades, bookstores and CD record shops. By contrast, the independent producer only has his little steel ball, and if he is not careful, he has to stand by and watch as all the others owning the contact points make money off his/her film. Describing the same phenomenon, Siegfried Zielinski uses an interestingly different metaphor: for him, a film is a *Durchlauferhitzer,* a machine that heats up cold water, brings it to the boil, and then lots of people turn on the tap and out comes a shower.

Combined with television, cable, home video, and DVD, what the cinema heats up is the temperature of popular culture, by giving certain of its products (brand name) recognition value. After bringing together text production and social experience, capital and desire, commodity and service, the blockbuster generates recognition value and thus cultural capital. Yet as a generator of cultural capital, it is not only a moneymaking but also a meaning-making machine. A third characteristic of the blockbuster is therefore that it is a movie engineered for maximum meaning, which is to say its different parts function as a cultural database, in a process that is both "analytical" (it breaks down culture into separate items and individual traits) and "synthetic" (it is capable of apparently reconciling ideologically contradictory associations). Often, the parts are attractions, which come together in the film's story line, but which in the process of marketing can be exploited separately. Sometimes, the parts are cultural assets, assembled specially for the occasion, validating and authenticating everything they touch. And invariably, the floor plan or chassis is the myths and templates of religion and Western culture. My tag that "everything connects," but not "everything goes" alludes to the fact that whoever the guests at the party, in the minds and bodies of the audience, the parts must reassemble themselves: their final "fit" is what makes the movie an event.

CATCH THEM YOUNG, KEEP THEM FOREVER: THE DISNEY FORMULA AND THE SPIELBERG CONCEPT

This final fit returns me to the "internal connections" or the micro-level. For not only the money, the corporate clout, the production values, or the stars make a movie "big." It is what these entities represent, what they can "realize." If delivery of recognition value or cultural capital is the way the "market" puts it, the more metaphysical move would be to say that what these values, accumulated in the blockbuster, realize is "time"—paradoxically, not so much the time of the viewing of the film, but time past and time future.

Foremost among the strategies with which the blockbuster multiplies, but also organizes the different temporalities, are precisely the kinds of "doubling" or repetition effects with which I started. The souvenir-display-within-the-film, as in the example from *Jurassic Park*, is only one such enfolding. The same goes for the internal repetitions of the "film-within-the-film," as in the opening scenes of *Titanic*. Another modality would be the event-within-the-film doubling the situation of the viewer (as in the films that are released around Christmas and feature wintry celebrations, e.g., *Gremlins*, 1984), or the films that feature vacations and are released for the vacations, such as *Home Alone* (1990) and the granddaddy of all modern blockbusters, *Jaws* (1975).

The special thing about a film like *Jurassic Park*, then, is not the doubling itself, but how tightly all this enfolding activity is synchronized and orchestrated, how neatly the different aspects of engineering and technology, of entertainment and adventure, of fantasy and merchandising fit into each other around the time-shifting axis of past, present, and future. Such films systematically "double" the levels of their referentiality, making us aware that we exist in two places at once: watching a movie and remembering ourselves watching a movie. But instead of "breaking the illusion," the split actually deepens our fascination. It catches us in multiple mirrors, but it is not necessarily only a visual effect. The folding movement is also emotional and cognitive, in that it joins anticipation with repetition, and mimesis with memory. I am tempted to call this type of effect not mise-en-abîme, but to think of it as a sort of "situation-synergy"—to join all the other kinds of synergy discussed above.

One reason a blockbuster is so often concerned with topics of childhood and adolescence, with major disasters and the forces of nature is that it prefers themes that dramatize time and temporality, that connect the past with the future. But what America has learned from the European fairy tales is not only their insights into the world of childhood fears and longings, of wonder and the need to "return home." It has also appreciated the fact that if you get children used to something early, they'll stick with it all their lives. What we do in our formative years will always remain a utopia, maybe a backward utopia since we always will want to go home. To make our childhood synonymous with the cinema: this has been the secret of the Disney principle. Earlier than any other studio, the Disney Corporation had "realized" that the modeling—and marketing—of time is the cinema's deepest fantasy.

In Disney films and in Disneyland, it is always "now," and every film is an instant "classic." As such, the Disney principle looks set to be the global master plan: each generation of Americans since the 1930s has in effect not only grown up with Disney cartoons, but has had the first and formative encounter with the cinema thanks to one of the company's key films, from *Snow White* (1937) to *Fantasia* (1940), from *Bambi* (1942) to *Cinderella* (1950), from *The Jungle Book* (1967) to *The Lion King* (1994), from *Aladdin* (1992) to *The Hunchback of Notre Dame* (1996). Only George Lucas, with *Star Wars* (1977), and Spielberg—with *E.T.* (1982) and his DreamWorks productions—has tapped as deeply into the roots of this fantasy structure of generational time "doing its work." By successfully adapting the Disney formula, Spielberg has expanded it to include wars and human disasters (*Schindler's List*, 1993; *Saving Private Ryan*, 1998), the boundaries between the human and the prehuman or post-human (*Jaws, Jurassic Park, Close Encounters of the Third Kind*, 1977). His special effects, soundscapes, and animatronics have realized to its fullest illusion of presence the cinema's ability to connect past and future into a mythic "now," extending it to stories taken from history, and making even the disasters of the twentieth century fit family fare for the theme parks of the future.

In the contemporary scene the blockbuster thus provides a focus for many conflicting forces. One of the minor miracles is how it rivals nature, by dividing the year and ringing the changes of the seasons. The big movies now colonize the holidays, such as Christmas and Easter, and they announce the summer vacation or the start of fall. Bringing home history, they are also becoming chronometers, the synchronizing gears of a media temporality that in many ways pick up on the mythic rhythms of the celestial clocks our ancestors used to live by: Stonehenge, the Pyramids, from DreamWorks to ClockWorks. As a billboard, pinball machine, or hot-water heater, a blockbuster may be the sign of a new kind of "vertical integration" in the audiovisual and entertainment industries. As pop and folkculture's timepiece, both at the level of the day-to-day and at the life-cycle level of childhood and its eternal returns, blockbusters want to be nothing less than our lifecalendar. The mise-en-abîme effect with which I started also works the other way round: movies take our everyday habits "by the hand" and mirror or fold them into so many temporalities and lifelines that our lives are at once miniaturized and magnified. Time as duration and time as intensity no longer appear to oppose each other, *chronos* and *kairos* come together in the space of the moment that mystics have always known about: the epiphany.

After the possible macro-links around the deals, the synergies and the diversifications, the point about the micro-links is therefore at once simple and complex. Between past and future, between childhood and parenthood, mainstream cinema has found its cultural function as the world's time machine, with the blockbuster the "engine" that simultaneously raises expectations, stirs memories, and unites us with our previous selves. Across mythical stories of disaster and renewal, trauma and survival, it thus reconciles us to our mortality. That is a tall order for the movies, but in a world where money is the bottom line and entertainment the generator of sky-high profits, the movies taking on the mandate of heading our secular redemption may not be too much to ask, not even of Hollywood. There, we are told, anything goes, but what matters is that sometimes it even connects.

2

Those Who Disagree Can Kiss Jack Valenti's Ass

Jon Lewis

> Salman Rushdie commented that the reason the State frequently wars
> with its artists is because the two represent two conflicting versions of
> the truth. . . . We of course do not have government censors—that
> would be totalitarian. It would also be unnecessary. What we do have
> is the MPAA.   —Wes Craven, filmmaker

IN THE SUMMER of 1999, two big films reached local theaters after celebrated bouts with the MPAA's Classification and Rating Administration (CARA): Stanley Kubrick's last film, *Eyes Wide Shut*, and Trey
Parker's animation feature, *South Park: Bigger, Longer and Uncut*.[1] First
cuts of both films received the NC-17 rating and, because of their contracts with their studio distributors, Kubrick and Parker cut their films
in order to obtain an R rating.

Kubrick's film is about the impact of sexual fantasies on even the
most perfect of couples and the ways sexual and erotic images both real
and imagined play on all of our minds. The nudity and sexual content
in *Eyes Wide Shut* were thus hardly, to coin the silly industry parlance,
gratuitous. (I'd argue that nudity and sexual content are never gratuitous. Cinema is a visual medium. No image, especially an erotic image,
however irrelevant to a film's plot, is, in the larger scheme of things cinematic, gratuitous.)

In order to obtain an R rating from the CARA board, Kubrick supervised the addition of computer-generated figures to obstruct our
view of the action during a long and wholly unerotic orgy scene.[2] While

23

Kubrick's distributor, Warner Brothers, insisted that not a single frame was cut—which is, after all, technically true—the effect of the computer-generated obstruction is comical. Indeed, the computer-generated figures seem only to be *standing in* for the CARA board, watching the film as we watch it, putting their torsos—their shrouded figures—in our way as we try to see what it is they can see that we can't. Jack Valenti, the MPAA's longtime president and CEO, maintains absolute secrecy concerning the identities of the CARA board members. The image of these board members as shadowy, shrouded figures seems at once appropriate and ironic.

When a number of well-known film reviewers complained about the computer graphics, Warner Brothers cochairman Terry Semel offered a succinct response: "We're not in the NC-17 business. NC-17 is a whole industry. It includes triple-X-rated porno films. So to us that's just not a business that we're in."[3] Semel's quip is disingenuous on so many levels it is difficult to know where to start. The NC-17 cut of the Warner Brothers film, released without the computer gimmick, was in theaters in Europe at the very moment Semel made his remark. In 2001, Warner Brothers released the "director's cut" on video and DVD. From the very start the plan at Warner Brothers was to cash in a second time on a film that really isn't very good the first time you see it. And that's fine with the MPAA, Semel, and the executives and shareholders at Time Warner.

A second question begs asking here. Why didn't Semel and Time Warner want the public to know that they are indeed in the NC-17 business? The NC-17 designation is a perfectly legitimate CARA classification. Its copyright is held by the MPAA. It was adopted in 1990 to classify and by classification legitimize studio-produced adults-only films. The first film released with an NC-17 tag was Philip Kaufman's *Henry and June* (1990), a frank if not all that graphic retelling of Henry Miller's adventures in Paris with two sexually liberated women, his wife, June, and fellow author Anaïs Nin. At the time, it seemed the perfect film to introduce the new designation: *Henry and June* was a gorgeously shot, serious bio-pic by a director with a considerable reputation.[4] It was a hard film to dismiss as just porn, but it was also a difficult and expensive art movie about an all too little-known American writer with no stars and no high concept. Though the NC-17 got *Henry and June* into the legit marketplace, the film, for reasons that had nothing to do with its rating, failed to make much of an impact at the box office.

In the summer of 1999, American audiences didn't get to see all of Stanley Kubrick's *Eyes Wide Shut* (Warner Brothers, 1999). Warner Brothers chairman Terry Semel reassured parents that his company was "not in the NC-17 business," at least not in theaters in the United States.

The most famous and historically important NC-17 title ever released in the United States was not *Henry and June* but *Showgirls* (1995), a film so bad and stupid there aren't words. Even with big studio money and advertising behind it, *Showgirls* bombed at the box office. The studios blamed the NC-17 rating because it was easier than blaming the film's writer and director. After *Showgirls* flopped, NC-17 became the designation for films that fall through the cracks in the regulatory process—films that are so pervasively NC-17 there is no way for filmmakers to cut to suit the CARA board.

NC-17–rated films face significant industrial obstacles. They don't play in most mall theaters (where leasing agreements prohibit such fare) or at many multiplexes (for fear of folks sneaking in after paying to see another title). None of the premium pay-channels—HBO, Cinemax, Showtime, the Movie Channel, Starz, etc.—screen NC-17 films. Blockbuster Video and Kmart won't shelve NC-17–rated videos. The studios have their reasons for writing contracts that prohibit filmmakers from producing NC-17 films. But such an industrial policy has nothing to do with sex or morality or larger legal questions regarding censorship and obscenity. In Hollywood, or so the saying goes, "when they say it's not about the money . . . it's about the money."

Semel's press release defending the alteration of Kubrick's film reveals the contemporary industry's all too industrial bottom line. The flap over *Eyes Wide Shut*, as Semel coolly implied, was not really about the integrity of the film itself, or of films in general. Nor was it really about the practice of film censorship, which has persisted here in the United States in a variety of forms since before the turn of the twentieth century. It's about box office and ancillary revenues. It's about the generation of profits and the complex ways cine-regulation (engineered in this and most other such cases by the MPAA) is designed primarily to serve the studios' best interests.

Like all the other MPAA member studios, Warner Brothers is committed to, as New York film writer Armond White has described them, "soft . . . American, box office friendly" films. Studio executives do not necessarily like such fare, but they are convinced that such films are the only sort that make money these days.

CARA's objection to the orgy scene in the director's cut of *Eyes Wide Shut* was anticipated; it was consistent with its classification of other similar scenes in other studio films. Kubrick made the film knowing that the orgy scene would most likely be cut to suit the industry censors.

And he understood that when the CARA board listed certain changes he might make to secure an R rating, Warner Brothers would force him to make the cuts or find someone else to do it for him. Kubrick also had the implied (if not explicit, contractual) promise of a properly preserved director's cut of the film, which is a whole lot more and better than directors could expect in the good old days under the Production Code Administration (PCA).

When the New York critics came to Kubrick's defense—a defense seemingly made stronger, to be brutally honest here, when the legendary director died before *Eyes Wide Shut* was released—they had little hope of effecting a change in policy at the MPAA, CARA, or the studios. The CARA board and the film rating system it has overseen at the MPAA's behest since 1968 have been widely and justifiably credited with saving Hollywood. However compelling the critics' argument, and however essential they have become in the entertainment marketplace, their efforts on behalf of the film were doomed to failure.

In their letter to Semel, the New York film critics excoriated the Warner Brothers executive for failing to protect *Eyes Wide Shut* from the industry censorship board. Copies of the letter were sent to the editors of several major newspapers and the industry trades. The letter asked why, especially given the film's larger historical importance, had Semel and Warner Brothers allowed the MPAA and CARA to alter Kubrick's final statement on film? The critics of course knew precisely why Semel did what he did. He is, after all, just a studio executive and in this case he was just doing his job.

The MPAA supervises the self-regulation of film content and does so solely to protect studio products in the marketplace. Cooperation with the MPAA is in every instance a practical as well as symbolic gesture. In the very act of adding those robed figures in the orgy scene, Warner Brothers expressed its continued commitment to the network of relationships that comprise the MPAA. Semel got Kubrick to alter his film because the network of relationships (between studios and other studios, between studios and the vast majority of American theater owners) that is maintained by the MPAA is and always will be more important than the integrity of a single movie.

The MPAA film rating system is technically voluntary. Since the classifications imposed by CARA are not legally binding, theater owners are free—at least on constitutional grounds—to ignore them. Of course they don't, for fear of breaking faith with a larger set of industrial relations with the MPAA that work very much to their economic advantage.

The New York critics' letter called attention to the ways such a practical business policy and procedure might have a larger cultural or political dimension. They described the CARA board as "a punitive and restrictive force [that] effectively tramples the freedom of American filmmakers." It is, of course, but that's beside the point.

The critics' collective indignation is at the very least interesting, mostly as an example of how the industry actually works these days. The studios participate in the rating system because they believe it is good for business. But while the primary task of the rating system is to support industry profitability and vertical and horizontal integration, the MPAA and its member studios have done well to define its classification of movies publicly in terms of social responsibility. That the critics oppose such a system thus speaks less to their critique of corporate-based censorship executed by the MPAA than to a mostly unpopular defense of dirty movies. In this little psychodrama, the studios play the part of good corporate citizens and in doing so successfully represent corporate collusion as responsible public relations.

An unsettling by-product of the studios' collective commitment to the economic imperatives of a safe and sensible movie culture (as envisioned by the MPAA) is, as the critics note, a pervasive "kneejerk Puritanism." The network of cooperative and collusive arrangements between the MPAA and the National Association of Theater Owners (NATO) that has at its foundation the CARA system has required of filmmakers and studio executives alike the delivery of watered-down, dumbed-down products. The principal and sole virtue of such a system is that it insures that all G-, PG-, PG-13–, and R-rated films move freely and profitably through the vast entertainment marketplace. Thanks to the MPAA, the art of cinema is institutionally subsumed by and rendered secondary to commerce. It's a matter of policy and standard business procedure.

A separate letter protesting the cuts to *Eyes Wide Shut* penned by the Los Angeles Film Critics Association was addressed directly to Valenti and the MPAA. It was met with a swift, succinct, and decidedly undiplomatic response. In a widely circulated press release, Valenti dismissed the West Coast critics as "a small band of constant whiners [who] talk to each other, write for each other, opine with each other and view with lacerating contempt the rubes who live Out There, west of

Manhattan and east of the San Andreas fault." For all those critics who would deign to disagree, who would dare to call for a less rigid, less inconsistent, less rigged production code, there is but one alternative. As Armond White put it in a piece on the *Eyes Wide Shut* controversy, they "can kiss Jack Valenti's ass."[5]

I use the term "rigged" here for a reason. All film distributors who want to get their films into mainstream American theaters—theaters more likely than not owned by one of a handful of conglomerates—must submit their film to the MPAA for classification. If you are not a member of the MPAA—if you are an independent distributor or foreign film importer—you still have to submit your film to an organization run by and for the major Hollywood studios. If you don't, your film is technically "unrated" and you will have no hope of securing screenings nationwide. If you do, the classification imposed ostensibly by your competitors—competitors who already have more money than you do—will very much govern the way your film moves through the marketplace.

South Park: Bigger, Longer and Uncut is comprised entirely of construction paper cutouts, crude animation that serves to highlight the animators' crude sense of humor. The film was screened by the MPAA six times. The first five times, the film was returned to Paramount with an NC-17. The sixth time proved the charm.

Dialogue between CARA and the studios is by policy confidential. The MPAA offices in New York guard CARA transcripts. All records of the ratings board since its inception in 1968 are kept secret. Researchers are never granted access to official CARA materials because Valenti believes that revelation, analysis, and/or discussion of how or why CARA rates a film R or NC-17 might compromise the board's objectivity.

In what may well have been something of a publicity gimmick, a series of confidential memos sent by the CARA board to Parker and co-writer Matt Stone were leaked to the press. In one of the memos, reprinted in part in *Entertainment Weekly*, the filmmakers were asked to change a line of dialogue from "God fucking me up the ass" to "God's the biggest bitch of them all." After careful consideration, the board approved the use of the word "fisting," so long as its definition was excised. One board member had trouble figuring out whether or not he/she should be offended by a scene in which a cutout depiction

Animators Trey Parker and Matt Stone had to recut *South Park: Bigger, Longer and Uncut* (Paramount, 1999) five times in order to get an R rating.

of Winona Ryder does something seemingly unspeakable with ping pong balls. Subsequent correspondence from the animators pointed out that Ryder's paddle, revealed in the last shot of the sequence, was the source of her expertise. The board accepted the explanation and okayed the scene.

The source of the leak, it turned out, was the film's executive producer, Scott Rudin, whose frustration with the board no doubt speaks for a lot of creative people in Hollywood: "The [memos were] like *Alice in Wonderland*, it was so crazy. I realize they're good people trying to do a good job, but the MPAA's not meant to be some moral arbiter of an entire culture."

Rudin and Parker and Stone are all savvy industry players and they made the most of their little drama with Valenti and the CARA board. "Hands down, the MPAA made our movie more graphic and subversive," the directors have boasted (and taunted) in the press. "We should send a thank-you letter to Jack Valenti. Our movie's funnier because of him." The MPAA chief doesn't argue the point: "They're trashing [the

MPAA] to get attention for their film, and guess what? They have brilliantly succeeded."[6]

However mad Valenti gets at Parker and Stone, he is no doubt happy for Paramount. *South Park* was a huge hit for the studio, even without an accurate tally of the youngsters who bought tickets at their local multiplex to G-rated films like *Tarzan* (1999) and then snuck into *South Park* when the theater manager wasn't looking. Even when filmmakers make a mockery of the process, as Parker and Stone have, the rating system is there to help everyone to make money. In the heat of a ratings controversy, we tend to forget that the true measure of the system lies not in its treatment of specific scenes in specific movies but in its maintenance of the larger network of relationships (between studios and other studios, between studios and their own subsidiaries, between studios and exhibitors) that comprise the new Hollywood.

In a press release revisiting the letters written by the New York and Los Angeles critics in the summer of 1999, Valenti bristled: "When I invented this system, which is totally voluntary, it was not to placate critics—it was to protect parents. I haven't heard from a single parent who said, 'Gee, I wish you'd kept that orgy in there,' . . . The ratings board isn't infallible, but I don't understand why a bunch of critics are so certain that an orgy is something the rest of America would find casual. I think this system is doing exactly what it was intended to do."[7]

Valenti can afford to be so glib. The system is indeed doing exactly what it was designed to do. As we marvel at the success of the studios these days, we need to remember that once upon a time not so very long ago the studios were not making any money. They are now. And they have Jack Valenti, the MPAA, and the film rating system to thank for it.[8]

NOTES

1. A third film bears mention here, *American Pie* (1999), though the tussle with the ratings board was at once weirder and easier to resolve than the two films discussed here. Warren Zide, the producer of the R-rated teen comedy, reflected on his exchange with the folks at CARA: "We went back four times before we got an R . . . we had to get rid of a few thrusts when he's having sex with the apple pie. The MPAA was like 'Can he thrust two times instead of four?'"

2. Though Kubrick died before the film was released, he is said to have supervised the post-production of the orgy scene himself.

3. Andrew Essex, "NC-17 Gets an F," *Entertainment Weekly*, August 13, 1999, 21.

4. Kaufman also directed *The Right Stuff* and *The Unbearable Lightness of Being.*

5. Armond White, "Those Who Disagree Can Kiss Jack Valenti's Ass," *New York Press and Arts Listings*, August 4-10, 1999.

6. The feeling is mutual: Valenti called the animators "hairballs" in *Entertainment Weekly*. See David Hochman, "Putting the R in Park," *Entertainment Weekly*, July 9, 1999, 16.

7. Essex, "NC-17 Gets an F," 20–21.

8. This essay recasts material covered at significantly greater length in Jon Lewis, *Hollywood v. Hard Core: How the Struggle over Censorship Saved the Modern Film Industry* (New York: New York University Press, 2000).

3

The Hollywood History Business

Jan-Christopher Horak

IN THE 1990s, film history became a viable commodity for the enter-tainment industry that could be marketed on television and other elec-tronic media. Previously relegated to the realm of the fan book publish-ing industry and the academic press, the film historical narratives reached a relatively small number of consumers. However, the prolifer-ation of cable networks and other new media, and the concomitant de-velopment of ever more specialized and fragmented audiences, forced distributors to turn to the collective movie past.

Old movies and documentary programming about the entertain-ment industry are inexpensive, at least in comparison to the costs of de-veloping and producing new product. Networks like American Movie Classics, Turner Classic Movies, and TV Land specialize in presenting old movies and television and also exhibit film historical "infotain-ment" as "wrap-arounds," or as independent programming. Other cable channels like Arts and Entertainment, E! and MSNBC present star biographies, supposed "behind-the-scenes" looks at the stars of yester-day and today. With the end of cinema as it has been practiced in the last century in sight, the history of the medium has gained currency on TV.

Such a glorified and schematized view of Hollywood film history had already been successfully peddled in theme parks like Universal Studios, Disney-MGM Studios Florida, and the Paramount Parks, theme restaurants like Planet Hollywood, and gambling casinos in Las Vegas and along the Mississippi. With the introduction of DVDs, the major studios have rushed to create added value for their most popu-lar catalogue titles with the production of film historical shorts. The Internet, apart from providing home pages for all the entertainment companies, has rapidly expanded a collector's market engaged in the exchange of film memorabilia through auction sites such as eBay and Amazon.com. In order to service all these myriad businesses, in the 1990s the studios began founding their own archives to protect their historical assets. For the first time, the studios became concerned with their own history.

While Disney has had a small archive for Walt Disney's personal collection for more than twenty-five years, the first studio to found a full-fledged archive was Warner Brothers, which hired a curator in 1994. Fox followed suit in 1996. Its archivist was primarily responsible for the extensive memorabilia tour surrounding the release of *Titanic* in 1997. Universal and Sony Columbia began to archive projects in 1998, leaving only Paramount without an official archive to protect and control its historical assets. At all the studios, the desire to collect film history was motivated and driven by marketing and branding considerations, rather than any altruistic urge to preserve history.[1]

By the late 1980s the work of film archives entered the public consciousness, thanks to the relentless self-promotion of the American Film Institute (AFI). The AFI has accomplished relatively little in terms of actual film preservation. But it has created a more acute awareness in the public mind of the ephemeral nature of the medium and the need for film preservation. Several high-profile restorations (and the publicity campaigns surrounding them), including *Napoleon* (1927 and 1981), *Lawrence of Arabia* (1962 and 1989), and *Vertigo* (1958 and 1996), and debates surrounding the "colorization" of black and white film classics also raised awareness in the general population.[2]

All this film historical activity has brought about an expansion of the labor market for film historians. But don't be misled. The studios have never been interested in film history per se, unless it can be used to market their product. For the studios, the exploitation of film history is never more than a short-term goal. The industry is structured only to achieve immediate profits, rather than invest in long-term strategies.

My goal in writing this essay is not so much to analyze the function and feasibility of film historical texts in the emerging mass media. Rather, it is to present a case study of one studio's relationship to its own history, as viewed from the vantage point of an insider involved in the founding of a studio archive. It is the story of a serious film historical experiment initiated by a major motion picture company, Universal Studios, which was summarily torpedoed, the victim of studio machinations and financial politics. The names have not been changed, since there are no innocents. This is a personal story, and this essay makes no claim to objectivity. Instead it offers a cautionary message on the stakes of film history in the 1990s.

Despite the fact that Universal Studios has existed as a company for nearly ninety years (an anniversary it will celebrate in June 2002), for most of its existence little thought was given to its history, traditions, and material culture. In 1936, after Carl Laemmle was forced to relinquish control, many of the production files from the silent era were thrown away. In 1949 Universal burned its entire nitrate holdings from the silent period in order to reclaim the silver. All 5,553 films that Universal produced between 1912 and 1930 disappeared in the flames. Around the same time, Universal sold much of its property department, which included material going back to the 1910s. With each succeeding generation of Universal managers, more and more historical material was lost or destroyed. As late as the early 1980s, Irving Thalberg's correspondence from his time as head of Universal disappeared when a New Jersey warehouse in which it was stored was sold.

In 1989 Beth Kennedy, senior vice president for administration at MCA (Universal's parent company), commissioned a feasibility study for the establishment of a Universal archive. The Winthrop Group was hired to conduct the study. The Winthrop Group surveyed for the first time Universal's historical assets, set parameters for the conditions necessary for their protection, and made recommendations for the establishment of an archive. The study was completed after five months of site visits to Universal City Studios, samplings of materials, interviews with corporate managers, and analysis of the situation at MCA. The report contained a wealth of information regarding Universal's archival-quality holdings as they existed in 1989-90. A not insignificant amount of the material described in the report would indeed disappear before an archive was actually established.

The Winthrop Report emphasized that the establishment of a corporate archive demanded a long-term budgetary and structural commitment from Universal's management, as well as the formulation of company-wide policies concerning the collection, maintenance, and use of archival collections. The Winthrop Report was presented to Lew Wasserman, MCA's aging chairman, in 1990. Wasserman rejected the proposal out of hand as too expensive.

Later the same year, Wasserman sold MCA-Universal to Matsushita Electrical Industrial Company of Japan for $6.59 billion. In 1995

Joseph E. Seagram Company purchased an 80 percent interest in MCA-Universal for $6.3 billion, leading ultimately to the retirement of Wasserman in April 1996. In December 1995, six months after Seagram purchased MCA, Seagram corporate curator Carla Ash sent a memo to Edgar Bronfman Jr., Seagram's thirty-nine-year-old CEO, which can be regarded as the founding document for the Universal archive. Ash, while on the Seagram payroll, reported informally to Phyllis Lambert, the sister of Edgar Bronfman Sr., a major stockholder in the family-controlled business and the director of the Canadian Centre for Architecture in Montreal, an institution she built and financed. It was through Lambert's influence that Seagram hired Mies van der Rohe to build its Park Avenue headquarters in the 1950s, created several corporate art collections, and established archives for all its subsidiary businesses. In the memo Ash made the following recommendations: (1) that company-wide guidelines be established for archiving Universal's history; (2) that a directory of archival holdings be created; (3) that conservation procedures be developed; (4) that an oral history program be instituted; and (5) that all artistic production materials be located and retrieved.

Although Bronfman's reaction to the memo is not documented in any available paperwork, it is assumed that he gave his blessing to the project, because in March 1996 C. Ford Peatross, curator of prints and photographs at the Library of Congress, began a yearlong study of the situation at Universal. In August 1996 Peatross proposed the formation of an Archives Committee, consisting of himself, Ash, and Maygene Daniels, chief archivist at the National Gallery of Art.

Meanwhile, in August 1996, an archives "working group" was set up at Universal (at Carla Ash's instigation) by Howard Weitzman, Universal's new executive president, and COO Ron Meyer. Richard Costello, a former Madison Avenue advertising executive and another recent Bronfman hire, was assigned the task of overseeing the founding of the archive. Independently of the Seagram initiative, an embryonic proposal for an archive had been made to Ron Bension, president of Universal Studio's theme park operations, which stated that such an archive could produce income for the theme parks. Another division of Universal, Consumer Products, also submitted to management a proposal for an archive, "Preserving the Magic of Hollywood."

A studio archives "working group" was formed, including representatives from Consumer Products, Recreation (theme parks), Strategic Marketing, Studio Operations, Corporate, and Corporate Communications. In a memo dated August 15, 1996, the committee suggested that an immediate moratorium be put on disposing of any company props or other studio materials, and that a studio archive be set up that would be exempt from operating on a profit/loss basis.

In February 1997 Carla Ash and the consulting team surveyed the historical materials and memorabilia at Universal. In almost every area the team identified historically valuable material that was in peril. A month later, Daniels and Peatross filed their report, "Archives and Collections: Recommendations for Action," which had been written in close conjunction with Ash. The recommendations included the following:

1. the establishment of an Archives and Collections Department;
2. the transfer to Archives and Collections of all files, photographs, manuscripts, posters, graphic items, and other materials that document the company's history;
3. The collection of signature props, costumes, and other memorabilia;
4. the maintenance of the best professional archival and curatorial practice to ensure preservation;
5. the hiring of a highly qualified senior-level archive director;
6. the establishment of offices (on-lot) and significant warehouse space (off-lot);
7. the immediate establishment of an exhibition space and long-term development of a museum facility;
8. the institution of Archives and Collections as a permanent department;
9. the establishment of a budget for all aspects of the department's work;
10. the immediate identification and transfer of historical materials at physical risk;
11. the establishment of programs and guidelines for the acquisition of historical materials from outside the company;
12. the establishment of policies and procedures for internal and external access to the collections;
13. the acquisition of key props from all new productions to ensure their preservation;

14. the development of products to draw on Universal's history; and
15. the participation in activities that improve corporate communications and increase a sense of corporate identity.

What immediately strikes one about these recommendations is that they insist on practices that are common in the nonprofit world of archives and libraries but are seldom put into practice in corporate archives. No motion picture studio had ever established archival practices in accordance with the guidelines of the American Society of Archivists (ASA). The committee's recommendations were based on the assumption that the archives would not generate income. Not even the nonprofit world can afford such idealism anymore, much less a corporation whose officers receive a bonus based on financial performance.

By the late spring of 1997 the archive project was well under way. In July 1997 Costello and Ash made a presentation to Weitzman, which called for the official establishment of an Archives and Collections Department divided into an archive subgroup and a marketing/resources subgroup. The proposal also included a first mission statement and a limited set of objectives. The list of objectives made clear a shift away from archiving the company's film history in favor of marketing concerns. It would not be the last time that archival and marketing functions would be debated.

In February 1998 I was hired as director of Archives and Collections, and officially began work in May. At my request, the marketing and archive areas were unified under one budget and management, with a staff of five. While the Universal Classic Film Series (the first of which was called "Universal Noir") was administered by an outside consultant, archive staff devoted time to both archiving and marketing efforts. I proposed a budget for fiscal year 1999, and on July 1, 1999, Archives and Collections officially became a department, reporting to Costello in Universal Corporate.

The budget included a list of long-term goals which were approved without discussion by Weitzman's replacement.[3] Since the archive was in Corporate, a division that does not itself generate income, but only assists and administers infrastructure for other income-generating departments, budget goals for generating revenues were included neither in the budget, nor in the attached goals.

In the summer of 1998 a warehouse was located near the lot. Initial capital improvements were completed in the winter of 1998, and in March of the following year, materials collected over the past two years were moved into the new archival space. At the same time, offices were set up in the basement of the Universal Commissary so that the archive would have the necessary on-lot presence. By the spring of 1999 the department had settled on a database system that was both robust and complex enough to handle the extreme heterogeneity of material coming into the collections.[4]

The technical aspects of founding, organizing, and creating a user base for the archive were relatively easy to accomplish, even with a small staff. Much more difficult was the navigation of the highways and byways of corporate politics. One of the first land mines was the issue of reporting structure. While I officially reported to Costello, Ash exerted influence over the decision-making process through the perceived power of her position as a direct link to Edgar Bronfman. Costello was more interested in the marketing aspects of the archive's corporate mandate, while Ash insisted that until exact surveys of all the company's historical materials had been made and the archive's infrastructure had been firmly established, the department should refrain from any marketing or outreach efforts. This managerial conflict bubbled under the surface in the archive's first fiscal year.

Several factors ultimately affecting the position of the archive changed in the beginning of the archive's second fiscal year. First, Edgar Bronfman's interest in Universal began to wane as he set his sights on the Polygram Music acquisition. Universal's dismal box office performance in 1997-98, encompassing seventeen months of flops, and the industry's cold shoulder to the Seagram CEO certainly didn't help to perk Bronfman's interest. Meanwhile, Seagram-installed executives began to disappear as quickly as they had appeared after the Seagram acquisition of MCA in 1995.[5] The executive control of Archives and Collections was shifted to Universal Studio Operations, the division responsible for maintaining and generating income from the studio's physical plant. This was not good news for a department that was a cost center, rather than a revenue center.

Studio Operations was controlled by executives who had worked for Lew Wasserman, none of whom had ever given their blessing to Seagram's archival project. Indeed, one can assume that they were unhappy about the archive's founding under Corporate, given the fact that Central Files, the Research Library, the Costume and Prop Departments, and the Film Vaults—all of which collected if not protected studio assets—were under their control. While paying lip service to cooperation and synergy, they frustrated the archive's efforts at every turn. For example, when the archive asked Studio Operations to turn over their poster collection for proper archival storage, they refused. The Property Department had been amassing original Universal posters for several years through purchase in the collector's market, in order to hang them in the offices of studio executives. While Studio Operations finally realized that it was not a good investment to expose a poster valued at $30,000 to UV light, and had begun a program of hanging photographic copies in public spaces, the originals were still being stored in a back room of the Prop Department.

At my first meeting with Jim Watters, president of Studio Operations, the executive stated that in his division "we do not eat our own," a comment meant to soothe and reassure. In point of fact, Studio Operations management would spend a good part of the fiscal year 2000 doing exactly that: eating their own.

By the winter of 1999 Bronfman began shopping the studio around. Universal was once again on a hit movie roll, having generated close to $1 billion in box office receipts, thanks to such blockbusters as *The Mummy* (1999), *Notting Hill* (1999), and *American Pie* (1999). But upper management began cutting costs anyway, so that the company would be more attractive to potential buyers. Quietly, a massive bloodletting began. In the spring of 2000, over six hundred jobs were eliminated. Archives and Collections lost two budgeted but not yet filled positions, and a third position through attrition. I was told to close the eighty-four-year-old Research Department (which was then sold to Lucasfilm). Then two researchers were let go and as a result I had to close the Research Library. Finally, the travel, exhibitions, and acquisitions budgets were either zeroed or cut back.

The Archives Department closed the fiscal year 2000 in June, 15 percent under budget. The museum project, which by July 1999 had progressed to an architectural drawing stage within Corporate Strategic Planning, was the first goal to be abandoned. When the department's manager for exhibition services resigned to take another position, all activities connected with servicing other departments were radically scaled back. Finally, when the French conglomerate Vivendi purchased Seagram in June 2000, Studio Operations felt they could abandon all pretense to following the lofty goals of the Seagram project. My position as director of Archives and Collections was eliminated, while the remaining staff was put under the administration of Central Files. While the archive continues to exist, its function is no longer to make history visible, but rather to bury it.

NOTES

1. Just why the entertainment industry put film history on its agenda in the 1990s bears some theoretical analysis, certainly more than will be discussed in this essay. The above articulated theory of an economic imperative is certainly one viable explanation, but it fails to account completely for the initial impetus to produce film historical programming and products. One need only remember that self-reflexive movies about the film, television or music industry's history were considered, with few exceptions, by industry insiders to be box office poison. My own possibly optimistic view is that the audience for film/TV history has grown, thanks to thirty years of film/media education at the secondary and university level, and historical film programming in countless museums, cinémathèques, art cinemas, and college film societies.

2. The U.S. Congress passed legislation pertaining to the distribution of classic Hollywood films, whether on film or video, which compels distributors to state whether a film has been altered or not. The legislation culminated after extensive hearings in 1993 on a national film preservation plan in the establishment of the National Film Preservation Board in 1998.

3. The goals included the following:

a. to establish an archive to collect, conserve, preserve, and catalogue all documents, visual materials, and three-dimensional objects pertaining to Universal's history;

b. to build a proper archival and research facility off-lot for long-term storage;

c. to repackage in archival housing and restore, where necessary, all historical materials;

d. to complete oral histories of the studio's longtime executives and employees;

e. to acquire historical materials from outside sources;

f. to create an outreach program to educate Universal employees;

g. to build a museum that would showcase Universal's history;

h. to develop access policies for internal and external users;

i. to facilitate other Universal departments to generate income from dormant historical assets.

4. The material included photographic stills, set and costume designs, production records, company correspondence, sets, costumes, props, memorabilia, posters, publicity materials, company publications, branded products, theme park designs, music cue sheets and scores, videos, DVDs, music videos, and awards.

5. Both Howard Weitzman and Dick Costello, two key players in the archive's founding, left the company, not necessarily at their own volition.

4

The Man Who Wanted to Go Back

Murray Pomerance

> When space feels thoroughly familiar to us, it has become place.
> —Yi-Fu Tuan, *Space and Place*

I AM TRYING to map my own experience and biography as memories of feeling-in-place. This involves, among many other things, trying to understand Hitchcockian narrative as an emplacement, a set storytelling. I am particularly interested in *Vertigo* (1958), a film that offers the problem of figuring out both where one is and whither one is going—two questions, Heisenberg warned, we could never answer at once. In particular it is *Vertigo: The Restoration* (1996) that fascinates me here, specifically, the film seen again—as Henry James would have put it, *revised*.[1]

Nowadays, a gripping predisposition for progress causes us to regard every space and meaning as a destination to which we might advance if only we had resources enough of understanding, sufficient light, the fuel to carry on. But as Yi-Fu Tuan cautions, "Human beings are not endowed with an instinctive sense of direction."[2] He goes on to quote James Feibleman: "The importance of events in any life is more directly proportionate to their intensity than to their extensity."[3] If we look at *Vertigo* as an unfolding of intensities, it is clear that its story rests on our ability to regard the past as something to contemplate returning to, a lure, even a target, rather than as a primordial source that lingers behind us and above. Above? Surely, to begin with an equation, *before is above*; and our fall is the gravity-bound depreciation of adventure, and surely of narrative. The Enlightenment posited life as a climb to ever purer, constantly and ineffably magnified Being, out of and in escape

Vertigo: The Restoration (Universal, 1996) reminded us that they don't make 'em like they used to.

from a "pit of Babel"[4] in which we hankered for freedom through ascent. But the image of our present and future as a glorious and golden prominence, a kind of sanctified crane shot, is a conceit, even sales pitch, calculated to feature the available (that is, well-distributed) present at the expense of the past. *Vertigo* shows clearly enough that futurity—the protagonist's and ours—is below, that progress (at least narrative progress) is a tumble. Paul Goodman was invoking this fall when he wrote of "probability and implication as important unifying relations" in literature.[5] The past is all improbable, and our experience as it unfolds is a gathering of probability.

The 1996 release of Robert Harris and James Katz's restoration of *Vertigo* recaptures and redeploys an earlier music. In so doing, it is a precise reflection of the themes of the film it restores, since *Vertigo* is explicitly about being restored while falling—falling in love, falling to death, falling for a performance. Scottie Ferguson's pursuit of Madeleine Elster is a fall toward certainty from a peak of suspicion and disbelief; and his relation with Judy Barton, ostensibly to him a voyage into the past, in fact hurls him toward his own creative ground. The "love story" of Scottie and Judy Barton—in which he uses her, as a film director might, for building up a characterization through gesture, hairstyling, costume, dialogue, posture, and situated action—echoes the earlier "love story" of Scottie and "Madeleine." Hitchcock establishes a vertical placement of these two tales on a scale of class and sentiment (preexisting for his audiences) and thus uses his narrative not only to drop us to a conclusion but also to inform us that we are being dropped. Judy is beneath Madeleine, and Scottie has "fallen." Hitchcock openly signals Judy, the rank actress, to be "low," making her a salesgirl at I. Magnin, giving her a harsh elocution, dressing her garishly.[6] This makes stratification itself the substance of the tale, and Kim Novak playing Judy playing Madeleine suggests directly Scottie's confusion about height, that is, his vertigo. Scottie's vertigo, however, is not ours, and it is *our vertigo* that is referred to in the film's title. We fall, but also loathe to fall, through the tale. To assist us, Hitchcock made the explicit choice to shoot in San Francisco, where it would be possible to have the story advance in a downhill direction.[7] Further, the "Madeleine" who seduces Scottie is unreal. He falls for someone who exists solely as a character concocted by Elster, and so his fall, a form of "reading," bears kinship with our own attraction to him, to Madeleine, and to the film.

It was precisely as a film lover who had seen *Vertigo* many times and felt its power, but had also failed to comprehend it deeply and who therefore needed to remember, *to re-vise* or see again, that Robert Harris entered into a project with James Katz to restore this film in the mid-1990s, a time when so much of human history was being reseen, reorganized, revised itself in memory of the twentieth century. So gripped was Harris by the possibilities of reproducing *Vertigo* as Hitchcock had originally conceived it to be seen, that the irony of laboring in restoration of a work about laboring-in-restoration entirely evaded him.[8] The intention of finding the original production materials and recrafting a print from them swept Harris into his own time trip, a systematic hunt through long-unopened storage boxes and rendezvous with now aged collaborators with both precise and faulty memories of their own early experiences working on this film.

From the start, the restoration of *Vertigo* posed problems. While mag tapes, color separation masters, original negatives, advertising materials, trailers, and sound stems for original effects, dialogue, and music tracks for most films of the 1950s and 1960s filled as many as one hundred large boxes, for *Vertigo* Harris and Katz found only ten. In 1967 the rights to the 1950s Paramount films reverted to Hitchcock.[9] In order to learn how best to keep the physical materials, the genetic fragments necessary for assemblage, Hitchcock consulted not an archivist but his business manager, Herman Citron, one of whose employees advised that he should store only the original camera negative, the black and white Technicolor separation masters, one for red, one for green, one for blue; a sixteen-millimeter optical track negative (for making prints); a thirty-five-millimeter soundtrack negative; and five positive prints. Everything else—original dialogue effects, original music stems, original Foley stems, original effects stems, original trailers, advertising materials, still photographs—was junked *worldwide.* Storage, after all, is expensive.

Ultimately, Universal spent $5 million to license the rights to the Paramount films from Hitchcock's estate. In 1983 James Katz, who was heading the Classics Division there, and who had not yet partnered with Harris, convinced the studio to make a license with him for *Vertigo.* Arrangements were made for Paramount to ship the stored materials to Universal from its vaults. But Hitchcock had everything in storage in a Los Angeles warehouse that was neither heated nor air-conditioned.[10] In summer, temperatures in the warehouse climbed to 105 degrees. The optical material faded, differentially according to whether the reel sat above or below other reels. Because of its Famous Music subsidiary, a substantial investment in itself, Paramount was assiduous about keeping the original music recordings, but of these the acetate backings were shriveled and the oxide was flaking off. Harris's assistant Mike Hyatt was able to get a sound dub by keeping his thumb against the mag stock as it rolled over the playback head in order to keep the contact consistent. For the entire picture the Foley track—an effects track incorporating footsteps on the stairs of the tower, Scottie climbing his ex-girlfriend Midge's banana yellow stepladder, and other "practical" sounds—had to be redone from scratch.

Certain specific sound effects were complicated to grab in 1995 with the authenticity that would have been possible in 1957. Restoration is a battle for authenticities. A period Karmann Ghia had to be located, for example, so that Midge's car stopping in front of Scottie's house at night would sound right. Some of the original soundtrack had dead spots unproblematic for theatrical speaker systems in the 1950s but impossible now, given the advanced Dolby sound equipment in most theaters.

Harris laid in the creaking of the tower stairs, a seagull near Fort Point, and the wind fluttering past the open tower window where they had never been before.

It is interesting that Harris's working process restoring *Vertigo* reflects Scottie's restoration of "Madeleine." In Judy, Scottie has only the shabbiest remnant of Madeleine to work with. To reinstate the more elevated Madeleine who he imagines preexisted Judy, Scottie must resort to a number of institutionalized resources designed for the specific purpose of restoration—such as the suit department at Ransohoff's. (It is, of course, exactly these resources Gavin Elster used with Judy in the first place.) As Harris had to calculate ways of rerecording and remixing sound, of reprinting imagery that made practical use of institutionalized resources already available, Scottie had to recalibrate a costume, reform a hairstyle, reconstruct a performance embodying a certain display of intent. When Scottie asks about a particular gray suit, the store manager has ready-made items to display and a model trained and prepared to display them. She is equipped to handle what might otherwise seem the eccentric or bizarre needs of a gentleman who "seems to know what he wants." Harris was another such gentleman.

By now—in the age of the genome project, the age of the GMO, a time when positivistic laboratory science has replaced *plein air* impressionism as our chief piety—we no longer find things, we make them. We have all become more acute observers of presentations, and have come to take at face value a world constructed of them: presentations of presentations, competitions for and manipulations of presentations— all commonplaces in an increasingly cynical, global, mercantile environment dominated by the routinization of performativity. Of all films to restore, it seems appropriate that Harris chose one about a cynical man murdering his wife for commercial gain then covering himself with an elaborate staging of beauty, fading youth, and entrapment by the past. *Vertigo: The Restoration* is stunningly appropriate to *its* time because it evokes so many other characteristics of the present age: its photographic reconstitution and rerecorded sound are exemplars of the passion for digitality and computerization that by the end of the twentieth century had swept the world (and the world of film). The diegetic focus on Elster's hucksterism is a reflection of the global frenzy for commercializing beauty and experience. The concentration on Scottie's crippling paralysis is a comment on the vertiginous panic of contemporary thought, self-conscious about narrativity itself and thus incapable of penetrating narrative. Scottie's obsession about Judy Barton's performance seems an evocation of the contemporary pressure for style and denigration of substance. The late 1990s were a time of general historical panic, too, and so the era embodied in Scottie's strange project seems ironically a struggling to go back while moving inexorably forward. His stance in the final shot, arms outstretched, eyes glazed open to the wind at the top of the tower, is a dream emblem of impotent desire.

We might return for a moment to the technological passions that made *Vertigo: The Restoration* possible and probable in 1996. Restoration involves *records*, not events; stored tape recordings and negative strips, tactile, actual, resistant. It is therefore a horticulture of sorts, invoking a millennial pastoralism or new ecological piety that privileges care for what has already been "planted" over the yearning to plant anew. This recent concentration on harvesting expressive outgrowths rather than reaching down for new and elemental materials in our mythic bedrock is an important feature distinguishing *Vertigo: The Restoration* from, say, the Gus Van Sant remake of *Psycho* (1998).

If it is remarkable that, working with such limited material as fell to them, Harris and Katz were able to bring *Vertigo* back to the screen, it is overwhelming that Hitchcock was able to conceive it in the first place. In 1957, Cold War panic was at its height. The cynical materialism of rampant performance that is our staple diet had not yet replaced innocent sweetness and genuineness for the middle-class viewing audience. For viewers then, *and for us now,* Scottie's zeal is his helplessness. We should remember that restoring the telling of a story is not the same as retelling it. In retelling, we fall *again* through time's gravity, accepting *again-ness*—that what came before *was prior. Retelling* is what Scottie is experiencing. In restoring, we climb against gravity until we fear falling once again. The film called *Vertigo: The Restoration* is an actual return, a going back by men who wanted desperately to go back to the tale of a man who wanted above everything to go back but could not find his way. This is a sip from the fountain of youth.

NOTES

1. Henry James, "Preface to *The Golden Bowl*," in *The Art of the Novel* (New York: Scribner's, 1934).

2. Yi-Fu Tuan, *Space and Place: The Perspective of Experience* (Minneapolis: University of Minnesota Press, 1977), 75.

3. James K. Feibleman, *Philosophers Lead Sheltered Lives* (London: Allen and Unwin, 1952), 55.

4. Franz Kafka, *Parables and Paradoxes* (New York: Schocken, 1961).

5. Paul Goodman, *The Structure of Literature* (Chicago: University of Chicago Press, 1954), 15.

6. The green outfit Novak wore was so unevocative of her "star" status it came ultimately to be stored beneath a Paramount soundstage in Rentals rather than Star Costumes. Robert Harris, in personal conversation, April 2000. For this, and a wealth of information and sensibility about *Vertigo,* I am deeply indebted to Robert Harris.

7. Murray Pomerance, "Vertigo in *Vertigo*" (paper presented at the Society for Cinema Studies, San Diego, 1998).

8. Harris.

9. *Rear Window* (1954), *To Catch a Thief* (1955), *The Trouble with Harry* (1955), *The Man Who Knew Too Much* (1956), and *Vertigo* (1958).

10. Harris.

PART II

THINGS AMERICAN (SORT OF)

5

"American" Cinema in the 1990s and Beyond

Whose Country's Filmmaking Is It Anyway?

Charlie Keil

AS AMERICAN CINEMA has redefined itself in the era of new technologies, bloated budgets, mergers and acquisitions, and relaxed cultural trade policies, one might easily overlook its role in the disappearance of the concept of national cinema. The preeminence of American cinema in virtually every other national marketplace has translated into the unassailable economic superiority of U.S.-based production and distribution and the near decimation of once mighty national cinemas, in both Europe and Asia. But if one examines the often overlooked case of another aspect of "American" film—cinema just north of the U.S. border—one can see clearly the other side of the equation.

My argument here does not involve the suspect claim that the Canadian activity I will describe threatens the U.S. film industry nor that American cinema risks imploding. Instead, I am suggesting that the push for reduced trade barriers that the United States has always championed inevitably contributes to the elimination of any sense of national cinema at all. Undoubtedly, proponents of American cultural trade policy have imagined the United States as the "last man standing," but they have not anticipated that this altered marketplace will also cause changes to American cinema. While we easily accept the commonplace notion that American film culture overcomes (other) national boundaries, seldom do commentators allow for the fact that whatever constitutes so-called American cinema may undergo a denationalizing process in the face of increased globalization. To explore this notion, I will examine American cinema from the perspective of

Canada, highlighting several aspects of contemporary trends that indicate the imminent dissolution of the concept of a U.S. national cinema.

CANADIANS AS AMERICANS: ABSORPTION VIA "GLOBAL MONOCULTURE"

Why Canada? Of all the nations affected by the American cultural juggernaut, Canada has probably proven the least resistant. Because the country possesses a negligible commercial film heritage, the Canadian government has found little to defend when attempting protectionist legislation. And the MPAA has quickly beaten back those few attempts with threats of reprisals. Current Canadian film production (particularly in English-speaking Canada) exists on the margins; typically, the highest grossing film made in Canada for any given year matches the earnings of a low-performing American independent release. In 1999 neither *Felicia's Journey*, directed by favorite son Atom Egoyan, nor *Sunshine*, recipient of numerous Genies, could even crack the $1 million mark.[1] Perhaps because of its proximity to the United States, a shared dominant language, and many surface similarities in their cultural makeup, Canada has never carved out a distinct filmic national identity. Ironically, lacking such an identity has not aided Canada in adopting the strategy Martine Danan has attributed to other filmmaking nations under siege:

> The "postnational" mode of production erases most of the distinctive elements which have traditionally helped define the (maybe) imaginary coherence of a national cinema against other cinematographic traditions or against Hollywood at a given point in time: for example, an implicit or explicit worldview, the construction of national character and subjectivity, certain narrative discourses and modes of address or intertextual references.[2]

In the postnational era, in lieu of emulating the U.S. production model, Canada has simply infiltrated it. Canadians figure prominently in every aspect of American popular culture. Two of the biggest stars in the American cinema at the close of the 1990s are Canadians by birth: Mike Myers and Jim Carrey. Canadian-born actors populate programming across broadcast schedules, from *Will and Grace* to *Felicity*, a graduate of the Canadian news system anchors a network prime-time news-cast, while Canadian-trained producers and writers guide shows as diverse as *Saturday Night Live* and *Family Law*.[3]

Singers whose careers began in Canada dominate radio playlists and sell tens of millions of units, no matter what the format: adult contemporary (Céline Dion), country (Shania Twain), or alternative (Alanis Morissette). Even the new Anakin Skywalker hails from Vancouver. Moving behind the scenes, one could find Canada's own Edgar Bronfman Jr., scion of the Seagram distillery dynasty, shaking the corridors of corporate power as mightily as Michael Eisner and Ted Turner; Bronfman, after acquiring control of MCA/Universal, tried to match movie-making might to domination of the recorded music industry by merging with PolyGram. Acknowledged as a Hollywood power player (quite literally, after being positioned at number 11 on *Entertainment Weekly's* 1999 Power List and 5 on *Premiere's*),[4] Bronfman most recently joined forces with the European media giant Vivendi.[5] And, if *Titanic* (1999) defines the 1990s in its global reach and transnational appeal, can we ignore the fact that the film's director, James Cameron, hails from the Canadian side of Niagara Falls?

While these might seem like isolated cases, they point to an altogether different truth: by internationalizing culture to the extent it has done so, the United States has also loosened its claim to defining that culture. It may be "American-styled,"[6] but it is no longer completely controlled by Americans and the sensibility may be less definably "American" than what emerged in earlier eras. If we restrict ourselves to the domain of movies, we can see that the comedy of Mike Myers, though ostensibly "American," is actually heavily inflected by his suburban Toronto roots (in *Wayne's World*, 1992) and his Anglo-expatriate parentage (in *So I Married an Axe Murderer*, 1993, and the Austin Powers films). As much as Céline Dion cannot entirely drop vestiges of her Québecois accent, Canadians do not lose all memories of the national context that produced them. And as much as the American cultural system might like to think that it merely absorbs and recasts, it may soon expand to the degree that there will be little that is definably American about American movies. Sony owns Columbia-TriStar. John Woo is one of the most commercially successful directors of American releases. Jet Li and Jackie Chan command top billing. The United States is now in the business of making international movies, and the question becomes, at what point does "inter" overwhelm "national"?

"HOLLYWOOD NORTH"

Naomi Klein has pointed to a pervasive trend in manufacturing, where-in companies put most of their effort into establishing brand loyalty, so that connotations of the brand supersede any qualities of the product or circumstances of its making.[7] Sportswear manufacturers have proven particularly successful in this regard, creating a desire for products bearing the logo "Nike" or "Reebok"; consumers remain willfully oblivious to the fact that the goods in question come from sweatshops overseas. Reduced manufacturing expenses allow for increased adver-tising expenditure, while the campaigns emerging out of the latter en-sure that the taint connected to the former goes unnoticed.

How does this notion of branding relate to the American film in-dustry? Arguably, moviegoers' notions of brand name identification have withered since the demise of the studio era. The end of long-term star contracts and studio-nurtured house styles has given way to deliberate corporate anonymity in the era of conglomerates and multimedia mergers. Yet the major distributors still exercise a form of branding. It may not matter which distributor releases, say, *X-Men* (2000), but it *is* important that ticket buyers recognize the film as the product of a system capable of providing films of a scale and nature no other competitor can match. The logos initiating the credits still matter: even if they are interchangeable in the minds of moviegoers. Collectively they signal "quality" in the same way brand names do on a sweatshirt.

But the American film industry is becoming increasingly reliant on its own version of the clothing manufacturers' sweatshops. The work-ing conditions may be better and the crews may be unionized, but the fact remains that more and more American films are being made just be-yond the border. Though moviemaking requires more specialized skills than sewing together a t-shirt, American production practices still fol-low the policy of chasing the lowest usable labor dollar, and that has brought more and more U.S.-based movie projects into Canada.

Despite the U.S. government's enthusiastic endorsement of NAFTA and other legislation aimed at liberalizing trade agreements, the flight of U.S. production dollars has caused concern among those who pre-fer expenditures to stay within the country. Protectionist-minded U.S. politicians have decried the current state of affairs; some have gone as far as threatening reprisals for what they see as Canada's unfair advantages in securing productions. Los Angeles–based unions have publicly upbraided American companies for shooting in Canada so often, and the situation became an issue in the recent elections for the SAG presidency.[8]

Film and television production in Toronto alone was valued at over $600 million in 1999, and trends in 2000 indicate a 15 percent increase over that figure. The Toronto Film and Television Office reports that 550 new projects at 1,587 locations have accounted for 3,229 shooting days as of the midpoint in 2000. Of this, 61 percent of the projects are American in origin, which means that U.S.-based production dollars are employing thousands of actors and crew members.

How does this differ from the postwar situation, when runaway production cropped up worldwide? At that time, various foreign filmmaking industries, responding to the growing numbers of Hollywood films flooding the crippled postwar international market, tried different remedies to limit the degree of American domination of their screens. One such solution was freezing funds earned by American releases, so that box office receipts in excess of a prescribed ceiling would need to be spent in that country. American producers were forced to film overseas to make use of funds that could not return to the United States. Changing fortunes in the domestic marketplace resulting in studio cutbacks and reduced overhead encouraged such production patterns and allowed Hollywood to benefit from other countries' protectionist impulses. In its current guise, Hollywood reliance on runaway production derives from the irresistible advantage offered by Canada's relatively low dollar and the tax credits extended to U.S.-based companies. American producers now embrace the notion of filming in Canada. Moreover, the steady supply of work has encouraged Canadian cities such as Toronto and Vancouver to establish themselves as alternative production centers to Hollywood or New York.[9] Though the percentage of total production that occurs in Canada remains in the minority, it continues to grow, showing no sign of abatement.

Should this trend continue (and extend to other nations in equal measure), eventually *U.S.-based* production will constitute a minority percentage of total activity. According to a survey prepared by Stephen Katz, films made in Canada accounted for 37 percent of the 161 films shot in North America with a production schedule of six weeks or more. In terms of miniseries and movies made for television, the majority are already filmed in Canada. While these altered production circumstances will not change the degree to which U.S. films dominate the international marketplace, they may well affect the kinds of films made (and the ways they are made). Canadian crews and supporting casts working for an American production render the product less "purely" American. American politicians (be they candidates for SAG president or the governor's mansion in California) recognize this when they try to make it into an election issue. But it's a losing battle. What defines an "American" movie in the future will have less to do with where it is made, who provides the financing, or even who stars in it than with its conformity to the broadbased model of global monoculture I alluded to previously.

"COMING SOON TO A THEATER NEAR YOU"

The IMAX theater chain is a model for successful alternative exhibition practice. A chain of large-screen theaters that involve massive projection systems, IMAX occupies a niche market in North America (and elsewhere), the theaters typically tied to "event" locations, such as museums, science centers, and theme parks. But toward the end of the 1990s, IMAX began to expand more vigorously, both by increasing the number of venues and also by integrating more conventional entertainments (exemplified by its exclusive showing of Disney's *Fantasia 2000*) into its exhibition schedule.[10] IMAX is a Canadian company, based in Mississauga, Ontario, a city just outside Toronto.

How do IMAX's success and its plans for expansion relate to the issues already introduced in the previous sections? Aspects of national identity have often manifested themselves in the exhibition sector as much as in (if not more so than) production. Even the Canadian exhibition market, which devotes approximately 98 percent of its screen time to American films, has until recently been dominated by Cineplex Odeon, a Canadian-owned company. (Its major competitor, Famous Players, though linked to Viacom/Paramount, employs a maple leaf, Canada's chief symbol, in its logo, to disguise its American roots.) With the recent move of AMC into the Canadian market, this may change, but for the time being, audiences seem to like the idea of their theaters assuming certain signifiers of national identity even when the films shown do not. The IMAX intervention involves insinuating itself into the arena of international exhibition by defining itself apart from conventional practice. IMAX posits that a changed theatrical experience need not have any defined national origin.

Moreover, IMAX may be more of a harbinger of things to come than we now realize. IMAX makes use of a distinct projection technology that necessitates the selection of specially made films for its screenings. With the advent of digital projection, some have speculated that the viewing situation may become more fragmented. As production shifts to a digital base we can expect changes to the nature of cinematic product and, concurrently, the nature of viewer response as well.[11] If that turns out to be true, niche exhibition may become the norm, and companies like IMAX will serve as a model of future practice.

In that case, possession of a salable/marketable technology could easily override the national/regional base of a theater chain's ownership. Which theater one chooses could be determined by which technology it employs, and as technology requires no national anchoring, the changes have the potential to render the notion of a definably American cinema, this time on the exhibition level, a relic of the past. The trend toward internationalism that IMAX's current expansion policy supports could open the door for similar niche exhibitors, with the result that the structure of exhibition a few decades from now could be one wherein technicians operating from a variety of Silicon Valleys located throughout the world serve as its chief architects.

With little to tie people to their theater of choice, the notion of a national cinema will become even more tenuous. See this film, made in one country, starring actors from another, and shown via technology developed and marketed by still another. The idea of a national film-making culture, already severely under strain, will have been reduced to the status of a quaint vestige of a bygone era. And who contributed to this? Blame Canada.

NOTES

1. The Genies are the Canadian equivalent of the Oscars. *Sunshine* enjoyed modest success in the U.S. market as an art house release, earning close to $3 million by the end of the summer 2000 season.

2. Martine Danan, "From a 'Prenational' to a 'Postnational' French Cinema," *Film History* 8, no. 1 (spring 1996): 78.

3. The Canadians in question are Eric McCormack (Will of *Will and Grace*), Scott Speedman (Ben on *Felicity*), *ABC News Tonight* anchor Peter Jennings,

Lorne Michaels (executive producer and creative force behind *Saturday Night Live*), and Paul Haggis (producer/writer for *Family Law*).

4. *Entertainment Weekly*, no. 509 (October 29, 1999): 33; *Premiere*, June 1999, 85.

5. Strictly speaking, Bronfman sold his interests to Vivendi, but he retains a role in the new corporation. The extent of his power as part of Vivendi Universal has not yet been revealed.

6. Both this term and "global monoculture," employed earlier, have entered the vocabulary of the media. For examples, see "Taking the Canuck out of the Superstar," *Toronto Star*, July 1, 2000, E1; "Planet America: All the World's a Screen," *Globe and Mail*, October 17, 2000, A16.

7. Naomi Klein, *No Logo—No Space, No Choice, No Jobs: Taking Aim at the Brand Bullies* (Toronto: A. A. Knopf Canada, 2000).

8. Incumbent Richard Masur, for example, warned that unless protectionist measures were adopted, "we could very easily lose this industry." Quoted in the *Toronto Star*, August 19, 2000, E4.

9. So much so that Toronto's mayor recently announced plans for a 1.5-million-square-foot production complex that would provide adequate soundstage facilities for larger-scaled productions. Industry officials (including the head of the Ontario Film Development Corporation) appeared to be caught unawares by this announcement, though a feasibility study released in January 2000 called for a $21 million production complex. *Toronto Star*, October 17, 2000, D4, 7.

10. IMAX's fortunes did experience a downturn in January 1999, when its stock price plunged 20 percent, spurring the company to seek new investors. The *Fantasia 2000* experiment helped to stabilize IMAX's share price. Its expansion plans for 2000 include adding approximately 45 screens to the 205 already in existence. *Globe and Mail*, February 17, 2000, B6.

11. For one such example, see Godfrey Cheshire, "The Death of Film/The Decay of Cinema," *New York Press* (http:\\ www.nypress.com, 2000), 1-7.

6

Marketing Marginalized Cultures

The Wedding Banquet, *Cultural Identities, and Independent Cinema of the 1990s*

Justin Wyatt

ACCORDING TO *VARIETY'S* 1993 Profit Chart, a ratio of return-to-cost reveals that 1993's most profitable film was not Steven Spielberg's dinosaur extravaganza *Jurassic Park* (with a return of 13.79:1), but rather the gentle cross-cultural social comedy *The Wedding Banquet*, directed by Ang Lee (with a return of 23.6:1). The film's financial success (a $30 million worldwide gross) was matched by widespread critical praise, including an Academy Award nomination for best foreign film and a most commercially significant "two thumbs up" from Siskel and Ebert.

The film's commercial and critical prestige was tied to the national and ideological position occupied by the film. It was a curious hybrid, classified as "United States/Taiwan" by distributor Samuel Goldwyn, a foreign film by the Motion Picture Academy, and (implicitly) an American film by the Independent Spirit Awards. Such is the fluidity of cultural production in the "communities" of independent film.

The film tells the story of two gay lovers—one Asian (Wai-tung), one Caucasian (Simon)—who fake a marriage to placate Wai-tung's traditional parents. The plot revolves comically around issues of sexual orientation, discrimination, and "family values." Critics generally applauded both the cross-cultural and sexual elements of the film. Consider Georgia Brown's assessment in the *Village Voice*: "If this movie doesn't become hugely popular and thereafter increase tolerance for gays, Asians, and emigrants, as well as reconcile the generations, it will make you glow just imagining that it might."[1]

This "glow" comes at a price, however. In this essay, I will address the commercial, economic, and aesthetic determinants of *The Wedding Banquet*, with an emphasis on how the larger institutional forces of independent filmmaking and marketing have created a work that replicates and reinforces dominant notions of cultural difference.

THE TRANSFORMATION OF AMERICAN
INDEPENDENT CINEMA

To better understand the box office success of *The Wedding Banquet* in the shifting marketplace of American independent cinema, we first must take a look back at the early 1980s, a time in which independents had great difficulty securing a market presence. As Myron Meisel wrote in *Film Comment's* sixth annual "Grosses Gloss" in 1980, "Independents generally had a hard time of it, with majors glutting the marketplace and competing with them in the horror and comedy genres."[2] Looming on the horizon, though, were cable and video, which, like the early days of television, seemed to provide an endless market for product of all kinds. The introduction of these various home box office markets did not lead immediately to an increase in production/distribution at the studios. But a dramatic increase occurred in the independent film sector. Suddenly, companies that had been either dormant or small in market presence (e.g., Cinecom, Goldwyn, DEG, Cannon, Vestron, Island, Alive, and Atlantic Releasing) increased their production schedules. The boost in independent film production (including titles released directly to video) created a market in which, by 1988, independently produced films accounted for 70 percent of the U.S. market, an increase of over 20 percent compared to only five years earlier.[3] The configuration of the market in 1993 developed from this volatile period—a period marked by a surge in independent production linked to the cable and video boom. As critic David Ansen commented in 1987,

> Why are there so many new companies joining the low budget bandwagon—companies like Cinecom and Island, Goldwyn and Alive, Skouras, Cineplex, Atlantic, Vestron, and Spectrafilm? The answer is home video. For one thing, the independent home-video companies need product to fill their pipelines. Since the studios already have their own video companies, new movie sources need to be created.[4]

At first, the dollars from video and cable acted as a large buffer so that, if the budget was comparatively low, an independent film could not fail to break even. But the video market has proven to be an "A" title market. Independents are viewed increasingly as a risky venture in terms of capital investment. Hemdale's John Daly described this situation in 1991: "It's tougher for independents to raise money today, no question about that. People are still in a hold-on-to-the-cash frame of mind."[5] In time, many of the companies once helped by video and cable severely cut production (Cinecom and Cannon) or exited from the market altogether (Island, Alive, FilmDallas, Vestron, Atlantic Releasing, Avenue, DEG). While the death of some companies like Vestron was due to overextension (in the wake of financial success), many more companies were simply unable to establish a presence in the theatrical, video, or cable markets.

Concurrent with the shrinking market for independent distributors was the founding in 1991 of a production company, Good Machine, by James Schamus and Ted Hope. Schamus and Hope based the company around the concept of "no-budget" production, enabling directors to work unrestrained by commercial determinants. As Schamus describes the modus operandi, "The budget is the aesthetic."[6] Similarly, Hope explains the method of making movies in the no-budget manner: "We produce movies by nonfinancing: low fees, deferrals. The easiest way to put together the money for a $1 million movie is just to cut the budget by $500,000."[7] The producers worked in association with several significant New York independent directors and producers in the early 1990s—most noteworthy, Hope with director Hal Hartley on films such as *Trust* (1990) and *Simple Men* (1992), and Schamus with producer Christine Vachon on films such as *Poison* (1991) and *Swoon* (1992). Projects completed within the parameters of the no-budget aesthetic (Claire Denis's *Keep It for Yourself*, 1991 and Dani Levy's *I Was on Mars*, 1992) were then placed with distributors specializing in the art house market.

Director Ang Lee, a New York University film school graduate, initially worked with Good Machine in 1992 on his first feature, *Pushing Hands*. Lee's screenplay, telling of an old t'ai chi master who moves in with his son and his son's white wife, received the first prize in the annual Taiwanese government screenplay contest. The government funded the project to the level of $500,000, while Good Machine was able to produce the film for a bargain basement $408,000.[8] Never released in the United States, the film was nevertheless very successful in Taiwan, allowing Lee to set up financing for *The Wedding Banquet* with the largest studio in Taiwan, Central Motion Picture.[9] Set at a slightly larger budget of $750,000, the film was coproduced by Lee, Schamus, and Hope. The film's commercial success worldwide—including $4 million in Taiwan (making it the highest grossing film ever in that market)—was matched by solid box office on the art house circuit in the United States. With the Samuel Goldwyn Company signing on as distributor, the film grossed slightly less than $7 million in North America, a figure comparable to the grosses of 1994's art house leaders, *Barcelona* and Lee's follow-up, *Eat Drink Man Woman*.

SELLING THE BANQUET: DIFFERENCE AND COMMERCE

The commercial triumph of Lee's film is inexorably joined to the careful negotiation of cultural, social, and sexual difference in the film. While *The Wedding Banquet* appears to be supporting the "lifestyle" of its male lovers, this position is actually more complicated than would be apparent in a simple plot summary. Consider that the domestic situation in the film—male lovers Wai-tung and Simon cohabiting in Manhattan— is presented initially as under threat, both inside and outside the confines of the upscale brownstone. The first conversation between Simon and Wai-tung is an argument over vacation plans and neglect, followed by a misleading gay-bashing remark—"Hey, you homo" to Simon as he takes out the garbage—which turns out to be a joke. This instability is multiplied by the zealous efforts of Wai-tung's mother to find her son a wife, long distance from Taiwan. Receiving audio letters bemoaning his fate as a single man and having his parents enroll him in a Taiwanese dating service are just two of many strategies hatched to make the son "settle down." The additional burden of Wei-wei's illegal immigration status leads Simon to suggest a marriage of convenience between Wai-tung and Wei-wei to placate the parents and solve the green card problem. The parents arrive unexpectedly, and, after a dull civil ceremony, an elaborate wedding banquet is planned for the couple by the father's old compatriot now living in the United States.

The narrative solution to Wai-tung's problems compromises a number of institutional and social forces: the law by falsifying the marriage and thereby deceiving the INS, cultural tradition by submitting falsely to the whole set of rituals presented by the parents on the day of the wedding banquet, and, most significantly from a narrative standpoint, the family from three perspectives: Wai-tung's nuclear family, the false family unit created by Wai-tung and Wei-wei, and the "family" of Simon and Wai-tung's union. Indeed, the film shifts from a comedy of deception to a much more solemn exploration of social transgression: the wedding designed to solve the familial and social pressures directly leads to an unwanted pregnancy, the splintering of Wai-tung's family, and a possible separation for Wai-tung and Simon. Further, these pressures are linked to the father's stroke, which extends the parents' stay with their son.

The resolution suggests a tentative reconciliation among the family members based on a clearer, though still incomplete, version of true romantic and sexual relationships. The parents each know about Wai-tung's true love, yet each steadfastly believes that the other does not understand the situation. Deciding to keep her child, Wei-wei plans to stay with both Wai-tung and Simon, looking at both as "the fathers" of her child. The final scene shows the three saying goodbye to the parents as they return at last to Taiwan.

Part of the film's commercial success derives from the manner in which the narrative complications are developed. The initial premise of the cross-cultural urban male couple seeking to overstep the boundaries of social convention may seem designed for a gay (and lesbian?) audience, a reading reinforced by the film's North American advertising campaign, which utilized the copy "Everybody wants to kiss the bride, except the groom. A little deception at the reception," and an image of a formal wedding photograph with best man Simon and bride Wei-wei seated, and the groom standing behind the couple. Unbeknownst to the bride, the groom and best man are holding hands. Presented as a joke at the expense of the bride, the ad positions the gay relationship and the homosexuality or bisexuality of the groom as central to the plot.[10] Apart from the film's first scenes, however, Lee foregrounds the deception, rather than the relationship, so that physical interactions and exchanges between Wai-tung and Simon are minimized.

Simultaneously, the film is constructed to accept and encourage "straight" readings. The moralistic attitude toward the characters' transgressions, along with the "don't ask, don't tell" position on the

Ang Lee's *The Wedding Banquet* (Samuel Goldwyn, 1993), a story about gay men and illegal immigrants, outearned *Jurassic Park* on a screen-by-screen basis. The market for independent films in the 1990s was indeed strange and unpredictable.

gayness of Wai-tung, falls firmly within the confines of conventional Hollywood constructions of homosexuality. As Vito Russo explains, "many mainstream films concerning homosexuality are refigured by the directors as they enter the marketplace—William Friedkin pronounces that '*The Boys in the Band* is not about homosexuality,' Gordon Willis: '*Windows* is not about homosexuality, it's about insanity,' or John

Schlesinger: '*Sunday Bloody Sunday* is not about the sexuality of these people, it's about human loneliness.'[11]

Similarly, *The Wedding Banquet*'s presentation in the press posed two angles: the similarities between the banquet in the film and director Lee's own wedding ceremony to his current wife (they are happily married with two children) and the banquet in the film, and the fact that Lee is not gay. Curiously, the latter element is underlined even further by Lee; as one article recounts, "Lee's biggest preproduction concern, however, was the reaction of the gay community. Although neither he nor his coworkers are gay, they based the script on the experiences of a friend who was."[12] As the film's North American run progressed, the print ad was augmented by strong quotes from both national and regional critics. These blurbs stressed the comedy of the film, whether as "a marriage of comedy and chaos" (*Newsday*), "seriously funny" (*New York Daily News*), or "funny and refreshing" (Siskel and Ebert). The sum of these strategies—the morality tale within the narrative, the press and publicity angles, and the focus of the critical acclaim—all strengthen the film's ability to broaden beyond a gay audience, and, indeed, beyond an art house audience also.

LOCATIONAL THEORY: ECONOMICS, AESTHETICS, AND THE INDEPENDENT FEATURE

The marketing strategies for the film were much closer to mainstream studio filmmaking than to the world of independent or avant-garde film. I would suggest, however, that the release of *The Wedding Banquet* illustrates the increasing centrism of independent cinema, defined as any project not distributed by one of the majors. This centrism configures "independent" films that are more and more similar to the products from the major distributors, with parallels particularly striking in the added commercial and marketing hooks present in many independent films.

This relationship is rooted in neoclassical economic theory, especially the work of Harold Hotelling. Hotelling's classic paper "Stability in Competition," published in 1929, introduces and defines the concept of locational theory.[13] The essay begins with the observation that firms tend to cluster together in their location or in the range and quality of their goods.[14] The near locations of gas stations, video stores, and supermarkets all attest to the basis of Hotelling's model. This clustering occurs not only in location, however, but also across products in each industry. Firms produce products that are only slightly different from each other. These products tend to be clustered in geographic space and in characteristic space.

To understand this model without a mathematical proof, consider the following intuitive example. In a certain economy, the geographic space of Main Street is one mile long. Along Main Street, customers are uniformly distributed across the entire mile.

Further, assume that there are two stores on Main Street, that each store offers the same product, and that customers prefer to minimize the distance that they travel to the store since cost of travel increases with the distance traveled. Hotelling's locational theory suggests that, under these circumstances, a stable location can be deduced. Suppose that Firm 1 is located nine-tenths of a mile along Main Street, while Firm 2 is located seven-tenths of a mile along Main Street. Because Firm 2 is located closer than its competitor to the midpoint and therefore commands a larger share of the market, it will remain in its location. However, because Firm 1 is initially located close to the end of the street, it will "leapfrog" its competitor and relocate adjacent to its competitor on the side closer to the midpoint. As a result of this move, Firm 2 will then supplant Firm 1 and recapture its market advantage. This process continues until both firms are located together at the center of the market.

The model can be generalized to a large number of other economic and noneconomic problems. Economist Kenneth Boulding expanded the initial model to consider situations beyond industrial location, building what became referred to as the principle of minimum differentiation. As Boulding recounts

> The general rule for any new manufacturer coming into an industry is: "Make your product as like the existing products as you can without destroying the differences." It explains why all automobiles are so much alike. It even explains why Methodists, Baptists, and even Quakers are so much alike, and tend to get even more alike, for if one church is to attract adherents of another, it must become more like the other but not so much alike that no one can tell the difference.[15]

Returning to the realm of the cinematic, the principle of minimum differentiation describes how *The Wedding Banquet* operates in relation to mainstream cinema. While appearing to be firmly within the domain of independent cinema, with the accompanying aesthetic and social differences from mainstream cinema, Lee's film actually utilizes its "independence" as just another marketing strategy. Consequently, in attracting the sum of a gay, art house, and most significantly a more mainstream audience by design, the film has bee⁻ pushed further and further to the center. While this centrism is no a ʾubt responsible for the widespread global appeal of the film, this movement carries certain implications for cultural identity politics.

While the economic centrism of independent film embodies a disturbing ideological shift to the morals, values, and credo of the majors, *The Wedding Banquet* doubles the stakes by juxtaposing the arenas of "Asianness" and "queerness." As Richard Fung argues, "Asian men have been desexualized for decades in Hollywood, leading to the question, 'If Asian men have no sexuality, how can we have homosexuality.'" In addition, Fung points out, in the world of gay and lesbian filmmaking, visibility is a huge issue, since "Asians are largely absent from the images produced by both the political and commercial sections of the mainstream gay and lesbian communities." Fung calls for an independent gay Asian pornography as a partial redress to the problem, yet he realizes that the ideological issues presented by porn are also most troubling.[16]

Whereas Ang Lee's film would seem to be a positive move in terms of visibility and awareness, its economic centrism effectively erases any representational difference from Hollywood's versions of gays and Asians. Cultural stereotypes of both groups are reinforced (i.e., family and ritual constructions of Asian society, the duplicity and emotional instability of gay men) in a manner that serves to separate both groups from the mainstream. There are clearly other representational possibilities for the conjunction of Asianness and gayness. Lino Brocka's *Macho Dancer* (1988), a story of one young man's involvement in the sex industry of Manila, refuses to present clear-cut distinctions between gay and straight. In doing so it makes a powerful argument for the social and economic forces that help to configure sexual orientation and attraction.

The Wedding Banquet's status as an independent film replicating the model of mainstream filmmaking illustrates the larger trend toward economic centrism in the world of independent film. With funding sources becoming more and more scarce, increasing attacks against government funding of the arts, and the shrinking market for art house and repertory theaters, perhaps it was inevitable that the American independent film would move closer to the world of commercial, high-stakes studio moviemaking. Indeed, one cannot overestimate the significance of the two independent companies that have survived and even progressed since the video/cable boom: Miramax Films and New Line Cinema.

In the 1990s, Miramax and New Line were able to withstand this shakeout by consistently developing movies with the potential to cross over beyond the art house market. As *The Wedding Banquet* demonstrates, by the midpoint of the decade, independent cinema was largely an illusion. Even supposedly groundbreaking and iconoclastic "indie films" were firmly located within the safe domain of dominant ideological and commercial practice.

NOTES

1. Georgia Brown, "The Wedding Banquet (review)," *Village Voice*, August 10, 1993, 49.

2. Myron Meisel, "Grosses Gloss," *Film Comment*, 1980.

3. "23-Year Production Pulse," *Variety*, June 26, 1991, 78.

4. David Ansen, "Hollywood Goes Independent," *Newsweek*, April 6, 1987, 66.

5. Michael Fleming, "Among Indies, Only the Strong Are Surviving," *Variety*, February 25, 1991.

6. Amy Taubin, "Art and Industry," *Village Voice*, July 9, 1991, 54.

7. Kit Carson, "Independents," *Esquire*, September 1992, 181.

8. Jeff Yang, "Wedding Dues," *Village Voice*, August 24, 1993, 67.

9. Ann Hornaday, "A Director's Trip from Salad Days to a Banquet," *New York Times*, August 1, 1993.

10. The dynamic suggested in the ad recalls Mary Ann Doane's analysis of Robert Doisneau's photograph *Un Regard Oblique*. While the woman's look appears to be foregrounded, her gaze is actually under the power of the male, who is slyly looking at a different picture than the woman. For Doane, the photograph encapsulates "the process of narrativising the negation of the female gaze." See Mary Ann Doane, "Film and the Masquerade: Theorizing the Female Spectator," *Screen*, September-October 1982, 84.

11. Vito Russo, *The Celluloid Closet* (New York: Harper and Row, 1987), 126.

12. Yang, "Wedding Dues," 66.

13. Harold Hotelling, "Stability in Competition," *Economic Journal* 29 (1929): 41-57.

14. B. Curtis Eaton and Diane F. Eaton discuss the long-term impact of Hotelling's theory in *Microeconomics* (New York: W. H. Freeman, 1991), 4-121.

15. Kenneth Boulding, *Economic Analysis* (New York: Harper and Row, 1966), 601.

16. Richard Fung, "Looking for My Penis: The Eroticized Asian in Gay Video Porn," in *How Do I Look? Queer Film and Video,* ed. Bad Object-Choices (Seattle: Bay Press, 1991), 148.

7

Hollywood Redux

All about My Mother *and* Gladiator

Hilary Radner

WHEN IS A film a "Hollywood movie"? Is there a relationship between Hollywood style and a national film style that we might identify as American? These are not new questions; however, filmmaking in the 1990s has underlined their significance. Two recent films, Pedro Almodovar's *All about My Mother* (1999) and Ridley Scott's *Gladiator* (2000) highlight these questions. Neither of these films was made in Hollywood. *Gladiator* was produced by Universal and DreamWorks but directed by an Englishman; it has a multinational cast and was shot in a number of locations, from Venice to Morocco. Almodovar is a Spanish *auteur* writer/director, often associated with a revival of Spanish culture in the post-Franco years; his film is a European coproduction.

The two films illustrate two distinct trends, neither of which originated in the 1990s but that might be said to represent two tendencies that characterize nineties cinema. The first trend involves the European *auteur* director. The director is the central creative force in these films. Paradoxically, she or he looks to classical Hollywood for her or (more often than not) his model. The *auteur* transforms the conventions of classical Hollywood in order to convey a personal message and vision. Auteurism, of course, emerged most clearly with the French New Wave in the late 1950s. However in the 1990s the figure of the director/author took on a canonical status—a status that Almodovar enjoys and that allowed his work to be immediately seized by critics in the United States and in Europe as an example of film culture at its best.

The second trend is exemplified by films with a Hollywood feel and an international cast, crew, and financial structure, like *Highlander*

(1986). These films constitute a genre that solidified in the 1990s and that depends on the creation of a single male character that becomes the focus of history. Inspired by the epic dramas of the 1950s, the genre developed over the 1990s with films like *Fortress* (1993) and *Fortress 2* (1999) and *Highlander* 3 (1994). The Academy Award winning *Braveheart* (1995) lends legitimacy to this genre as an alternative to the *auteur* film.

Family and freedom provide the pretext for *Braveheart*'s story of the thirteen-century rebel Scot William Wallace (played by Mel Gibson). But the film relies more heavily on displays of man-to-man violence that its hero pursues as his destiny, a destiny that is inevitably fatal. *Gladiator* looks back at this genre nostalgically.[1] The film provides a baroque and overtly artificial overstatement about the ideology of these films in which masculinity, nation, and history are mourned rather than celebrated. *Gladiator* is about the 1990s, recapitulating cinematic past rather than looking forward to the new millennium. The film's success at the Academy Awards underscores the significance of this idealized history and its cinematic representations.

Gladiator and *All about My Mother* reveal how film culture of the 1990s called into question concepts of national culture and national history. These two films have a common dependence upon Hollywood movies of the studio era. These old Hollywood movies have come to constitute a shared culture in which international audiences participate as part of their visual and narrative heritage. Universal defines Scott's film in terms of a Hollywood past. "It has been four decades since chariots raced and swords flashed across movie screens in epic dramas of a time long past."[2] The blurb refers specifically to *Spartacus* (1960) and more generally to the epic films of Cecil B. De Mille in the 1950s, such as *The Ten Commandments* (1956); however, this quote itself suggests an ambiguity in the notion of Hollywood.[3] *Gladiator* is also indebted to the Italian mytho-melodramas of the late 1950s and 1960s: *Ercole e la regina di Lidia* (1958), *Ercole alla conquista di Atlantide* (1961), *Ercole sfida Sansone* (1964), and so on, or even the United Kingdom's *Jason and the Argonauts*, produced by Columbia Pictures (1963).

Almodovar's title is an obvious reference to Mankiewicz's *All about Eve* (1950), its topic borrowed from the women's weepies of classical Hollywood such as King Vidor's *Stella Dallas* (1937) and Irving Rapper's *Now Voyager* (1942) that intertwine motherhood and destiny. These references to Hollywood and to its legacy as an international film style are not mere nods to the *cinéphile*; they speak eloquently about how film style and film genre create meaning for viewers by calling upon a shared Hollywood literacy. Hollywood movies, then, serve as touchstones, the marks of a culture that the viewers understand as enduring and valuable.

Perhaps, then, we should talk about Hollywood as an international cinema. Doing so raises a number of crucial questions: Is the primacy of this cinematic memory a sign of the dominance of a global, American consumer culture? Is the continued revision of these memories a testimony to the persistence of individual identity? Is interpretation a process by which the viewer both adapts to and resists the hegemonic imposition of American consumer culture, more specifically American film?

Here, two sets of issues seem of special importance. The first set involves the way that Hollywood classical films provide a bank of images and stories that constitute a source of cultural and intellectual capital for movies within an international market. The second regards a thematic thread: The family is a set of vexed relations that define the individual's identity and that hark back to the representations of maternity and paternity in classical Hollywood films.

MATERNAL MELODRAMA IN DRAG

Both *All about My Mother* and *All about Eve* emphasize the notion of quest and in particular the quest for identity. Typically, in *All about My Mother*, as in the women's films that it references, relations between characters are highlighted as the means by which self-realization must be achieved. *All about My Mother* shares this trait with other women's melodramas of the last decade, such as *Fried Green Tomatoes* (1991) or *Waiting to Exhale* (1995)—films that redefine the woman's place through her relations to other women. Family and community are interlocking grids from which men are largely absent. Manuela leaves her home in search of her destiny after the tragic death of her son, Esteban, in an auto accident. In penance, she undertakes to find the boy's father, who has never known his son. Along the way she encounters Rosa, a young nun, pregnant with Esteban's half-brother. This child comes to replace the child Manuela has lost. She finds not only a child, but also a new community. This community enables her to become a better mother, and to avoid the mistakes of her past, in particular that of hiding the sexuality of Esteban's father from her son.

This New World has no stability. Gender and sexuality are endlessly mutable. The only "masculine" father named as such, Rosa's father, is without memory and wanders the city accompanied and protected by his dog. The patriarch is a ghost, his identity lost even to himself. Esteban's father, Lola, is a transsexual, neither man nor woman, both more and less. Dying of AIDS, he is a mysterious and fascinating figure, seducing women and men, a glorious and damned Frankenstein who enjoys the unholy beauty that Mary Shelley originally attributed to her monster in the nineteenth-century novel.

In this film, authenticity emerges only through the extreme plasticity of a frenzied body that gives itself over to the surgical and cosmetic interventions of consumer culture in a delirium in which pain and pleasure become one and the same. Herein lies the importance of *All about Eve*, in which a younger woman attempts to become a star by patterning herself after an older successful actress, who is played by Bette Davis. The philosophical mother of cinema is the star exemplified by Bette Davis—the eternal and yet ever-changing woman whose performance of femininity is more compelling than its reality. The star is mother to modern woman; she teaches the girl or, as the case may be, the boy, how to perform femininity. In *All about Eve*, the women characters fail to understand their common destiny. They are pitted against each other, competing for the attentions of a man, whose interest is necessary to their status as feminine. In contrast, *All about My Mother* emphasizes the emotional bonds established between the star, Huma, who is barren, and the mother, Manuela. The film offers two mothers: one who models femininity as performance (Huma, patterned after Bette Davis in *All about Eve*) and the other an idealized femininity of sacrifice (Manuela, patterned after Barbara Stanwyck in *Stella Dallas*).

All about My Mother demonstrates how the question posed by Simone de Beauvoir more than fifty years ago—What is woman?—is not the exclusive property of feminists. Cinema has been in dialogue with woman and her efforts to define her place in twentieth-century society since its inception. Hollywood cinema has done so perhaps even more convincingly than its avant-garde counterparts because of its proven capacity to speak *to* if not *for* women. Cinema itself is an instrument of analysis that permits us to ask whether or not the category woman retains any specific meaning. Perhaps, as in the case of Lola, femininity as the object of desire is better performed than inherited as a set of traits.

Is Lola the best woman—the most desirable? What is his relationship to parenthood?

Almodovar invokes the Hollywood tradition as the means by which traditional gender roles have been called into question. Like Universal's *Gladiator*, his film conjures up the great Hollywood dramas of the 1950s—the films of Douglas Sirk, Nicolas Ray, Vincente Minnelli, and Elia Kazan—and John Cassavetes in the 1960s and 1970s. *All about My Mother* produces an energy, a kinetic explosion that carries the narrative from shot to shot, echoing Minnelli's more excessive productions. The vitality and the emphasis on gesture and expression recall Kazan; the stylization of the mise-en-scène owes much to Sirk. The placement of the figure within the frame, the choreography of human form, and the evocation of the family, remind us of Nicholas Ray's *Rebel without a Cause* (1955) and *Bigger Than Life* (1956). Yet unlike these films, in which an element of social critique inevitably emerges, *All about My Mother* celebrates performance as an essential gesture that defines the individual.

Even the angelic mother, Manuela, is inhabited by an energy that is over the top. She recalls Gena Rowlands's inspired performances for John Cassavetes, most notably in *Woman under the Influence* (1974). Manuela is as excessive in her grief as in her happiness. The close-ups of her face, lined by tragedy, are naked to the camera. This nakedness is as much a performance as is the glamour look and lighting that define Lola's features.

The joy of performance and the joys of consuming these performances, these are the means by which Almodovar recreates a Hollywood that is not simply the celebration of consumer culture. The film's irony authorizes these excesses and legitimates its aesthetic of performance. This aesthetic constitutes a legacy that unites mother and child, fascinated in front of a television watching Hollywood movies, in a scene from the beginning of the film. Initially, Almodovar appears to question femininity and motherhood; by the end of the film, motherhood as a value is reaffirmed. The family is remade in the image of a new community. Gender is freed from the constraints of the oedipal triangle of father, mother, and child. This new society, however, is a society without politics in which only individual relations are important. We are encouraged to understand the world as a set of personal choices and relationships. Economic, political, and social structures seem non-existent and without effect. The myth of individual autonomy and agency, the power to act, is reworked in terms of gender itself.

INADEQUATE PATRIARCHS: FAMILY MELODRAMA IN IMPERIAL ROME

The figures of father, mother, and child provide the defining terms of *Gladiator*'s story. However the implications of its conclusion, in spite of the apparent happy ending, are far more pessimistic than those of *All about My Mother*. The film encourages us to understand imperial Rome in terms of a family dynamic. The dysfunctional family breeds totalitarianism.

Here is a political world but one in which the individual and his place in the family determine the course of history. History and politics are collapsed, united into one universal concept, the family. This concept is hollow, a cover story; scenes of violence depicting men among men visually and dramatically dominate the screen. Vital family relations, those that determine history, are themselves between men.

The ailing Marcus Aurelius, father to his country, intent on restoring the republic, deems his son, Commodus, unfit to rule and wishes to leave the empire in the hands of one of his generals, Maximus, the ideal son. He confides this wish to his daughter, Lucilla. Commodus kills his father and assumes the throne. Only Maximus and Lucilla know that Commodus is a usurper and guilty of patricide. Maximus escapes death but becomes a slave. At this point, his life takes the form of a double quest, to kill Commodus and to rejoin his family, which was murdered by Commodus's followers. Actions, rather than relationships (as in the woman's film described above), determine the outcome of his quest, which recalls masculine Hollywood genres, such as the western.

Marcus Aurelius as the inadequate father assumes responsibility for his son's weakness. If the film borrows its scope and setting from the epic adventure film, its plot derives from the family melodramas and social problem films of the same period. This conflict between father and son mark the melodramas of the 1950s and early 1960s, such as *Rebel without a Cause* (1955) and *Bigger Than Life* (1956), Douglas Sirk's *Written on the Wind* (1956), and Elia Kazan's *Splendor in the Grass* (1961). In *Gladiator*, as in *Written on the Wind*, the ideal son and the daughter must right the wrongs perpetrated by the father and son. Lucilla must come to realize her moral responsibilities. Maximus must restore order, and in so doing reestablish the republic as a government for the people.[4] Having triumphed over Commodus, Maximus, dying, is urged by the weeping Lucilla to join his family. In death the father, mother, and child triangle is restored; however in life, as in Almodovar's film, only the mother and son survive. Lucilla and her son inherit Rome.

The family that is reunited in death is a family that exists only in Maximus's memory.[5] We are first introduced to Maximus's family near the beginning of the film when Marcus Aurelius asks Maximus to describe his home. At this point we understand that the first image of the film, a hand passing through a field of grain, is associated with the ideal imaginary family.[6] This image, as well as others, a wall with a door, a woman with dark flowing hair, a young smiling boy, presented early in the film will be repeated at its conclusion, at the moment when the dying Maximus has fulfilled his quest. This cluster of signs borrowed from the imagery of advertising alludes to another ideal world where all desires are realized, where desire and memory are one and the same. These recurring disjointed images disrupt the sense of real time and space, created through the use of classical Hollywood editing conventions, that allows the bulk of the film's action to be understood as plausible. There is only one sequence that shows the real family, Maximus, his wife, and son reunited. Here, we see only the blackened legs of the dead mother and son, their bodies outside the frame. The focus of the shot is on Maximus, positioned between the two bodies, frozen by what he sees, what we cannot see, the tortured bodies of his murdered wife and son in their entirety.[7] In this film, family is not a set of relations in life but a dream realized in death, a set of corpses that appear only fleetingly, a wistful vision of what might have been.

This dream of the family that the film posits as ideal and universal lends cohesion to the film and enables it to create a concept of morality and humanity that appears to transcend time and culture. This concept of family permits Maximus to become a charismatic leader and to triumph against all odds. This ideal creates the bond that will make allies of such diverse figures as Juba, the African hunter, and Lucilla, the emperor's sister and lover. Commodus's father, Marcus Aurelius, claims that Commodus is not a "moral man" precisely because he cannot incarnate this ideal of family. Commodus's failure to understand the moral concept behind the notion of family results in his crimes: patricide and incest. Not coincidentally, Commodus's character unites a number of traits stereotypically linked to male homosexuality, indirectly associating alternative sexual identities with criminality and heterosexuality with morality.

Commodus's crimes against the family are also linked to his position as a despot. In an Internet advertisement, Ridley Scott comments on the role of the despot, associating himself and Commodus as entertainers and criminals: "Entertainment has frequently been used as a tool of leaders as a means to distract and abuse citizenry. The most tyrannical ruler must still beguile his people even as he brutalizes them."[8]

Ironically, *Gladiator* upholds this ideal of brutality in a story that can have no other purpose than to excite a lust for violence because, as in *All about My Mother*, this is a film without politics. Unlike *All about My Mother*, however, this film devotes its energies, not to the depiction of family and community, but to scenes of frenzied violence that exhaust themselves in death.

In *Gladiator*, any specific notions of social responsibility are lost in a spectacle of violence that is neither moral nor political and that places family drama at the heart of all narrative. Family relations, as Hollywood has defined them, offer an ideal that makes the world meaningful and above all distinguishes good from evil. Family is literally a religion in this film. Maximus prays to little figures who represent family as the unattainable ideal. My point here is not to critique a given interpretation of history; *Gladiator* of course is fiction. The film's principal goal is to offer a series of spectacular and violent scenes to a mesmerized viewer, lulled by the false sense that he is viewing a moral tale.

A CITIZEN WITHOUT POLITICS

The many points that these two dramatically different films hold in common suggest how categories such as studio production versus independent film, American movies versus European cinema, genre narrative versus *auteur* fiction, have been thrown into question by recent cultural and industrial developments. Is this a general "Americanizing" of film culture? It seems more accurate to see Hollywood itself as an international terrain. *All about My Mother* offers a Spanish rendition of the maternal melodrama that moves beyond national boundaries by taking up the questions of gender and performance. *Gladiator* is concerned with creating a story that subscribes to a humanistic vision, the family of man, in order to create an alibi for its morality of violence. Both films throw into question the role of paternity and its relationship to masculinity. In *Gladiator*, the film attempts to shore up a traditional

Hollywood definition of masculinity, echoing the great masculine genres such as the western. *All about My Mother* is less universal in its perspective, putting forward the importance of subcultural concerns and their viability.

All about My Mother is more optimistic; its Hollywood is forever subject to change and reinterpretation. In the end, however, both *All about My Mother* and *Gladiator* refuse the viewer a sense of how collective social and political structures might be understood as forming individual destinies. Neither film attempts to define a set of moral principles that encompasses the complexities of contemporary global culture, extending beyond family and individual. This is perhaps Hollywood's most enduring and most pernicious legacy and one that marks the 1990s as a whole. It dictates the limits of moral responsibility. Individual fulfillment is its goal.

NOTES

1. In many circles, Ridley Scott would be evaluated as an *auteur* director; however his popular (as opposed to critical) successes depend on genre as much as personal vision. *Gladiator* is considered at best a weak example of his work, though it won him the Academy Award for Best Picture, 2000.

2. Internet advertisement, July 2000.

3. Many famous cameramen, directors, actors, and actresses of the Hollywood classical era were European in origin.

4. The film does not emphasize the notion of democracy, a government "by the people," but (anachronistically) suggests it by implication.

5. The film presents the wife and son through Maximus's description. They exist for him and us primarily as memories. He has seen neither for almost three years; nonetheless, the film shows us not the child whom Maximus left almost three years ago, but rather, a young boy whom he has never known, as Maximus *imagines* him to be.

6. Michael Rogin drew my attention to the fact that the ring is on the fourth finger of the left hand, thus, for all intents and purposes a wedding ring according to Hollywood (if not Roman) convention.

7. The previous sequence in which the soldiers arrive at Maximus's home is shot and edited to give it a dreamlike feel. This sequence is perhaps yet another moment in which Maximus imagines his family's fate. It does not have the force of an event that occurs in real time (such as the battle scenes or later scenes of violence in the arena), pointing to the ambiguous status of that family's reality.

8. Internet advertisement, July 2000.

PART III

FOUR KEY FILMS

8

The Zen of Masculinity—Rituals of Heroism in *The Matrix*

Pat Mellencamp

I FIRST SAW, or experienced, *The Matrix* in New York, in the summer of 1999, the day it opened to a packed theater of savvy, sophisticated movie fans from the Upper East Side. I loved the film immediately, from the opening credits' alteration of the sacrosanct studio logo, followed by the torrential strings of green computer code, the matrix itself, cascading down the huge screen. On the soundtrack is a telephone connection that sets up Trinity's (Carrie-Anne Moss) daring rooftop escape from the police and the smarter, stronger agents/bots—a dash through a maze-like building and a death-defying leap between buildings, *Vertigo* (1958) meets *Street Fighter*.[1] It is an energizing scene, an adrenaline rush.

It will be ten minutes of this exhilarating chase before the film's star, Keanu Reeves, is introduced.[2] Groggy, disheveled, he is slouched, dozing in front of his computer monitor, barely conscious. (Some critics might say this state is a constant for Reeves.) Subsequently, we are never certain whether Thomas Anderson/a.k.a. Neo is asleep or awake, in reality or virtuality. It will take the entire film before he gets up to this woman's speed, fighting skills, awareness, and black-leather fashion.

Immediately, it is apparent that the film's energy, its artistic invention, is considerable. It could be that John Gaeta (visual effects supervisor) and Zach Staenberg (editor) are right on when they claim *The Matrix* as the "first film of the millennium, monumental, groundbreaking, with a new visual style that will be remembered."[3] To them, *The Matrix* is art, made by artists, the Wachowski brothers, who have a consistent, unswerving, and clear vision—an auteur imprimatur.

At first glance, *The Matrix* is postmodern punk—high-tech, over-the-top aggression, martial arts fights tempered by a narrative of minimalist facial expressions, flattened emotions, and few words. Agent Smith speaks his pithy epigrams in a modulated, singsong monotone: "Human beings are a disease, a plague, and we are the cure." Or, my favorite, "Never send a human to do a machine's job." Bots are better fighters than humans because they never die; they instantly reproduce and multiply, like bacteria. The "real world" is a mise-en-scène of black and blue/green, a grunge techno aesthetic, exemplified by the S and M club in Sydney where Trinity, in black leather, first meets Neo/Thomas Anderson.

The Matrix eclectically blends Asian and American film genres (particularly action adventure, sci-fi, Kung Fu/Hong Kong martial arts), live action and animation (Japanese anime, Warner Brothers cartoons), and other media (comic books, TV, and computer/video games, in the latter, particularly architectural form and visual style). The Wachowski brothers, the film's writers/directors, wanted to bring Japanese animation to life, to add flesh to a cartoon and soul to a machine. They love and know film history, particularly genre films, which they cite, mix up, and alter.

The title, *The Matrix*, suggests more than computer code, its main referent. It represents a confluence, a grid, of aesthetic and structural forms—theater, film, graphic arts (particularly comic book drawings and stories), television, and centrally, I think, computer games. It seamlessly merges analog and digital effects and forms, live action with CGI (computer graphics) so that it is "virtually" impossible to discern any difference between staged and computer-generated stunts, between real and computer-generated bodies fighting. This synthesis between live action and CGI, between film and TV, like the theme of the film itself, joins realities by passing through portals, images of screens and windows, transversing one dimension, and one medium, into another.

I see the film as a hybrid, mutable object—simultaneously old and new, physical and ephemeral, real and virtual, analog and digital, an intermix of Western and Eastern thought and practices. Interestingly, the technology that is essential to the narrative and to the characters' lives is a nineteenth century invention—the telephone. The only way to get out of virtual reality is to make a telephone call back to the home base, the mother ship *Nebuchadnezzar*. (The telephone call is a key structuring narrative principle of the 1998 German film *Run Lola Run* as well.)

While 110 digital artists and 40 photographic artists worked on individual shots in *The Matrix*, making what is called "dimensional film," special effects are not primarily used for "razzle dazzle." On the contrary, they move the narrative and tell the story, which is rare. The special effects are critical to the movie. They are very costly and much discussed (winning Academy Awards and other plaudits), *The Matrix* celebrates the paradox of so many science fiction films—criticizing technology in the narrative while using it to entertain us in the movie theater. Set in the future, 2090 to 2139 (after humans have destroyed the environment and the intelligent machines have rebelled, resulting in the apocalyptic Machine War, begun when a droid killed two humans), *The Matrix* enacts the contradictions of contemporary technology—it decries the effects of technology on humanity, while at the same time deploying the most advanced technologies to make its point in dazzling, moneymaking images. Back through Fritz Lang's *Metropolis* (1927), films have depicted technology other than cinema as dystrophic. In fact, for the past fifteen or so years, films attacking the evil, dehumanizing effects of computer technologies almost form a Hollywood genre. (Only now is Hollywood jumping on the digital, Internet bandwagon.)

In the film's black world of the machine, human bodies are produced for energy, grown in machine fields as adult embryos, as fuel cells. The embryo field is the most complicated computer graphic shot—all painted. The field is what humans don't see, reality. As Morpheus says, "For a long time I wouldn't believe it but then I saw the fields with my own eyes." Seeing is still believing, and sight is knowledge. Intelligent, voracious machines with grasping tentacles right out of *20,000 Leagues Under the Sea* (1954) and *Aliens* (1986) rule the sunless world. Human minds and imaginations are deceived and held captive by virtual reality, computer programs of an illusory modern city and its inhabitants—the Matrix of the title. That the city (and the citizens), the Matrix, is virtual, a computer simulation, is signaled by its green hues, without any blue in the sky. "There is no blue in the Matrix, it is sucked out, monochromatic, no sun, no life." It is green-toned, like the earlier Warner Brothers logo. The virtual world is very bright, starkly white, perfect, sharp-edged, and sterile. It is symmetrical, mathematical, repetitive, and predictable—like computer code. The real world is old, worn-out, tattered, and eclectic; reality is dark, mystical, mythical, and messy (a young, or adolescent, man's rendition). The line between the synthetic and the organic, like that between the virtual and the real, is one of imperfection, awkwardness, and clutter. Unlike humans, computer programs never make a mistake. When they do, like déjà vu, the glitch signals that something has been changed. And that is what cannot happen—change.

As realized by the set designer, Owen Patterson, the mythical, blue-toned, German Expressionist world of the *Nebuchadnezzar* is beat-up, dingy, dark, claustrophobic, filled with computer screens and old electronic machines that crowd the small spaces. Morpheus looks directly out, at us, at Neo, during his and our initial visit to the ship. In these rare shots of looking at the camera, at the audience, our subjectivity is elided with Neo's—thus this story is about us, about our empowerment. We meet the motley crew, the usual band of punk rebels, from a point just this side of the screen, a position of first-person subjectivity comparable to computer games, where we are on a quest, or holding the gun, where we are the main character searching for truth and the princess in a labyrinthine structure containing clues and traps. We grow stronger or we die, only to live again to repeat our actions, practicing, gaining mastery, as the levels of the game intensify in difficulty and speed. We are singular characters while our enemies lack individuality and are interchangeable; among their superpowers is their ability to multiply and replicate. In computer games, we continually die; thus, death is virtual, merely a stage in the journey, a temporary lull in the action.

The scene at the Oracle's apartment is typical of the strange-way stations in computer games, a notion that *ExistenZ* (1999) develops in greater detail. It encapsulates what's going on in the entire film—we are whom we believe we are. As the Spoon Boy, in monk's attire and shaved head, says, "Don't try and bend the spoon. That's impossible. Try and realize the truth. There is no spoon. It is not the spoon that bends, it's only ourselves." Another visual motif occurs here—the reflections on the spoon, like the many reflections on the sunglasses, suggest that this world is illusory.

When Morpheus takes Neo to the Oracle's flat, an inner-city project setting, he offers the following advice: "Try not to think in terms of right or wrong. . . . I can only show you the door. You have to walk through it." Two key principles—the problem with dualistic, moralistic thinking and the necessity for us to choose right action—emerge here. In the background the song "Beginning to See the Light" is playing. In her grandmotherly way, the Oracle says, "You're waiting for something. Your next life, maybe." (The Eastern philosophical premises also

"Try not to think in terms of right and wrong. . . . I can only show you the
door. You have to walk through it." Laurence Fishburne as the inscrutable
Morpheus in Larry and Andy Wachowski's *The Matrix* (Warner Brothers, 1999).

include reincarnation, which could be thought of as the base of many computer games where death is followed immediately by rebirth, as characters become stronger with each reincarnation.) After telling him he is not the one, the Oracle guides Neo with a prophecy that is a narrative riddle, both a test and a clue: "Without Morpheus we are lost. One of you is going to die. The choice is yours."

Thus, just beneath the black-leather toughness, kick-ass attitude, and heroic technique is a sweet message of self-empowerment and even self-sacrifice. Through the guidance of a teacher and the counsel of a grandmother, the true prince or warrior will encounter and overcome obstacles, becoming stronger and more skilled in the process. In the end, if he does his duty by taking right and selfless action, with humility and discipline, he achieves the impossible, is rewarded with the love of the princess, and lives to star in another film already in production. While his fighting skills come from technology—implanting computer programs directly into his brain—his real strength comes from within, from the belief in himself, in his own greatness, in the self-awareness that he is "the one."

The words of the last scene are "You're afraid of us, of change. I came to tell you how it will begin, a world without you, without borders." Neo is wearing sunglasses, talking on his cell phone, wearing his black outfit. Keanu Reeves's transformation—from Thomas Anderson, computer programmer in a cubicle of an anonymous software corporation, to Neo, his online name as a computer hacker/purveyor of illicit digital material, to finally "the One," an invincible warrior—is exemplified by his costume. He goes from wearing the dark gray suit of a midlevel computer programmer by day, to the generic baseball jacket of the anonymous hacker by night, to the ultimate, the long black leather coat of an avenging savior/warrior in the lobby shoot-out scene.

When I taught *The Matrix*, my male students were quick to distance themselves from Keanu Reeves, his persona, and his performance as Neo. They repudiated any identification, any affective response, with this self-realized hero in the making—a great spiritual and martial arts teacher with a powerful girlfriend in black leather. But I think their response was too fast, too dismissive. Old-fashioned identification with such an ideal, with such a beautiful man, is uncool to admit, despite the fact that freshman and sophomore guys often speak with the same expressionless faces and voices.

The film was made by two unknown, young directors. Larry and Andy Wachowski are unpretentious, even nerdy, regular guys, formerly carpenters, brothers from Chicago who wear shorts and baseball caps, and laugh a lot. The story behind their making of *The Matrix* resembles the film's theme of believing in oneself and hence accomplishing the impossible. They have taken the very advice Neo takes at the end of the film to become Hollywood movie directors with studio support, artistic freedom, personal control, a big budget, and wide release on only their second film.[4]

In "Zooming Out: The End of Offscreen Space" Scott Bukatman sees the logical congruence between science fiction and new media, as movies extend "into a multimedia, global consciousness."[5] In an argument similar to Tom Gunning's now axiomatic assessment of early cinema, Bukatman refers to John Belton's analysis of technological spectaculars in which "plot is replaced by audience envelopment."[6] In large-format events, the causal chains of narrative are displaced by a more participatory, bodily engagement.[7] The function of the entertaining technology is to inscribe "new, potentially traumatic . . . perspectives onto the familiar field of the film spectator's body." In relation to the increasing prevalence of computers and other intelligent machines in our lives, as well as in filmmaking, this could be one mission of *The Matrix*, a warning about the replacement of our real lives with sterile virtual simulations.

Bukatman accords science fiction a significant role in forming subjectivity (which is the principal theme of *The Matrix*): "the genre of science fiction denaturalizes the world, constructing new subjects, new beings in cyberscapes." His term for this new self is derived from computer thought—the very literal "terminal identity"—which is a great way to think about the relation between the person working in a corporate office and the computer hacker, searching for the meaning of life and death. Terminal identity includes both the end of the "traditional self and the emergence of new definitions," all "constructed at the computer station and television screen."[8] Through science fiction, "the shock of the new is aestheticized and examined." It is intriguing that the film industry views the new technologies as both dystopic stories and utopian technical feats. As Bukatman explains these contradictions, the genre's narrative is often conservative while the delirious techniques can "speak" other meanings entirely.[9]

To a degree, Bukatman's very creative essay inadvertently performs this same contradictory strategy of containment—taking concepts from computer thought and then making a conservative argument about this technological shift. He argues that delirium, immersion, and kinesis all refer to modernity, to turn-of-the-century urban industrialism.[10] Via Jonathan Crary, he adopts the term "kaleidoscopic perception" to include all three. As much as I like this metaphor of "kaleidoscopic perception," I question whether "immersion," a key term for gamers, digital thinkers, and virtual reality builders, can so easily be placed into an older context, without acknowledging its updated forms and effects that elide or make irrelevant the distinction between the real and the virtual. In addition, I think there is a huge difference between the spectacular, kinetic effects of events like big-budget, big-screen sci-fi spectacles and the interactive, everyday, and ongoing subjectivity of the computer and of two-way interaction that computers involve. Although both are participatory, the first events focus on vision, while we remain in the dark; the second ones are more tactile.

Bukatman concludes that film is becoming something to "inhabit rather than watch."[11] The narrative "enhances cohabitation with the film's world"; its expansion into "a more environmental, ambient form" fosters "sense of presence, the replacement of urban space by cyberspace." For Bukatman, cyberspace is the "new referent for the immersive entertainments founded on some form of kaleidoscopic perception."

"What interests me about these effects," Bukatman concludes, "is that they are addressed to me: they acknowledge my presence in the theater and emphasize the experience of viewing. . . . They license an adventure of perception that is not voyeuristic but exploratory. They reintroduce cinema as a public space; they provide a release from causal structures like narrative."[12] I love the notions of "kaleidoscopic perception," "terminal identity," and films as spaces or worlds we inhabit. But I disagree about the displacement of narrative, or the relegation of narrative to a subservient status. If anything, the opposite is true of the film I am considering here.

Clearly, the narrative of *The Matrix* is central. But it is a narrative in which conventions of cause-effect logic, like reality itself, are rapidly and inventively changing. The same can be said about *Being John Malkovich* (1999), *Run Lola Run*, and *ExistenZ*. In one sense, these films are questioning the causal structure of narrative, as well as fashioning new forms, emerging in the digital era of hypertext, hyperlink, and two-way (at least) interaction/participation. For Bukatman, they are not revolutionary; they are playful.

In *zeros + ones: digital women + the new technoculture*, Sadie Plant poses the continued viability of Marshall McLuhan's assertion that "Times of great technological change always tend to be marked by the feeling that 'the future will be a larger or greatly improved version of the *immediate* past.'" Plant reminds us through McLuhan that "the present is viewed through a rear-view mirror that conceals the extent of contemporary change."[13]

For Plant, multimedia are addressing "an entirely new sensory environment" in which "'touch' is not skin but the interplay of the senses . . . a fruitful meeting of sight translated into sound and sound into movement, and taste and smell." There is no longer the hierarchical system of knowledge and media in which vision is superior but a "synaesthetic, immersive zone in which all the channels and senses find themselves," leaving the spectator "with no private protection, not even his own body, to protect him anymore." While sight is organized around the organs that see and the things that are seen, touch is not a localized sense. "It is dispersed and distributed across the skin . . . the skin is both a border and a network of ports. . . . Sight depends on separation, the possibility of distinguishing what is touching from what is touched. . . . Sight is the sense of security which tactility completely undermines" and thus, "touching is the principal prohibition." Disavowal is a visual mechanism, no defense at all for the experience of "tactility" in that New York movie theater.[14]

I felt defenseless in front of *The Matrix*—and I am a film professor, long familiar with disavowal (the use of "it's only a movie" to quell anxiety). As Plant points out, this is precisely "what the history of technology was intending to avoid . . . the fear of the 'alien touch.'" (The scariest, most terrifying part of the Alien exhibit/event at Disneyworld is not the magnificent and detailed holograph of the Alien, or any other hi-tech devices. It is the old-fashioned claustrophobia of being strapped into a seat, including heads and necks, the blast of air in one's face, the slight rumble of the seats, and the intense darkness, together triggering "fear of the 'alien touch.'" It is also our loss of movement, our feeling of having no control—all, however, intensified by the high-tech hologram.)

Plant's view of virtual reality and immersion is almost diametrically different from *The Matrix*. In her virtual reality, we surrender to the perceptual realm, "celebrating the bodily freedom of cyberspace as the final frontier," a "haven waiting to welcome its users to a safe computer-generated world in which they could finally be free as their finest fantasies. It promised a zone of absolute autonomy in which one could be anything, a space without bodies and material constraints, a digital land fit for heroes and a new generation of pioneers."[15]

This is the zone of computer hackers, of visionaries, of online gamers and programmers. And although the digital world in the narrative of *The Matrix* is a means of containment, a mechanism for keeping humans captive in a sunless machine world, it is the choice Morpheus offers Neo in the film, the same choice we make on opening the DVD: "You take the blue pill and the story ends . . . you wake up in your bed and believe what you want to believe. You take the red pill and stay in Wonderland and I show you how deep the rabbit hole goes." We interact by clicking on the pill, we make a choice, and no matter how limited, contained, or authored our choice, we do take action.

Perhaps even more than films, computer games are interactive, impressive, and kaleidoscopic. The opening sequence of *The Matrix*, like all of *Run Lola Run*, is almost directly derivative of a game. And this is not surprising given the influence of Japanese comics and animation on the computer gaming world as well as the Wachowski brothers. In the action adventure game, we make our way through a fantasy world of graphic design by creating and developing a character as we go, picking up clues and magical tokens, often hidden in the graphics, in the very architecture of the game. Although there can be a princess in the end, the quest matters more than the prize; in fact, winning the princess is quite incidental. The narrative of *The Matrix*, along with its mythology, is similar.

In the twitch, or click and shoot games, we can charge through mazes firing at the bad guys who suddenly confront us, die and then multiply, our goal being to get through various levels of difficulty. To achieve this, we will die numerous times before we complete the game. Death in a computer game is not high drama or emotive, although it can be a surprise. It is a lull in the game, a space between repetitions of the same moves, but with a difference—we can learn from our errors, we can be resurrected, regularly, and eventually, if we persist, we can win the game. Critically, the subject position is first-person, from the player's point of view, which is invoked often in *The Matrix*. In the opening sequence, when Trinity runs through the hotel corridors, turning corners only to meet agents, the set design, its space and tone are just like the graphic architecture of a computer game with its telescoped corridors, a labyrinth of halls leading to cavernous rooms.

The Matrix touched a chord in my students, including their love of computer games (which very few of my students will initially admit to liking or still playing) and their dream of making a Hollywood movie. Their enthusiasm for the film's technical and aesthetic accomplishments and its message of self-empowerment through the auspices of a benevolent teacher represents the New Age philosophical paradigm—high-tech meets ancient Eastern discipline and practices. This mix of Eastern thought in Western genres and characters is at the core of so much contemporary culture, including that of self-help, suggesting a move, perhaps even a longing, similar to the counter-artistic cultures of the 1960s, which united technology, particularly video, with Eastern thought. The overriding message of the film is that if our belief in ourselves remains steadfast, there is nothing we cannot accomplish or become. Our thoughts, which we will learn to focus and discipline, create and determine our world—a distinctly Eastern philosophical premise. Each obstacle we surmount will make us stronger and will give us the awareness we need to go forward. In terms of vision as knowledge, Neo learns to "see" himself in a new way—he is given insight and comes to see the world differently. It is insight that matters the most.

Popular culture is in flux; the forms are changing into multimedia, and with this will come altered subjectivity. *The Matrix, Being John Malkovich*, and *Run Lola Run* are reconfiguring narrative, and refiguring difference differently. They are all vanguard films, cultural signposts of change. They are also terrifically entertaining.

NOTES

1. This powerhouse sequence, which encapsulates the style of the movie—in the editor's vernacular, "it kicks ass and never stops"—took four days of shooting and six months of training; it energized the entire production, and galvanized front office support.

2. This sequence demonstrates the prowess of the cinematographer, Bill Pope, and the split-second editing of the film.

3. These quotations are taken from the supplemental, voice-over analysis

on the DVD, which parallels some information on the Web site, recent and re-constructed.

4. The heroic mythology in the film is replicated again and again by the tales of "rocket science" technical achievement for the film.

5. Scott Bukatman, "Zooming Out: The End of Offscreen Space," in *The New American Cinema*, ed. Jon Lewis (Durham: Duke University Press, 1998), 249.

6. Bukatman, "Zooming Out: The End of Offscreen Space," 252.

7. This distinction between narrative and participatory performance is very close to my analysis of a low-tech small-TV format, *I Love Lucy*.

8. Bukatman, "Zooming Out: The End of Offscreen Space," 253.

9. Bukatman, "Zooming Out: The End of Offscreen Space," 267.

10. Bukatman, "Zooming Out: The End of Offscreen Space," 255.

11. Bukatman, "Zooming Out: The End of Offscreen Space," 266.

12. Bukatman, "Zooming Out: The End of Offscreen Space," 267.

13. Sadie Plant, *zeros + ones: digital women + the new technoculture* (New York: Doubleday, 1997), 180.

14. Plant, *zeros + ones: digital women + the new technoculture*, 186.

15. Plant, *zeros + ones: digital women + the new technoculture*.

9

Ikea Boy Fights Back

Fight Club, Consumerism, and the Political Limits of Nineties Cinema

Henry A. Giroux and Imre Szeman

IF IT HAS now become easier to imagine the end of the earth and of nature than the end of capitalism, as Fredric Jameson has argued in *The
Seeds of Time*, it is due in large part to the redoubled efforts of a global,
neoliberal capitalism.[1] The breathless rhetoric of the global victory of
free market rationality spewed forth by the mass media, right-wing intellectuals, and governments alike has found its material expression in
an all-out attack on democratic values and on the very notion of the
public. In the discourse of neoliberalism, issues regarding persistent
poverty, inadequate health care, racial apartheid in the inner cities, and
the growing inequalities between the rich and the poor have been either
removed from the inventory of public discourse and public policy or
factored into talk show spectacles that highlight private woes bearing
little relationship either to public life or to potential remedies that demand collective action.

As the laws of the market take precedence over the laws of the state
as guardians of the public good, the state increasingly offers little help
in mediating the interface between the advance of capital and its rapacious commercial interests, on the one hand, and those noncommodi-
fied interests and nonmarket spheres that create the political, economic,
and social conditions vital for critical citizenship and democratic public
life on the other. In the prevailing discourse of neoliberalism that has
taken hold of the public imagination, there is no vocabulary for political or social transformation, no collective vision, no social agency to
challenge the ruthless downsizing of jobs or resist the ongoing liquida-

tion of job security, no spaces from which to struggle against the elimination of benefits for people now hired on a strictly part-time basis. In
the midst of this concerted attack on the public, the market-driven consumer juggernaut continues to mobilize desires in the interest of producing market identities and market relationships that ultimately appear as, in the words of Theodor Adorno, nothing less than "a prohibition on thinking itself."[2]

It is this context of the ongoing assault on the public, and the growing preponderance of a free market economy and corporate culture that
turns everything it touches into an object of consumption, that David
Fincher's film *Fight Club* (1999) needs to be considered. Ostensibly, *Fight
Club* appears to offer a critique of late capitalist society and the misfor-
tunes it generates out of its obsessive concern with profits, consumption, and the commercial values that underline its market-driven ethos.
It seems to be opposed to capitalism and consumer culture in a direct
way that is seldom if ever seen on the big screen in America, which is
no doubt why the premiere of *Fight Club* was accompanied by an onslaught of reviews that celebrated it as a particularly daring example of
social critique—the filmic equivalent of magazines like the *Baffler* or *Ad-
busters*, or even of the protests in Seattle, Washington, Philadelphia, and
Los Angeles.[3] But *Fight Club* ultimately manages to offer a critique of the
social and political conditions produced by contemporary capitalism
only in a way that confirms capitalism's worst excesses and legitimates
its ruling narratives. *Fight Club* is, finally, less interested in critiquing the
broader material relations of power and strategies of domination and
exploitation associated with neoliberal capitalism than it is in rebelling
against a consumerist culture that dissolves the bonds of male sociality
and puts into place an enervating notion of male identity and agency.
As much as the film invites cultural critics, art house sophisticates, and
academics to read it against the grain, in the end, *Fight Club* has nothing
substantive to say about the structural violence of unemployment, job
insecurity, cuts in public spending, and the destruction of institutions
capable of defending social provisions and the public good.

Fight Club, along with films such as *American Beauty* (1999), *Rogue
Trader* (1999), *The Big Kahuna* (1999), *American Psycho* (2000), and *Boiler
Room* (2000), inaugurates a new subgenre of film narrative that combines a fascination with the spectacle of violence, enlivened through
tired narratives about the crisis of masculinity, with a superficial gesture toward social critique designed to offer the tease of a serious inde-

pendent/art film. While appearing to address important social issues, these films end up reproducing the very problems they attempt to address. Rather than turning a critical light on important social issues, such films often trivialize them within a stylized aesthetics that revels in irony, cynicism, and excessive violence. *Fight Club* can also be seen as the latest in what has now become a sizable body of recent films that explore American consumerism and its discontents by taking seriously the idea that the cultural and social landscape has been entirely overtaken by the mass media. The political message of films such as *To Die For* (1995), *Cable Guy* (1996), *Pleasantville* (1998), *The Truman Show* (1998), *The Matrix* (1999), and *Ed TV* (1999) is that in the face of the intractable dead-zone reality of shopping malls, freeways, and suburbs, it is only possible for *some* of us to reinvent our lives. It is never imagined that a whole culture could or should change how it organizes the lives of members. These films attempt to reinforce the individualism of neoliberal capitalism by allowing each of us to identify ourselves with their exceptional protagonists, those true individuals who are able to separate themselves out of the mass fantasy of contemporary consumerism and who can thus live out a genuine life in spite of the anxieties and dissatisfactions of the present moment. Among all these films, what makes *Fight Club* so dangerously seductive is that, by contrast, it seems that its protofascist cells at least offer a possible vision of a collective response to the crisis of the neoliberal order, however disturbing such a response might be. But even here, in its perverse imagination of an anticonsumerist skinhead army, *Fight Club* simply reinforces our sense of defeat in the face of contemporary capitalism by making a regressive, vicious, and obscene politics seem like the only possible alternative.[4]

Based on the 1996 first novel by Chuck Palahniuk, *Fight Club* narrates the story of an insomniac, bored corporate drone, Jack (Edward Norton), who finds meaning in his life through his newly found relationship with Tyler Durden (Brad Pitt), a thrill-seeking Everyman. Durden rails against both consumer society and the ongoing feminization of men, both of which contribute to men's feelings of disenfranchisement. In response to these assaults against masculinity, Durden and Jack create an underground bare-knuckles club where men can beat their sufferings out of each other. Eventually the violence escalates into a terrorist bombing campaign against banks, credit card companies, and other corporate holdings.

Though it is problematic in all sorts of ways that demand further

A deft critique of corporate capitalism or just a defense of authoritarian masculinity? David Fincher's stylistically hyperkinetic, thematically ambiguous *Fight Club* (Twentieth Century Fox, 1999).

analysis, particularly in its signature violence and deeply conventional views of gender relations, what we would like to concentrate on here is the way *Fight Club*, in its abject failure to carry out the critique that it purports to undertake, very powerfully reveals the astonishing limits of our political imagination, especially as this is represented in mass media forms like Hollywood films. *Fight Club* understands consumerism, which it takes to be the defining problem of contemporary politics, primarily as an attack on masculinity. Its challenge to the boredom, shallowness, and emptiness of a stifling consumer culture thus necessarily passes through an exploration of what it might mean for men to resist compromising their masculinity for the sofa or cappuccino maker that partly defines them, in order to establish a sense of community in which men can reclaim their virility and power. By trying to think about consumerism and masculinity as phenomena that are linked—a notion of the reigning cultural *Zeitgeist* that it shares with books like Susan Faludi's *Stiffed: The Betrayal of the American Man*—*Fight Club* manages to create a narrative centered around the kind of hip, stylishly violent action that is so attractive to today's filmgoers. It tells us very little, however, about the real circumstances and causes of our discontent, which lie in a very different place than in the seeming emasculation of that social group that wields perhaps the most concentrated power the world has ever seen—urban, upper-middle class, white, male technocrats.

The central protagonists in *Fight Club*, Jack and Tyler, represent two opposing registers that link consumerism and masculinity. Jack is representative of a generation of men condemned to corporate peonage whose emotional lives and investments are mediated through the allure of commodities and goods. No longer a producer of goods, Jack exemplifies a form of domesticated masculinity—passive, alienated, and without ambition. On the other hand, Tyler exemplifies an embodied masculinity that refuses the seductions of consumerism, while fetishizing forms of production—from soaps to explosives—the ultimate negative expression of which is chaos and destruction. Tyler represents the magnetism of the isolated, dauntless antihero whose public appeal is based on the attractions of the cult personality rather than on the strengths of an articulated, democratic notion of political reform. Politics for Tyler is about doing, not thinking. As the embodiment of authoritarian masculinity and hyperindividualism, Tyler cannot imagine a politics that connects to democratic movements, and is less a symbol of vision and leadership for the next millennium than a holdover of early-twentieth-century fascism. Tyler's obsession with power and celebration of violence as the only registers of resistance make him an appropriate founding father of Operation Mayhem, a vanguardist political movement, hierarchically organized through rigid social relations and led by a charismatic cult leader. If Jack represents the crisis of capitalism repackaged as the crisis of a domesticated masculinity, Tyler represents the redemption of masculinity repackaged as the promise of violence in the interests of social and political anarchy.

While *Fight Club* registers a form of resistance to the rampant commodification and alienation of contemporary neoliberal society, it ultimately has little to say about those diverse and related aspects of consumer culture and contemporary capitalism structured in inequitable power relations, material wealth, or hierarchical social formations. *Fight Club* largely ignores issues surrounding the breakup of labor unions, the slashing of the U.S. workforce, extensive plant closings, downsizing, outsourcing, the elimination of the welfare state, the attack on people of color, and the growing disparities between the rich and the poor. All these issues get factored out of *Fight Club*'s analysis of consumerism and capitalist exploitation. Hence, it comes as no surprise that class as a critical category is nonexistent in this film. When working-class people do appear, they are represented primarily as brownshirts, part of the nonthinking herd looking for an opportunity to release their tensions and repressed masculine rage through forms of terrorist violence and self-abuse. Or they appear as people who willingly take up jobs that are dehumanizing, unskilled, and alienating. There is one particularly revealing scene in *Fight Club* that brings this message home while simultaneously signaling a crucial element of the film's politics. At one point in the story, Tyler takes Jack into a convenience store. He pulls out a gun and forces the young Indian clerk to get on his knees. Putting the gun to the clerk's head, Tyler tells him he is going to die. As a kind of parting gesture, he then asks Raymond, the clerk, what he really wanted to be in life. A veterinarian, Raymond replies, but he had to drop out of school for lack of money. Tyler tells him that if he isn't on his way to becoming a veterinarian in six weeks he is going to come back and kill him. He then lets Raymond go and tells Jack that tomorrow morning will be the most important day in Raymond's life because he will have to address what it means to do something about his future. Choice for Tyler appears to be an exclusively individual act, a simple matter of personal will that functions outside existing relations of power, resources, and social formations. As Homi Bhabha points out, this notion of agency "suggests that 'free choice' is inherent in the individual [and] . . . is based on an unquestioned 'egalitarianism' and a utopian notion of individualism that bears no relation to the history of the marginalized, the minoritized, the oppressed."[5]

This privatized version of agency and politics is central to understanding Tyler's character as emblematic of the very market forces he denounces. For Tyler, success is simply a matter of getting off one's backside and forging ahead; individual initiative and the sheer force of will magically cancel out institutional constraints, and critiques of the gravity of dominant relations of oppression are dismissed as either an act of bad faith or the unacceptable whine of victimization. Tyler hates consumerism but he values a "Just Do It" ideology appropriated from the marketing strategists of the Nike corporation and the ideology of the Reagan era. It is not surprising that in linking freedom to the dynamics of individual choice, *Fight Club* offers up a notion of politics in which oppression breeds contempt rather than compassion, and social change is fueled by totalitarian visions rather than democratic struggles. By defining agency through such a limited (and curiously Republican Party) notion of choice, *Fight Club* reinscribes freedom as an individual desire rather than the "testing of boundaries and limits as part of a communal, collective process." In the end, *Fight Club* removes choice as a "public demand and duty"[6] and in doing so restricts the public spaces people are allowed to inhabit as well as the range of subject positions they are allowed to take up. Hence, it is no wonder that *Fight Club* is marked by an absence of working men and women who embody a sense of agency and empowerment, focusing instead on largely middle-class, heterosexual, white men who are suffering from a blocked hypermasculinity.

Consumerism in *Fight Club* is criticized primarily as an ideological force and existential experience that weakens and domesticates men, robbing them of their primary role as producers whose bodies affirm and legitimate their sense of agency and control. The importance of agency is not lost on director David Fincher, but it is restricted to a narrowly defined notion of masculinity that is as self-absorbed as it is patriarchal.[7] Fincher is less interested in fighting oppressive forms of power than he is in exploring how men yield to it. Freedom in *Fight Club* is not simply preoccupied with the depoliticized self, it also lacks a language for translating private troubles into public rage, and as such succumbs to the cult of immediate sensations in which freedom degenerates into collective impotence. Given Fincher's suggestion that men have no enduring qualities outside their physicality, resistance and affirmation are primarily taken up as part of a politics of embodiment that has little concern for critical consciousness, social critique, or democratic social relations. In *Fight Club*, the body is no longer the privileged space of social citizenship or political agency, but becomes "the location of violence, crime, and [aggression]."[8] What changes in *Fight Club* is the context enabling men to assault each other, but the outside world remains the same, unaffected by the celebration of a hypermasculinity and violence that provide the only basis for solidarity.

Fight Club's critique of consumerism suffers from a number of absences that need to be addressed. First, the film depicts capitalism and the ideology of consumerism as sutured, impenetrable, and totalizing, offering few if any possibilities for resistance or struggle. Consumerism, for David Fincher, can function only with the libidinal economy of repression, particularly as it rearticulates the male body away from the visceral experiences of pain, coercion, and violence to the more "feminized" notions of empathy, compassion, and trust. Hence, the film defines masculinity in opposition to both femininity and consumerism while simultaneously refusing to take up either in a dialectical and critical way.

Second, *Fight Club* functions less as a critique of capitalism than as a defense of authoritarian masculinity wedded to the immediacy of pleasure sustained through violence and abuse. Once again, *Fight Club* becomes complicitous with the very system of commodification it denounces since both rely on a notion of agency largely constructed within the immediacy of pleasure, the cult of hypercompetitiveness, and the market-driven desire of winning and exercising power over others.

Third, *Fight Club* resurrects a notion of freedom tied to a Hobbesian world in which cynicism replaces hope, and the survival of the fittest becomes the clarion call for legitimating dehumanizing forms of violence as a source of pleasure and sociality. Pleasure in this context has little to do with justice, equality, and freedom, but with hyper modes of competition mediated through the fantasy of violence. More specifically, this particular rendering of pleasure is predicated on legitimating the relationship between oppression and misogyny, and masculinity gains its force through a celebration of both brutality and the denigration of the feminine. Hence, *Fight Club* appears to have no understanding of its own articulation with the very forces of capitalism it appears to be attacking. This is most evident in its linking of violence, masculinity, and gender. In other words, *Fight Club*'s vision of liberation and politics relies on gendered and sexist hierarchies that flow directly from the consumer culture it claims to be criticizing.

Fight Club may be just one film. However, what we would like to assert here—against the sometimes too simple claims about the indeterminacy of all interpretation—is that the politics imagined in *Fight Club* is symptomatic of a wider symbolic and institutional culture of cynicism and senseless violence that exerts a powerful pedagogical influence on the imagination.[9] As a form of public pedagogy, films such as *Fight Club* bridge the gap between private and public discourse, putting into play particular ideologies and values that resonate with broader public conversations regarding how a society views itself and its political possibilities and potentialities. *Fight Club* reminds us of the need to reclaim the discourses of ethics, politics, and critical agency as important categories in the struggle against the rising tide of violence and human suffering and the specter of fascism that threatens all vestiges of democratic public life. Precisely because of its ideological implications, *Fight Club* posits an important challenge to anyone concerned about the promise of democracy, particularly for critical intellectuals who want to both engage the dominant media and provide opportunities to develop what Paul Gilroy calls, in another context, "minimal ethical principles."[10] At the heart of such an engagement is the need to accentuate and highlight the tension between the growing threat to public life and the promise of a democracy that both remembers the history of human suffering and works to prevent its reoccurrence. The political limits of *Fight Club*'s attack on capitalism and consumerism should point to the need for a more sustained and systematic critique of the dire conditions of contemporary social life.

NOTES

1. Fredric Jameson, *The Seeds of Time* (New York: Columbia University Press, 1994), xii.

2. Theodor W. Adorno, *Critical Models* (New York: Columbia University Press, 1993), 290.

3. See, for example, Janet Maslin, "Such a Very Long Way from Duvets to Danger," *New York Times*, October 15, 1999, B14; and Amy Taubin, "So Good It Hurts," *Sight and Sound*, November 1999, 16.

4. The initial political activities of the fight clubs are carried out in the form of "culture jamming," an ostensibly left-leaning practice of turning consumer culture, and in particular, advertising images, against themselves for political ends. By parodying targeted ad images, culture jamming recontextualizes them and offers a different set of associations through which they can be read. See Kalle Lasn, *Culture Jam: The Uncooling of America* (New York: Morrow, 1999).

5. Homi K. Bhabha, "The Enchantment of Art," in Carol Becker and Ann Wiens, eds., *The Artist in Society* (Chicago: New Art Examiner, 1994), 33.

6. Both of these quotes are from Bhabha, "The Enchantment of Art," 33.

7. For some excellent commentaries on the politics of masculinity, see R. W. Connell, *Masculinities* (Berkeley: University of California Press, 1995); Maurice Berger, Brian Wallis, and Simon Watson, eds., *Constructing Masculinities* (New York: Routledge, 1995); and Paul Smith, ed., *Boys: Masculinities in Contemporary Culture* (Boulder: Westview, 1996).

8. Paul Gilroy, "'After the Love Has Gone': Bio-Politics and Ethepoetics in the Black Public Sphere," *Public Culture* 7, no. 1 (1994): 58.

9. See Henry Giroux, *Impure Acts: The Practical Politics of Cultural Studies* (New York: Routledge, 2000).

10. Paul Gilroy, *Against Race* (Cambridge: Harvard University Press, 2000), 5.

10

The Blair Witch Project, Macbeth, and the Indeterminate End

Eric S. Mallin

> Present fears
> Are less than horrible imaginings.
> —William Shakespeare, Macbeth (1.3.137–38)

THE BLAIR WITCH PROJECT (1999), directed by Eduardo Sanchez and Daniel Myrick, exploits certain limitations of the film medium by setting them against our imagination's resistance to limitations. As most everyone knows by now, this wildly successful faux documentary follows three student filmmakers—actors Heather Donahue, the "director"; Joshua Leonard, the cameraman; and Michael Williams, the sound engineer—into the woods outside Burkittsville, formerly "Blair," Maryland. They search there for the truth behind the legend of the Blair Witch, a figure (even in the movie's terms) of uncertain provenance and debatable historicity. The Witch may or may not exist, haunt the woods, and terrorize the three youths as they become wretchedly and irretrievably lost in darkness. The "project" is the record of a spectacular failure, film footage that the crew could never complete, which paradoxically secures its success as a documentary: to grasp some definitive information about the Blair Witch, the filmmakers need to encounter this ineluctably hostile force. The movie pretends cleverly to be the last word in documentary realism because its reality is so great that the filmmakers could not survive it.

Or could they? While unsteady camera work and inelegant, apparently unscripted conversation bolster the movie's pretense of unmediated recorded truth, the fates of the filmmakers, and simply *what happens* on the level of plot, remain unclear. The conviction of "reality" grows and tracks with the movie's refusal to show any agent of terror or even any unambiguous shape of terror's material effects.[1] Out of hanging stick figures, ominously placed clumps of stones, and a mounting sense of the characters' helplessness the film forges its frights, and something more: it makes the fact of *not* seeing the proof of a malevolent otherworldly presence. The movie lures the viewer into "horrible imaginings" of the unseen, the occulted. And so it shares a noble representational lineage.

I believe we can understand much of what happens in *The Blair Witch Project* through analogy with an older, evocative text of the uncanny: Shakespeare's *Macbeth*. As a progenitor of the horror genre, *Macbeth* haunts high and mass cultural texts alike, providing an archetype for equivocal meanings in the context of supernatural events.[2] While Shakespeare's stage business is never as fuzzy as the events of *The Blair Witch Project*, the play almost obsessively thematizes the literal and moral miasma, the radical uncertainty, that envelops Scotland at the end of Duncan's regime: "Fair is foul and foul is fair," the witches famously intone, "Hover through fog and filthy air" (1.1.11–12); and Lady Macbeth, surprised by her own guilty conscience, says in her sleepwalking reverie near the end of her life, "Hell is murky" (5.1.36).[3] The movie does not remake or consciously reformulate the primary semantic energies of Shakespeare's play, and it contains no direct references to the Scottish tragedy.[4] Yet through the confluence of witchcraft, interdicted knowledge, childhood, the equivocal, and other thematic clusters, *Macbeth* may be said to haunt, or at least echo in, the recent horror film. Both texts are about partial truths, paltering revelations.

Witchcraft or occult stories are always familiars of the uncertain. Interviewing two fishermen about the Blair Witch legend early in the film, Heather receives confirmation and contradiction. The first man says, "Anybody worth their salt around here knows that this area has been haunted by that old woman." The second responds testily, "Oh, that's bullshit." The indeterminate character of the myth thus receives play from the beginning of the movie, reinforced by the physical position of the men here: they are fishing standing back to back. Further interviews with witnesses of varying credibility similarly disrupt certitude. A woman holding a small child claims to have seen a

The most successful independent film of all time, Eduardo Sanchez and
Daniel Myrick's *The Blair Witch Project* (Artisan, 1999).

documentary about the Blair Witch on the Discovery Channel;[5] but
then as she tells the story, the child reacts badly:

> The creepy [*little girl puts her hand on her mother's mouth, mother pulls the*
> *hand away*], the creepy story that I heard was that two men were out
> hunting, they were camped near the cabin she's supposed to haunt
> [*child cries now: "No! No! No"*], and they disappeared off the face of the
> earth. It's OK, Ingrid, I'm just telling a scary story, but it's not true.

Heather, off camera, repeats for the child's sake, "It's not true," as the
woman mouths conspiratorially to the camera, "It's true." The tale, told
in an oscillating affirmation and denial of its own truth, seems plausible because of the terrified youngster's response, which seems authentic and prescient. But even this "scary story" narrates only a disappearance, an evaporation; the Witch herself notably goes missing from the
telling. In fact, almost every aspect of the Blair Witch legend concerns

disappearance, culminating in the fate of the filmmakers; the tale comprises aporias of horror, gaps designed to be filled by the hearer, the audience. The story is about the need to complete the story, the absence of certitude.

So the eponymous figure at the heart of the "project" seems shadowy at best. But her legend does bear a determinate meaning, heralded by the little girl's reaction: it terrifies children. And at first glance the movie itself assumes a naturalistic style appropriate to this meaning: "It's a simple movie, almost childishly so," writes Michael Atkinson in *Film Comment*. Atkinson describes the film as "an ordeal of raw innocence" that evokes "better than any movie has before the reawakened sense of being 10 and shaken rigid by a bogeyman story."[6]

If *The Blair Witch Project* assumes a "childish" stylistic simplicity in the service of reproducing preadolescent terrors, it is a mimesis that sorts well with the historical meanings of witchery. The German word for witch, *die Hexe*, "was not originally applied to human beings at all, but to child-devouring demons, corresponding to the Roman *lamia* . . . till the 14th century."[7] The witch—from Medea to the Russian Baba-Yaga, from Hansel and Gretel's tormentor to the weird sisters in *Macbeth* and Burkittsville's scourge—figures an implacable and irrational threat to youth.[8] The Blair Witch began, we hear, as Elly Kedward, who in the late eighteenth century was accused by neighbors of performing bloodletting on children; she was summarily blindfolded, tied to a tree in the woods, and left to die. But her body was never found, and soon children of the town began disappearing. The ensuing mass hysteria virtually emptied Blair of its denizens. This foundational myth cunningly forms the movie's thematic base: as the filmmakers grow more terrified they become ever more childlike, and as they regress, their vulnerability to the Witch increases, and their chances for survival diminish. Their only hope, as Heather instinctively senses, is to live in representation and continue filming ("It's all I've fucking got left," she cries). The movie charts arrested development, painfully evident in the filmmakers' petulance, their profane shouting matches, and finally their paralyzed sense of helplessness. To find a way out of the woods would not only mean staying alive, but growing up.

The antithetical relation of witches to children operates in *Macbeth* as well. The great warrior comes to lament his childless status because the witches, who prophesy his kingship (and who, incidentally, make potions with "finger of birth-strangled babe" in them), also mention that his friend Banquo will have the more impressive legacy:

1. WITCH: Lesser than Macbeth, and greater.
2. WITCH: Not so happy, yet much happier.
3. WITCH: Thou shalt get [i.e., beget] kings, though thou be none.
So all hail, Macbeth and Banquo!
. . .
MACBETH: Stay, you imperfect speakers. Tell me more. (1.3.65–70)

The witches speak more perfectly than Macbeth knows, their paradoxes calculated both to tell the truth and to leave chasms in understanding that his future gory actions must fill. Because fatherhood gives Banquo the "happier" condition, Macbeth grows miserable at the built-in, heirless limits of his kingship. The witches' information inspires Macbeth to purposeless child killing. For when he fails to murder Fleance, Banquo's son, he senselessly assaults his rival Macduff's estate and puts Lady Macduff and, shockingly, her children to the sword, superfluous deaths that carry immense symbolic freight. Eventually he will be killed by the father of the children he slaughtered, and succeeded as king by the son of the father he murdered.

In light of the determinate or knowable, children represent a node of ambivalence. They are on one hand fixed, elemental, sometimes without guile, their desires dark and bright displayed like banners; on the other, they are in flux, human potentiality in its purest form, and thus signatures of hope or at least the not-yet known. They are fragile yet threatening replacements. Macbeth's juvenicides are therefore at the imaginative center of the play. His deepest wish, revealed in child killing, is not for mere kingship but for literal and symbolic permanence without the danger of being superseded. When he finds that Fleance has escaped, he laments the new disorder:

Then comes my fit again. I had else been perfect,
Whole as the marble, founded as the rock,
As broad and general as the casing air;
But now I am cabin'd, cribb'd, confin'd, bound in
To saucy doubts and fears. (3.4.19–24)

To Macbeth, the failure to kill Fleance means loss of control: suddenly, his certitude fractures. He hopes for solidity ("whole as the marble"), omnipresence, and ungapped knowledge, an expansive yet statuary ontology that no child could threaten; in some way, his dream of being "perfect" in Fleance's death is the dream of being at once inanimate and immortal. Macbeth, childless and tortured by the idea of what heirs could figuratively provide, irrationally needs to kill other people's children. We can see him as a witchy agent of rage against progeny.

The Blair Witch, too, targets children, but we have no psychology for her, only a symbology. Yet by the end of the film, we can be sure that, if she exists, she has found more juveniles to dispatch. The movie's most frightening effect is neither the sounds of children's voices outside the tent where the filmmakers cower, nor the tiny handprints on the walls inside the Witch house, but rather, the reduction of Heather, formerly self-confident documentarian, to a blubbering, snot-dripping child, begging maternal forgivenesses in the best-known scene from the film:

> I just want to apologize, to Mike's Mom, to Josh's Mom, and my Mom, and I'm sorry to everyone. I was very naive. I am so, so sorry for everything that has happened, because in spite of what Mike says it *is* my fault, because it was my project, and I insisted, I insisted on everything. . . . And it's all because of me that we're here now, hungry, and cold, and hunted. I love you Mom, and Dad. I am so sorry.

Heather's dedicated apology to the *mothers* of the filmmakers ("Dad" is but an afterthought) echoes a history that resounds in the film: because witches were always inimical to children, Heather surprisingly inscribes *herself* here as the sacrificial witch, the force who, having destroyed children, now seeks amends with their mothers. Writing about the history of the occult in early modern Germany, Lyndal Roper has noted that "relations between mothers, those occupying maternal roles, and children, formed the stuff of most . . . witchcraft accusations."[9] Incapable of saving or properly caring for her crew, Heather confesses herself to be the fully (if unintentionally) destructive force. Earlier, Josh had filmed her behind some brush; he says into the microphone, "Is that the Blair Witch? No, I think it's Heather, taking a piss." In his mind, the domineering and urinating woman who has doomed them all to probable death is contiguous with the figure they once sought and now flee.

As both symbolic child and witch, Heather bodies forth a riven identity. Missing from her tragic apologia, and indeed from the movie's profile of her or Mike, is any reference to lovers, to adult erotic attachment. She refers at one point to her sound man as "our little Mikey," and when she first meets him outside his house she calls out from the car, "Don't we get to meet your momma?" The movie suggests not only Heather's child status, but even her infancy. Early in the expedition, she records their trip to the grocery store for supplies, and her camera zooms in much too close on a bag of marshmallows in the shopping cart: "Mmm, marshmallows, feel how soft," she says, drawn to the sweet food as if it were an irresistible breast. But if Heather and Mike are figured as endangered children, Josh evokes another psychological stage altogether. Just before he disappears (the victim, presumably, of supernatural foul play), the three characters are sitting around in extremis, shivering, commiserating, talking about what they miss eating, drinking, or doing. Josh says, "You know what I'd love? Mashed potatoes. My Mom's mashed potatoes." He pauses. "And a piece of ass." He does not have another line in the film, and vanishes in the very next scene.

In the logic of the movie, his last words not only seal his fate, but set him off from the presexual others as a threat. Josh resides in a turbulent space between the infantile need of simple oral gratification (his Mom's mashed potatoes) and crude adult sexuality (a piece of ass). In this he plays Macbeth, dependent and yet berserk, to Heather's conscience-stricken Lady Macbeth, apparently independent and yet impotent; and like Shakespeare's male hero, he may be a plausible candidate for supernatural singling-out. Josh's absence from the last quarter of the film makes him a likely suspect for the presumed murders that occur, either as crazy independent agent or tool of the free-floating iniquity that is the Witch. Finally, if psychotically snarky Josh is on the cusp of adulthood in a way the others are not, it makes symbolic, psychological sense that he would wish to kill them; the Witch and her agents are dedicated destroyers of children and optimism. Yet we cannot know what becomes of him, and as in *Macbeth*, fantasies and deeds of infanticide secure nothing certain, and certainly nothing good, for the murderer.

Indeterminacy pesters but also structures both *The Blair Witch Project* and *Macbeth*. From the witches' equivocal prophecies to the extraordinary moral casuistries of all the main characters, Shakespeare's play occupies the interstices of tragic certitude (i.e., physical death or nightmarish criminality) and evaluative impossibility. In seeking to become perfect, invulnerably *without doubts*, Macbeth produces only the murky hell that signifies ever greater unclarity, and he opens Scotland to governance by men of intensely suspect ethics. He knows he has sinned, knows he will die; he does not know what that means.

The dramatic climax of *The Blair Witch Project* sustains similar equivocations. It shows Heather and Mike dashing wildly through a dilapidated house in the woods in search of Josh; palsied cameras catch creepy images, and soon we hear the thump of a dropped microphone, which may be a fallen body. But even after Mike's camera hits the floor, we presently see him, his back to the frame, facing into a corner like previous child victims who, it was said, were made to turn away from Witch-possessed murderers. His motionless form only makes sense (if at all) in terms of the Blair Witch myths; it does not make intelligible, narrative sense. The film's crowning sequence effects an admirable indeterminacy: we cannot know what happened, and so we cannot, even in the end, know what it means.

CONCLUSION

What could account for the sustained indeterminacy of the movie? A glance at the historical moment of *The Blair Witch Project* might help here. As the filmmakers first set off on their investigation, Heather brags about how well equipped they are: "We've got so much fucking battery power we could fuel a small-world [*sic*] country for a month," she says. Such "power" would have seemed enviable in the summer of 1999, for this was when American citizens had begun stockpiling supplies, including food, generators, and ammunition, in anticipation of a massive national chaos. Heather's reference to her own preparedness is an encoded glance at "Y2K" anxiety and hubris, and the reference carries a dismal irony emplotted in the movie: there are wounds beyond the reach of technological cures, and no periapt or amulet of science can provide salvation. Ironically, of course, the Blair Witch exposes not technology's threat but its failure, and (remaining undetected by the camera) she demonstrates the totemic power of the pretechnological past to wreak murderous havoc. One sensible way to historicize this movie is to see the Y2K crisis lurking beneath the film's incertitude and atmospheric dread; the Blair Witch elicits doubts about self, one's fellow travelers, the future, and especially technology. Map, compass, lighting,

sound and camera equipment all become useless in discovering or combating her.[10] Indeed, the resolutely low-tech movie repeatedly shows
the *burdens* of the technological. Heather insists on lugging the camera
and sound equipment, and refuses to turn them off. Her vision through
the view-finder (her "filtered reality," as Josh calls it) subtends a
sharply, dangerously limited horizon.

Witchcraft intimately connects with themes of indeterminacy at
century's end partly because of its participation in the aptly named "occult," but more centrally because of its profound transcultural history
as a practice destructive to children. This menace produces reticulated
forms of *cultural* indeterminacy, a radical demolition and thus not-
knowing of the future that children, by most any measure, represent.
Fear of children in *Macbeth* plainly enough describes a phobia about
legacy and posterity, and the depredations wrought by the Blair Witch
may code similar anxiety with different cultural coordinates. At the
precise historical moment of *The Blair Witch Project*, nervousness about
the end of things dovetailed with a sense that meaning would be revealed in the year 2000: the predicted disasters of technological collapse
signified, for many evangelical readers and social Darwinists, the assurance of revelation. But in *The Blair Witch Project*, the end brings no
clarity at all, no truth—just a spastic camera frame, the ticking of film
stuck in a loop, the sight of nothing in particular. Witchcraft devours the
future and stands on the millennial cusp for an occluded present, where
we wait for our disappearance in, at best, uncertainty.

NOTES

1. Even when the camera stares directly in its jittery way at something, the
content of the frame may not be clear, such as the bloody body part (or banana
fragment? plastic wedge? game piece?) wrapped in a bundle of sticks left by the
hostile force pursuing the film crew. The movie causes further unease in the
viewer by conducting its documentary style in, as one reviewer puts it, "perhaps the only media that Americans still associate with reality—home video
and 16 mm film." Christina Bieber, "Witching Hour," *Christian Century*, August
25, 1999, 821.

2. See Stephen Booth, *King Lear, Macbeth, Indefinition, and Tragedy* (Berkeley: University of California Press, 1983) for the question of ambiguity and incoherence in the Shakespearean drama and its audience. For a historicized reading of the extensive ambiguity ("amphibology") in the play, related to the early-

modern Jesuit practice of equivocation, see Stephen Mullaney, "'Lying Like Truth': Riddle, Representation and Treason in Renaissance England," *ELH* 47, no. 1 (1980): 32–47.

3. Quotations from *Macbeth* are from G. Blakemore Evans et al., *The Riverside Shakespeare* (Boston: Houghton Mifflin, 1974). The parenthetical numerals after the quotation indicate act, scene, and line number respectively.

4. Having made this claim, I would like to modify it: after she discovers and unwraps the bloody bundle of sticks laid outside the tent, Heather is filmed washing her hands maniacally. As a visual recollection of Lady Macbeth's renowned "out, damn'd spot!" sleepwalking sequence (5.1.35), this shot implies the vast weight of guilt (as well as terror) Heather feels about the encroaching, dismal fate in which she has involved her fellows.

5. This witty nod to the film's extensive ancillary publicity materials refers to *Curse of the Blair Witch* (directed by Sanchez and Myrick, 1999), a fake "documentary" about the fake documentary; it consists of outtakes from *The Blair Witch Project* and was in fact televised on the Sci-Fi Channel.

6. Michael Atkinson, "*The Blair Witch Project*," *Film Comment*, July 1999, 74–76. See also Jay Carr, "Mockumentary Does Good Horror on a Budget," *Boston Globe*, July 16, 1999, C4, for a convincing account of the characters' helplessness: "at a certain point it becomes clear that power plays are irrelevant, that any idea that they are going to wield any power or control is only an illusion."

7. Northcote Whitridge Thomas, in *The Encyclopedia Britannica*, 11th ed., 29 vols. (New York: Encyclopedia Britannica Co., 1911), 28: 755, s.v. "Witchcraft."

8. See Bruno Bettelheim's interesting reading of "Hansel and Gretel" through the lens of child developmental psychology, in *The Uses of Enchantment* (New York: Vintage Books, 1989), 159–66.

9. Lyndal Roper, *Oedipus and the Devil: Witchcraft, Sexuality, and Religion in Early Modern Europe* (London: Routledge, 1995), 201. Roper mentions too that "the witch could be a kind of evil mother who harmed instead of nourishing her charge" (207).

10. See David Banash, "*The Blair Witch Project*: Technology, Repression, and the Evisceration of Mimesis," at http://muse.jhu.edu/journals/postmodern_culture/v010/10.1.r_banash.

11

Empire of the Gun

Steven Spielberg's Saving Private Ryan *and American Chauvinism*

Frank P. Tomasulo

The cinema, as the world's storyteller *par excellence*, [is] ideally suited to project narratives of nations and empires. National self-consciousness . . . [is] broadly linked to cinematic fiction.
      —Ella Shohat and Robert Stam, *Unthinking Eurocentrism:*
                                   Multiculturalism and the Media

AS THEY HAVE throughout literary and cinematic history, nationalistic and patriotic sentiments persist in today's historical dramas—particularly in the Hollywood spectacles of the 1980s and 1990s. Indeed, the war movie and action-adventure genres underwent a resurgence in that era, paralleling and epitomizing the "America First" and "U.S.A.! U.S.A.!" ethos of the Ronald Reagan–George Bush era and its immediate aftermath.[1] Despite Steven Spielberg's early reputation as a "popcorn" director of "kidult" movies and his more recent incarnation as a "serious" filmmaker and liberal "FOB" (Friend of Bill [Clinton]), his oeuvre stands as one of the chief cinematic purveyors of American exceptionalism and triumphalism in contemporary filmdom. He could rightly be called the American Kipling.[2] Six of the top twenty box office hits of all time have been Steven Spielberg films. In addition, eight of his seventeen features to date have dealt with the World War II epoch.[3] In most of Spielberg's feature films, the Americans win the day—either through their quick wits or superior firepower—a resolution that the Pentagon could be proud of.[4] Thus, in most of his movies, as in most Hollywood films of the 1980s and 1990s, the United States is the empire of the gun.

Even Spielberg's flops contain the seeds of a chauvinistic and possibly racist worldview. In *1941* (1979), for instance, the focus is on the possibility that a Japanese submarine is going to attack the coastline of California. Though Americans had no actual fear of a Japanese *military* invasion in 1979, there *was* popular hysteria over the much-reported Japanese *economic* invasion of U.S. markets for automobiles, electronic equipment, cameras, and other consumer goods, not to mention the purchase of landmark U.S. buildings, corporations, and motion picture studios. In that context, *1941* became a disguised national allegory about the perils of globalization and world trade that tapped into a putative mood of economic xenophobia.[5]

SAVING PRIVATE RYAN

As Spielberg's first major contribution to the DreamWorks SKG company, in which he is a partner, *Saving Private Ryan* (1998) grossed more than $30 million domestic in its opening weekend. Within a year, domestic gross receipts reached $216 million and more than $224 million in the rest of the world.[6] When one factors in the various videocassette, DVD, and other ancillary merchandising commodities (including the soundtrack album, the novelization, the "making of" book, and the ever-popular "G.I. Joe" action figure), the movie's profitability was impressive, even against the backdrop of its $70 million production budget. In addition to its box office success—but linked to it—*Saving Private Ryan* garnered a number of critical kudos and prestigious nominations and awards: Oscars for best director, best cinematography, best film editing, best sound, and best sound effects editing; Academy Award nominations for best actor, best picture, art direction, makeup, music, and screenplay; the Directors Guild of America Award for best picture; the Golden Globes for best picture and best director; a Grammy for best instrumental movie score; the New York Film Critics Circle Award for best film; the Chicago Film Critics Association Award for best picture; among many others.[7]

Hero, martyr, schoolteacher: Tom Hanks as the ever decent Captain John H. Miller in Steven Spielberg's nostalgic war epic, *Saving Private Ryan* (Dream-Works, 1998).

(ALL-)AMERICAN VALUES

Saving Private Ryan begins—and ends—with a close-up shot of a translucent American flag blowing in the breeze, an image and narrative positioning that suggest that the United States is the alpha and omega, the be-all and end-all, of human civilization. To say that the film is a sentimental "flag-waver" may therefore be stating the obvious. Nonetheless, the visual transparency of the "Stars and Stripes" used in the opening and closing images may just reflect Spielberg's transparent and obvious propagandistic meaning: in the Second World War, America saved the world, pretty much unassisted, and emerged victorious despite great sacrifices. As a first point to consider, we never see any other nation's troops, even though a "realistic" depiction of the D-Day invasion on June 6, 1944, should have focused on the *collective* Allied military effort. Rather, as presented in the film, D-Day is an all-*American* operation.[8]

The modern-day framing episode, used at the start and again at the end of the movie, shows an unidentified older man and his family wandering in the military cemetery above Omaha Beach. The camera isolates on the elderly gentleman as he drifts away from his relatives, peruses an American flag, and scans a veritable field of identical crosses and an occasional Star of David. As the man drops to his knees and begins to sob, Spielberg cuts to three separate shots of crosses before zooming in slowly on the man's eyes.[9] The sound of the sea lapping against the shore triggers the flashback memory that constitutes the rest of the three-hour movie.[10] The calmness and serenity of the elegiac setting, the measured pace of the editing, and the steadiness of the camera are in marked contrast to the chaotic scene that follows: the landing on Omaha Beach. Suddenly, the camera is handheld and shaky, several soldiers vomit in fear, and explosions get louder and louder as the landing crafts approach the shore. Instead of the stately crosses above the beach, we see one G.I. kissing the crucifix around his neck for luck; and instead of the serene grassy site on the bluff, we view pandemonium as men jump into the water in full battle gear, swimming for their lives amid slow-motion blood and horror.

These fictional cinematic images—of the contemporary scene in the cemetery and of the 1944 assault—serve to recall two images that were broadcast far and wide: Ronald Reagan's fortieth anniversary speech at that very cemetery on June 6, 1984, and Bill Clinton's fiftieth anniversary address at the same locale on June 6, 1994. Two other cultural events are worth noting in this context, namely, the rise to best-seller status of *The Greatest Generation*, NBC broadcaster Tom Brokaw's book about World War II veterans; and former U.S. senator Bob Dole's efforts to build a National World War II Memorial on the Mall in Washington, D.C., an endeavor that actor Tom Hanks has endorsed.[11] Spielberg was clearly not alone in harking back to those thrilling days of yesteryear when American hegemony was undisputed. With the tepid end of the Cold War, the natural place to turn to for enemies was the "Good War," with its sadistic Nazi enemies typecast in the role of evil villains.

As in the Indiana Jones cycle and *Schindler's List* (1993), the Germans in *Saving Private Ryan* are depicted as depraved monsters. The much-celebrated opening montage, for instance, shows waves of G.I.s being mowed down by Nazi machine guns, blown out of the water by powerful enemy mortar fire, and shot through their helmets, incinerated, dismembered, or disemboweled by unseen enemy ordnance.

Although we occasionally see a shot from the physical point of view of the Axis gunners, we are clearly not in their moral viewpoint; the POV shot from behind the German troops preserves their anonymity, prevents any identification with their predicament, and leaves them faceless automatons, no more human than their weapons. The opening battle scene thus establishes empathy for the "underdog" U.S. forces, who are far below the enemy stronghold on the cliffs of Normandy and hardly able to wrest a foothold on the heavily fortified Omaha Beach without suffering intense carnage and massive casualties. Both the film's narrative structure, which opens on a gore-filled and ostensibly "antiwar" scene of death and destruction, and the natural geography of space—the "Huns" above, the Yanks below—create an immediate sense of epic heroism amid despair. Private Caparzo emphasizes this underdog status when he says, "We don't have a frickin' chance and that ain't fair!"[12]

The opening battle scene is thus a setup for the Americans' counteroffensive as they begin to advance on the Germans' positions. In short, twenty-five minutes of seeing and identifying with Americans killed and maimed as cannon fodder in an apparently futile assault paves the way for their eventual brutal and unmerciful retaliation against their adversaries—even if they do not play by the accepted international rules of engagement or the code of conduct Americans usually expect of their screen heroes.[13]

"THEN EVERY SOLDIER KILL HIS PRISONERS"

King Henry V's pre-battle speeches to his outnumbered army in Shake-speare's famous history play are well known for their clarion rhetoric about patriotic duty and honor on the battlefield. ("Once more upon the breach, dear friends, once more."[14] "We few, we happy few, we band of brothers; for he today who sheds his blood with me shall be my brother.")[15] Less well remembered is the scene that occurs *after* the defeat of the superior French forces at the Battle of Agincourt. In victory, Henry orders the cold-blooded murder of all French prisoners.[16] The first person to speak after Henry's brutal edict, Captain Fluellen, states, "'Tis expressly against the law of arms. 'Tis as arrant a piece of knavery, mark you now, as can offert."[17] Now, as then, the wanton killing of prisoners of war is considered a violation of the "laws" of combat. In Henry's time, the unwritten rules of medieval chivalry provided the norms by which to treat prisoners, civilians, and the slain; today, nations rely on more formal documents, specifically the Geneva Conventions and the international legal principles laid down at the Nuremberg war crimes trials.

It is therefore interesting—and instructive—that in *Saving Private Ryan* the "heroic" Americans violate the rules of the Geneva Conventions on several occasions by killing surrendering combatants and prisoners of war in cold blood. The first such instance occurs when the platoon under the command of Captain John H. Miller (Tom Hanks) fires point-blank at surrendering German machine gunners. Hand grenades and a flamethrower are then used against those who remain inside a machine-gun nest; one G.I. sadistically suggests, "Don't shoot. Let 'em burn!" As more Nazis surrender to the advancing U.S. forces, they are routinely shot in cold blood in or around their foxholes, while the Americans make fun of the German prisoners' palms-up gestures of submission ("Look, I vashed for zupper") or pretend not to comprehend the unarmed Germans' verbal pleas for compassion ("I'm sorry, I can't understand you"). The "good guys" even summarily execute a surrendering Nazi officer, whose hands are in the air. How does the film get audiences to identify with these acts of "barbarity," even in the context of an inhuman war and the brutality of the Nazi regime?

Part of the explanation can be found in a scene toward the beginning of the film. Miller's special squadron approaches a radar site and spots an enemy machine-gun post nearby. One of the men suggests detouring around the position: "This isn't our mission . . . an unnecessary risk." But Miller insists on checking it out: "Our mission is to win the war." Private Reiben, the platoon's Brooklyn-born chronic griper, spouts the clichéd line from so many war movies: "I just don't have a good feel about this." But Miller insists they proceed: "When was the last time you felt good about anything?" The unit does engage in a brief battle with some German troops, and they lose their medic, Wade, in the process. His anguished death, filmed in handheld close-up as he begs for his mother, angers one G.I. so much that he bashes a wounded German soldier with his rifle butt. Again, the death of an "innocent" American provides the provocation and justification for retaliation.

One German prisoner is taken in the action, and he is ordered to dig graves for the dead. The expectation is that he will be executed and tossed into the hole he has dug; but Corporal Upham, the unit's interpreter, challenges Miller's unspoken order: "Sir, you're gonna let them kill him? This is not right!" While digging his own grave, the enemy captive tries to ingratiate himself with his captors and would-be executioners by spouting what little English he knows, a smattering of popular culture: "I like America!" "Fancy, schmancy," "Steamboat Willie," "Betty Boop—what a dish," "Betty Grable—nice gams," "Oh, say can you sink . . . ," and even "Fuck Hitler!" Upham, the translator, once again makes his case to take the German as a prisoner of war: "He says he's sorry about Wade. It's not right! He surrendered to us." Miller finally relents and reluctantly agrees to release the German: "He's a POW. We can't take him with us." Despite a near-mutinous reaction from most of the men, the German is blindfolded and set free, with the assumption that he will be captured by advancing Allied forces.

That one act of "kindness" comes back to haunt Miller's detail—and the audience—at the end of the film. That same prisoner (referred to in the cast list as "Steamboat Willie") returns to action and kills Private Mellish, the Jewish G.I., who had earlier relished taunting enemy prisoners by waving his Star of David and shouting "Juden" as they marched past. Mellish is stabbed to death by "Steamboat Willie" in a strangely sexualized—almost tender—yet grueling and excruciating hand-to-hand struggle in a bombed-out building. In her review of the film for *Film Quarterly*, Karen Jaehne suggested that this *mano a mano* contest shows the German in a nonsadistic, humanized light. According to Jaehne, the Nazi says, *"Lass uns es beenden"* (Let's just end it all), offering Mellish an easy death, but that dialogue—which is lost on

"This time the mission is the man." Captain Miller rationalizes his orders in *Saving Private Ryan* (DreamWorks, 1998).

non-German-speaking viewers—can also be regarded as a verbal tactic by the Nazi to get his rival to surrender without further struggle.[18] Rather than showing mercy to the unarmed Mellish, "Steamboat Willie" plunges a knife into his heart. Worse yet, in the final battle scene at the bridge in Ramelle, the same German kills Captain Miller (after spotting the man who had freed him earlier and shouting, "I know that guy!"). The moral is not lost on the cowardly Corporeal Upham, who had interceded earlier on behalf of the "Americanized" German POW. At the end of the film, when his knowledge of German allows him to take control of a group of Wehrmacht captives, Upham spots "Steamboat Willie" and shoots him dead in cold blood. The niceties of the "Good (and moral) War" are soon forgotten; bloodlust and vengeance trump honor and *esprit de combat*. Although Captain Miller had earlier mused, "If God's on our side, who's on theirs?" such ephemeral ethical speculation is abandoned when Americans are clearly in the right.

"THIS TIME THE MISSION IS THE MAN"

Captain Miller's quixotic mission is clearly established at the outset. Once the U.S. forces take the plateau above Omaha Beach and begin to mop up, the scene shifts suddenly to a stateside locale. On the home front, army secretaries type up death notices while a voice-over narrator reads the KIA announcements aloud. Eventually, we learn that three such telegrams are being sent to the same address in Iowa, to the home of "blue star" mother Mrs. Ryan, who now has only one surviving son left, Private James Francis Ryan (Matt Damon). As a car containing an officer and a minister approaches her pastoral Norman Rockwell–like farmhouse, Mrs. Ryan senses the bad news. These sepia-toned and redolent images of down-home Americana segue to army chief of staff George C. Marshall, a revered patriarchal figure in U.S. military history, as well as the author of the Marshall Plan to rebuild postwar Europe (and thus prevent communists from gaining a foothold there). Marshall's compassion is evident as he recites from memory a letter of condolence written by Abraham Lincoln to a mother whose five sons had been slain during the Civil War. The invocation of Lincoln, with solemn, almost ecclesiastical, musical accompaniment is punctuated by a zoom in on Marshall's face as he emphatically states, "We're going to get him the hell out of there!"

This scene sets up the "point of attack," the hermeneutic of the narrative: will Private Ryan be saved and returned to the safety of his mother's bosom? It also demonstrates what the boys are fighting and dying for on Omaha Beach: their beloved mothers, their beloved country, their beloved religion, and their beloved superior officers. There are frequent reminders throughout the narrative that these things *are* worth fighting for, despite an occasional cynical remark from the troops. But patriotism is taken for granted here, not extolled in fancy speeches.

The mission is set: find Private Ryan and "get him the hell out of there." Despite some griping by Private Jackson about the "serious misallocation of valuable military resources," Miller rounds up a squad and they march together, their silhouettes set against a scenic horizon filled with dramatic storm clouds ahead. A similar use of the pathetic fallacy occurs shortly thereafter when those storm clouds burst and raindrops fall on the leaves. As the rain falls harder and thunder is heard, Spielberg and his sound editors blend the sounds of nature with the percussive explosions of grenades and bombshells.[19]

The omen is fulfilled as the detail finally encounters evidence of the enemy in a bombed-out village. Some civilian victims are also found: a French family hiding on the second story of a demolished house. Private Caparzo wants to take the little French girl with them, against Miller's explicit orders:

> MILLER: Caparzo, get that kid back up there!
> CAPARZO: Captain, the decent thing to do would be take her over to the next town.
> MILLER: We're not here to do the decent thing; we're here to follow fucking orders!

While tending to the child, Caparzo is shot by an enemy sniper and dies in the street, his blood mixing with the raindrops, his letter to his father soaked with blood and rain. To avenge Caparzo's death, the unit's resident sharpshooter and religious zealot, Private Jackson, is called on to retaliate against the hidden German marksman. Jackson, another stock character out of countless combat movies, prays out loud for accuracy before lining up his rifle: "Be not that far from me, for trouble is near; haste Thee to help me. . . . Blessed be the Lord my strength, which teacheth my hands to war, and my fingers to fight . . . O my God, I trust in Thee; let me be not ashamed, let not my enemies triumph over me."[20]

Unlike Miller, Jackson has no doubts about which side the Lord is on: "Sir, it seems to me, God gave me a special gift, fashioned in me a fine instrument of warfare." Jackson prevails by killing the enemy sniper.

Right after this incident, Miller's men meet up with other G.I.s in the same town. As they relax and lean on a precarious structure, a wall caves in, revealing a German unit playing cards. Tension mounts as the soldiers aim their weapons and shout at each other in very close quarters. The Germans yell, "Don't shoot!" but no one besides Upham, the translator, can understand them. Speaking German, he orders them to surrender: "*Haende hoch; ohne zu scherzen!*" (Hands up; no kidding!). Just then, a burst of gunfire rings out, mowing down all the Nazis in a brutal *danse macabre*. It is unclear who fired the first shot, until we see another group of Americans entering the structure from the second floor.

Shortly after this horrific scene, there is a moment of comic relief when the squad seems to have found Private Ryan; it turns out that *this* soldier's brothers are all in grammar school. This semicomic snafu allows the audience to forget the slaughter of surrendering prisoners and sets up another rationalization scene. While Miller is bivouacking in a candlelit church, his hand shakes—a recurring motif to suggest his slight imperfection and thus his humanity, the emotion behind the façade of quiet masculine strength he must present to his men—as he reflects on his company's casualties: "Ninety-four men lost under my command, but that means I've saved the lives of ten times that many, doesn't it? Maybe twenty." He adds, "That's how you rationalize making the choice between the mission and the man." Miller's second-in-command, Sergeant Horvath, responds with the remark that became the tag line of the film, "This time the mission is the man." Such conscientious leadership seems to justify the entire American war effort. Miller also comments on the specifics of this mission: "This Ryan better be worth it. He better go home and cure a disease, or at least invent a longer-lasting light bulb." The other rationale for the assignment, of course, is Ryan's grief-stricken mother at home.

Once the diminished unit finally locates the true Private Ryan in the bombed-out French village of Ramelle, the seeds are planted for the final confrontation. Ryan refuses to be shipped home, at least not until reinforcements arrive to help his tiny platoon defend the hamlet's tiny bridge, the last bastion of liberty in this strategic town.[21]

Another cliché of Hollywood cinema—the last-minute rescue—crops up at the end of *Saving Private Ryan*. Instead of the cavalry

appearing at the eleventh hour, the *deus ex machina* arrives in the form
of U.S. P-51 warplanes, which strafe and bomb the Panzer tanks and
Nazi troops into submission.[22] Unfortunately, the reinforcements are
too late to save Miller, but the strategic bridge is held. In the final
skirmish, the battle-weary captain loses his character-revealing hand
tremor in death and his "thousand-mile stare" becomes frozen in premature rigor mortis. Although the film has been praised for its gritty
"realism," it also contains oodles of melodrama, particularly in its tear-
jerker climax. Perhaps there is a fine line—in real life and in cinema—
between legitimate human sentiment and bathetic sentimentality, but
Miller's stoic death scene seems to cross the line into pathos. Miller's
demise in the service of a larger cause makes him another in a series of
sacrificial "Spielbergian Christ surrogate[s]."[23] So, in the end, back at
the Normandy cemetery, the elder Private Ryan salutes the crucifix that
marks the grave of his savior, the reluctant warrior, Miller. And Spielberg dissolves from the cross to Old Glory, the star-spangled banner,
still gallantly streaming "o'er the ramparts we watched." This retrospective cinematic linking of God and Country in *Saving Private Ryan*
closely parallels the coupling of deity and nation in the fourth stanza of
the American national anthem: "Blest with victory and peace, may the
heav'n rescued land / Praise the Power that hath made and preserved
us a nation. / Then conquer we must, when our cause it is just, / And
this be our motto: 'In God is our trust.'"

CONCLUSION

Every individual and social group, including nation-states, seems to
need an enemy against whom to define itself. If those enemies do not
exist in reality at any particular historical conjuncture, they are often invented or created by a process akin to psychological projection. Because
all history is, ultimately, contemporary history, mainstream movies
often draw on the past to comment on the present episteme. In a post-
Vietnam and post–Cold War epoch, the Hollywood cinema of the 1990s
used both current and past historical events to re-create and conciliate
a collective delusion that reflected—as well as displaced—real socie-
tal problems and contradictions. Mainstream American cinema of the
1990s resolved those antinomies by invoking a filmic relegitimation
of the U.S. military and the state war apparatus after the real-life recla-

mation of those forces during the invasion of Panama and the Persian Gulf War.

In particular, even though *Saving Private Ryan* is set in the glorious past, when the U.S. army saved the world and extended America's economic and cultural hegemony/dominion over Europe and the Third World, its contemporary moral and political effectivity seems clear: to hark back to those "days of yesteryear" in order to renew and revivify America's mythic rightness as a nation, particularly as U.S. and NATO forces bombed Serbia and ground troops were sent into Kosovo. Although set in the past, Spielberg's "antiwar" film has ideological ramifications that affect spectators now and in the future, and provide the self-perpetuating jingoistic justifications for future unilateral military invasions, incursions, and interventions.

NOTES

1. For more on the nexus between Spielberg's cinema and Reaganite policies, see Frank P. Tomasulo, "Mr. Jones Goes to Washington: Myth and Religion in *Raiders of the Lost Ark*," *Quarterly Review of Film Studies* 7, no. 4 (fall 1982): 331–40, and "The Gospel according to Spielberg: Postmodernist Escapism in *E.T.: The Extra-Terrestrial*," *Quarterly Review of Film and Video* 18, no. 3 (Summer 2001), forthcoming.

2. Tomasulo, "The Gospel according to Spielberg."

3. World War II is the subject of two of Spielberg's earliest efforts: *Fighter Squadron* (1960), an 8mm. tribute to Castle Films documentaries about the 1940s, and *Escape to Nowhere* (1962), an award-winning forty-minute-long movie, made when the budding director was only sixteen.

4. In *Raiders of the Lost Ark* (1981), Indiana Jones (Harrison Ford) nonchalantly shoots an Arab brandishing an immense scimitar in the streets of Cairo. Although played for comedy, the incident conveys the implicit message that the United States' superior gun power can and should be used against foreign enemies, even if it is not a fair fight. Furthermore, given the release date of *Raiders*, the slaying of this Arab can be linked allegorically to the Iranian hostage crisis of 1980–81, the OPEC oil embargo, and the failed "rescue mission" of the American embassy hostages in Tehran. Tomasulo, "Mr. Jones Goes to Washington," 335.

5. Unfortunately for Spielberg, the American public apparently was *not* as distressed over Japanese gains in the global marketplace; after all, Americans were frantically purchasing Japanese products, and the United States relied heavily on overseas investment to sustain its economic growth. In this case,

then, patriotic appeal did not translate into box office success. Indeed, *1941* grossed only $23.2 million (domestic) on a production budget of $35 million. These figures come from the Internet Movie Database, better known as <imdb.com>, an Amazon.com company.

6. Ibid.

7. Ibid.

8. Many other Allied nations participated in the D-Day invasion, including England, France, Canada, and Australia. In addition, segregated African American units also landed on Omaha Beach, although there is no evidence of any black soldiers in Spielberg's epic.

9. Spielberg allegedly witnessed just such a scene during a visit to France in the 1970s. Richard T. Jameson, "History's Eyes: *Saving Private Ryan*," *Film Comment* 34, no. 5 (September–October 1998): 23.

10. We later learn that the man is the grown-up title character, but, although we are led to believe the flashback is from his perspective, he had no direct knowledge of the events we witness until he enters the narrative as a young man, two hours later.

11. Ironically, architect Frederick St. Florian's monumental design for the proposed memorial is reminiscent of the work of Albert Speer, the chief architect of the Nazis. It features a sunken stone plaza ringed by fifty-six stone pillars, each seventeen feet high, and a pair of triumphal arches as tall as a four-story building. See Paul Goldberger, "Not in Our Front Yard," *New Yorker*, August 7, 2000, 27–28.

12. The film's gut-wrenching (and gut-*spilling*) opening battle sequence has been praised for the stark "antiwar" realism of its representation of the calamitous contingency of combat—an *effet du réel* enhanced by the use of desaturated film stock that conveys the look of old 1940s black and white newsreel footage. In addition to the visual "realism," *Private Ryan* reveled in "the period authenticity in arms, vehicles, uniforms, and insignias," as well as "wartime vernacular and military lingo." Thomas Doherty, *Projections of War: Hollywood, American Culture, and World War II*, rev. ed. (New York: Columbia University Press, 1999), 303.

Just as important to this realism effect is the presentation of supposedly random acts. For instance, when one soldier is struck in the helmet by a bullet, he miraculously survives and removes his helmet in disbelief; a nearby soldier, equally amazed, says, "Lucky bastard." Just then, another (digitally animated) German bullet hits the G.I. square in the forehead, killing him instantly. Although meant to suggest the accidental nature of life and death on the battlefield and to portray the jeopardy of the innocent G.I.s, the scene is highly calculated to demonstrate the precision of the German sharpshooter and the long odds of taking the beach from the Teutonic hordes on the bluff above.

13. In this regard, *Saving Private Ryan* is not an isolated instance of a contemporary Hollywood film in which the "virtuous" protagonists break all the classical ethical laws of fairness by killing unarmed, albeit villainous, people. In Kathryn Bigelow's *Blue Steel* (1990), for instance, the policewoman heroine (Jamie Lee Curtis) shoots her male nemesis (Ron Silver) point-blank in the heart rather than arrest him, even though, as Linda Mizejewski notes, "he is out of ammunition, wounded, and barely able to stand up." See Mizejewski, "Picturing the Female Dick: *The Silence of the Lambs* and *Blue Steel*," *Journal of Film and Video* 45, nos. 2–3 (summer–fall 1993): 16. Similarly, in Curtis Hanson's *L.A. Confidential* (1997), the self-righteous, "goody-goody," by-the-book detective (Guy Pearce) shoots his disarmed rogue captain (James Cromwell) in cold blood, just as a slew of other officers arrive on the scene to sort things out. Finally, in Joel Schumacher's *8mm* (1999), a private investigator (Nicolas Cage) goes on a veritable killing spree to avenge the murder of one young woman who ended up in a pornographic "snuff" film. The vigilante hero captures one of the accomplices (James Gandolfini), pistol-whips him unmercifully, soaks him in gasoline, and incinerates him, rather than turn the sleazebag over to the proper authorities.

14. William Shakespeare, *Henry V*, act III, scene i, lines 1–2. The line quoted in the section heading is from *Henry V*, IV, vi, 37.

15. Ibid., IV, iii, 60–62.

16. At the real-life battle, however, the king's knights hesitated and Henry had to call in archers to carry out his barbarous order.

17. Shakespeare, *Henry V*, IV, vii, 3–5.

18. Karen Jaehne, "*Saving Private Ryan*," *Film Quarterly* 53, no. 1 (fall 1999): 39–41.

19. World War II newsreel footage was always shot silent because existing sound recording equipment was cumbersome to carry around in combat situations. Spielberg's use of three-dimensional digital THX sound effects is, therefore, anachronistic and inauthentic, even though its goal is "realism." Bill Nichols, "The Ten Stations of Spielberg's Passion," *Jump Cut* 43 (2000): 10.

20. Jackson's religiosity, Old Testament locutions, and hillbilly roots are reminiscent of another famed movie sharpshooter, World War I Medal of Honor–winner Alvin York (Gary Cooper) in Howard Hawks's *Sergeant York* (1941). *Sergeant York* was a propagandistic film made on the eve of World War II that suggested that the United States had to give up its pacifistic, isolationist ways (York was a Quaker) to defeat the Huns in a second outing.

21. This scene raises a significant military question: Who destroyed this small French village? At the beginning of the war, Paris fell after a six-week campaign in 1940 and the Germans occupied France thereafter. There was no need for the Nazis to obliterate a small village in the far west during the D-Day

invasion. Although unstated in the film, Allied bombers probably "took out" the town (and possibly its civilian population) as part of their assault on retreating Axis forces—"destroying the village in order to save it."

22. Initially, before seeing—and hearing—the bombers, we are confused by the sudden explosion of the approaching German tank. The dying Captain Miller, here behaving more like an underdog David to the Nazi Goliath (or an outmanned Davy Crockett to Santa Ana's Mexican forces at the Alamo), fires his .45 at the menacing Panzer, only to see it blow up.

23. Robert Kolker, *A Cinema of Loneliness,* 3d ed. (New York: Oxford University Press, 2000), 306, 324. Bill Nichols makes a similar point about Spielberg's penchant for "white male heroes of gentle character, empathetic nature, and altruistic impulse: Christ figures." Nichols, "The Ten Stations," 9. Finally, my essay "The Gospel according to Spielberg" makes overt comparisons between the space alien E.T. and the biblical Jesus.

12

Saving Private Ryan Too Late

Krin Gabbard

AS THE TWENTIETH century was coming to an end, so were the lives of many of the men who fought and survived World War II. For many of their children, anxiety about a dead or dying father may have precipitated a new view of the war years. Some honored their fathers as "the greatest generation," suggesting that their own generation had achieved less. Steven Spielberg went even farther, directing a film that implicitly blames his peers for renouncing those values that led their fathers to victory in 1945. As has often been the case in Spielberg's career, his conservative message paid off. *Saving Private Ryan* was the number two box office hit of 1998 and was honored with five Academy Awards.

Spielberg's revisionist project begins only a few minutes into the D-Day landing sequence that opens *Saving Private Ryan* and that shocked many with its graphic depictions of violence. When the front of the first landing craft drops open, virtually all the infantrymen in the boat are immediately hit with machine gun fire. When several men jump into the sea as they try to escape from another landing craft, two are shot underwater and a third drowns under the weight of his backpack and gear. These are the film's most powerful images of war, exploding conventional notions of heroism and the role of the individual soldier in battle. At this point *Saving Private Ryan* seems to suggest that war is senseless slaughter, something that pacifists and antiwar artists have been saying for a long time, especially during the Vietnam War and its aftermath. But after the opening minutes of the first battle scene, the American soldiers in *Saving Private Ryan* begin to fight back, and we get to know them. For the rest of the film the slaughter ceases to be senseless. As in the vast majority of war movies, the possibilities for heroism and the contribution of the individual soldier are constantly available. Spielberg departs from the more recent paradigm of war films in the 1970s and 1980s by suggesting, sentimentally and without irony, that war is about building character and not about brutality and stupidity. Most disturbingly, he joins those who have promoted conservative retrenchment through nostalgia for the war years.

In this context, the figure who has been continually brought forth to authenticate Spielberg's vision of war in general and of World War II in particular is Stephen Ambrose, the author of hagiographic biographies of Dwight Eisenhower and Richard Nixon, and a harsh critic of the antiwar movement during the Vietnam years. Ambrose has also written a collection of books about World War II that now amounts to a mini-industry. In July 2000, clicking on "Stephen Ambrose" at the Amazon.com Web site brought up ninety-three items, most of them about the European theater in World War II and at least half of them published or republished since Ambrose was prominently mentioned in the publicity for *Saving Private Ryan*. Spielberg and Robert Rodat, who is credited with the film's screenplay, found many of the details for their script in Ambrose's work, especially his best-selling books *Citizen Soldiers, Band of Brothers*, and *D-Day June 6, 1944*.[1]

Written in a style so colloquial as to be sometimes incoherent, Ambrose's books build sketchy histories of Americans in World War II around anecdotal accounts from veterans. Ambrose does not hesitate to catalogue the horrific and antiheroic aspects of the war, even the criminal incompetence of those who made command decisions, but he consistently glorifies the individual behavior of the men who fought. He is especially fond of stories about the industriousness of American soldiers who tinkered together ad hoc solutions to problems they encountered in the field. In writing *Saving Private Ryan*, Spielberg and Rodat have relied on Ambrose's approach when, for example, they show Captain Miller using chewing gum to attach a mirror to a bayonet so that he can look around a corner and safely observe a German machine gun nest, or when he instructs his men on the bricolage technique of making "sticky bombs."

John Gregory Dunne has suggested that Spielberg, trying to avoid a plagiarism suit like the one that sullied the reception of his previous film *Amistad* (1997), invited Ambrose to a preview screening of *Saving Private Ryan*.[2] Ambrose's reaction to the opening battle scene has been widely reported. Not only did he not sue; he said that he was so affected by the film's realism that he crawled under his seat and asked the projectionist to shut down for a moment.

One might suppose that Stephen Ambrose himself landed at Omaha Beach on June 6, 1944. In fact, Ambrose was born in the mid-1930s and knows the war only from the stories he heard first from the ex-GIs in his neighborhood when he was growing up, later from his father's friends who took the young Ambrose along on hunting trips, and more recently from the many veterans he sought out in his research. Significantly, in his own autobiographical statements, Ambrose does not report the stories he heard from his father, who was a navy flight surgeon in the Pacific theater during the war. I would speculate that the senior Ambrose is one of those veterans who preferred not to talk about what happened to him during the war. When Ambrose interviewed the men who *did* want to talk about it, their accounts were several decades old and surely revised and elaborated, as is always the case with oral culture. Nevertheless, Ambrose reproduces their stories without question. If he has modified their accounts, he does not say so. Not surprisingly, the romantic view of American men in battle that emerges from Ambrose's books is entirely consistent with the mythologies of the Hollywood cinema. Ambrose's subjects, like Ambrose himself, have watched a lot of war movies, and their war stories have surely been influenced by the conventions of the film genre.

Stephen Ambrose has much in common with Steven Spielberg, who has also seen a lot of war movies, and whose father was a radio operator with a B-24 squadron in Burma during the Second World War. Like Ambrose seeking out hundreds of veterans, Spielberg has obsessively returned to World War II with *1941* (1979), *Empire of the Sun* (1987), and two of the Indiana Jones films. Victor Fleming's *A Guy Named Joe* (1943), which reassured American audiences that their fighting men were not really dying in World War II, was remade by Spielberg in 1989 as *Always*. These films may have been Spielberg's way of working through his relationship with his father, just as Ambrose was probably engaged in something similar in his pursuit of World War II veterans.

How different *Saving Private Ryan* might have been if Spielberg had read a less credulous war writer, such as Paul Fussell. Unlike Ambrose, Fussell actually saw combat in World War II. In *Wartime: Understanding and Behavior in the Second World War*, Fussell reports incidents such as the shooting down of twenty-three American planes by American gunners who panicked during the invasion of Sicily in

1943, and the incident when B-24s dropped their bombs on American soldiers trying to break out of a Normandy beachhead near Saint-Lo a few weeks after D-Day, killing almost two hundred Americans.[3] Fussell also catalogues what he refers to as the "chickenshit" behavior of officers who regularly endangered the lives of their troops by insisting on spit-and-polish discipline at the most inopportune moments. As Fussell shows, there was more than one occasion when enraged soldiers killed their own officers, a practice that we now associate almost exclusively with the American invasion of Vietnam.

Fussell is especially convincing as he dispels myths of heroic behavior under fire. He argues that soldiers seldom had their wits about them during battle and that men who rushed enemy machine guns acted as much from desperation, panic, and/or fear of shame as from what is usually called courage. The Allies won the war not just because of Yankee ingenuity and true grit but because America had the men and material to wear down a German army that was already depleted and exhausted from years of fighting, especially on the eastern front. America's politicians and generals were willing to draw on a huge population of eighteen-year-old boys, giving them minimal training and then throwing them into the war as cannon fodder. Fussell also exposes the myth of World War II as "the good war," pointing out that few Americans had *moral* convictions about the need to fight Hitler. In general, white Americans harbored deep racial hatred for the Japanese after their "sneak attack" at Pearl Harbor and regarded the Japanese as inferior to everyone except perhaps African Americans. The United States fought Germans primarily because Germany had declared war on America after Pearl Harbor. "The slogan was conspicuously *Remember Pearl Harbor*," Fussell writes. "No one ever shouted *Remember Poland*."[4]

Fussell continues,

> Now, 50 years later, there is so much talk about "The Good War," the Justified War, the Necessary War, and the like, that the young and the innocent could get the impression that it was really not such a bad thing after all. It's thus necessary to observe that it was a war and nothing else, and thus stupid and sadistic, a war, as Cyril Connolly said, "of which we are all ashamed . . . a war . . . which lowers the standard of thinking and feeling . . . which is as obsolete as drawing and quartering. . .": further, a war opposed to "every reasonable conception of what life is for, every ambition of the mind or delight of the senses."[5]

Guilty nostalgia for the good war: the multiethnic American GI heroes fight the good fight in *Saving Private Ryan* (DreamWorks, 1998).

The opening moments of *Saving Private Ryan* contain brilliant sound design and point-of-view cinematography. As always, the technical skills of Spielberg and his staff are extraordinary. But stripped of the cinematic immediacy made possible by Industrial Light and Magic, Spielberg's images should be familiar to anyone who has seen a lot of war movies. Moments in *Saving Private Ryan* recall scenes in films such as *Catch-22* (1970), when Yossarian carefully patches up the leg of an airman only to see his intestines fall out; *Full Metal Jacket* (1987), when a sniper prevents men from saving a wounded soldier; and Samuel Fuller's *The Steel Helmet* (1951), when American soldiers unrepentantly kill prisoners of war. In fact, Fuller anticipated Spielberg by eighteen years when he showed the legendary red tide on Omaha Beach in *The Big Red One* (1980). And as many critics pointed out, innumerable films have populated an infantry squad with a country boy, a Jew, a wiseguy from Brooklyn, a college boy, a tough sergeant, and so on.

Other than the high-tech immediacy of its action sequences, what *is* new in *Saving Private Ryan* is what Jacques Derrida would call "guilty nostalgia" for the war years. Unlike most of the infantrymen in World

War II, the men in *Saving Private Ryan* admire and protect their captain, who fits into an organic chain of command that stretches seamlessly upward to General George Marshall (Harve Presnell). Bringing the moral authority of Abraham Lincoln into an idealized headquarters inspired by Norman Rockwell, and backlit like a saint in a Baroque painting, General Marshall orders the saving of Private Ryan with such moral certainty that any cynicism expressed by a member of the squad (or the audience) can only sound hollow. In those days, the film tells us, and unlike today, the film implies, the system worked and morality was unambiguous.

Similarly, the film reassures us that war is in fact a test of manhood and courage and that a warrior aristocracy will naturally emerge, even if Captain Miller has to take a moment to sob in private. His heroism and that of the men in his squad are in sharp contrast to the cowardice of Corporal Upham, the intellectual played by Jeremy Davies, who, at least according to the *Village Voice* writer Richard Goldstein, symbolizes the Baby Boomers who sat out their war with II-S deferments and refused to be tested in the crucible of battle.[6] Corporal Upham can redeem himself only by shooting "Steamboat Willie," the German whose life he had previously argued was worth saving. In fact, the film's refusal to show any sympathy for individual German soldiers allows Spielberg to paint the war as moral and necessary.

The film is most consistent with the old cinematic myths when Captain Miller dies. The film had previously shown a number of "realistic" death scenes, including the bloody demise of Medic Wade (Giovanni Ribisi), who asks for morphine and then for his mother as he dies. But when Captain Miller (Tom Hanks) passes away, he not only dies a conventional, bloodless movie death, he doesn't cry out for his mother, his wife, or even himself. Instead, he devotes his last words to dispensing life-changing advice to a man he barely knows. In *Wartime*, Paul Fussell critiques a newspaper story by Ernie Pyle about the death of a captain. In one of his most famous dispatches, Pyle writes of a Captain Waskow of Belton, Texas, who died and whose body was brought down from a mountain on muleback. According to Pyle's account, one man sat by the body holding the dead captain's hand and looking into his face. "He reached over and gently straightened the points of the captain's shirt collar, and then he sort of arranged the tattered edges of the uniform around the wound."[7] Fussell then wonders about what Pyle has omitted from his account, "Where was his wound? How large was it? [Pyle] implies that it was in the traditional noble place, the chest. Was it? Was it a little hole, or was it a great red missing place? Was it perhaps in the crotch, or in the testicles?"[8] Even with all its blood and viscera, no one in *Saving Private Ryan* is shot in the crotch. Captain Miller, of course, dies from a "noble" wound in the chest.

Because of what may be an unconscious oedipal agenda, Steven Spielberg has spent much of his career trying to make sense of World War II, even experimenting with the giddy satire of *1941*. But with *Saving Private Ryan* he has uncritically idealized the role of the United States in World War II at a time when many Americans were experiencing the death or imminent death of a parent or grandparent who played some role in that war. Tom Brokaw's book *The Greatest Generation*, written out of a similar impulse, was on the *New York Times* list of best-selling nonfiction hardcover books for at least ninety-three weeks, beginning in the winter of 1998. During the end-of-the-century impeachment proceedings against Bill Clinton, two Congressmen, Lindsay Graham and Henry Hyde, invoked the men who fought for America—especially the men who landed at Normandy on June 6—as they argued for the removal of that best-known of all Baby Boomer draft dodgers. Of course, this opened the way for the president's attorney, Charles Ruff, to trump the Republicans by invoking his own father's actual landing at Normandy.

Nevertheless, for Steven Spielberg, Stephen Ambrose, Tom Brokaw, Lindsay Graham, and the rest, insisting that World War II was the Good War is at the very least a means of reconciling with fathers who may have made real, face-to-face reconciliation difficult. It is also a good example of what Herbert Marcuse has called "surplus repression."[9] Americans were being asked to repress much more than their oedipal hostility toward fathers who participated in World War II. They were also being asked to accept the superiority of the old order represented by the fathers over what Americans had achieved by the end of the century. Appropriately, in the world of *Saving Private Ryan*, white males go about their work unencumbered by affirmative action guidelines and civil rights laws, and they recount their sexual exploits without self-consciousness or concern for women.

But if many of the critics who praised *Saving Private Ryan* were right, and if Spielberg has made a film that can discourage young Americans from going to war, he is several years too late. His message may change the minds of soldiers elsewhere who still look their victims in the eyes as they kill them. But Americans no longer fight that kind of war. Shortly after *Saving Private Ryan* opened in theaters, Bill Clinton ordered attacks on Afghanistan and Sudan, launching Tomahawk cruise missiles from American ships well out to sea. No American soldier came near the borders of the countries being bombed. Why warn young men and women about the danger of machine gun bullets when they are likely to see the war on a computer screen, if at all? An important message of *Saving Private Ryan* is that war is a necessary and life-defining experience, even if it's a bloody one. Today, when war is no longer bloody for American soldiers—or for the American civilian watching the scrupulously sanitized broadcasts on CNN—the message is simply that war is necessary and life-defining. As an apparatus of the state, *Saving Private Ryan* does what it has to do: it re-creates a fascination and reverence for war so that, someday in the not too distant future, the state can put this fascination and reverence to use once again.

NOTES

1. Stephen E. Ambrose, *Band of Brothers: E Company, 506th Regiment, 101st Airborne from Normandy to Hitler's Eagle's Nest* (New York: Touchstone, 1993); *Citizen Soldiers: The U.S. Army from the Normandy Beaches to the Bulge to the Surrender of Germany, June 7, 1944–May 7, 1945* (New York: Simon and Schuster, 1997); *D-Day June 6, 1944: The Climactic Battle of World War II* (New York: Simon and Schuster, 1995).

2. John Gregory Dunne, "Virtual Patriotism: Feeling Good about War," *New Yorker*, November 16, 1998, 98–103.

3. Paul Fussell, *Wartime: Understanding and Behavior in the Second World War* (New York: Oxford University Press, 1989).

4. Ibid., 139.

5. Ibid., 142–43.

6. Richard Goldstein, "World War II Chic," *Village Voice*, January 19, 1999, 46.

7. Fussell, 287.

8. Ibid., 287.

9. Herbert Marcuse, *Eros and Civilization: A Philosophical Inquiry into Freud* (Boston: Beacon, 1955).

PART IV

PICTURES AND POLITICS

13

The Confusions of Warren Beatty

Dana Polan

AT THE END of the 1990s, Warren Beatty's career intersected explicitly with politics in a series of striking events. First, although he is known as a left filmmaker and participated, for example, in that guise in an issue of the *Nation* on political filmmaking in Hollywood,[1] Beatty pointedly was one of the audience members who stood up and applauded when HUAC name-namer Elia Kazan was given a controversial lifetime achievement award from the Academy of Motion Picture Arts and Sciences.

Second, Beatty got caught up in intense media coverage when he was pushed to consider running as a Democratic candidate for the 2000 presidential election. Interestingly, in another blurring of political lines, it was journalist Ariana Huffington—at that point most closely allied to a conservative position—who first planted the idea of a Beatty campaign in her column and on her Web site. The media flurry around a Beatty run for the presidency was quite intense until Beatty finally made it clear that he was not a candidate. Subsequently, when Beatty was awarded an Irving Thalberg Life Achievement Award from the Academy, some commentators joked that it was being given in appreciation of Beatty sparing Hollywood the spectacle of a presidential campaign.

But the most significant event was Beatty's production and direction of one of the most bluntly committed films to come out of the Hollywood dream machine: *Bulworth* (1998). Explicitly political, but not necessarily successfully political, *Bulworth* is a complicated and even contradictory film. It is precisely the film's failure (both ideological and, in fact, financial) that is itself revealing of some of the possibilities and limits of *liberal* politics—and, more particularly, for a liberal politics in the cultural realm—at the end of the century. Just as Beatty's support for Kazan and his flirtation with a presidential campaign blur categories—for example, that of radicalism and anticommunism in the former case, and that of entertainment and politics in the latter—so does Beatty's cinema offer a narrative that is intriguing yet inevitably incoherent.

But to talk of films this way—to say, for instance, that what a film like *Bulworth* is doing parallels what its director is doing in his life might seem to partake of auteurism, that seemingly discredited approach that would study films as most determined by the creativity of their directors rather than, say, the broader institutions of the film industry or the even broader ones of social and cultural context. I would want to argue, however, that in the case of certain directors, the very fact that their films are presented as authored, are offered up as the vision of a lone artist, is part of the meaning that must be analyzed. In an age where the director's name can be a salable attraction for a film, auteurism becomes not a tool of analysis but an object of analysis. To take one example, Terrence Malick's *The Thin Red Line* (1998) is among other things a film about a fantasy of the endurance of auteurist creativity, the sheer beauty of the images making an argument for the aesthetic power of the visionary director in a world that has little room for the aesthetic dimension.[2]

In fact, if auteurism traditionally has been contrasted to a political approach to film insofar as it centers on myths of individual creativity, *Bulworth* is evidence that individual creativity itself can be put forward as a political act. In an age seemingly geared to standardization, one way to stand out is by cultivating one's image as a special creative figure, as an artist. There is even a complementariness of liberalism and auteurism. Both structure the world according to a binary opposition in which, opposed to the crush of systems of authority and governance, there stand solitary figures who by their force of will try to stand up for personal identity and self-worth.

Liberalism and auteurism both start with the personal, with the potential for the individual to fight to make a difference. In two big Beatty films of the 1990s, *Bugsy* (1991) and *Bulworth*, for example, the central figure is a dreamer who struggles to gain respect for his vision and fights against the resistance of figures of power. In the case of *Bugsy*, with its emphasis on a creator who wants to build up a new world of leisure culture and runs into budget problems, it is particularly tempt-

Warren Beatty: movie star, ladies' man, presidential candidate. The explicitly political *Bulworth* (Twentieth Century Fox, 1998) seemed to suggest Beatty's plans for life after Hollywood.

ing to see here an allegory of filmmaking: the artist struggles to complete his project as the men in power worry about cost and eventually remove him from the scene.

The personalism of liberal politics can lead to a concern with solitude, with the visionary's abandonment by people around him (as when Bugsy is alone with his dreams in the last scene, vulnerable to his killer's bullets). But liberalism also presents itself as a coalition building, in large part through a faith in emotional bondings between like-minded dreamers. Bulworth, for instance, finds his dream to be a contagious force that sweeps up other individuals in its path. Significantly, the content of his dream is itself about coalition: he imagines a world in which sexual love will tear down racial barriers. Here, we might note the racial *fantasy* at work in *Bulworth*'s notion of love across race lines: where a common feature of much nineties culture is white admiration for a blackness that is taken to be the epitome of seductive cool (as in the films of Quentin Tarantino), *Bulworth* goes further and imagines that the performance of a minstrel blackness by whites makes those whites so cool they become contagious objects of veneration by the blacks whose culture they've appropriated. Thus, to take one example, the inner-city crime boss (Don Cheadle) ends up adopting Bulworth's philosophy as a mission statement for rebuilding the ghetto. Newspaper coverage of *Bulworth*'s production took note of the fact that Beatty was able to ingratiate himself with local rappers because of his reputation as a "Daddy Mack," a man who's made it big with women. (A classic example of gender—and the seductions of a charismatic celebrity—trumping race.)

In the world of Beatty's liberalist creativity, the contagion of charisma is a force that breaks boundaries and challenges forces of authority. Hence, the importance of stories of love in Beatty's cinema: not so much a rejection of the political, love is imagined as a way a politics of the personal is established, building up from the unity of the heterosexual couple to larger coalitions. It is revealing that one major plot line of *Bulworth* has to do with the way Bulworth's potential assassin Nina (Halle Berry) comes to fall for him (and his dream) and becomes part of his "team." Significantly, though, love in Beatty's films builds from an attraction at a distance—in *Bugsy, Bulworth,* and *Love Affair* (1994) alike, the Beatty character spots his future love from across a room, rendering the core of coalition as an activity of seduction and fascination, mysterious, ineffable, romantic.

But if heterosexual love as an intuitive reaching out to another person is the purest incarnation of coalition building in Beatty's cinema, there is also a faith in less intense forms of friendship and partnership as bases that one can build a vision upon. *Bugsy*, indeed, is filled with characters who come to share some part of Bugsy's dream and form bonds with him—not only Virginia Hill (Annette Bening), whose relationship to Bugsy is both amorous and corporatist since she collaborates on his project, but Mickey Cohen (Harvey Keitel) and Harry Greenburg (Elliot Gould). In the ways Beatty's career blurs boundaries between the films and the man himself, the bonds of creative friendship function centrally in his life as well as his art. Hence, the importance of a cohort of buddies (for example, Dustin Hoffman, who introduces him at his speech on the presidential campaign, or Jack Nicholson, who presents him with his Thalberg award). Hence, too, the recurrent use of such buddies in the crews and casts of film projects.

Most important, this emphasis on close friendship as the seed out of which larger politics blossoms helps explain Beatty's standing up for Elia Kazan. Kazan was the first person to give Beatty a role in a Hollywood film (*Splendor in the Grass*, 1961) and, as Beatty explained in a question-and-answer session at the University of Southern California, you don't betray the friends who stood up for you in the beginning. Central to the liberalist ethos is a philosophy of honor: one does not renounce the people one has pledged friendship to. For example, when Bugsy kills his pal Harry it is in fact to save him from worse violence on the part of the mob, and the killing is highly tinged with tragic regret.

But Kazan is important to the liberalist ethos for an additional reason. He is a symbol of the old Hollywood, of a mythology, indeed, of the old Hollywood as a place where friendship meant something. For all its vision of better-things-to-come, Beatty's liberalism is also heavily caught up in nostalgia—in particular, a nostalgia for an old filmmaking past in which it is believed that creative people made well-crafted stories. The liberal conception of history frequently imagines a past golden age that has been lost under the pressures of governance and authority and can be returned to only by active effort. It is fitting, for instance, that Beatty's *Love Affair* is a remake of Leo McCarey's 1939 film, also titled *Love Affair*, and remade by McCarey in 1957 as *An Affair to Remember*. The nostalgia is for both a certain kind of filmmaking practice—a unity of friends working as a team to express creative vision—and a certain kind of film (well-structured narratives in which people bond together in friendship and love and offer their bonds as resistance to establishment power). Moreover, insofar as Beatty's liberalism works from an irremediable opposition between dreamers and establishment figures, there is also a nostalgia for what is imagined to be the clear, unambiguous morality of older narrative cinema. Significantly, Beatty began the 1990s with *Dick Tracy* (1990), a film that invokes the binary oppositions of the original law enforcement comic strip and reinvigorates square-jawed mythologies of the effective male hero. Revealingly, *Dick Tracy* has the eponymous hero, played by Beatty, riddling the cars of bad guys with a machine gun. The image is a stark ideological reversal of the most celebrated image of a machine gunning in cinematic history—*Bonnie and Clyde* (1967), where Beatty is a victim of the establishment, rather than its fervent upholder.

But nostalgia is limited as a politics that one can build on for the present and future. Insofar as nostalgia has to do with a mythologizing of a past that it supposes got corrupted by a more modern age, it presents difficulties in imagining that the lessons of the past have a relevance in the present. At best it can inspire the present with its ideals but cannot itself be converted into a political praxis.

Beatty's nostalgia is for a world that is no more. Indeed, at USC, after explaining that it was friendship that had led him to stand up for Kazan, Beatty went on to argue that one shouldn't make too much of the blacklist since it had to do with issues and events of over fifty years ago—issues and events, that is, of purely historical, rather than ongoing political, interest. This sense of the irrevocable pastness of the past is captured in *Love Affair* by the casting of Katharine Hepburn in a rare screen appearance in the role of Beatty's elderly aunt, who lives away from civilization on an idyllic isle. Coming into the film as a cameo, Hepburn appears as a deeply admired relic from the past but one whose pertinence to the contemporary world is limited. By the end of the film, the aunt has passed away and so too, the film implies, has a whole way of life (which it does not acknowledge has all the trappings of an imperial colonialist fantasy, the white person as proud possessor of a conflict-free fiefdom).

A direct corollary in Beatty's films to the idea that the things in the past that we love nostalgically have no sway in the present has to do with the ineffectiveness in that present of the characters he plays. The past may be inspirational but primarily for incapable heirs who are not equipped to make the lessons of the past live. The Beatty character has often a fundamental character flaw that mars his ability to accomplish things: Bulworth and Bugsy are, for instance, idiosyncratic figures whose visions for change are not that far from mad, unrealizable fantasy.

But even in more mundane contexts, the Beatty hero seems fundamentally awkward, unable to perform even ordinary activities with skill or efficiency. Significantly, this seems to be another arena in which actor and persona merge. When Beatty gave his big speech at the Beverly Hills Hotel to indicate whether he was running for president or not, many journalists commented on his awkwardness at speech—the stuttering, the inarticulateness of ideas, the jumps in logic, the lapses and dead spaces that broke up the flow. Like Bulworth, who spits out his hip-hoppin' politics through a convulsive effort, Beatty himself seems clumsily to be trying to formulate a position out of chaos.

One highly indicative way the Beatty character manifests his awkwardness at negotiating the demands of modernity has to do with a constant emphasis on that character's scrambling. *Shampoo* (1975) in the 1970s had already depicted the hectic world of a man trying to hold different parts of his life together, and all of Beatty's 1990s films give great prominence to scenes of frantic scrambling. As in a classical French farce, the Beatty character is always rushing crazily from place to place to sort out events or experiences that are simultaneously making demands on his life. In *Bugsy*, a key scene has Bugsy frantically zigzagging back and forth between his daughter's birthday preparations and complicated discussions over his casino plans with Mafia chieftains; in *Love Affair*, the hero has to find a way to meet his paramour while avoiding the inquisitive camera of a tabloid journalist, and, in classic farce manner, he does this in part by sneaking out a window; in *Bulworth*, most of the plot has to do with Bulworth's unpredictable veering around sectors of Los Angeles and trying to tie different parts of his life together. The Beatty character's desperate rush to try to keep up, to try to connect, suggests that he is living in situations that surpass him, that are beyond his control. These situations can be political as well as existential (the randomness of a universe that is unpredictable), but they are ones that defeat mastery, that put the lie to effective action.

Defeat, indeed, is a central component of the narratives of Beatty's films: a character tries to buck the system and loses. It is striking to note how many Beatty films across the range of his career end with his character killed, as if to a very great degree the prowess and capability of the hero are fundamentally in thrall to an inescapable fatalism. As a comedy, *Love Affair* shies from this model, although, as I've noted, there still is a mourning for a whole (Hollywood) way of life represented by the Katharine Hepburn character. In contrast, both Bugsy and Bulworth are unceremoniously shot down at the end, their visions shattered by forces of inescapable fatality.

Actually, in *Bulworth*, it is not precisely the case that the Beatty hero is shot down *at the end*. *Bulworth*, in fact, ends with a coda in which Amiri Baraka, standing outside the hospital we assume Bulworth's body has been taken to, exhorts the audience in a direction of hope. But the fact that this last moment of hope is a separate bit tacked on to the rest of the film is significant. Narrative resolution in Beatty films comes off as arbitrary, not structurally integrated. The political confusions—how can one deal effectively with and in the present?—are manifested as narrative confusions. Beatty's films give themselves over to a series of plot reversals, unexpected twists, meanderings, as if no one narrative direction is assumed to be logical, inevitable, necessary. *Bugsy*, for instance, has several narrative climaxes, each of which has a different signification: Bugsy's casino fails and everyone abandons him; Virginia returns to Bugsy and makes amends for embezzling from him by admitting she does love him; Bugsy returns to Los Angeles and is gunned down. Likewise, with its debt to both farce and melodrama, *Love Affair* has sudden reversals of fortune as its guiding narrative principle. And in *Bulworth*, the arbitrariness of narrative progression is taken to an extreme as the "ending" breaks into a series of "resolutions": Bulworth wins his senatorial bid; Bulworth seems to come out of his folly; despite seeming to have returned to normal, Bulworth suddenly asks Nina to come with him; Bulworth is shot dead; the homeless man offers up his exhortation.

For all his love of the golden age of classical Hollywood filmmaking, there is also something baroque, even modernist, about Beatty's cinema, as if it knows that the modern age cannot sustain a combination of clear-cut storytelling and clear-cut political agenda. A film like *Bulworth* proceeds by fits and starts, its abrupt and ragged structure mimicking the stuttering hesitancy of its main character and the liberal actor playing him. The confusions here are the unavoidable conditions not only of a man and his cinema but of a whole way of conceiving politics and change at the end of the twentieth century.

NOTES

1. *Nation*, 5–12 April 1999, 13–20.

2. I discuss the example of Malick at greater length in Dana Polan, "Auteurism and War-teurism: Terrence Malick's War Movie," *Metro*, no. 119 (1999): 58–63.

14

Movie Star Presidents

Thomas Doherty

ONCE CAST MAINLY in marble or paper money, the president of the United States doubled as a motion picture star in the 1990s. A Hollywood POTUS landed featured roles in romantic comedies (*Dave* [1993], *The American President* [1995]), big-budget science fiction (*Independence Day* [1996], *Mars Attacks!* [1996]), and a spate of suspense thrillers (*Absolute Power* [1997], *Murder at 1600* [1997], *Air Force One* [1997], and *The Contender* [2000]). Central casting–wise, the person of the chief executive was suddenly as popular as hit men, architects, and hookers. Plotwise, the dynamics of White House intrigue beckoned as alluringly as the theatrics of a backstage musical.[1]

The filmic incarnations of the president in the last decade of the twentieth century were striking not just in quantity, or in range across genres, but in outlook: they showcased the figure of the commander in chief as a dramatis persona, sometimes as a solid member of the ensemble, more often as lead actor in the play. Against expectations, the sheer imagistic ubiquity of the modern, televisual president only enhanced the box office appeal of a fictional surrogate.

Though Hollywood and Washington have never been strange bedfellows, the motion picture industry traditionally treated its presidents respectfully, even reverently. A dignified walk-on in a colorful costume drama or a stolid portrayal in a worshipful bio-pic was the preferred means of representation. The transcendent personality in the presidential pantheon was Abraham Lincoln, the beloved martyr of the Republic, who alone inspired artistically worthy and financially successful screen treatments. Among the many Lincoln memorials on film are his canonization as the merciful "great Heart" in two D. W. Griffith films, silent and sound, *The Birth of a Nation* (1915) and *Abraham Lincoln* (1930), and as the demigod in embryo in both John Ford's *Young Mr. Lincoln* (1939) and John Cromwell's version of Robert Sherwood's *Abe Lincoln in Illinois* (1940). But Lincoln aside, full-length presidential features were rare entries and tough sells. Not even wartime patriotism could turn Andrew Johnson into a matinee idol in William Dieterle's *Tennessee Johnson* (1942). The president who kept us out of war kept moviegoers out of theaters in Darryl Zanuck's epic flop, *Wilson* (1944).

Dealing with living presidents in office called for special delicacy in depiction. Elected in sync with the maturity of the sound motion picture, Franklin Roosevelt was the first president to make a true cinematic impact. Not just a familiar radio voice, or the benevolent visage on the New Deal posters, he became a vibrant film personality via the newsreels. Within weeks of his inauguration, two newsreel specials were rushed into theaters, MGM's *Roosevelt—the Man of the Hour* (1933) and Universal's *The Fighting President* (1933). For the next twelve years, the newsreels projected FDR as the marquee name in a motion picture friendly administration. Appropriately, FDR's newsreel life was reviewed and commemorated in a feature-length documentary, *The Roosevelt Story* (1947), the prototype for what was to become a sturdy film genre. "The impact is startling," marveled *Variety*, sizing up the pioneering archival bio-pic. "It is surprising how the editors of this motley collection of silent and talker newsreel shorts . . . have managed to catch and sustain the heroic spirit of the late president."[2]

FDR's charismatic newsreel presence carried over into the entertainment feature film, notably at Warner Brothers, where Democratic partisan Jack Warner fortified the New Deal by genuflecting to its point man. Typically, FDR was portrayed pretty much the way God appeared in biblical epics—a shimmering silhouette accompanied by the strains of a hymnal anthem, a profile glimpsed in a halo of light. In Michael Curtiz's *Yankee Doodle Dandy* (1942), when George M. Cohan (James Cagney) is ushered into the August chambers of the Oval Office, the FDR lookalike emanates an almost divine glow. Thus too the portrait of a later president in John Ford's *The Long Gray Line* (1955), when West Point's Marty Maher (Tyrone Power) is granted an audience with former plebe and current commander in chief, Dwight D. Eisenhower. In deference to the office and the man, the motion picture camera kept a respectful distance.

Only in the realm of wild fantasy or dark satire might a presidential character appear less than presidential. Spawned in the depths of the

Great Depression, Gregory La Cava's *Gabriel over the White House* (1933) starred Walter Huston as a demonically possessed chief executive who solves the nation's problems by abolishing Congress, declaring martial law, and summarily executing gangsters. Not until the irreverent 1960s would Hollywood again hallucinate so outrageously about the chief executive. In Stanley Kubrick's *Dr. Strangelove: Or How I Learned to Stop Worrying and Love the Bomb* (1963) Peter Sellers wickedly impersonates a hapless Adlai Stevenson figure named President Muffley ("Gentlemen!" he yells at two wrestling officers. "You can't fight in here—this is the war room!"). Moving from black comedy to tie-dyed psychedelia, Barry Shear's youth rebellion film *Wild in the Streets* (1968) conjures a dystopic future where rock star president Max Frost (Chris Jones) consigns the elderly—that is, everyone over thirty—to concentration camps and forces them to imbibe LSD.

Yet even in the anti-establishment 1960s, the president was more liable to be a stalwart leader than a scoundrel or dolt. In John Frankenheimer's conspiratorial *Seven Days in May* (1964), the president (Fredric March) is forceful and principled, concerned more with protecting the Constitution than himself as he outmaneuvers a military coup. Likewise, in Sidney Lumet's thriller *Fail-Safe* (1964), the president (Henry Fonda) sacrifices his own family (and New York) in order to save the world from nuclear conflagration. Even in Theodore J. Flicker's irreverent psycho-comedy *The President's Analyst* (1967), the (offscreen) patient is treated with kid gloves.

It was Richard Nixon, of course, who dispersed the reverent aura and left behind the bad smell around the Oval Office. From secret tapes to tell-all memoirs, the revelations about President Nixon exposed not just political chicanery but personal failings, undressing the imperial presidency and laying bare a graphic image of a broken man: drunken ravings, foul language, late night conversations with oil paintings. After Nixon, the picture of the president was not "warts and all," as that other president had joked to a photographer, but all warts.

Nonetheless, even as a wave of Watergate-inspired antigovernment scenarios proliferated during the underachieving administrations of Presidents Gerald Ford and Jimmy Carter, the president still mainly escaped personal indictment and on-screen caricature, as if filmmakers and audiences alike still retained a residual respect for the office, if not the man. In Alan J. Pakula's adaptation of Bob Woodward and Carl Bernstein's *All the President's Men* (1976), Nixon is a lurking offstage presence, spotted backscreen on television monitors. Faceless bureau-crats, despotic generals, and shadowy figures running secret agencies were the preferred vessels of federal villainy. The next steps, moving down the corridors of power and into the sanctum of the Oval Office it-self, was facilitated by a president who thrived on a new level of tele-filmic intimacy.

Ronald Reagan, the motion picture star turned star president, is the obvious nexus for the merger of screen status and political stature. Where Nixon made the president hissible, Reagan made him accessible. In the resonantly titled essay *"Ronald Reagan, the Movie,"* the cultural historian Michael Rogin argued that "Reagan's easy slippage between movies and reality is synechdochic for a political culture increasingly impervious to distinctions between fiction and history."[3] But Reagan's gift wasn't so much slippage as synergy. More significant than his back-story as an actor in A (not B) movies at Warner Brothers in the 1940s, or even the serene telegeniety of the Great Communicator, was the ongo-ing revolution in moving image entertainment during Reagan's presi-dency. His term in office between 1981 and 1989 coincided suggestively with the ascent of cable television. In the 1980s, the Olympian domi-nance of the American president—a leader who could once command network airtime virtually by fiat—was undercut by dozens of nonpres-idential options on rival channels. Yet while all future presidents would be diminished by the medium's ever expanding menu of tantalizing al-ternatives, Reagan added a uniquely surreal element to the televisual collage. A restless televiewer might channel surf from the president de-livering a State of the Union address to—zap!—the image of the self-same man slapping Angie Dickinson in *The Killers* (1964) on Turner Classic Movies or strutting as a U.S. cavalry officer in an old episode of *The Big Valley* on the Family Network.

Cumulatively, the cupidity of Nixon, the stupidity of Ford, the ti-midity of Carter, and the (media) promiscuity of Reagan left a legacy of diminished expectations and open disdain.[4] By the 1990s, condescen-sion vied with contempt in the typical Hollywood portrait of the presi-dent. Whether the tale came from the Left—Alan J. Pakula's version of John Grisham's *The Pelican Brief* (1993)—or the Right—Philip Noyce's version of Tom Clancy's *Clear and Present Danger* (1994)—the American president was apt to be a very inept or very bad man.

Making a timely comeback, Nixon himself was kicked around for an emblematic flaying in Oliver Stone's patho-bio-pic *Nixon* (1995).

Screening the American presidency: Oliver Stone's epic historical melodrama, *Nixon* (Cinergi, 1995).

Unlike the deceptively titled *JFK* (1991), a tale of conspiracy, not personality, *Nixon* purported to delve deeply into the checkered psychology of America's most perversely fascinating president. Stone dissected Nixon as a bourbon-soaked, unscrupulous neurotic. The director, said critics, had gone soft on the guy.

Yet what was new about the cluster of presidential films that emerged in the 1990s was not their by now familiar cynicism but their intrusive familiarity. In film after film, romantic comedy or high-octane thriller, the president was an active agent, a protagonist whom audiences were to cheer or despise, not a background figure who functioned as a deus ex machina at a crucial plot twist. Front and center, his character was an emotional fulcrum for the entire narrative—our hero, our villain.

Here the cultural link to the manner and mettle of the keeper of the keys to the Lincoln Bedroom between 1993 and 2000 seems more than coincidental. After all, Bill Clinton was the most camera-ready of all presidents: talk show host, master of ceremonies on C-SPAN, in shades with sax on *Arsenio*, in boxers or briefs on MTV, in less than that in the Starr Report. JFK may have been the first television president, Reagan may have been the first president to exploit a television career for political capital, but Clinton was the first television-bred president. A baby boomer to the medium born, he evinced a cool and easy manner on the small screen that worked both ways: the corollary to the president who feels your pain being that you're prepared to feel his. The video JFK was glamorous and unattainable; the video Clinton was ordinary and approachable. Little wonder that the Oval Office and its custodian became fit subjects for all kinds of screenplays that refuse to keep a respectful distance.

As to political sympathies, the president-on-film cycle follows a schematic set of party lines. The main ideological divide is between the Capraesque optimism of *Mr. Smith Goes to Washington* (1939) and the Stoned paranoia of the executive branch twinpack, *JFK* and *Nixon*. Good father/bad father, heartwarming leader/bloodcurdling monster, hail to the chief/rail at the chief.

In Ivan Reitman's *Dave*, when the unscrupulous real president is incapacitated, a lookalike Everyman takes his place. The imitation soon proves better at serving the nation—and the First Lady—than the original. Great with kids, a natural on television, he wrangles with the federal budget like Dad balancing the family checkbook.

The kinder and gentler version is also on flag-waving display in Rob Reiner's *The American President*, a Hollywood liberal fantasy of what Bill Clinton would be like if he were only less like Bill Clinton and more like Michael Douglas—a romantic dude with great pickup lines, no cumbersome First Lady to crimp his style, an adorable daughter, and a kamikaze devotion to left-wing causes. Tender and empathetic even when ordering air strikes, he is sensitive but strong, of sturdy principle and good humor, as dexterous at a press conference as on the dance floor. (CBS's hit situation comedy *The West Wing*—dubbed "The Left Wing" by resentful right-wingers—bespeaks the same unrequited impulse for a Washington actor parroting a Hollywood script.)

Against that star-spangled image, the tattered version of the American president exposes a man behind the curtain who is either sinister or simpering. In what cannot be mere happenstance, Clint Eastwood's *Absolute Power* and Dwight Little's *Murder at 1600* both linked kinky sex and mysterious death to the highest levels of White House authority. In *Absolute Power* the presidential partner in a bout of rough sex is shot dead by overprotective Secret Service agents. Cover-up and murder ensue. In *Murder at 1600* a milquetoast president manipulated by a

Rasputin aide watches his administration unravel when a beautiful blonde turns up dead in a White House bathroom. Cover-up and murder ensue. In both films, criminal conspiracy and lethal sex play are as much a part of the job as photo ops with Boy Scouts and Miss America.

However, the approach taken by the blockbusters *Independence Day* and *Air Force One* suggests not only that Americans still retain a reservoir of idealism when they imagine the president but that they prefer a model with alpha male prowess to sensitive guy empathy. Both films conjure up combat-ready presidents who turn gladiator in mano a mano death matches with the enemies of the United States.

The highest grossing film of 1996, Roland Emmerich's FX extravaganza *Independence Day* toplined a president who was (1) a likable and approachable guy; (2) a former fighter pilot who personally leads a multiethnic squadron against extraterrestrial invaders; and (3) an honest leader totally unaware of the alien corpses kept in cold storage in Roswell, New Mexico. Forced to evacuate headquarters when celestial lasers score a direct hit on the White House, the president (Bill Pullman) rallies the armed forces to spearhead a counterattack against the alien hordes. In a rousing speech to his fighter squadron on D-Day—July 4th—he proclaims the dawn of a new independence day for all the people of the beleaguered planet. If the architecture around Washington, D.C., absorbs a terrific blasting, the ethos remains as solid as the Puritans' City upon a Hill. America is still the last best hope of mankind.

In the ostensibly more realistic realm of the action adventure genre, *Air Force One* carried on board an exceptionally resourceful chief executive (Harrison Ford) who becomes—literally—a fighting president. When terrorist wackos hijack the title airplane, he initiates a *Die Hard*–like one-man insurgency to regain control of the ship of state. "Get off my plane!" he snarls as he wallops the terrorist leader into oblivion. Back at the White House, unsteadily manning the helm, a female vice president wobbles indecisively while her superior throttles the invaders. Not incidentally, no matter how stormy the turbulence aboard Air Force One, the First Lady and First Husband are devoted spouses, still lovey-dovey after years of marriage.

Throughout the 1990s, at the box office if not always the voting booth, the best policy for a successful presidency was a combination of good family values, progressive domestic policies, and swift retaliation against terrorists, global or intergalactic. For a vivid picture of the cozy symbiosis between the televisual president and the motion picture president, consider the moment in Robert Zemeckis's science fiction film *Contact* (1997), when a clip from an actual speech by President Clinton is seamlessly edited into the action, a trick that seems less a rude infringement than a gracious cameo appearance. For a likely coming attraction, contemplate the all-but-inevitable credit line of a future production: starring, as himself, the President of the United States.

NOTES

1. A subspecies of the presidential genre that also thrived in the 1990s was the race-for-the-White House film, a kind of electoral college road movie built around political process and media manipulation. Descendants of Frank Capra's *State of the Union* (1948) and Franklin Schaffner's version of Gore Vidal's *The Best Man* (1964), the list includes the prophetic *Wag the Dog* (1997), film à clef *Primary Colors* (1998), the Warren Beatty trial balloon *Bulworth* (1998), and the allegorical *Election* (2000).

2. "The Roosevelt Story," *Variety*, July 2, 1947, 13.

3. Michael Paul Rogin, *Ronald Reagan, the Movie and Other Episodes in Political Demonology* (Berkeley: University of California Press, 1987), 9.

4. A widely quoted wisecrack also captured the prevailing zeitgeist. Looking over the delegation sent to the funeral of slain Egyptian leader Anwar Sadat in 1981, Senator Bob Dole took the measure of the three living ex-presidents in his line of sight, Ford, Carter, and Nixon. "There goes See No Evil, Hear No Evil—and Evil."

15

The Fantasy Image

Fixed and Moving

Maureen Turim

IN A SHORT essay, "A Mythological Parallel to a Visual Obsession" (1916), Freud explores the case of a patient whose obsessive thoughts and images, whenever he saw his father coming into a room, involved both a verbal association and an image.[1] The patient either would think of the compound word *vaterarse* (fatherass) or imagine the image of a man's nude torso cut off at the waist, viewed from behind, with his father's face superimposed on the buttocks. Word and image, so intricately connected as signifiers, did not necessarily both appear together; Freud tells us that word and image could coincide for his patient, or either one could appear independently.

Freud goes on in this essay to explore the word *vaterarse* as a Germanic translation of "patriarch." He then notes parallels for the visual image in terra-cotta figurines of Baubo found in Asia Minor that show her as a nude torso whose face is superimposed on her abdomen.[2] The difference between a goddess viewed frontally and a father viewed from the rear does not receive comment. The suggestive yet incomplete aspect of this short essay serves as an invitation to further speculation.

We might append Freud's analysis with more references from modern art, such as René Magritte's face/torso series and Hans Bellmer's involuted bodies. We might equally explore the significant issues it raises about word/image connections in psychoanalysis, and make connections to Jean-François Lyotard's *Discours, figure* essay "Le désir dans le discours," which discusses similar fragmentation and blending of body parts, human as well as animal, in the construction of words in the rebus.[3] My reason for citing it here, however, is to explore precisely the theoretical issue of images within fantasy that it suggests, in particular the question of fixation of the fantasy image, known as obsession.

If the scene of fantasy presents itself as visual, is it fixed, or does it move? Is it more like a tableau, a still, or a filmed scenario, a narrative image, a dream? Freud himself notes in recommending the examination of child play to understand fantasy life: "People's phantasies are less easy to observe than the play of children." So if we now ask, "When is the fantasy image fixed, and when does it move?" this is not a question empirically answerable as regards actual fantasies, but one that instead takes as its focus representations of fantasy in analysis and in fictional forms. When are fantasies displayed as unique and isolated, or conversely, part of a narrative flow?

In returning to the example mentioned above, it seems as if word and image are bound to each other, the image in some ways an illustration of the verbal thought, in some ways a product of it that incorporates other material. By turning the epithet "fatherass" into an image, the subject infuses the pejorative with sexual prowess and desire, superimposing the face, the site of vision, voice, and reason not on the frontal genitalia, as in the goddess figure, but on the buttocks and anus, inverting the phallic associations and perhaps the power relations. The fantasy image thus does much more than the word association alone and can be seen as both informing and transforming it. It is also a prime example of a fixed image that recurs in an obsessive manner. Statue or illustration of a statue, it hovers in front of the actual father each time he enters a room.

We must take into account here that in describing the fantasy, psychoanalysts use the term "fixed" in a metaphorical rather than a literal sense. This very metaphor has significant implications for a theory of desire and of visual imagination. I hope to open this question to its conjunction with theories of the image and visual representation. Specifically, I want to investigate the power of stopping motion in the articulation of a fantasy, using examples drawn from art, film, and photography.

Still images become fixed in photography as the culmination of a process of design and craft. Now that image production is likely to be a digital process rather than a plastic and chemical one, the metaphors we might draw from the fixative baths of nineteenth- and twentieth-century photography will be joined with new metaphors from digital inscription and encoding. If I linger, however, over the fixation of images in the past, it is to hold on to a metaphor that has its moment fixed in history, a period precisely obsessed with a change in recording processes *and* in recording change, stopping our view of space and time to enframe it as image. Photography implies so much as historical metaphor, so much that affects our thoughts and psyches. We use its fixity to slice out parts of our lives, parts of our landscapes and cityscapes, holding them still as metonymies. It frames our relationships, cementing bodies as statues in relation one to another.

For psychoanalysis a fixation is linked to the notion of repression, arrested development, and obsession; it indicates how fantasy has at its core an element that determines the very images that may be produced. In Freud's case histories, fantasies may take numerous forms. Sometimes they are conceived of with metaphors borrowed from the theater, such as scene and staging. In fact fantasy is defined as a scene in which the subject is actor. Sometimes fantasy is a narrative, a story that is formed or retold in language. The specificity of the language chosen becomes more significant than the scenography, as in Freud's essay "A Child Is Being Beaten" (1919). In this essay four case histories are condensed into a model narration, the elements of which are rendered in phrases that Freud articulates as phases of the fantasy. These phrases are, in Freud's analysis, (1) "A child is being beaten," (2) "My father is beating me," and (3) "My father is beating the other child; he only loves me."[4] That these phrases themselves condense elaborate fantasies into simple sentences is evident from Freud's comment that abruptly introduces the notion of the patients' various daydreams all being preoccupied with male characters: "In both cases of day-dreaming—one of which rose almost to the level of a work of art—the heroes are always young men; indeed women did not usually come into these creations at all, and only made their first appearance after several years, and then in minor parts." So the actual fantasies that lie behind Freud's structural and linguistic analysis were in fact narrative elaborations, creations that we are tantalizingly told could be quite "artistic," though no specifics of the form of this artistry are provided.

Take, for example, "A Case of Paranoia Running Counter to the Psychoanalytic Theory of the Disease" (1915). Here the fantasy is a recounted narrative, a story told in which Freud sets out to aid a legal process of detection, to separate what actually happened from what is the fantasy image embellished by the patient.[5] The story is of a tryst between the patient and her lover, interrupted by a knocking that the patient believes is someone hiding behind the curtains of her lover's room, taking photos of her in a compromising position. The click of the shutter, a sound, becomes Freud's focus as fantasy image, an element not without its own poetic consequences for our consideration of the relationship between fantasy and image. That a modern woman should find her fantasy occupied by the sound of a camera's shutter, the sound that indicates that she has been captured as part of a shameful scene that others will then regard, links the technology of the still photograph with paranoiac structures. The photo slices through her sexual experience, eliciting her fear, framing her knowledge that instances are open to framed recording and uncontrollable dissemination.

Freud asks the patient to tell the story a second time, hoping for more details. He is gratified to receive the additions, including the introduction of an older woman into the scenario who supplies this case with the mother figure and lesbian dynamic he felt had been missing, and which had made this case seem to run "counter to the disease."

Worthy of our notice, "fixation" appears dramatically as the last word of this essay.[6] This psychic inertia, arrested development, stubborn symptom, holding onto the fetish, and fixation form a nexus of terms in which the stopping of motion is the dominant metaphor. The work of Jacques Lacan propels this metaphorical use of stopped motion even further.

In *Le séminaire de Jacques Lacan*, book 4, *La relation d'objet: 1956–1957*, Lacan evokes a specific definition of the veil, the curtain in front of or over an object, as in the veiling of a work of art, particularly a statue, prior to its presentation, its unveiling.[7] He then links this notion of the veil to another related image, the screen, and thus to the notion of a screen-memory in Freud. Lacan uses these images of suspended cloth to help him portray aspects of concealment and projection operative in the structure of perversion, and specifically the fetish. Now for Lacan the fetish is related to a moment in a story. As he puts it, "It's the moment of the story where the image stops." (C'est le moment de l'histoire où l'image s'arrête.)[8] The implied comparison with a film that suddenly halts is shortly made even more explicit, as an "arrêt sur l'image," in English "a fixed frame," as Lacan retells Freud's scene of the origination of the fetish as if it were a film being projected: "Just before the moment at which what one looks for in the mother would be seen, that is the phallus that she has and doesn't have, as presence absence, and absence presence. The rememorizing of the story stops and suspends itself at the moment just before."⁹ Lacan's pursuit of this metaphor takes one more turn as he defines the fetish as an interruption of the story at the moment where it stops and becomes fixed, as where it indicates the pursuit of its movement beyond the veil.

Historical and socially specific contexts might drive the choice of the form of a fantasy. With photographs, billboards, films, and video games, with each new apparatus of representation establishing its own contextual universe from which an individual might learn to draw her fantasies, comes more external shaping of the form individual fantasy might take.

Consider the recent debate in the United States over the influence of violent imagery on teenagers. Empirical evidence of two youthful mass murderers' obsessions with specific media images have formed the basis of a national obsession with three specific productions; two of these, *The Basketball Diaries* (1995) and *The Matrix* (1999) are films, while *Doom* is a video game. New groups of potential perpetrators of mass crimes seem to model themselves after these images, following the lead of the last group to obtain the public's attention through media coverage of their destruction and the analysis of its causes. Cause and effect, the relationship between individual psychology and mass psychology, is here in such a short and uncertain cyclical pattern that only by stopping the images themselves do we as analysts seem to be able to grasp at understanding the phenomenon.

The images in question are all of "shooters," young men sporting automatic weapons dressed for their kill in black trench coats. There is both an uncanny similarity to these images and distinct differences among them, particularly in the context in which they are embedded. In *The Basketball Diaries*, directed by Scott Kalvert from a novel by Jim Carroll, the shooter, Jim (Leonardo DiCaprio), appears in a dream sequence, as an element of represented fantasy within a narrative biography. The protagonist, a future musician/writer, suffers alienation in high school, an alienation epitomized by his imagining a violent revenge through storming a classroom and blasting bullets to silence his tormentors. In *The Matrix*, directed by Andy Wachowski and Larry Wachowski, the shooters appear in continual kinetic repetition as sci-fi guerrilla fighters seeking to overturn the evil cannibalistic rule of automatons and their central cybernetic programming. Though the hero, Neo (Keanu Reaves), sometimes appears in a solitary but two-fisted aiming of his guns, he is just as often doubled by a female partner shooter, Trinity (Carrie-Anne Moss).

Doom, on the other hand, is an animated interactive game in which the player is represented by a realistically rendered figure armed with automatic weapons whose task it is to chase down fleeing victims and annihilate them. As such it works on repetitive image cycles rather than narratively specific contexts, though it is clearly the outgrowth of cumulative comic book fantasies of superheroic avengers.

U.S. discussion of these violent images has for the most part ignored their iconography, if you will, their complex heritage and its functioning. They are the outgrowth of an archetypal U.S. image of the gunman in the western, split as he was between outlaw and law enforcer. This gunman's antiheroic offshoot dominates the gangster film, trading his frontier setting for an urban or road-movie itinerant one. He permutates from cavalry officer battling Native Americans to World War II foot soldier. As a collective image he is an emblem of both pride and shame, with sometimes the separation between hero, antihero, and villain far less distinct than the mythic, epic, or melodramatic structures these genres might suggest. Given that the iconography is so complex historically, these recent manifestations need to be read for their contemporaneous reiteration of a major national icon conjoined with a basic phallic signification as a fantasy of power and omnipotence.

Yet their difference deserves our attention. The shooting in *The Basketball Diaries* fulfills a symbolic narrative function within a revenge fantasy later successfully sublimated as artistic creativity, while *The Matrix* fulfills a function of humanist melodrama, as human good overcomes mechanical, industrial evil. These film images are carefully contextualized, while *Doom's* primary context is that of ritual reiteration. Action, fighting, and shooting computer games do surround their quest and labyrinthine confrontational schemas with mission narratives that fall into two major types: one simply presents destroyer-combatants, while the other poses the player's identification with a savior figure who must fight to save humanity from evil forces. Such symbolic coding seems vital to their need to elevate the fantasy of shooting beyond the mechanical challenge of the shooting games of sideshows and penny arcades. In addition it provides other levels of intrigue for the player and an alibi for the company that distributes the game. From another perspective, the narrative bears minimal importance in *Doom* and similar shooter games, as it serves as a convenient platform through which to introduce an episodic structure of violent encounters with a variety of rules that govern their circumstances, but not their basic structure. Temporality is also a factor here.

The Basketball Diaries in context is not reiterative, but rather contains its violent revenge imagery within a brief segment. This segment is marked as a fantasy within a psychological biography. While such markers seemingly limit its potential for being read as a superfluous exploitative endangering of those susceptible to influence, after the carnage in Littleton the film was pulled from video distribution. The sequence provided an uncanny representation of the Littleton massacre, whose perpetrators chose to forgo the encapsulation and eventual sublimation the fantasy shooting spree receives in the narrative. Instead, they favored writing their fantasy in blood, a move that distinguishes them from other spectators and players, but a move that is proving to be hardly unique to these particular borderline personalities.

Doom is reiterative virtually ad infinitum. *The Basketball Diaries* is contained and limited, but paradoxically charged with adolescent potential identification. *The Matrix* structures its violent shooting imagery somewhere between these two extremes of framed iteration and infinite reiteration. It uses its shooter as a repetitive motif, providing as much reiteration as the linear structure of a narrative film will allow, performing its repetitions as choreography to a brilliant soundtrack. Its hero defies gravity, marshaling mental powers to shoot and kick-fight through space unlimited by the weight that normally constrains a human body in a less virtually plotted universe. This dance of violence mesmerizes. All these shooting images are moving images, kinetic choreographies, and kinetics are the bases of their appeal. Yet each is in a sense static, still, iterated and reiterated in a frozen conjunction, one that links the specificity of the action pose to the monumental stasis of the icon. So while we may see them as different, we cannot use that difference to simply align the films with one function, while the game is assigned another. There is no easy separation of good and evil images once one begins to theoretically explore how these images function.

Once the borderline personality takes hold of these images, their differences of inscription are further mitigated. Literally, our borderline subject can stop the image anywhere he likes or run them over and over again. He can import them onto his Web page as stills, thereby simply making manifest what processes are occurring in his psyche. He stops their specific functioning by obsessing on them as his fantasy. He collects them, frames them, fixes them.

I will end this speculation, though, with the discussion of the portrayal of fantasy within a far more feminist framework, the treatment the fantasy image gets in Lynn Hershman Leeson's *Conceiving Ada* (1997), a virtual exploration of the biography of Ada Byron, granddaughter of the poet Byron, and a woman who contributed to the invention of early prototypes of the computer. The film owes much—far too much, perhaps—to Virginia Woolf's *Orlando* and Sally Potter's film adaptation of that book (1992). Yet it contains at least one splendid sequence, in which a photo of Ada in the hallway of her home is programmed by a contemporary feminist computer scientist to move and therefore to virtually re-create its historical actual place as a slice of Ada's life and thought. The still photo becomes the moving fantasy, which the film then endows with a magical power to interact with the present. For a moment this cybernetic and historical obsession with Ada proves dangerous for our contemporary programmer, interfering with the genetic coding of her fetus, as the film plays with the trope interchangeability of computer codes and genetic codes. But the danger is only briefly entertained, yielding to the safe image of a Berthe Morisot–style portrait of mother and daughter years later seated lovingly in front of a computer monitor. We learn that the daughter, named Ada, regularly engages with their computer game reanimation of her namesake Ada, but in a manner the mother fully regulates so that she will have a "normal childhood."

Of course the fantasy here is a happy ending in which obsession can be controlled. Finding a sweet ending rather than a horrific one to a game like *Doom*, however, may be more than a matter of ideological reprogramming. At risk in the game is the subject's formation before gaming, the desires and conflicts the child brings with him before cursors are ever moved. What is left out of all the debates on the effects of external images on violent fantasies is the way such images work as a trial acting out of the fantasy rather than its invention.

Users praise a new competitor game of *Doom*'s named *Half-Life* for doing away with all the interruptions of the action disguised as body count tally screens and informative communications that previous levels of programming development necessitated. Seamless realistic three-dimensionally rendered action in space, mobility, kinetics, and depth seem ironically now necessary components to such fantasy images.

If the psyche fixes images like the snapshots that Freud's patient imagined being taken of the sexual encounter of which she was ashamed, I am suggesting that this fixative can now be applied to the most mobile of images, and that the false mobility and multidimensionality of these new images are part of their psychic deception. They disguise the hold they have on certain subjects with an illusion of going through a journey, accomplishing a quest, solving a puzzle, or conquering all obstacles thrown in one's path. All our fantasies of animating such fixations to our will, be they of control, contextualization, or censorship, seem to miss some fundamental understanding of the very hold of the fantasy image before such computer images ever supplied themselves as supplements.

I have tried to open up many questions here about the relationship between fantasy images on one hand and external images with their historically changing technologies on the other. Movement, rapidity of change, and greater simulation of reality are elements of these technological changes that I believe deserve more consideration in our case histories. Perhaps we will learn from the analysts who work with the boys who survived writing out their fantasies in blood.

NOTES

1. Sigmund Freud, "A Mythological Parallel to a Visual Obsession (1916)," in *The Standard Edition of the Complete Psychological Works of Sigmund Freud*, trans. and ed. James Strachey (London: Hogarth Press, 1916), 14: 337–39.

2. These figurines are presented in Salomon Reinach, *Cultes, mythes et religions* (Paris: Ernest Leroux, 1923) (first published in 1912) in connection to the myth of Demeter's search for her abducted daughter; Baubo, her hostess on her journey, performs the lifting of her skirts to amuse Demeter, distracting her from her distraught state. In the excavations at Priene in Asia Minor some terracottas were found that represented Baubo. They show the body of a woman without a head or chest and with a face drawn on the abdomen: the lifted dress frames the face like a crown of hair.

3. Jean-François Lyotard, "Le désir dans le discours," in *Discours, figure*, Collection d'esthétique (Paris: Klincksieck, 1971), 281–326.

4. Sigmund Freud, "A Child Is Being Beaten" (1919) in *The Standard Edition of the Complete Psychological Works of Sigmund Freud*, trans. and ed. James Strachey (London: Hogarth Press, 1919), 17:175–204. See the discussion of this essay

in Serge LeClaire, *A Child Is Being Killed: On Primary Narcissism and the Death Drive*, trans. Marie-Claude Hays (Stanford: Stanford University Press, 1998).

5. Sigmund Freud, "A Case of Paranoia Running Counter to the Psychoanalytic Theory of the Disease" (1915), in *The Standard Edition of the Complete Psychological Works of Sigmund Freud*, trans. and ed. James Strachey (London: Hogarth Press, 1915), 14:261–74.

6. Ibid., 274. Freud explicates the "psychic inertia" that Jung sees as the fundamental condition of neurosis: "this specialized 'psychic inertia' is only a different term, though hardly a better one, for what in psychoanalysis we are accustomed to call 'fixation.'

7. Jacques Lacan, *Le séminaire de Jacques Lacan*, book 4, *La relation d'objet: 1956–1957* (Paris: Seuil, 1994), 157 (my translation).

8. Ibid., 157.

9. Ibid., 157 (my translation).

16

Men with Guns

The Story John Sayles Can't Tell

Ralph E. Rodriguez

> Half the movies ever made could be called *Men with Guns.*
> —John Sayles

I WANT TO begin by explaining how I am situating my discussion of *Men with Guns* (1998). First, I'm less concerned with simply reading the film than with thinking about its potential political effects and the history it attempts to engage, to allegorize. To take up these issues means to place *Men with Guns* in a particular context.

I will be talking about *Men with Guns* against an implicit backdrop of other films about revolutionary Latin America: *Under Fire* (1983), *Salvador* (1986), and *Romero* (1989). Like these films, *Men with Guns* comments on the political unrest and terror during U.S.-backed "dirty wars." But unlike these films, Sayles avoids a specific geographical setting or historical time frame.

Second, I want to think about *Men with Guns* in the context of contemporary Hollywood films that wax political and historical (e.g., *Fight Club* [1999] and *The Patriot* [2000]). *Fight Club* feigns to be political, but it undermines its own critique of consumerism through an endless chain of product placements. Its conclusion shrouds itself in a far too comfortable cloak of cynicism and despair. *The Patriot* refigures history by reducing the American Revolution to catchphrases like "No Taxation without Representation" and a testosterone-driven tale of personal vengeance. I won't even go into its gross misrepresentations of race relations in colonial America.

In an industry replete with such vapid films, John Sayles has built a career on a body of work recognized for its political vision. He tells compelling stories that tackle complicated issues. Like some of the best, contemporary, independent-minded filmmakers—Spike Lee and Oliver Stone, for example—Sayles has a take on politics that is visionary without being naïve. His progressive politics get hamstrung, however, in *Men with Guns*.

Men with Guns is the story John Sayles can't tell. I want to consider what that implies for the film's audience.

Men with Guns explores the atrocities committed in an unnamed Latin American country during a period of political unrest. Rather than approach this topic as a documentary, Sayles investigates these atrocities and their impact on the indigenous communities through his principal character, Dr. Humberto Fuentes. A denizen of one of the country's metropolises, Dr. Fuentes quickly enters into unknown territory as he searches for the student doctors he trained to help the Indians in his country's backlands. As he moves from village to village, he finds that "men with guns" have executed all his students. Though the film sometimes indicts the revolutionary guerrillas, more often than not culpability for these killings rests with the army. As Dr. Fuentes journeys through the countryside, a number of "pilgrims" join him—an orphan boy (Conejo), an army deserter (Domingo), a former priest (Padre Portillo), and a mute woman (Graciela). They are all in search of better lives, lives to be found "más adelante" (further ahead). Each of the fellow travelers helps the woefully ignorant doctor learn more about his country and his students. The pilgrimage concludes when the characters reach what they believe is the safe haven of "Cerca del Cielo" (Close to Heaven). Here the doctor dies and Domingo and Conejo are left to assume his legacy of caring for the people. The closing shot sees Graciela contentedly smiling as she gazes at the blue sky and neighboring mountain peaks. Perhaps Heaven *is* just a little further ahead.

Critics fall into two camps when evaluating *Men with Guns*. In the first and more dominant camp, they read the film as a political awakening for Dr. Fuentes. The doctor's journey from the city through the country displaces his nearly implausible naïveté about his own country's politics. Critics like Janet Maslin of the *New York Times* are quick to read the film as a "voyage of discovery."[1] While they are right to note the doctor's political awakening, they unfortunately tend to subordinate the film's political critique to the doctor's developing *Bildung*.

Those in the other camp, mostly academic critics, skewer Sayles for failing to elaborate a critique of U.S. intervention and complicity. Writing in *Cineaste*, Susan Ryan maintains that "Placing the blame solely on the ownership of guns avoids any systemic criticism of the powers that allow it to happen."[2]

In an essay in *Discourse*, Marcus Embry pushes the point a step further. He argues that "*Men with Guns* leaves the viewer with a pile of rubble growing ever larger, a tremendous amount of violence and oppression with no suggestion that it will ever cease nor that we can stop to fix what is broken." Ultimately, Embry determines that the film makes the audience complicitous in the very violence it represents.[3]

Between these two camps lies a middle ground that neither reduces the film to one man's voyage of discovery nor completely hangs Sayles out to dry. To stake that ground out, we have to consider Sayles's deployment of allegory versus history, issues of faith and narrativity, and the film's political agenda.

While the plot of *Men with Guns* is easily enough followed, matters become complicated when one considers the film's allegorical dimensions. Since Sayles opts to shoot a "realistic fable," he effaces all specific historical and geographical traces from the narrative. Attempting to justify this narrative strategy, Sayles maintains that "If you set a film in a specific country, you create the responsibility of addressing the specifics of that country." Moreover, he adds that the realistic fable is maintained precisely "by not announcing that this is Guatemala, El Salvador, or Argentina."[4] This swerve away from specificity and toward allegory or fable complicates the film's political import. For instance, the film's allegorical generality opens Sayles up to criticism that his film "mystifies rather than illuminates." As Susan Ryan asserts, "Allegorical treatments of sensitive subjects have a long history in socially conscious filming, particularly in Latin America (e.g. *Land in Anguish, The Promised Land*), but the lack of historical specificity in *Men with Guns* mystifies rather than illuminates the treatment of indigenous people."[5] This is a trenchant appraisal of a filmmaker with a long record of committed filmmaking. But Ryan is right: the film is ahistorical.

By opting for allegory rather than specific history, Sayles allows the audience to assume a too cozy stance toward the very atrocities he represents. I could imagine a moviegoer, ignorant of the history of political unrest in Latin America, leaving the film saying, "See I told you, honey, those brown people really are savages. Given the opportunity to kill each other they will." The narrative makes no attempt to historicize or contextualize the atrocities it limns. Rather, it seems to assert that men who are willing to use their guns will control the country. Consequently, the film's political agenda, which I believe to be about a history of "dirty wars" and a legacy of U.S. intervention in sovereign nations, is easily lost. Conversely, if Sayles imagines an audience already conversant with the atrocities committed in, say, Guatemala, El Salvador, or Nicaragua, the film really can have no political persuasion. For that audience, *Men with Guns* would be like preaching to the choir.

It may be helpful to think about Sayles as analogous to his very own Dr. Fuentes. Bravo, the first student who abandons the doctor's program, tells him that if he wants the "whole story," he should find Cienfuegos. Thus, the doctor's journey begins, and soon he learns that each of the remaining student doctors has been killed. But how exactly does he learn about these students' fates? Through stories. Only once does he ever see tangible evidence (bones and a torture table) of the atrocities committed. More often than not, he must rely on the villagers' and his fellow pilgrims' narratives. A tension obtains between empiricism and faith, a tension that runs throughout the film. Can Dr. Fuentes trust the stories he hears, or must he see evidence? Certainly, his trip to the boneyard has a dramatic effect. As Conejo nonchalantly sifts through and even plays with the bones, the doctor registers his shock. "People should know about this," he says. Conejo matter-of-factly responds, "Everyone knows. The army brought us to see what could happen." Still amazed, Fuentes complains, "I didn't know anything about it." Then the boy tellingly fires back, "'Cause you're a stranger." This scene emblematizes almost exactly the very dilemma Sayles encounters in trying to tell the story of men with guns. Like the doctor, he must rely on stories, for the material vestiges of the army's crimes are often covered up.

Sayles makes valiant attempts to relate a centuries-long history of murder in the name of big business, oligopolies, and globalization. Again, however, like Dr. Fuentes he can never get the "whole story," for *Men with Guns* is the story Sayles can't tell. It eludes him because he's a stranger. No matter how fluent his Spanish or how comprehensive his understanding of Latin America, he remains an outsider come to Mexico to shoot a film about the rampant murders of indigenous peoples in Latin America. While Sayles employs a number of Indians as actors and while he shoots his film almost entirely in Spanish, Nahuatl, Maya, and

Kuna, these efforts do little to change his outsider status. Unlike *Matewan* (1987), for instance, where the history of those coal miners is some eighty years old, Sayles covers incidents in *Men with Guns* that have contemporary residues and survivors who experienced the terror his film tries to capture. His endeavor, then, is riddled with the problems of contemporary ethnographers. The avenues to access the story he wants to tell are restricted to the willingness of people to speak with him about the atrocities. Simply put, *Men with Guns* is not a lived experience for Sayles. Yet this is a story he recognizes needs to be told, and one that even films about the region such as *Under Fire, Salvador,* and *Romero* have yet to tell. These other films have sought to narrate the atrocities largely through Western eyes. Sayles wants to tell the story through the voices, languages, and eyes of the inhabitants of the region.

At a certain level, the fabulistic quality of *Men with Guns* speaks to the respect with which Sayles approaches his subject. Because he is a stranger he opts not for a specific history he can't access, but for a general fable, a moral tale about the consequences of political upheaval and the extent to which men with guns will go to assume power. Respecting the limits of his knowledge, he doesn't attempt to speak *for* the region's Indians, but he offers his power and talent as a filmmaker to share what he can of their story. Coming into political consciousness, Fuentes recognizes that "There should be somewhere that white people aren't allowed." So too does Sayles. White signifies throughout the film not a particular phenotype or complexion, but rather a feeling of entitlement and impunity. Rather than assume "white" privilege, Sayles recognizes that there are some places he can't go and some stories he can't fully tell.

This is not a turn to some crude authenticity politics that would only permit people who have lived certain experiences to tell their stories. On the contrary, it is to recognize that Sayles has an interesting story to tell, but it is only one story among many about men with guns. Unlike Fuentes, who believes he can find the "whole story," neither Sayles nor any storyteller or historian can tell the whole story; all stories have limits. We must read a number of stories and talk to as many people as possible to understand any topic, let alone a tale as complicated as the one Sayles tries to tackle in *Men with Guns.*

It is disappointing that this film fails to implicate the United States for its role in shattering the lives of innumerable Latin Americans. But this failure doesn't vitiate the power of the story Sayles does tell. One might even think of it as fomenting the outrage the Nicaraguan Red Cross nurse calls for at the end of *Under Fire*. Confronting the American journalist crying over the army's murder of her husband, the nurse says, "Fifty thousand Nicaraguans have died and now one Yankee. Perhaps now Americans will be outraged at what is happening here. [. . .] Maybe we should have killed an American journalist fifty years ago." While *Men with Guns* won't necessarily help the noninitiate know where to direct their anger, it can't help but outrage them, and that's a start.

A comment Sayles makes in the introduction to the published screenplay of *Men with Guns* disheartens me. Sayles justifies Dr. Fuentes's death by noting that he is "drawn further and further into the dark of his own society's violence, until there is no honorable way he can return to his former life."[6] If Fuentes, armed with his new knowledge, can't return to his former life, how does that augur for the moviegoers whom the film has carried on a similar journey? Can they, too, no longer return to their former lives? In one sense, we hope they can't return to a life of blissful ignorance regarding foreign affairs. Return, however, they must, for the film's political agenda depends on them taking the fable they have seen and considering its implications for their everyday lives. If the film is to be effective, they must be pushed to ask, for instance, how they might set out to change the political violence committed in the name of big business and the opening of global markets. Unlike the jingoistic fever *The Patriot* stirs up, the aim of *Men with Guns* is not to make us celebrate the superiority of the United States; rather, it wants to critique the very project of the nation-state and the violence committed in its name, even if it doesn't explicitly indict the United States.

Certainly, the allegorical nature of *Men with Guns* runs the risk that some viewers will miss the point of the film and the political and historical context that underwrites it. Consider, for example, Peter Howell's concluding question about the film: "Can anything we do really make a difference to the Third World?"[7] Indeed, it can. U.S. intervention in Latin America is responsible for toppling a number of democratically elected governments and perpetuating civil wars and the deaths of far too many innocent people. Perhaps a more historically situated film would have made it impossible to ask a question as ludicrous as Howell's.

Nonetheless, *Men with Guns* remains the story John Sayles can't tell, yet must tell. And though I'm torn by the conundrums the film creates,

I admire Sayles for telling *any* story about men with guns. His fable is one piece in a complex narrative puzzle. By not naming a particular country or time, he asks us to consider how his tale ramifies beyond one country and continent. Further, it implicitly questions how men with guns, in the name of empire (and even at times in the service of revolution), have wiped out indigenous communities. If Sayles doesn't capture these accounts in all their explicit details, it is because there are some stories "white" people can't tell.

NOTES

A number of friends and colleagues graciously and patiently listened to me talk tirelessly about *Men with Guns*. For their kindness and insights I thank Jo Nutter, Kathryn Hume, Philip Jenkins, Paul Youngquist, Jillian Smith, Susan Searls, and Jane Juffer.

1. Janet Maslin, "An Unsuspecting Traveler Loses His Illusions, Step by Harrowing Step," *New York Times*, 6 March 1998, E29.

2. Susan Ryan, "Men with Guns," *Cineaste* 23, no. 3 (1998): 44.

3. Marcus Embry, "A Postcolonial Tale of Complicity: The 'Angel of History' and *Men with Guns*," *Discourse* 21, no. 2 (spring 1999): 178.

4. Thompson, op cit., 81.

5. Ryan, op cit., 44.

6. John Sayles, *Men with Guns and Lone Star* (London: Faber and Faber, 1998), vii.

7. Peter Howell, "Difficult Questions in Any Language: *Men with Guns*," *Toronto Star*, 27 March 1998, D3.

17

The End of Chicano Cinema

Chon A. Noriega

THE EARLY 1990s witnessed the end of Chicano cinema, a film movement that had its start in the civil rights struggles of the 1960s, entered the public sphere via television in the 1970s, and saw a brief flirtation with low-budget integration into a so-called Hispanic Hollywood in the 1980s. In all these periods, Chicano cinema worked against the specter of the gang film—and not the western as one might suppose—since this genre and its gangster predecessor more closely corresponded to the urban milieu for Chicano political struggle.

With the release of Edward James Olmos's *American Me* (1992), followed closely by Taylor Hackford's *Bound by Honor* (1993; available on video under its original title, *Blood In, Blood Out*), Hollywood effectively co-opted Chicano cinema, recuperating it into the very genre it had struggled against for nearly three decades.

In these films, the prison is refigured as the site of Chicano "home" and "family," while the barrio itself becomes little more than a place where disaffected family members bide their time. Domestic and institutional spaces not only interpenetrate each other, but are interchanged wholesale.

Insofar as these films constitute a decisive shift in Chicano representation, it is important to start with some background. In earlier Chicano-produced feature films, prison often stands as the displacement of domestic space and the interruption of couple formation. Here I'm thinking about films such as *Zoot Suit* (1981), *The Ballad of Gregorio Cortez* (1982), *Born in East L.A.* (1987), and *Break of Dawn* (1988). This combined displacement and interruption operates on two levels: historiography and genre conventions.

On the first account, the eighties films are all based on actual events and attempt to articulate and situate these local histories within some notion of "American" history. If the protagonists have all been denied the rights of citizenship, these films are insistent that that "true story" is a decidedly "American" one. The Chicano community functions as a spatial counterpart in the narrative to the culpable legal system. This is why, in part, the Chicano protagonists fluctuate between two noncontiguous spaces, the barrio and the prison.

In terms of genre conventions, the few Hollywood films "about" Chicanos have been courtroom dramas or have had pivotal scenes of trial and imprisonment. Most of these films fall into the gangster-to-gang genre. This is a well-worn observation. But what I find interesting in the wake of *American Me* is the degree to which Chicano directors have suddenly accepted the industry's premise that the gangster and gang genres represent the Ellis Island of Hollywood cinema. In short, these genres represent something every new "immigrant" group must pass through on its way to assimilation, acceptance, and the romantic comedy.

If so, these films also occupy what George Lipsitz calls the "dangerous terrain" between history and myth: that of counter-memory. In contrast to Foucault, Lipsitz defines counter-memory as a process in which the particular (local, personal, hidden histories) continually attempts to reframe the universal (dominant narratives).[1] What is of interest in the Chicano films of the 1980s is that the "dangerous terrain" of counter-memory is not so much a metaphoric space as a material one. Counter-memory oscillates between the social environment and its textual representation. Here, in other words, Lipsitz's proposed "suspicious" interplay between history and myth takes place in the representation of a local struggle between a minority culture's "home" and the dominant culture's "prison." At stake, of course, is the space—both narrative and institutional—from which Chicano history will be told. That struggle also delimits or frames the spaces from which it can be told.

The same can be said of an earlier group of social problem films about Mexican Americans: *Bordertown* (1935), *The Lawless* (1950), *My Man and I* (1952), and *Trial* (1955). In these films, the "prison" represents the point of entry for Mexican Americans into the dominant culture, or, in the language of the times, "first-class citizenship." The courtroom became the space and place within which Mexican Americans might begin to speak within the national discourse—as a citizen, as a laborer, as an adolescent or student. These statements were a form of public per-

The penitentiary serves as the site for an emerging cultural politics and the institution of social control in Edward James Olmos's gangster-to-gang picture *American Me* (Universal, 1992).

formance (that is, an instance of freedom of speech), but its consequences—the judgment—returned the Mexican American subject to nonpublic spaces: prison or back to the barrio. Here, free speech becomes not so much a shared or universal right—almost an end in itself—but rather an act that can only take place in order to constitute the courtroom as the nexus of two discrete, nonpublic spaces outside civil society (i.e., government or family). In this manner, the prison and the barrio are juxtaposed in a liberal-to-progressive cinema that constructs a dual moral: ideological assimilation and social segregation.

The Chicano-produced feature films of the 1980s evince a similar dual moral, though the perspective is radically different. Here, in its most extreme form, there is a demand for structural assimilation and cultural separatism. In general, both sets of films agree that the Mexican American or Chicano subject should return to the barrio, though for quite different reasons. In the former, ideological assimilation ensures that the barrio becomes the site of "a collection of separated individualities" (to borrow Foucault's description of the effect of the panopticon).[2] In the latter, structural assimilation becomes the object of cultural identity and collective politics.

As I mentioned at the start, Olmos's *American Me* and Hackford's

Bound by Honor represent a radical shift in both Chicano cinema and the gangster-to-gang genre. These films invert panopticism, wherein the panoptic prison imposes an axial visibility (from the supervisor) and implies a lateral invisibility (among prisoners).[3] Prisoners are seen, but do not see; they are the object of information, but never the subject of communication. In these films, prison and panopticism are represented as the very condition for the "collective effect" they are supposed to abolish.

In these films, the protagonist is no longer exiled either to or from the barrio; and, in fact, the courtroom that interrelated and mediated these spaces in the earlier films disappears altogether here. Instead, the barrio itself is conflated with the prison, so that the minority culture occupies, infiltrates, or produces itself within that institutional space. In both films, the prison becomes the space for the emergence of a cultural politics rather than for the enacting of social control (at least, not in a direct sense within the narrative). These films are perhaps the first to situate the discourse of the Chicano civil rights movement—a movement to gain control over (or access to) public spaces and institutions—within rather than in opposition to dominant institutions. But while the narratives are strikingly similar (a fact that has occasioned a lawsuit), each film is different in how it envisions the prison as the space of domestication for the (male) Chicano community.

Bound by Honor conflates the rhetoric of the Chicano civil rights movement with prison culture to a degree that is truly shocking, in part because neither the Chicano movement nor its discourses has ever been represented in mainstream narrative and documentary. The only exceptions are, not surprisingly, two gang exploitation films from the late 1970s: *Boulevard Nights* and *Walk Proud* (both 1979). But in *Bound by Honor*, there is no indication whatsoever that the cultural politics within the prison emerged first and foremost as a broad-based public movement, one that was aimed initially at education, employment, and property rights. The film does, however, offer alternatives within the public sphere, although they are dependent on some notion of surveillance rather than access or rights. In short, the two "good guys" who emerge from the original delinquent triumvirate become a police officer and a neo-expressionist painter (one who kicks both his drug habit and photorealist documentation of barrio culture). Both watch the barrio, the former on behalf of the state, the latter with an eye toward the marketplace.

Taylor Hackford's family melodrama *Bound by Honor* (Buena Vista, 1993).

With *American Me*, Olmos's highly stylized poetic narration be-comes unstable vis-à-vis his very different roles as character, star, au-teur, and celebrity. Olmos's Santana does not rehearse the rhetoric of the Chicano movement. As Chicana and other feminist critics have noted, *American Me* decouples the discourse of the Chicano movement from prison culture in such a way that also challenges its overt gender poli-tics. By the end of the film, Julie—Santana's would-be girlfriend—chal-lenges his rhetoric of "la raza, education, revolution" and identifies him as nothing more than "a fucking dope dealer." But, unlike *Bound by Honor*, *American Me* offers scant alternatives, ending with a nihilistic vi-sion of the barrio-as-prison. Even Julie and Santana's father are shown, in close-up, to have the telltale gang tattoo between their thumb and forefinger. No one escapes. Or, in the case of Julie, who covers her tat-too with makeup, only individuals escape. As Carmen Huaco-Nuzum argues, the film's "implicit" analysis is that "the barrio functions as a form of social containment built into the socio-economic apparatus to prevent . . . integration with the rest of society."[4]

Rosa Linda Fregoso notes the shift in the film's cultural politics and, ultimately, in its mode of address. The film is not, she concludes, a "cel-ebration of the Chicano nation," but rather "disturbs and disrupts our

[Chicanos and Chicanas] imaginary self-coherence." But at the same time, neither is the film "for 'ideal' white middle-class males (or females) like Siskel and Ebert." Instead, "its race and gender specificity speaks mostly to young Chicano males." Citing Teresa de Lauretis, Fregoso concludes that "These are the viewers 'inscribed in the film-maker's project.'" Fregoso, however, does not follow up on the full implications of de Lauretis's statement about the address of feminist cinema, namely, that the film would have to address *all* viewers as young Chicano males, not just literal "Chicano males."[5]

So what about these young Chicano males? In contrast to the "noncorporal" penality of the modern prison, in these films anal rape functions as a return to the spectacle of punishment within an economy of the criminal. Spectacle and pain return, not as the meta-logic of the criminal system, but as the inner logic of the criminal *class* itself. Or rather, that is how it is represented in these films. In *American Me*, in what is clearly the film's worst pun, prisoners repeat the aphorism "Control the inside, you own the outside." Thus, the spectacle and pain of anal rape lead prisoners to conform to the codes of the criminal class in their *outside* behavior, whether they reside in the prison or in society-at-large.

But rather than take the film's aphorism at face value, we need to pay attention to how such a logic resituates the outside (barrio/body) within the inside (prison/anus). This logic does not so much reverse causality as, in fact, establish one—mapping the Chicano movement onto prison "culture" and the barrio onto the prison—enacting, historicizing a literal present.

By way of a provisional ending, it is of note that the prisons in both films are at some remove from East Los Angeles—Folsom State Prison and San Quentin—and yet that geographical distance is never represented, let alone suggested. Crimes are committed in the barrio, fade out, fade in, and we're in prison. This begs the question, "Where are the long bus rides from East L.A. through the agricultural belt on the way to prison?" Indeed, would the bus stop in San Juan Bautista, where El Teatro Campesino might perform a revival of *La Gran Carpa de los Ras-quachis*, a tale of farmworkers who become urban poor whose children become gang members, drug addicts, prisoners, and then die? Where, in short, are the highways? The dissolve—a common enough effect in narrative cinema—works within the overall strategy of both *Bound by Honor* and *American Me* to conflate two noncontiguous spaces as well as the history between them. Here we return to the "dangerous terrain" of counter-memory wherein this absence speaks to the topographical history of East L.A. itself: to the state appropriation of the private home in order to make the public highway; and now to similar efforts to impose state prisons within that space as well.

Despite their liberal impulses—or, perhaps, because of them—these films articulate a rationale for these state actions. Like the riddle of the chicken and the egg, it hardly matters which came first, the barrio or the prison, since, as the films argue, we know that their relationship is both organic and cyclical—that is, that they produce each other. In the final analysis, the two are the same. They belong together, by no less than the same logic that made Chicano cinema isomorphic with Hollywood (and its genres) in the 1990s.

NOTES

1. George Lipsitz, *Time Passages: Collective Memory and American Popular Culture* (Minneapolis: University of Minnesota Press, 1990).

2. See Michel Foucault, *Discipline and Punish: The Birth of the Prison*, trans. Alan Sheridan (New York: Pantheon, 1979).

3. Ibid.

4. Carmen Huaco-Nuzum, "Despair in the Barrio: *American Me* (Edward James Olmos, 1992)," *Jump Cut*, no. 38 (1993): 92–94, see p. 94. In contrast, Kathleen Newman argues that to the extent that the film foregrounds female survival and homoerotic love it also signals the "reterritorialization" of Chicano subjects. See Kathleen Newman, "Reterritorialization in Recent Chicano Cinema: Edward James Olmos's *American Me*," (1992), in *The Ethnic Eye: Latino Media Arts*, ed. Chon A. Noriega and Ana M. López (Minneapolis: University of Minnesota Press, 1996), 95–106.

5. See Rosa Linda Fregoso's discussion of *American Me* in *The Bronze Screen: Chicana and Chicano Film Culture* (Minneapolis: University of Minnesota Press, 1993), 122–34. Fregoso engages Teresa de Lauretis's argument about an aesthetics of reception in *Technologies of Gender: Essays on Theory, Film, and Fiction* (Bloomington: Indiana University Press, 1987).

PART V

THE END OF MASCULINITY AS WE KNOW IT

18

Being Keanu

R. L. Rutsky

IF THERE IS such a thing as an exemplary figure of U.S. cinema in the 1990s, Keanu Reeves may be it. In the context of this volume, such a statement may seem rather like a cheap joke, as if Keanu—dismissed as a "slacker Ken doll" whose acting skills and general intelligence have often been the object of ridicule—were symptomatic of a premillennial degeneration of cinema: "the end of cinema as we know it." In such a joke, Keanu would be cast as symbolic of not only a cinematic but a cultural decline, in which prettiness triumphs over intelligence, style over substance. Keanu, in other words, would stand as the very emblem of the banality and sheer stupidity of the postmodern culture industry.

It is not, however, my intention to launch yet another critique of the obvious shortcomings of contemporary U.S. cinema and culture. Nor do I wish to make any argument concerning the intelligence, or presumed lack thereof, of Keanu Reeves. If Keanu is emblematic of anything about 1990s cinema and culture, and I believe that he is, it has much less to do with vague notions of stupidity or banality than with important cultural changes in how identity is portrayed and perceived. Indeed, over the course of the last decade, Keanu's films—from the Bill and Ted movies (1989, 1991) to *Point Break* (1991) to *Speed* (1994) to *The Matrix* (1999)—have exhibited a consistent concern with issues of identity and its instability, with a lack of fixity that is often figured in these films' emphasis on movement.

At the same time, the case of Keanu highlights certain assumptions concerning identity that underlie a good deal of "serious" film—and cultural—studies, including the often unstated idea that "auteurs" and "actors" are active, thinking subjects (i.e., artists) while "movie stars" are passive objects, mere products of the culture industry. My point, however, is not that stars, with their increasing power in Hollywood and the consequent ability to shape their own careers, should now be considered artists or auteurs.[1] Rather, I want to suggest almost the opposite: if we wish to understand the movements of popular culture, it may be more productive to disregard our old notions of purposeful authorship—and identity—and to look instead at the fortuitous cultural patterns and associations that swirl around a star's persona and body of work.[2] I am not, then, arguing for Keanu Reeves as some sort of auteur, but for the cultural significance of the links and associations that make up his persona.[3]

BEYOND STUPIDITY

Much of the derision aimed at Keanu is a result of the perception that he is dumb or, at the least, flaky. Keanu has, in fact, often described himself as "goofy."[4] Much of that perception was clearly a result of his role as Ted in the Bill and Ted movies. As Michael Shnayerson noted in his touchstone 1995 article about Keanu in *Vanity Fair*, "The dumbness rap grew out of *Bill and Ted's Excellent Adventure*. So well did he play the Valleyspeak teen and air-guitarist *extraordinaire* in the 1989 hit and its sequel that [many] assumed Keanu *was* Ted."[5] In fact, in many of his early interviews, Keanu seemed to be playing Ted off the screen as well as on. As Gus Van Sant, his director in *My Own Private Idaho* (1991), noted for a 1991 article on Keanu, "Keanu can lapse into Ted. Sometimes he can be momentarily possessed."[6]

As time has passed and Keanu has played more varied roles, the perception of Keanu-as-Ted has faded somewhat, but the conception of him as none-too-bright has remained. Indeed, both *Speed* and *Feeling Minnesota* (1996) have jokingly played on this perception. Even in *The Matrix* his character is portrayed as, if not exactly stupid, then certainly something of an innocent. A number of his directors have, in fact, commented on this sense of "innocence." Kathryn Bigelow, his director in *Point Break*, has noted that there is "a purity and an innocence to him."[7] Similarly, Bernardo Bertolucci felt that "Keanu has an innocence I felt was crucial to the role of Siddhartha—his innocence is on his face and it goes to the core of his personality, and that's why I cast him."[8] Yet, if a certain innocence translates well into such proto-messianic figures as Siddhartha and Neo, it can also be read as a kind of emptiness. Thus, for example, Lisa Schwarzbaum, in her review of *The Matrix*, can speak derisively of Keanu's "serene blankness" and can complain that she "can't get [Keanu] in focus as an actor."[9]

Charles Taylor, in his defense of Keanu in *Salon*, quotes a film critic who told him that "he thinks people look at Reeves and see nothing going on."[10] Keanu, in other words, is continually depicted in terms of vacuity and superficiality: as a kind of pure, blank surface, lacking all depth. In this, Keanu's persona is oddly similar to what Steven Shaviro has written of Andy Warhol's films and art: "*it has no latent content at all. His surfaces are impenetrable precisely because there is nothing beneath them, no depth into which one could penetrate.*"[11] Given this context, it is perhaps not surprising that one of the earliest interviews with Keanu appeared in what was, at the time, still called *Andy Warhol's Interview*.

Perhaps, too, it is not coincidental that in his discussion of Warhol, Shaviro—following the lead of Michel Foucault—has recourse to the very term that has so often been applied to Keanu: *stupidity*. For Foucault, stupidity was that which is beyond categories—a "magma" or "amorphous fluidity" that "carries one gently along and [whose] action is mimed in the abandonment of oneself."[12] Similarly, Shaviro figures stupidity as an "emptying out" of representation and significance, so that one is left with "something that freely offers itself to all categories of thought and representation, allows them to invest it and pass through it, yet somehow always effortlessly evades them" (208). Shaviro finds this notion of stupidity particularly relevant to Warhol's films:

> All of Warhol's films . . . are marked by the *literalism* with which they evacuate all other significance and content in order to capture, record, and display the sheer, stupid, inert presence of bodies. . . .
>
> The body before the camera is a mute appearance, devoid of consciousness, will, or interiority. Warhol's "subjects" are emptied out, distanced and absented from themselves, drained of their subjectivity, and reduced to a silent (yet insistent) spectacle of bodily presence. (210, 212)

Rather like the "superstars" that appear in Warhol's films, one might read Keanu in terms of this stupidity of the body, which presents nothing except its own materiality, which says nothing beyond its own

His serene blankness, Keanu Reeves. *The Matrix* (Warner Brothers, 1999).

physicality. The emptiness that is often perceived in Keanu's persona is precisely a matter of this insistent, mute—or, more appropriately, *dumb*—physicality. Numerous interviewers have noted his persistent reticence to speak, the long pauses between his answers. As a recent interview (titled, significantly enough, "The Quiet Man") observes, "A conversation with Keanu Reeves is not always easy."[13] Thus, Keanu is often presented as inarticulate, lacking the words to speak, lacking even something to say. He becomes little more than a face, a body—without depth, without an interior. More than one interviewer has noted that with Keanu, "what you see is what you get"—which is, of course, one definition of stupidity. Stupidity, in this sense, is always *blatant*.

OUTSIDE BEAUTY

This stupidity cannot be dissociated, in Keanu's case, from his obvious physical beauty. Much of the antipathy toward Keanu—including the perception of his dumbness—seems traceable to the sheer fact of his attractiveness. Indeed, by the traditional standards of masculine good looks, where "ruggedness" is supposed to demonstrate "character," Keanu is perhaps too perfect, too pretty. His good looks are too obvious, too visible.

Keanu therefore seems to fall victim to some of the same stereotypes that have commonly been attached to feminine beauty—particularly in Hollywood, where being beautiful has often been figured as being empty-headed, dizzy, or downright dumb. Charles Taylor has argued, in fact, that much of the resentment directed at Keanu is precisely the result of the fact that his beauty "represents a subversion of traditional sex roles."[14] As Taylor observes, "performers who have offered themselves most willingly to the camera have almost always been women. . . . Men, on the other hand, have traditionally acted to deflect attention from themselves, as if doing anything less would seem unmanly or feminine." As "one of the few contemporary male stars whose presence acknowledges that people are out there in the dark looking at him," Keanu has a physical attractiveness that is, by traditional standards of masculinity, too visible, too *out*. Thus, the very visibility of Keanu's beauty may help to explain not only the persistent rumors that he is gay (most notably, that he was secretly married to David Geffen) but also the resentment and ridicule that have been directed at him, which Taylor reads as a manifestation of homosexual panic. Here, the idea that Keanu is so pretty that he must be gay overlaps with the notion that being so pretty, he must be stupid. For being beautiful, being gay, and being stupid have all been consistently associated with superficiality, with outward appearances, with manifest rather than latent content.

Portrayed both as ingenuous, without ulterior motives, *and* as without depth or character (even, or perhaps especially, in his on-screen roles), Keanu comes to be seen as lacking "identity": as an empty shell, a superficial image concocted by the mass media and the culture industry (which are, of course, well known as repositories of stupidity). There is, however, a certain seductiveness to this lack, as Shaviro notes of the body's stupidity: "we are incited to keep on looking, again and again, precisely because our desire for comprehension and control is never satiated. The more we look the less we are able to make anything of what we see; we can only abandon ourselves to it" (209). Thus, the very fact that Keanu's identity seems so superficial, so obvious, makes it difficult to comprehend; we are unable to "make anything of it." Keanu's supposed lack of identity therefore comes to be seen as something of an enigma.

In fact, as Keanu's star persona has drifted away from its early identification with Ted, it has become increasingly difficult for interviewers and critics to get a fix on him. The question of whether or not he is gay is merely one aspect of this instability. *Vanity Fair*, for example, described him as "a man who earns millions, yet lives out of a suitcase; a heartthrob who dates few women, yet fends off rumors of a gay marriage; an actor who can appear in *Bill and Ted's Excellent Adventure* and *Hamlet* with equal conviction and appeal" before posing what it called "the essential question" about him: "just who is Keanu?"[15] This sense of mystery persists even today, as evidenced in the subtitle of a recent *Rolling Stone* interview: "The Riddle of Keanu Reeves."[16]

Keanu, for his part, often seems to encourage this haziness about his identity. When asked by Dennis Cooper in *Interview* if he were gay, he denied it, but then added, "But ya never know."[17] When asked if it wouldn't "be useful to shoot the rumors down cold," Keanu was reportedly taken aback, replying, "Well, I mean, there's nothing wrong with being gay, so to deny it is to make a judgement. And why make a big deal of it?"[18] More generally, Keanu has said that "I want to fall into all categories—and no categories!"[19]

Similarly, Michael Shnayerson reports the following exchange:

> I wonder aloud if there isn't in Keanu some central struggle between
> discipline and nihilism—devotion to acting versus motorcycles, Bud-
> dhism versus sex, drink, rock 'n' roll. A *dynamic*. Keanu looks at me
> with bemusement. "I get one dynamic?" he says. "Can I have more
> than one? I want at least nine!" (148)

Perhaps even more telling, however, is Keanu's take on his own celebrity. Asked how he manages to deal with the constant intrusions by fans
and autograph seekers, he replied, "I'm Mickey [Mouse]. They don't
know who's inside the suit" (148).

Of course, even when played by an actor in a suit, Mickey Mouse
has no "interior." He *is* his public persona, and that persona, much like
Keanu's, is based on a certain naïveté, which persists throughout the
different roles he plays. Yet this very shallowness (and Mickey is, essentially, a two-dimensional creature, born on the screen) seems to stir
the urge to discover deeper desires, hidden proclivities, true identities.
To some degree, the very act of being a star involves a superficiality, a
public mask, that inevitably stirs interest in the "real identity" behind it.
Yet Keanu's star persona—in its superficiality—seems at once to exac-
erbate and confound this desire to know "just who he is."

THE MOVEMENT OF THE OTHER

For all the attempts to categorize Keanu, his identity remains difficult to
pin down, evading attempts at defining him. He remains little more
than a face, a body, a name. Of course, as every fan knows, Keanu's
name is Hawaiian, and means, as virtually every article or fan Web site
on Keanu seems obliged to repeat, "cool breeze over the mountains."
Yet despite the ethnicity of his name, Keanu is often perceived as a
"middle-class white boy," perhaps because of his early roles as an alienated teenager. Indeed, so strong is this perception that some have assumed that Keanu is simply an "exotic-sounding stage name."[20] As the
son of a Hawaiian-Chinese father, however, Keanu could easily be described as a person of color, although he rarely is. One might view this
perception of Keanu's identity as yet another example in Hollywood's
long history of effacing the ethnicity of its stars while retaining some

measure of their "exoticism." In this context, however, it is worth re-calling that, much as with (feminine) beauty, the "exotic" is generally associated with a physicality or sensuality that evades intellectual cate-gorization or meaningful articulation. This notion of dumb, if usually happy, physicality has often been attributed to "other" races and cul-tures, but is particularly pronounced in Western portrayals of Hawaiian and Pacific Island cultures as Edenic paradises filled with beautiful, sensual natives, untroubled by depth or thought.[21]

If Keanu's name and persona continue to evoke these kinds of stereotypes, it is also the case that his persona raises certain questions about the division between the intellectual and the physical on which Western notions of identity, of the thinking subject, are based. Many of the roles Keanu has undertaken have in fact dealt explicitly with issues of identity. *The Matrix* and *Little Buddha* (1993) are, for example, cen-tered on questions involving the falsity of reality and identity, and the transformative possibilities of recognizing what might be called the "stupidity" of what is taken to be "real." In *Point Break*, as well, the story revolves around questions of true and false identity, with Keanu cast as a former star quarterback who becomes an FBI agent. The football player who has become an FBI agent masquerades as a surfer to foil surfers who have become bank robbers—robbers who disguise them-selves by wearing masks of former presidents.[22]

Yet I am less concerned here with the explicit thematization of iden-tity issues than with the way most of Keanu's films seem to highlight the significance of sheer speed and movement. From the surfing and skydiving of *Point Break* to the speeding bus of *Speed* to the techno-ac-robatics of *The Matrix*, Keanu's films often seem to emphasize a kind of fluid kineticism over character depth, over any fixed notion of "iden-tity."[23] Indeed, while in most action films, movement serves as a dem-onstration of the hero/star's power and control, Keanu's action films often involve his being carried along by the movement, "surfing" it, at times even losing himself in it.

Of course, it is also true that Keanu's own movements seem to con-vey a grace that is almost entirely missing in the dynamics of action stars such as Stallone and Schwarzenegger. Charles Taylor, whose essay on Keanu is titled "Something in the Way He Moves," has written elo-quently of the cinematic "erotics" of Keanu's movements and physical-ity, particularly in a film like *The Matrix*, which "allows us to revel in his physicality, which has always been such a strong component of his acting."[24] Yet, as Taylor notes, while movement is an accepted part of the performance of dancers and stage actors, when it comes to cinema, "having a sensual or kinetic response" is often viewed as an abandonment of critical or intellectual rigor. To enjoy such movement, to become caught up in it, is to lose one's critical position, one's ability to know. It is to be carried stupidly along. This is, in a sense, the critical equivalent of the fear of "going native," only in this case what is feared is the loss of one's ability to think critically, to be a critical subject, when one is immersed in the stupidity of popular culture. What Keanu perhaps shows us, then, is that identity need not be based solely on a position of knowledge, on an opposition to what is seen as inarticulable, as stupid, or as other.

In a world that some would say is increasingly stupid, we must be willing, as Keanu seems to be, to take the risk of being caught up in the indeterminate currents of that "amorphous fluidity" that Foucault associates with stupidity. Indeed, this risk—the risk of losing one's self in the stupidity of the motions and images that stream around us—has perhaps always been inherent to the cinema, and to popular culture more generally.

NOTES

1. Obviously, the increasing clout of stars extends beyond just cinema. Consider, for example, the case of Madonna, who is often considered the ultimate example of a star shaping her own career.

2. Indeed, it seems to me that such a procedure is to some degree similar to Jacques Derrida's practice of playing on the associations inherent in the *names* of writers and philosophers for unsuspected clues to their work. In thus giving a place to what might appear to be chance connections, Derrida often discovers new ways of thinking about the work under consideration.

3. For this reason, also, I have followed the usage of his fans, and much of the press, by referring to him throughout this essay by his first name.

4. See, for example, Chris Willman, "The Radical Reality of Keanu Reeves," *Los Angeles Times*, July 17, 1991, Calendar Section, p. 1.

5. Michael Shnayerson, "Young and Restless," *Vanity Fair*, August 1995, 96.

6. Quoted in Willman, "The Radical Reality of Keanu Reeves," 1.

7. Quoted in Willman, "The Radical Reality of Keanu Reeves," 1.

8. Quoted in Kristine McKenna, "Keanu's Eccentric Adventure," *Los Angeles Times*, June 5, 1994, Calendar Section, p. 3.

9. Lisa Schwarzbaum, "Techno Prisoners," *Entertainment Weekly*, April 9,

1999. Available at http://www.ew.com/ew/archive/1,1798,1 | 25536 | 0 | The_ Matrix,00.html (5/25/00).

10. Charles Taylor, "Something in the Way He Moves: In Defense of Keanu Reeves," *Salon*, April 29, 1999, 2. Available at http://www.salon.com/ent/ movies/feature/1999/04/29/keanu/ index1.html (5/25/00).

11. Steven Shaviro, *The Cinematic Body* (Minneapolis: University of Minnesota Press, 1993), 206.

12. Michel Foucault, "Theatrum Philosophicum," in *Language, Counter-Memory, Practice*, ed. Donald F. Bouchard, trans. Donald F. Bouchard and Sherry Simon (Ithaca: Cornell University Press, 1977), 188–89.

13. Chris Heath, "The Quiet Man: The Riddle of Keanu Reeves," *Rolling Stone*, no. 848 (August 31, 2000): 52.

14. Taylor, "Something in the Way He Moves," 2.

15. Shnayerson, "Young and Restless," 95.

16. Heath, "The Quiet Man: The Riddle of Keanu Reeves."

17. Dennis Cooper, "Keanu Reeves," *Interview* 20, no. 9 (September 1990): 134.

18. Shnayerson, "Young and Restless," 146.

19. Jim Turner, "Much Ado about Keanu," *Detour*, May 1, 1993, available at http://keanuweb.com/reports/19990258.htm (3/31/00).

20. See "Cool Breeze," at www.keanunet.com/cool.htm (3/25/00).

21. As Avital Ronell has noted, the issue of stupidity inflects everything from "contemporary debates on affirmative action" to "seemingly less lacerating assertions of stupidity (shallow, airhead, bimbo, braindead, etc.)," all of which are part of "a sinister history" that puts into question the aptitude, educability, and intelligence of those who are seen as other. "The Uninterrogated Question of Stupidity," *Differences: A Journal of Feminist Cultural Studies* 8, no. 2 (1996): 3.

22. Clearly, both *My Own Private Idaho* and *Johnny Mnemonic* (1995) also focused on issues of memory and identity. *Feeling Minnesota* also might be said to touch on the relationship of stupidity and identity.

23. I leave aside here the trips that Bill and Ted take, the continual, frantic running of *Chain Reaction* (1996), as well as the odyssey of *My Own Private Idaho*.

24. Taylor, "Something in the Way He Moves," 1.

19

Woody Allen, "the Artist," and "the Little Girl"

David R. Shumway

> The heart wants what it wants.
> —Woody Allen, quoted in the *New York Times*,
> September 1992

> The real world is a place that I've never felt comfortable in. I think that my generation grew up with a value system heavily marked by films. . . . My ideas of romance came from the movies.
> —Woody Allen, *Rolling Stone*, September 1993

IT BECAME HARDER in the 1990s to separate Woody Allen's life from his art. Allen seems to have spent most of his professional life denying that he is in real life the person he plays on screen. But his affair with Mia Farrow's adopted daughter, Soon Yi Previn, and the events that followed are awfully similar to those depicted in his 1992 film *Husbands and Wives*.

Allen's films do make frequent use of materials from his life, but the films aren't autobiographical merely because we can find similarities between events in them and in his life. They seem to be autobiography because Allen repeatedly invokes the conventions of that genre, or, to be more precise, he invents filmic equivalents for them.

I am interested here in a particular character, whom I call "the artist," appearing in *Annie Hall* (1977), *Manhattan* (1979), *Husbands and Wives* (1992), and *Deconstructing Harry* (1997). These films present Woody Allen in this key role, but through a differently distorting and revealing lens. All make careful and self-conscious use of various conventions that lead the viewer to experience them as autobiography. The four films form a coherent body of work that explores the same themes using different kinds of narrative framing. But if we are meant to experience these films as autobiography, the films exist at a significant distance from the director's life. The distance exists not in the details, but in the form that the filmmaker gives to them. This transformation is exactly what we would expect of a filmmaker who understands himself as an artist in high modernist terms.

All four films depict what might be called a pedagogical relationship between the artist and a younger woman. In *Annie Hall* the age disparity is smaller, but the teaching role is quite explicit. The other three films depict relationships between an older man and a much younger woman, and in both *Husbands and Wives* and *Deconstructing Harry* the young woman is also the older man's pupil.

Manhattan first establishes explicitly Allen's interest in and ambivalence about relationships between older men and younger women. (The "little girl" in the essay of my paper comes from *Manhattan*, where it is applied derisively by Mary [Diane Keaton] to Isaac's [Woody Allen] seventeen-year-old girlfriend, Tracy [Mariel Hemingway].)

These relationships represent for Allen and for many in his audience an ethical dilemma. On the one hand, many believe in a version of Pascal's "The heart has its reasons which reason knows nothing of," which Allen has articulated as "The heart wants what it wants." Though obviously not invented by a modernist, it is a characteristic pronouncement of the modernist artist. Modernism has enlarged the significance of this view by claiming that there is a realm of personal experience—the erotic— that is not only beyond personal control (as romance would have it) but also properly outside social or public regulation or judgment.

On the other hand, there is the feminist claim that the personal is the political. The modernist position seems to make the private space of the erotic free of the contamination of political struggle. Feminism sees society riven by imbalances of power between classes, races, and, especially for purposes of this question, genders. Individuals are unable to leave these determinants behind when they relate to each other erotically. These considerations have led to new forms of regulation and a new ethics. Relations between an older man and a younger woman, especially between teacher and student, boss and employee now come into question. Allen's films take seriously the ethical problems raised by such relationships, even as they also express the desire that produces them.

Husbands and Wives is in many respects a rewriting of *Manhattan*, telling more or less the same story in different styles, tones, and outcomes. Both movies feature a writer, the "artist" (played by Allen himself), who becomes romantically involved with a "girl" less than half his age. In both, the writer is a friend of another couple whose marriage is in trouble. In both, a third party (Mary in *Manhattan*, Michael [Liam Neeson] in *Husbands and Wives*) becomes involved with two of the protagonists. Each film features a woman who is "too cerebral" (Mary in *Manhattan* and Sally [Judy Davis] in *Husbands and Wives*), and one who is too emotional (Tracy in *Manhattan*, Judy [Mia Farrow] in *Husbands and Wives*). The films have differing attitudes toward these characters and their problems, but the stories are also told from different perspectives and in radically contrasting styles. Where *Manhattan* is told from outside marriage, *Husbands and Wives* is told from inside marital relations, where its most important struggles are located. Extramarital relations in this film are just that: they are defined by the marriages to which they are tangential. As a result, each film poses a different central question about intimate relationships. *Manhattan*'s question is "Who is the right person?" *Husbands and Wives* asks whether there is a right person. Thus, the earlier film remains to some extent a romantic analysis of romance, where the later one is antiromantic.

Husbands and Wives takes the form of a case history, or, perhaps, of a group of case histories. It works as hard at looking like a documentary as *Manhattan* works at looking like a collection of art photographs. The first thing we notice is the handheld camera, which gives a cinema verité feel to much of the film. In the opening scene, for example, the camera darts around from character to character as if it were reacting to the strife it is filming. The documentary-like photography is supplemented with objective voice-over narration and interviews with the film's characters, in which they comment on their lives and each other. The handheld camera and frequent instances of actors addressing the camera remind us that we are watching a movie.

A certain alienation effect results. Even though we are meant to identify more strongly with the "artist," Gabe Roth, than with the other characters in this film, he is not its center. The interviews give voice to most of the major characters. We as spectators are asked to evaluate their differing interpretations and claims. It seems as though nothing that happens in this film goes without being analyzed, often from more than one point of view. This makes *Husbands and Wives* far removed from the conventions of romantic comedy. Indeed, perhaps the chief popular objection to the film on its release was that it wasn't funny but depressing.

The film opens with two couples meeting for dinner at Gabe and Judy's apartment. When Jack (Sidney Pollack) and Sally arrive, they announce rather blithely that they have decided to separate. This has a powerful impact on Judy, who takes the news very badly and has to be cajoled into going ahead with the dinner plans. This scene sets in motion a series of events in which we find Jack and Sally experimenting with other partners and returning to each other, while Gabe and Judy break up. Gabe is a respected novelist who teaches at Columbia. The "little girl" in *Husbands and Wives* is Rain (Juliette Lewis), one of Gabe's students. Rain is clearly the pursuer. She is sexually experienced, having previously had affairs with older men who had power over her— her father's business partner, her analyst, and so on. Rain says that her interest in Gabe is different, and the mutual admiration they have for each other's writing gives some credence to this claim. Nevertheless, Gabe must recognize, as we do, that there is a dangerous pattern here. Rain is not innocent, and she is not overly awed by Gabe's reputation. She dares to criticize the manuscript he has given her, and he responds as if wounded. Rain seems here more secure and stable than Gabe does. But, as Gabe tells the interviewer, her criticism of him makes her much more attractive. In this, Rain combines traits that *Manhattan* had attributed to Tracy and Mary. It would seem to make her the ideal object of desire, and, as such, more fantasy than reality. That status is confirmed by the fact that Rain is one of the few characters who are not the subjects of interviews.

Where *Manhattan* had made student-professor relationships into a joke, the matter is addressed directly in *Husbands and Wives* when Gabe explains in an interview that he knows of professors who regularly seduce their students. Gabe, however, has never before been involved with a student. Moreover, he insists that he has never cheated on Judy. This gives Gabe the high moral ground compared to Jack, who has been with prostitutes and had a mistress at the time he and Sally separated. Gabe's moral judgments seem to be affirmed, and yet they are not rewarded. His physical relationship with Rain consists of one long kiss;

An older man, a much younger woman . . . sound familiar? Woody Allen and Juliette Lewis in the inevitably autobiographical *Husbands and Wives* (TriStar, 1992).

he knows literally the taste of this desire, but he will not act on it. The heart here is refused by the head. Rain represents the possibility of romance, a possibility this film rejects.

The end of the film finds Gabe alone, divorced from Judy, who has since married Sally's former lover. Jack and Sally are back together again. It seems that they can't live without each other, but the problems in their marriage persist. The last scene is an interview with Gabe, who describes himself as out of the game for a while. He also comments that he "blew it with Judy." But that comment is hard to understand because we don't know what Gabe could have done better. Gabe describes a new novel that he is writing, having abandoned the one he had shown to Rain. In a revealing exchange, the interviewer asks Gabe on the heels of this, "Is it different?" Gabe's answer, "What, the novel?" makes it clear that the interviewer meant his life, and that Gabe wants to dodge the question. He says that the new novel is "more political and less confessional," and then asks, "Is this over, can we stop now?" At that moment one has the sense that Gabe experienced the interview as torture, and that he is fundamentally a victim, though perhaps only of his own repression. He wants to stop confessing and wishes to retreat into the more impersonal realm of politics.

Husbands and Wives literally ends with a confession, the absolute antithesis of the Hollywood ending. There is no hope for romantic marriage at the end of *Husbands and Wives*; we have seen nothing to make us believe that even the new couple will escape the traps into which the others have fallen. Romance itself—outside marriage—comes off no better. But if *Husbands and Wives* is powerfully antiromantic, it does not escape from confession into politics, for it offers nothing by way of an alternative. The film, then, verges on cynicism or despair. At best, it suggests that we can only hope to muddle through relationships that will inevitably be painful and unsatisfying. But even if *Husbands and Wives* does not end happily for Gabe, like *Manhattan*, it has depicted the relationship between Gabe and Rain in an idealized way. Art has once again transformed life.

Although it includes a therapy session that could have been one of the interviews from *Husbands and Wives*, *Deconstructing Harry* in the main lacks such documentary conventions. Rather than adopt the conventions of nonfiction, it concerns itself with the conventions of fiction and fantasy. *Deconstructing Harry* is an explicit meditation on the relations of life and art, and a response to the public's perception of Allen's use of his own life as material. The "artist" here seems to be someone who, like Allen, uses materials from his life without regard for the hurt they might cause the people who have shared it.

Virtually all the people Harry knows are unhappy about their all too obvious appearance in his latest book. But Harry's stories are also fantastic embellishments of the real. In one of them, Death appears to take Harry's young alter ego away when Death mistakes him for the regular occupant of the apartment borrowed for a meeting with a prostitute. In another, Harry finds himself on a tour of Hell guided by his friend Larry (Billy Crystal), the "devil" who "stole" the "little girl," Fay (Elizabeth Shue), from him. This scene is key because here the separation of the film's different ontological levels disappears entirely.

In *Deconstructing Harry*, the relationship between Harry and Fay is perhaps less central than the one between Gabe and Rain. Since this film is essentially a retrospective of the title character's relationships, none of them stands out entirely from the pack. Still, it can be argued that Fay is the most important to Harry because she is the one he is still in love with as he is telling us the story. Moreover, Harry treats

Fay very differently than the other women in his life. Unlike Allen's other "artists," Harry is not finally an admirable character. We repeatedly see him treat badly those who love him, and, perhaps worse, offer lame excuses for the behavior. This surely inhibits the audience's identification with Harry.

Fay was a fan of Harry. He describes her as moving from fan to pupil all during a period when they were lovers. But unlike the previous movies of the cycle, questions of the ethics of such relationships are not explicitly raised. The issue of power is represented, however. It is clear that Harry dominates the relationship in its early stages, but in the end, the power relations are reversed. Harry repeatedly cautions Fay that she should not fall in love with him. This advice is a version of what Isaac tells Tracy in *Manhattan*. The problem this time is that Fay listens, while Harry falls in love with her. This renders Fay a familiarly romantic character, the woman the man wants all the more because he cannot have her. As a result the film does not offer the analysis of the relationship with "the little girl" found in the other films. The idealization here is more traditional. Fay is the woman who should have been Harry's salvation, though the film strongly suggests that she is better off with Larry.

Fay differs from Harry's other exes in that she is an artist—an artist whom Harry has helped to form. This makes her, paradoxically, like the fictional characters who populate this film. They are, of course, completely Harry's creations. But Fay has a mind of her own. One reading of the film's conclusion, in which Harry is honored by a convocation of the characters he has invented, is that made-up people are much more reliable than real ones.

Deconstructing Harry returns to the relationship between life and art depicted at the end of *Annie Hall*, where that film's failed relationship is rewritten in a play with a happy ending. But where the artist in *Annie Hall* was mildly apologetic about his revision of the truth, Harry in the end seems to prefer fiction to life. Thus, the new novel he begins to write, which we might be entitled to believe is *Deconstructing Harry*, is the story of a novelist who is at home in his writing but not in the world. The artist's life is thus quite properly grist for the mill out of which the fictional world is churned. But that material, once it is transformed, can no longer be properly comprehended as a reference to the life. Woody Allen can assert that his films are not autobiographical because they are not for him about his life; they use his life to create other worlds in which he would perhaps rather live. Yet this film treats fiction as a form of autobiography. Thus it quite intentionally also offers the opposite reading: that Woody Allen's films are about his life and almost nothing else. Like a good deconstructionist, Allen does not attempt to resolve this contradiction.

Deconstructing Harry takes up as a theme the transformation of life that art renders. This may make it seem like a postmodernist film, and perhaps it is. The position that a world constructed by the artist is preferable to the real one may be the *reductio ad absurdum* of modernism, and, thus, beyond modernism. Moreover, the fictional world that Harry creates differs from the idealized ones that Allen and other modernists have made. And yet, as in high modernism, art is finally a redemptive process for Harry. In this sense, *Deconstructing Harry* is of a piece with Allen's other portraits of the "artist."

20

Affliction

When Paranoid Male Narratives Fail

Marita Sturken

A CULTURE REVEALS its underlying values in those aspects of its social fabric that are understood to be in crisis. In American culture, there has been in the past few decades a constant media focus on childhood in crisis, the family in crisis, memory in crisis, and, inevitably, masculinity in crisis. Indeed, during the twentieth century, masculinity has been seen as always moving from one crisis to another, never secure and safe, always under threat. This is paradoxical, given the power awarded to masculinity in American culture, and its central role in the construction of national identity. Yet the trope of crisis has remained a constant; from the Great Depression to the Vietnam War, historical events have been understood as traumatic to the social role of masculinity. This reached an accelerated pace by the late twentieth century, with the rise of feminism and the shift from an industrial to a postindustrial economy, which proved devastating to the jobs of working-class men.

In 1999 Susan Faludi published *Stiffed: The Betrayal of the American Man*, in which she argues that the baby boomer generation was betrayed by the society of its fathers.[1] Her work prompts the question, What is it about our overinvestment in masculinity that makes it always come up "short," that asks it to be more than it possibly can be?

The contemporary version of masculinity in crisis has emerged hand in hand with several other distinct social trends: identity politics and paranoid narratives. The public discussion of white men as victims of feminism, affirmative action, queer politics, and multiculturalism has fueled concerns of masculinity under siege. In addition, the 1990s saw a fascination in popular culture with paranoid narratives, including such television shows as *The X-Files, Dark Skies*, and *Millennium*, the historical films of Oliver Stone, and more recent cyberfilms such as *The Matrix* (1999); the continuing credence in a government cover-up of the crash of an alien spaceship in Roswell, New Mexico, in 1946; the rise of conservative and right-wing conspiracy groups in the United States; and a preoccupation with narratives of millennial apocalypse and natural disaster. This new version of paranoia, which is distinct in many ways from the 1950s paranoia that centered on the external threat of communism, is inextricably tied to contemporary discourses about race and identity, and the emergence of the white male as a figure in crisis.

I would like to explore in this essay the relationship of narratives of masculinity and paranoia through an analysis of the 1998 Paul Schrader film *Affliction*, starring Nick Nolte, which is faithfully based on the Russell Banks novel.[2] The novel and film center on the character of Wade Whitehouse, a white forty-one-year-old divorced man living in Lawford, a small New Hampshire town, working as the local policeman, snowplow driver, well digger, and general handyman for a local businessman and selectman, Gordon LaRiviere. Wade is a fading American archetype, and he begins the film angry, troubled, and restless, as if he knows that all that shores him up as a man is about to unravel. He is the father of a daughter he rarely sees, the son of an abusive father, and unfulfilled and unhappy in his work and life. He drinks too much, and his erratic moods are tolerated by the people around him. He is, in essence, the symbol of masculinity in crisis, and one has to wonder if Banks meant to suggest through his naming that we should consider him to stand in for the American male of the late twentieth century.

The film chronicles in a deliberate and painful fashion the stripping away of the masculine postures that hold Wade's life together. He is a big man, played by Nolte as always on edge, his body often hunched over in anger, his clothes and boots always undone, as if carelessly thrown onto his hefty frame. There is also a charm in his character, the kind of charisma carried by men who appear to inhabit their bodies carelessly yet powerfully, a quality that is central as well to James Gandolfini's portrayal of Tony Soprano in *The Sopranos*. As the film begins, we see Wade first attempting to cajole his way into his daughter Jill's good graces, making excuses, as he always does, for being late, screwing up, letting someone down. When she calls her mother, Lillian (played by Mary Beth Hurt), to pick her up, Wade is confused by Jill's

The angry, troubled, and restless men in Paul Schrader's *Affliction* (Lions Gate, 1998).

rejection, angry that Lillian has the upper hand over him, and shamed by the incident. It is this rejection of him as a father that sends Wade into a downward spiral.

Wade's investment in himself as a good father, even in the context of an ugly divorce, is deeply tied up with his relationship to his own father, an abusive alcoholic played by James Coburn (who won a best supporting Oscar for the role). He is deeply invested in knowing that he is not like his own father, that he is better, kinder, and more loving. Pop is a huge, barrel-chested man, drunk and spiteful, constantly calling his sons "candyasses" and taunting their very existence. There may be an explanation for Pop's anger, but the film does not provide it for us. We see him rather through the eyes of Wade, in grainy flashbacks in which he towers over the camera, bellowing, always ready to raise his fists in violence. The film places the viewer in the position of the frightened child, so that these flashbacks overpower the more pathetic image of Pop as a confused and addled, though still angry, old man. The film thus defines Wade as marked for life by the fact that he was a boy beaten by his father. Stories of Pop's cruelty even follow him as an adult in the form of gossip at the local bar, stories that send him angrily stomping toward the door like a child. It is the fear of his own capacity for such cruelty that motivates Wade. As his brother Rolphe, who narrates the film, states at the end, Wade was one of those boys,

> beaten by their fathers, whose capacity for love and trust was crippled almost at birth, whose best hope for connection with other human beings lay in detachment, as if life were over. It's how we keep from destroying in turn our children and terrorizing the women who have the misfortune to love us, how we absent ourselves from the tradition of male violence, how we decline the seduction of revenge.

Wade's spiral downward begins with his daughter's rejection, and then continues at a relentless pace. He begins the film with the fragile illusion of authority, with the belief that he is needed in, if not crucial to, the running of the town. His coworker Jack jokes with him that LaRiviere, his boss, would go broke without him. Wade is nominally the town policeman, a post that is more of a uniform than actual authority. He plows the streets when it snows and serves as the crossing guard in the mornings for the schoolchildren. His sense of worth is deeply tied to a sense of the civic.

As the film progresses, this veneer of male authority is stripped from Wade. He fantasizes about starting a custody battle over his daughter, eventually to no avail. His mother dies of the cold in his parents' unheated home, as his father sits confused downstairs. He flails increasingly out of control, eventually losing all his jobs. He is left by his girlfriend, Margie (Sissy Spacek), and so frightens his daughter that she hits him in fear. Throughout this time, Wade is fighting a toothache, the pain of which keeps him strangely rooted in the present. Yet, when he finally takes a pair of pliers and pulls out the tooth himself, the release from the pain has the effect of taking him further down, almost in search of pain itself.

Importantly, Wade's downfall gets caught up in a paranoid narrative that he constructs about the world around him, one that is suggested and even fostered by his brother Rolphe from a distance. Wade's coworker Jack takes a wealthy man from Massachusetts, named Twombley, out deer hunting on the first day of the season. Twombley stumbles on the trail and shoots himself by mistake. Wade becomes convinced that this was not an accident—that Jack was paid by someone to kill the man and make it look like an accident. He harasses Jack, damaging La Riviere's truck while chasing him, and finds out that LaRiviere and Twombley were in business together buying land. In Wade's mind, there are connections between all of these seemingly arbitrary events—the shooting, the land purchases, Jack's behavior. Everything, in light of this paranoid narrative, becomes meaningful.

It is crucial to the film's effect that the viewer is taken up by Wade's notions of conspiracy, and pulled into it. Wade's gradual disintegration in the film is painful to witness, and one begins to feel that the film will spare us his inevitable self-destruction and turn thankfully into a story of intrigue instead. Masculinity, the film seems to say, needs a detective story. It is with relief that the viewer participates in Wade's theory, seeing the clues and expecting the story to act as redemption for him, to prove his worth that we as viewers have been doubting. Wade believes that this conspiracy is passing him over and setting him up to fail. His fantasy of intrigue and shadowy dealings is much more interesting than the mundane routine of his life in a small town. It provides him—and the viewer—at least temporarily, with meaning and purpose.

But Wade is wrong; there is no conspiracy or connection between these events. They are simply arbitrary and unimportant. Yet Wade's need for a conspiracy to provide meaning in his life is instructive. He is empowered by his paranoid narrative. It is as if he can reaffirm his masculinity with the discovery of plots and conspiracy; they can account, then, for his own failure too. (After all, people are conspiring against him.) In this, Wade's character is emblematic of the way that paranoia functioned in the 1990s as a means for disempowered citizens to feel that their lives have meaning.

One of paranoia's defining features is its dependence on a state of prior innocence. Paranoia follows the moment when we were innocent, unknowing, and believing in the good. It is the result of the bitter shock that comes from having been naive about structures of power. In the late twentieth century, paranoid narratives have been situated in large part on the right, with right-wing conspiracies about government oppression acting as a strange echo of left 1960s anti-establishment politics. Narratives of paranoia are most often read as culturally disruptive stories that powerfully evoke the alienation of everyday life and the terror of citizenship. Yet it is also possible to see them as providing a particular form of comfort. Paranoid narratives assert structure where there is none. They see master plans in the arbitrariness of everyday life. They provide narratives of motivation for events that ultimately are meaningless. As such, they ironically act to shore up the system even as they critique it, since the illusion that there is structure rather than chaos, a plan, however evil, rather than arbitrary pain, allows the system to appear intact.

The prevalent paranoia of the 1990s was, among other things, a means through which citizens mediated their identification with the nation. This paranoia can be seen as the direct outcome of the daily infantilization of citizenship.[3] For Wade Whitehouse, a paranoid narrative about the dealings of his small town serves to counter the infantilization of his daily life, in which he is beholden to LaRiviere and his ex-wife, and treated like a child by each. It allows him to deny the sad truth that his authority as a policeman and as a man is fake, seen through by everyone around him. As such, he stands in for the frustrated citizen of late-twentieth-century American culture.

Freud defined paranoia as an aspect of narcissism and linked it to the "delusion of being noticed."[4] This is crucial in relation to citizenship, for who is the citizen but someone who is rarely noticed, who is absented from the public debates and replaced by cultural figures and stereotypes—the welfare recipient, the soccer mom, and so on. The paranoid citizen assumes that others get all the attention and all the benefits of the system. When this paranoid citizen gets angry he does something to up the ante, to be noticed forever—sending mail bombs, bombing a federal building filled with people going about their unnoticed daily lives, or gunning down schoolmates. Wade Whitehouse plays out this narrative in his small way. He kills his father in a fight, burns his body in the barn, and then seeks out his former friend Jack and shoots him dead. He makes himself, his anger at his father, and his belief in conspiracy noticed. Then he disappears, never to be seen again. Life has been altered by Wade, but then it inevitably returns to its routine, as if he had not been there. Only his brother Rolphe, the teller of the story, remains to try and give the story meaning. This is, inevitably, the paranoid person's ultimate nightmare, that their story will not be noticed and finally have no effect.

Affliction depicts the struggle of sons against fathers in ways that reflect Faludi's argument regarding betrayal, anger, and disappointment. As Wade stands in the driveway, watching Margie and Jill drive away, his father comes stumbling out of the house to claim him as a "real" man. "You've finally done it like a man, like I thought," he says. "I love you, you mean son of a bitch." This final embrace, a hideous expression

of love, takes Wade to the edge. Wade represents the men described by
Faludi who are still and always sons, still defined by the narratives of
their fathers, still shocked that the system that was supposed to make
them has turned out to be so flawed, so fickle, and so disinterested in
their well-being. The shock of prior innocence permeates this crisis of
masculinity in its post-Vietnam understanding that the system cares so
little for its citizens, no matter what their privilege. Wade Whitehouse
disappears into the landscape of forgotten men, a painful reminder of
the fragility of the impact of one man's life. *Affliction* shows us the crucial role that paranoia plays in the construction of masculinity, and the
trauma that ensues when the belief in masculinity's power to discover
an underlying truth fails.

NOTES

1. Susan Faludi, *Stiffed: The Betrayal of the American Man* (New York: William Morrow, 1999).

2. Russell Banks, *Affliction* (New York: Harper Perennial, 1989).

3. The concept of the infantilization of citizenship is defined by Lauren
Berlant in her important essay, "Theory of Infantile Citizenship," *Public Culture*
5 (1993): 395–410. It is reprinted in her book *The Queen of America Goes to Washington City: Essays on Sex and Citizenship* (Durham: Duke University Press, 1997).

4. Sigmund Freud, "On Narcissism: An Introduction," in *The Freud Reader*,
ed. Peter Gay (New York: Norton, 1985), 559.

21

The Phallus UnFetished

The End of Masculinity As We Know It in Late-1990s "Feminist" Cinema

Alexandra Juhasz

THE PHALLUS UNPLUGGED

The telling moments from my two favorite feminist films of 1999:

1. David Fincher's *Fight Club*. Marla and Tyler are about to rush out of her seedy flophouse, just steps ahead of the police. He's saved her from suicide. Sort of. He eyes a dildo on her dresser. "Don't worry, it's not a threat to you," she states impassively.
2. Trey Parker's *South Park: Bigger, Longer and Uncut*. Saddam Hussein and his lover, the Devil, are in bed, arguing once again about sex. Saddam wants to fuck all the time; the Devil would rather communicate, maybe cuddle. But this time, Saddam wants it so bad, he pulls his penis out from under the covers and waves it in the crisp night air. "I'm just fucking with you. It's not real," he snickers as he chucks aside what is, it turns out, a dildo.

DILDO TIME

Two telling dildo moments. That's what did it; that's what told me these films were *feminist*. These two free-floating phalluses (the unlikely possessions of a whacked-out girl and a tyrannical Arab fag) generated a space carved into their elegant late-1990s misogyny that was made especially for the likes of me: 1980s-style feminist film professor. A dildo

210

puts something close to a penis into the hands of anyone who desires one. Masculinity, revealed as an effect of signification, becomes available to all.[1]

Academic feminism and its more sordid sister, queer theory, applaud all acts that unlink genitals from their gendered homes, that sever biology from destiny. They instruct us that a proactive political practice can occur whenever bodies (or body parts) are separated from their culturally determined duties. In these late-1990s movie manifestations of male gender angst, the sex/gender/sexuality system reaches a feminist apex, so fully destabilized that unanchored genitals are up for grabs. The films accomplish the complex theoretical/political project of detaching bodily organs from their host organisms and presenting them, instead, as fully dependent on discourse. Throughout *Fight Club* the narrator enjoys addressing the audience as his disembodied vitals: I am Jack's medulla, Jack's nipple, Jack's colon. "My father dumped me, Tyler dumped me, I am Jack's broken heart." Meanwhile, Stan, from *South Park,* spends most of his time in search of the clitoris, which finally does appear to save the day at movie's conclusion—this enormous, doughy, pink mound, fashioned after a men's bowler, who expounds moralistic half-truths: "Behold my glory. I am the clitoris. Have confidence in yourself. Chicks love confidence. The clitoris has spoken."

These films are decidedly feminist in the sense that they are aggressively self-conscious (and self-confident) about the mobility of gender. The super-wimpy protagonist of *Fight Club* (Edward Norton), the unnamed narrator who sometimes calls himself Jack, is so uncertain about his masculinity that he opts for schizophrenia to refashion himself as male through the hypermasculine Tyler Durden (Brad Pitt). In *South Park,* so unformed, so emasculated are the film's ideas and desires that the protagonists could only be the presexual, homosocial little boys Kenny, Eric, Stan, and Kyle.

A PROSTATE CHECK AIN'T NO CURE FOR THE POSTMODERN CONDITION

The postmodern condition is, it turns out, fundamentally a *male* condition involving nothing more than the loss of masculinity. Both *Fight Club* and *South Park* center on worlds-of-men fully peopled by un-males, quasi-males, uncertain-males, males-in-waiting. "At least we're still men," snivel the divorced, bankrupted, pathetic members of the testicular cancer survivors group—Remaining Men Together—who make up the community where Jack hopes to begin to eradicate the feminine within. "Yes, we're men. Men is what we are." But we all know they're not; they're hugging, crying, whining, and one even has breasts. ("Bob. Bob had bitch tits.") Sure, they don't have balls, but a deeper loss is indicated by their behavior. "Not just male hysteria in relation to sexual lack," write Arthur and Marilouise Kroker in their study of early-1990s male hysteria, "but as the emblematic sign of a more primordial lack in postmodern society."[2]

It turns out that most men are women in the current world order, not because of what they *have*—balls or breasts, no matter—but because of what they *lack*: immediate access to their own masculinity. In our contemporary consumer (multi)culture—increasingly dominated by women and gay men whom we are forced to tolerate according to the dictates of p.c. ideology—all roads lead to the feminine. While Jack may not have suffered the more obvious biological loss of his fellow support group members, he has suffered one even harder to rectify, a cultural one. Tyler exposes Jack to the deep reaches of this effeminization: he knows the meaning of the word *duvet*, he's never been in a car crash, and most significantly, and from whence Fight Club is born, he's never been in a fistfight either. Yet even after the establishment of Fight Club, Jack continues to disregard Marla as a sexual object. When she makes him fondle her breasts (a potential cancerous lump as excuse), he stays flaccid. "Do you feel anything?" she asks. "You feel nothing?" "No, nothing." "I'll check your prostate," she offers. He is unmoved: "I'm okay. Are we done now?"

THE DILDO AND THE DICK

Let's return again to the dildos and what they might signify. In *South Park*, after Saddam tosses off the first dildo, the Devil is disgusted. "That is not appropriate," he snaps. So Saddam pulls out his dick: "And this?" Is it less or more appropriate when this penis turns out to be another detachable dildo? Does he have two dildos because he lacks a dick or because he's been given permission to greedily grab extras?

Meanwhile, in *Fight Club*, before Jack has even begun his masculinity quest, he is held up by airport security as he tries to claim his luggage. He has been delayed because something inside his bag vibrated. While security checks to see if it is a bomb, a guard informs Jack that they are on to him: "It's usually an electric razor but once in a while it's a dildo." "But I don't own a . . . " Dick? Dildo? Is it that clear that he's missing something?

It turns out that Marla is the one with the phallus at hand: "Don't worry, it's not a threat to you." She assures Jack that she uses *her* dildo for pleasure, not power. At the same time, even though Jack actually does have a penis (but not, however, a dildo), he doesn't use his for power either. This is what he's lost the ability to do; this is what Fight Club is organized to rectify; this is what *Fight Club* is about.

In "Phallus/Penis: Same Difference," Jane Gallop writes, "As long as the attribute of power is a phallus which can only have meaning by referring to and being confused with a penis, this confusion will support a structure in which men have power and women do not."[3] In the late 1990s, straight white male filmmakers introduced a "new" kind of masculinity, one previously imagined by feminist and queer theorists. Imagine a phallus that does not refer back to a penis. Imagine a penis that does not refer back to a man.

PENILE ASSAULTS

Let's return to the dildos yet again. Let's say that for Marla, Saddam, the Devil, and Jack, they serve less as a phallus than as a fetish. For Freud, a fetish is an object that substitutes for the missing female penis. "The horror of castration," Freud writes, "has set up a memorial to itself."[4] A fetish is always linked to the threat of castration, as embodied visually by the penis-less woman. As women (and gay men) move ever closer to the phallus (through ownership of dildos, for example), women no longer function as a signifier of penile loss.

In these two films, the dildo is a postmodern fetish that stands in for the missing *male* penis. Thus, the unplugging of (male) genitals from their rightful homes is made visible. Castration and other potential penile assaults abound: bigger, longer, and uncut. The joke is, of course, that by 1999 they've gotten smaller, shorter . . . shorn! Cut clean away. *Fight Club* organizes two of its more violent scenes around attempted castrations. In both, a pack of bloodthirsty men hold down their quarry and threaten him with a rubber band and shining steel knife. The second potential victim of this inconceivable act is none other than our narrator. However, the film's narrative has gone to such great lengths to suggest that he lacks his balls already that this scene is played with much less horror and much more irony than the earlier scene it imitates. Meanwhile, *South Park* casts its leads as prepubescent boys whose penises are necessarily cut short—no need for the dreaded act—because the boys are still in the early throes of biological development.

Fight Club's most egregiously reflexive scene—showing us its inner workings—focuses on penis cuts of a slightly different sort. "Let me tell you about Tyler Durden," says the narrator. There is an edit to a flash frame of a massive erect penis. Durden is directly linked to his privates; Tyler *is* the phallus. We then return to Jack, now looking directly at us in the foreground while Tyler busies himself with a film editing machine in the shot's background. The fourth wall completely broken down, Jack uses this portion of *Fight Club* to illustrate for us how his pal Tyler, while working his job as a film projectionist, cuts single frames of "a nice big cock" into family movies, "splices sex organs into Cinderella." We see the disembodied member again, and lest we forget, again: first in Tyler's hand, then on/as our screen. We observe our doubles—the viewers of the movie he is projecting within our movie—appearing understandably shaken, but uncertain as to why, as the nasty frame is subliminally cut into their movie. Their faces of horror and disgust speak for the film: this severed member is disturbing beyond words. The film is organized around this crisis: the capacity to disengage and arbitrarily insert free-standing penises anywhere.

However, it is the reintroduction of this frame-of-a-penis at film's end that is most significant. If you catch it (and it is easy to miss), it is there to behold yet again, spliced into the last seconds of our movie, now functioning as it did for our surrogate audience: leaving us vaguely, distastefully unsettled as we view our hero and his putative love interest, Marla, truly united for the first time. We feel there is something a little bit off as we watch the happy couple watch the destruction of the world—albeit chastely, hand in hand, bodies separated by an inexplicable gulf. This member-burst uses its brief moment of film time to stand erect as it perfectly inserts itself into the space left in the frame between the newly unified heterosexual couple. Although Jack has assassinated Tyler by a gunshot to (their) head only minutes earlier, the phallus/Tyler returns, demanding his birthright—all that Jack will never own, all that Jack can never be.

The impact of the briefly visible but unattainable phallus, recognizable solely *as* representation, is what divides the happy couple (along with Jack's virtually explicit homosexuality, of course). It speaks what the film really believes: that while Marla may have a dildo, and Jack never did actually lose his penis, neither lovebird ends the movie attaining what access to a penis really should promise. Now that the penis is fully ambulatory, it turns out to be unmoored from what it used to anchor and what it used to signify. In this late-1990s dystopia, having a penis does not insure masculinity or even what masculinity used to shore up: power.

A PHALLUS GRAFT

While the dread of castration has long organized male subjectivity, *Fight Club* and *South Park* attest to a world where castration is no longer an empty threat. We've returned to Freud's early phallic phase with a twist.[5] We reside in a new kind of one-sex era where all are castrated. Thus, in *Fight Club* and *South Park,* the penis/dildo is as much the rightful property of women and gay men as it is of real men.

While the films contend that masculinity can be easily taken from a man, they suggest that it is not nearly so easy to get it back. When the boys' super-fey teacher, Mr. Garrison, enrolls in the army to fight Canadians—a sure route from penis to phallus throughout (modern) history—*South Park* knows he is no more manly for his costume. "This uniform makes me feel like a tough brute man," he cockily assures his puppet-friend, Mr. Hand. "I can't wait for shore leave to get me some fucking Poontang."

At the same time, the more contemporary (postmodern) male costume of washboard stomach and bulging biceps, easily bought at any gym (empty signified referring to no real signifier), is also not a route to masculinity. "Is this what a man looks like?" wonders Jack as he looks up to see a black and white photograph of one such torso, selling jeans or underwear on a bus. His is a rhetorical question. He has learned from his nights at Fight Club that a man need not look like anything: it's not the jeans he buys but the genes he owns that count.

Both films speak a need to regain a brute, violent, asocial (biologically male) body living outside (female) culture. One film advocates senseless, uncensored violence, the other, childish locker-room potty

"We're a generation of men raised by women. I wonder if another woman is what we need?" Apparently not. Brad Pitt and Edward Norton square off and then pair off in David Fincher's *Fight Club* (Twentieth Century Fox, 1999).

humor as solutions to an overly feminized postmodern culture. They accomplish their procedures in single-sex worlds where women are eradicated, absented, unnecessary. Marla is the only female who appears in *Fight Club* and she takes up surprisingly little screen space, given that she is assigned the narrative function of Jack/Tyler's love object. Rather, Jack first accesses his virility through his deep and destructive attachment, intimacy, and passion for Tyler (at this point in the movie, understood to be a distinct character). The two men set up house together; the movie's sexiest scenes occur between Jack and Tyler. After they fight for the first time—no rules, shirts off, a little drunk—the men enjoy a postcoital smoke. The parking lot is suddenly bathed in a soft yellow light, and wisps of smoke filter through the night air: "We should do that again sometime," Jack says longingly, as he reclines against the curb, their makeshift headboard. Cast as the true-woman to Tyler's real-man, it is Jack who is the film's heroine.

Of course, it is Jack's very femininity (and by association his homosexuality) that is the problem Jack and Tyler seek to cure through Fight Club, their roaringly homosocial invention built on the bodies of sweaty, nearly naked men, touching, pummeling, rolling, and bleeding together in a dark basement. If you don't have a penis, and you want access to the phallus, you'll need to get close enough to another man to share his, to finger his entrails, to get inside him and find the primal traces of his maleness swimming within his blood and guts. The film's anxiety is rooted in the dilemma that its homophobic, biology-based mission is impossible to accomplish outside homosexuality.

MEN AGAINST FEMINISM

As uncertain as these two films may be about the relation between their homophobia and homosexuality, they are dead set in their interpretation of where women fit into the new world order. "If the *phallus* is distinct from the *penis*," writes Jane Gallop, "then feminism's battle against phallocentrism is not a battle against men."[6] Our current situation begs one important turn on her 1970s equation: if the penis is not a phallus then men must be in a battle against feminism.

In *South Park* the object is always transgression: to shock by tearing down political correctness, to participate in aggressive antisociality where acceptance and tolerance have become the rule. No rarified, respected minority group is spared a joke: Jews, fags, African Americans, women, and feminists. These boys may not know how to find the phallus, but they do know that it's best to prohibit women's gaining of it through political action. "Was my mother careful when she stabbed me in the heart with a clothes hanger while I was still in the womb?" asks the Mole, the nihilistic child-spy who helps the boys in their effort to save the raunchy, wrongfully imprisoned Canadian movie idols, Terrance and Phillip.

The postmodern era disperses authority so that it is intangible, scattered, the possession of faceless multinational corporations. Without a clear enemy, male anxiety must re-roost locally, at home. For instance, *South Park* initially tries to remedy its postmodern anxiety by offing Bill Gates, the czar of the home computer. "Fucking Windows '98," sneers the army general who executes Bill point-blank in front of a crowd of cheering G.I.s. But this is not a final solution. The evil roosts deeper within. The solution: the boys must quiet their domineering mothers. Kyle's mother, the villainous Jewess, Sheila Brotslowski, subject of her own song, "Stupid Bitch: The Biggest Bitch in the Whole Wide World," is reassigned to the position of secretary of offense by Bill Clinton during the war on Canada, which she originated. But what exactly is her offense? Answers Kyle at *South Park*'s finale, "You never take the time to talk to me. You keep going off and fighting all these causes. I don't want a fighter, I want my Mother." *South Park*'s position against political women and the politics of women could not be made more clear. The only "political" message that is expressed clearly, and without humor or sarcasm, in the entire film is "Kyle, you have to stand up to your mother."

There's another kind of woman who also needs to be told what's what. Postmodern (multi)culture is rife with a new breed of females who have helped in raising these boys to be the girls that they are. The vast majority of male role models for the *South Park* boys are themselves most clearly modeled after gay men: from pansy-ass Mr. Garrison, to Big Gay Al, whose number "It's Super to Be Gay" is the tour de force of the G.I. Show, to homosexual Canadian figure skating champion Brian Boitano, who is himself the honored subject of a song where his virile heroism is presented as exemplar for the boys. Of course, homosexuals, Saddam and the Devil, take up a good deal of screen time with their relational bickering: "Let's fuck," says butch-top Saddam. "Is sex the only thing you think about?" whines the Devil in response. It is the film's martyrs, the Canadian comedy duo Terrance and Phillip, who most clearly model the dangers for boys who grow up in a society where feminists and fags have refashioned popular culture. "We want to be just like Terrance and Phillip," the boys whine. They are referring, of course, to the very Terrance and Phillip who have introduced our susceptible young friends to cool new playtime activities like ball sucking, rim jobs, and ass-ramming uncle-fucking.

THE NEW WOMEN

Whatever happened to the missionary position? Let's face it: masculinity as we knew and loved it is *over*. "I can't get married," explains Jack to Tyler in *Fight Club*. "I'm a thirty-year old boy. We're a generation of men raised by women. I wonder if another woman is what we need?" How closely linked is threatened heterosexuality to threatened masculinity?

In conclusion, I'd like to look briefly at one more gender-anxious, same-sex dystopia, *The New Women* (2001), a film written and directed by Todd Hughes, a gay white male. Unfortunately (for my analysis), there are no dildos in *The New Women*, but this is because in this film men's penises *are* dildos. For the lucky new women in the film's title, the penis has become a dildo-plus. After a strange storm, all the men in the world have gone to sleep and women can access men's penises with complete abandon. It turns out that until the men die of dehydration or starvation, their penises continue to stiffen every forty-five minutes, these penises are not fully detachable, but completely available. They can be taken by women for stimulation and also impregnation (that's the plus).

Early in the film, Lisa La Strada (Mary Woronov), the film's heroine, returns home from a town meeting where the women have attempted to create a new social order. They decide that women will be given the public roles once held by their husbands. This means Lisa gets to be the law; her husband was sheriff. "I felt so alive, and I made sense," she explains, as she relays to her still snoozing spouse how she took control of the meeting. Before the meeting things had been rough. The post-male society looked like the all-male society, "with the same meanness and greed, but without the men to blame." At the meeting, Lisa suggests to the group that rather than continuing the current survival of the fittest model, every woman in town should share her food and other provisions, so that all might have a chance at survival. As the women drop their crackers and candles into cardboard boxes in the high school gymnasium, we see the one moment in the film when something other than a patriarchal (capitalist, violent) political vision organizes the world. Her husband responds to this vision with his on-the-hour erection. "Baby, I get it! You *want* me to be in charge," she croons, as she mounts and fucks him.

There is an immediate cut to a series of extreme close-ups of parts of her body as she dons his sheriff outfit to the sound of a military march: holster, gun, mirrored glasses, big smile. Unlike Mr. Garrison, who was no more a man for wearing military fatigues, Lisa is the only lead character across these three films who accesses the phallus as it should rightfully be done: by enacting a powerful political deed. *The New Women* imagines its post-male world, at this one moment, as a meritocracy. Any person can have the phallus when she does something that deserves it, when she wields power through principle. In all the films, it is only Lisa who for the briefest of moments lets us see that the phallus is attainable for anyone who deserves and earns it through actions of power enacted outside the aggression, violence, and bigotry that have always cemented dominant, patriarchal power.

All these films imagine dystopias where men's intrinsic hold on the phallus has ceased. This is as it should be. But our straight boys can't imagine how to get back the phallus outside the traditional (messed up and anachronistic) ways that always worked before: violence, cruelty, hatred, scorn, biology. They loathe politics, and would rather fuck things up than figure out how to make them work. "Nothing was solved, but nothing mattered," explains Jack about the successes of Fight Club. The political philosophy of Fight Club—anarchy and situationist pranks—results in a totaled, not a better, world. *South Park* is even more uncertain as to a solution to the loss of male power—outside mother-bashing—and until the bitter end, merely mocks those who might imagine a better world. The movie ends by placing our heroes into a satiric utopia. As flowers, rainbows, doves, and luv return after the devastation wrought upon the earth by the Devil and his lover, the boys' friend, the African American Chef, speaks the film's final parodic sentiments: "Let's all join hands and knock oppression down."

Of course, given the mood of our era, *The New Women* is as dark, self-reflexive, and cynical a comedy as are either of the straight boy flicks. It pretends it believes in nothing, too. It mocks all that it champions. That said, Lisa's attempted socialism *is* rewarded with the phallus. And later, at the all-women's Goddess-worshiping Camp Gaia, the tambourine-pounding, hippie-girl campers circle a bonfire and sing to the sounds of pipes and an acoustic guitar:

> *We are the New Women, working together, Goddess meant it that way.*
> *When the rain came and washed the world for us, no more fighting, and no*
>   *more fuss. Females from far and wide realized they could work together,*
>   *side by side.*
>
> *We are the New Women, loving together. Finally we're having our say.*
> *Through clarity, hard work and common sense, we've aligned together in our*
>   *own defense. We are the New Women.*

NOTES

1. Male anxiety in 1990s cinema has a history. Several academic studies of the early 1990s set about theorizing what were even earlier, "new" kinds of

male trouble. For instance, in the introduction to *Male Trouble* (Minneapolis: University of Minnesota Press, 1993) editors Constance Penley and Sharon Willis look to *Pee-wee's Playhouse* as an example of new possibilities for men in feminism: a place of "male subjectivity as nonmonolithic and even capable of positive or utopian moments" (vii). Pee-wee belongs in a long line of men who work through masculine anxiety through wimpdom: from Jerry Lewis to Jim Carrey to *Blue's Clues'* Steve. But what makes Pee-wee special is exactly what Tyler and the *South Park* boys can't abide. Penley and Willis explain that Pee-wee "puts camp to work arguing for an ethics of tolerance for all differences by making fun of the standard categories governing what counts as sexual identity—especially straight masculinity—and 'normal' family relations" (xiii).

Meanwhile, in her book *Spectacular Bodies* (New York: Routledge, 1993), Yvonne Tasker seeks to understand the antithesis of Pee-wee's breed of "new man." She studies the hypermuscular action heroes of the late 1980s and early 1990s who "reassert, mourn or hysterically state a lost male power" (109) through what she terms "musculinity." Unlike the wimps, these action heroes exhibit "a fascist idealization of the white male body" (1). In the late 1990s, Tyler Durden proves that such a fully masculine figure can register only in the imaginary, and Jack and Tyler's dual personality creates one body in which to work through the contradictions between these two models (as does both Jerry Lewis's and Eddie Murphy's body in *The Nutty Professor*).

2. Arthur and Marilouise Kroker, "The Hysterical Male: One Libido?" in Arthur and Marilouise Kroker, eds., *The Hysterical Male: New Feminist Theory* (New York: St. Martin's, 1991), xi.

3. Jane Gallop, "Phallus/Penis: Same Difference," in Janet Todd, ed., *Men by Women* (New York: Holmes and Meier, 1981), 246–47.

4. Sigmund Freud, "Fetishism" (1927), in *On Sexuality*, trans. James Strachey, ed. Angela Richards (Harmondsworth: Penguin, 1983), 353.

5. Gallop, 244–45. According to Gallop, Freud theorized that the phallic phase was based on a monosexual logic, and a child recognized people by the opposition phallic/castrated (as opposed to masculine/feminine).

6. Gallop, 244.

PART VI

BODIES AT REST AND IN MOTION

22

Bods and Monsters

The Return of the Bride of Frankenstein

Elizabeth Young

THE FRANKENSTEIN PLOT has been a remarkably protean one, sub-ject to constant remaking, since the publication of the novel *Frankenstein* in 1818. Film has been an especially generative medium for such re-making. There have been well over a hundred films based on Mary Shelley's novel, beginning with the 1910 Edison *Frankenstein* and rang-ing, more recently, from the comic burlesque of Mel Brooks's *Young Frankenstein* (1974) to the Blaxploitation drama of William Levey's *Blackenstein* (1972), and from Kenneth Branagh's *Mary Shelley's Franken-stein* (1994), a doggedly faithful adaptation, to Tim Burton's *Franken-weenie* (1984), the inspired story of a boy and his reconstituted dog. In its more general form—as a narrative about the construction of mon-strous bodies—the long cinematic arm of the Frankenstein plot extends even further. For example, Jonathan Demme's *The Silence of the Lambs* (1991) features a serial killer who attempts to play Dr. Frankenstein to himself.[1]

My focus in this essay is on one striking feature of this cinematic ge-nealogy: films that depict a female monster. In Mary Shelley's story, this possibility is invoked but never realized. Late in the novel, Victor Frankenstein reluctantly agrees to the monster's demands for a bride, but then, realizing that such a figure "might become ten thousand times more malignant than her mate," he aborts the female monster before animating her.[2] This "malignant" figure is nonetheless alive in many Frankenstein films, from James Whale's horror classic *Bride of Franken-stein* (1935) to such later spin-offs as *Frankenstein's Daughter* (1959) and *Frankenstein Created Woman* (1966). Often these films focus specifically on monstrous brides: one is simply entitled *The Bride* (1986), and another announces its debt to Whale with the title *Bride of Re-Animator* (1989).

When the monster is female, I suggest, two structural elements of the Frankenstein story are heightened: dismemberment and reanimation. While these elements are central to the making of *any* monster, they take on an added charge when they are applied to female bodies. In films with female Frankenstein monsters, dismemberment and reanimation are at once theme and technique: their narratives include sequences of men taking apart and reconstructing female bodies, while their cinematic form disassembles and reimagines the imagery of the Frankenstein story through parody and pastiche. Yet even as these films organize fantasies of male control over female bodies, I argue, they also undermine those fantasies. This unstable dynamic is already implicit in Whale's *Bride of Frankenstein*, the template for imagery of a female Frankenstein monster. It is further realized in divergent directions in two films of the last decade: Frank Henenlotter's 1990 low-budget cult movie *Frankenhooker* and Bill Condon's 1998 art film success, *Gods and Monsters*. In "low" and "high" cinematic registers, these films reveal some radical uses of the figure of the bride of Frankenstein. *Frankenhooker* suggests the feminist potential of the bride of Frankenstein story, while *Gods and Monsters* develops the gay male possibilities of Whale's original film. From its cinematic inception to its more recent incarnations, I argue, the bride of Frankenstein bridles at norms of both gender and sexuality. In so doing, this figure provides a valuable laboratory not only for studying the gendered anatomy of monstrous bodies, but also for understanding the ongoing cinematic modes through which such bodies continue to be brought to life.

In James Whale's *Bride of Frankenstein*, the monstrous bride appears only once, at the end. The climax of the film is a creation scene in which two scientists, Drs. Pretorius and Frankenstein, bring to life a female monster who is to be a companion to Boris Karloff's lonely male monster. But the bride—played, unforgettably, by Elsa Lanchester in a long white dress with a Nefertiti hairdo, glazed eyes, and jerky movements —recoils from the monster; enraged and despairing, he blows up the castle, killing all but Dr. Frankenstein and his bride, Elizabeth. This scene is notable for, among other things, its comically hyperbolic gender relations. The bride is a female body trafficked between men: the monster himself, Dr. Pretorius, and Dr. Frankenstein, whose own bride, Elizabeth, is abducted by the monster, in an intertwining of two women

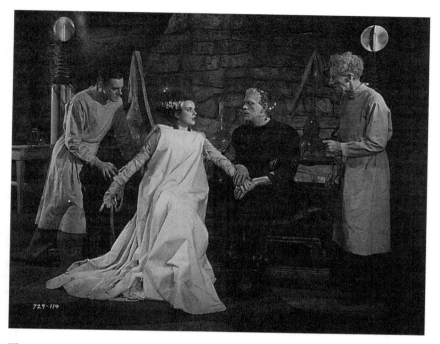

The original *Bride of Frankenstein* (Universal, 1935).

who both qualify for the title "bride of Frankenstein." Both brides are animated by men, a process that also functions reflexively, in the implicit parallel between male scientist and filmmaker. Like the scientist, the filmmaker animates lifeless images, or rather, *re*animates them, since *Bride* itself reprises and expands on images from Whale's own 1931 film *Frankenstein.* Yet if *Bride* seems to literalize a set of gender asymmetries, it also contests them. For one thing, the bride recoils not once but twice from the monster's touch. With her repeated shriek and her returned gaze, the bride incarnates from within the force of what Mary Russo has termed "the female grotesque" and Barbara Creed "the monstrous-feminine." The bride's rejection suggests the potential for resistance inherent in performing the role of the scary woman. In the initial cinematic incarnation of the bride of Frankenstein, monstrous female bodies are so powerful that they literally bring down the house.[3]

The potential power of female monstrosity is realized in unusually vivid form in the low-budget cult film *Frankenhooker.* In this loose rendering of the bride of Frankenstein story, a young man named Jeffrey

The lobby poster for Frank Henenlotter's hilarious low-budget monster picture, *Frankenhooker* (SGE, 1990).

Franken reconstructs his recently decapitated girlfriend, here called Elizabeth Shelley, by grafting her head onto the body parts of prostitutes. The reconstituted monster, Frankenhooker, runs amok and kills her male clients. In the climax of the film, Frankenhooker engages in an act of monstrous violence against her creator, when she straps Jeffrey to a laboratory table, anesthetizes him, and transforms him into a woman using spare female body parts. In the final scene of the film, Jeffrey wakes up, looks into a mirror, and sees that his head is attached to a naked, voluptuous female body. Despite Frankenhooker's attempts to soothe him, he screams with horror as the screen goes black. This scene is characteristic of *Frankenhooker*'s combination of comedy, horror, and pornography. As in *Bride*, dismemberment and reanimation characterize both theme and technique, but here in a deliberately crude register. This is a proudly lowbrow film about the legacy of a low-browed monster.[4]

Like Elsa Lanchester's over-the-top shriek in *Bride of Frankenstein*, the closing scene of *Frankenhooker* destabilizes the potential passivity of a bride of Frankenstein figure. In this case, however, the reversal is much more direct, as male scientist becomes female monster. When Jeffrey looks in the mirror and sees his female body, he is positioned as the object of his own horrified gaze. The moment is a comic literalization of the psychoanalytic narrative of the monstrous-feminine. For the mirror forces Jeffrey to see what the monstrous female body is often meant to hide: that is, the possibility of his own castration. Although Henenlotter is the actual creator of this scene, its on-screen author is a female monster. That this monster has the voice and face of Jeffrey's dead girlfriend suggests that even the story's supposed ingenue may be disingenuous, and female "brides," like female monsters, may be more cutting than they at first seem. *Frankenhooker* exemplifies, then, one possible expansion of the original instabilities of Whale's *Bride of Frankenstein*, into a film that emphasizes the potential power of the female monster. Through lowbrow parody, this version of the bride of Frankenstein takes male fantasy so far that it castrates itself.

If *Frankenhooker* expands the cutting force of Elsa Lanchester's shriek, then Bill Condon's *Gods and Monsters* takes the legacy of *Bride of Frankenstein* in a different direction, toward a radical examination of bonds between men. *Gods and Monsters*, based on the 1995 novel *Father of Frankenstein* by Christopher Bram, imagines the last weeks of British director James Whale in Los Angeles in 1957. *Gods and Monsters* is struc-

Director James Whale (Ian McKellen) and his gardener, Clay Boone (Brendan Fraser), at George Cukor's garden party in Bill Condon's deft examination of male bonding, *Gods and Monsters* (Lions Gate, 1998).

tured around a series of encounters between Whale (Ian McKellen) and a fictional character, a naive gardener named Clay Boone (Brendan Fraser). The film's present-day of 1957 is intercut with a series of flash-backs to Whale's childhood and World War I experience. It ends with his suicide by drowning, followed by a scene of Clay some years later.

Gods and Monsters is a complex film, whose exploration of sexuality, memory, art, and mortality demands full discussion in a variety of con-texts, particularly those of gay male representation; this is a film about a gay director by a gay director, starring an out gay actor and based on a book by a gay novelist.[5] I focus here on the figure of the bride of Frankenstein in *Gods and Monsters*, a figure that is thematically central to the gay possibilities of the film. This centrality is suggested in two ex-traordinary sequences. In the first, two groups of characters watch the original 1935 *Bride of Frankenstein* while it is shown on television. In a diner, Clay and his friends watch the film for the first time; meanwhile, in Whale's home, the director introduces the film to his skeptical house-keeper, Hanna, played by Lynn Redgrave. In this skillfully edited three-minute sequence, director Bill Condon crosscuts among *Bride of Frank-enstein*, the diner, and Whale's home; among characters within these settings; between point-of-view close-ups and long shots of groups; and between unmediated close-ups of *Bride of Frankenstein*, in which the film image exceeds the frame of the television, and longer shots in which the television is revealed as such. To return to the terms I've been using, Condon dismembers the Whale film and reanimates it through its new televisual context. As seen on TV within the diegesis of *Gods and Monsters*, James Whale's *Bride of Frankenstein* is a cinematic mirror through which we see the characters, as well as the original Whale film, reflected back in new form.

More specifically, the dozen clips excerpted from the original *Bride* in this sequence bring out the gay possibilities of Whale's film. A number of critics, including Vito Russo, Rhona Berenstein, Harry Benshoff, and Mark Bronski, have articulated gay readings of *Bride of Frank-enstein*; Condon's ingenious contribution is to offer such a reading through his very abridgement of the original.[6] Thus the first substantial clip focuses on Dr. Pretorius and his invocation of "a world of gods and monsters." With his effete, aesthete ways, Pretorius is a connotatively gay figure, unmistakably camp and homoerotically linked with Dr. Frankenstein throughout the film. If the scientist-gods of the film seem queer, so do its monsters. In the next clip, the monster holds up a skull and poignantly asks, "Woman—friend—why?" His query moves away from heterosexuality as the only prized affective bond, toward the more general category of "friend." ("Friend" is also the epigraph to Bram's novel *Father of Frankenstein*.) The final two scenes excerpted from Whale's *Bride* show the monster's self-inflicted death and the clos-ing embrace of Dr. Frankenstein and Elizabeth. Completing Condon's abridgement, these images suggest the cost of gayness in a world that sacrifices both gods and monsters in the relentless drive toward hetero-sexual closure.

This version of Whale's *Bride of Frankenstein* both draws force from and further shapes the two diegetic worlds with which it is crosscut, Clay's diner and Whale's home. The scene of the monster asking, "Woman—friend—why?" is viewed by Clay, who responds, "The mon-ster's lonely. He wants a friend—girlfriend—somebody." As this echo suggests, the monster's quest provides a framework for understanding

Clay's own nonnormative status as an unmarried adult, as well as his growing closeness to Whale. Whale is himself affiliated first in this sequence with gods, not monsters. He describes Karloff as "the dullest figure imaginable" and laughs appreciatively after seeing Dr. Pretorius. But Whale is also identified with the monster; the shot of the monster declaring, "I love dead—hate living," for example, is followed by a close-up of a deeply moved Whale, suggesting that the monster's line provides a gloss on Whale's own sense of mortality and his memories of the dead. Elsewhere, the connection is even more direct, when Whale describes himself as "a freak of nature."

If Whale is monster as well as god, then Clay is god as well as monster. In a film that emphasizes, as Mark Bronski argues, a belief in "the healing nature of homoeroticism," Clay's status as an object of desire and conduit to memory makes him a godlike figure to the older man.[7] When Whale later dreams that both men are in the Frankenstein story, Clay plays Dr. Frankenstein to Whale's monster. As both gods and monsters, moreover, the two men are also linked to each other. This linkage is advanced through the editing of response shots: a shot of Whale laughing at Pretorius cuts to one of Clay looking puzzled at the same image, while Clay's defense of the monster cuts immediately to Whale's pensive response. The film *Bride of Frankenstein* is not only an animating narrative for each man, but a medium of homosocial exchange bringing them together.

And what of the bride? In an interpretation focused on the gay possibilities of Whale's film, the bride's shriek is less a resistant moment of female power than a voice of conservative reaction against the ostensible sexual unnaturalness of the monster. Both Betty, Clay's erstwhile girlfriend, and Hanna, Whale's housekeeper, reprise this version of rejecting the bride. Condon cuts from Elsa Lanchester rejecting the monster to a shot of Betty's approving response, talking back to Elsa Lanchester, "You don't want him." Hanna, herself a mixture of funny and scary, is another bride figure, positioned here with Whale in comic two-shots that make them seem a parody of an old married couple watching TV. Although Hanna calls the bride of Frankenstein "horrible," it is she who occupies the space of the grotesque, with her heavy makeup, her malapropisms, and, most important, her attitudes. Like Betty, she dislikes *Bride of Frankenstein*, and her harsh final review—"the bad people are dead, good people live"—indirectly reinforces the judgment that she elsewhere declares overtly, when she tells Clay that Whale will "suffer the fires of hell" for his homosexuality. Hanna is treated parodically, but the target of the parody is serious. Hers is the monstrosity of homophobia.

Like *Frankenhooker*, *Gods and Monsters* pays affectionate homage to the imagery of the bride of Frankenstein story. Where *Frankenhooker* takes a hyperbolically lowbrow approach to this legacy, *Gods and Monsters* dramatizes the place of the "low" Frankenstein story within higher cultural registers, from James Whale's self-construction as a British gentleman in America, to the cultural capital associated with the casting of Sir Ian McKellen, to *Gods and Monsters'* own positioning as an art film. In both *Frankenhooker* and *Gods and Monsters*, moreover, bride figures have power over the telling of the story. The television-watching sequence begins with Betty turning on the television in the diner, and it ends with Hanna turning off the television in the house. But unlike *Frankenhooker*, these bride figures do not challenge gender norms in the service of enlarging female authority. The role of Hanna seems misogynist, not only because she looks and sounds grotesque, but also because she assumes the voice of homophobia for the film as a whole. Rather than extend the *female* power of the bride, this sequence suggests that the truest inheritors of Elsa Lanchester's legacy in *Gods and Monsters* are its gay men—from the actor playing Dr. Pretorius, Ernest Thesiger, who proudly announces her birth, to Whale, who declares, "She's beautiful." Unlike Jeffrey in *Frankenhooker*, who is outraged to see himself in female form, the gay men in *Gods and Monsters* happily embrace the legacy of Elsa Lanchester for themselves. To put it another way, what *Frankenhooker* sees as a fear of becoming female is in *Gods and Monsters* a fantasy of creating femininity.

The cathartic relation of Elsa Lanchester to the film's gay men is made more explicit in the sequence that immediately follows the television-watching one, when Whale has a flashback to the set of *Bride of Frankenstein*. Having transformed *Bride* by placing it within a new viewing context, Condon takes the next step, and reconstructs the making of the original film. We see the set of *Bride of Frankenstein*, with actors portraying Elsa Lanchester (the bride), Ernest Thesiger (Pretorius), and Colin Clive (Frankenstein), as Whale prepares to film the creation scene. Upon first seeing Lanchester costumed as the bride, Thesiger launches a witty exchange:

THESIGER: My god, is the audience to assume that Colin and I have done her hair? I thought we were mad scientists, not hairdressers.

LANCHESTER: Only a mad scientist could have done this to a woman. [. . .] In the sequel, James, two lady scientists should make a monster. Our monster will be Gary Cooper.

THESIGER: I thought Leslie Howard would be more your line.

LANCHESTER: More your line, I think.

THESIGER: My line nowadays runs to Rin-Tin-Tin.

[Colin Clive enters]

THESIGER: I gather we not only did her hair but dressed her— what a couple of queens we are, Colin.

WHALE: Yes . . . a couple of flaming queens. [To Colin Clive] Pretorius is a little bit in love with Dr. Frankenstein, you know?

This scene reanimates the gay potential of the film *Bride of Frankenstein* by making explicit its links to 1930s Hollywood. Mad scientist becomes gay hairdresser, Ernest Thesiger chooses between Leslie Howard and Rin-Tin-Tin, and Doctors Frankenstein and Pretorius are named as "a couple of flaming queens." Together with the uncanny visual re-creation of the original actors, the dialogue both draws from and reinforces the excessive, exaggerated, parodic, and otherwise camp possibilities of the original Whale film. The gay references of the dialogue gain extra charge from the obliviousness of Colin Clive, who is scripted as the scene's straight man in both senses of the term. Named as "flaming queen" by Thesiger and object of Pretorius's desire by Whale, Clive anchors this scene's evocation of gay possibilities both on the set and in the story of *Bride of Frankenstein*.

As before, the figure of the bride of Frankenstein is central. Elsa Lanchester's character, the bride of Frankenstein, is presented as the creation of the two overtly gay men, her birth proudly announced by Thesiger and lovingly staged, filmed, and remembered in flashback by Whale. But Lanchester also has a more active role, bantering archly with Thesiger and Whale and imagining a reversed homoerotic world with "two lady scientists" making a Gary Cooper monster. This characterization undercuts the misogyny with which Hanna is scripted, and moves the figure of the bride toward greater agency. The film's step outward from the diegesis of *Bride of Frankenstein* back to its movie set moves the bride beyond her shriek. In Condon's meticulous homage to the world of James Whale, Elsa Lanchester both reanimates Whale's memory and speaks in an animated voice of her own. The female voice is, to be sure, briefly heard: the character of Elsa Lanchester stops speaking by the end of this scene. The ending of the film, meanwhile, has a silencing effect on its sexual themes; showing Clay years later with a wife and son, the last scene seems to undercut the narrative of gay male possibility that precedes it. But even in a slightly misshapen state, *Gods and Monsters* suggests the continuing cinematic lifeblood, as well as the transgressive possibilities, provided by the figure of the bride of Frankenstein.

In combining analyses of these two films, I have aimed to generate some reanimating connective tissue of my own. Ideologically, these films suggest the salience of both gender and sexuality to the bride of Frankenstein narrative, and to films about female monsters more generally. Formally, these films suggest a congruence between "low" and "high" uses of the monstrous bride, not only because *Gods and Monsters* is "high" to *Frankenhooker*'s "low," but also because *Gods and Monsters* plays with the high/low distinction itself. Subject to incision, amputation, and decapitation, the body of Whale's *Bride of Frankenstein* is also available for constant rebirth. In this ongoing cycle of dismemberment and reanimation, the figure of the bride of Frankenstein remains highly charged, vivifying film at the end of the century.

NOTES

1. For an overview of Frankenstein films, see Donald F. Glut, *The Frankenstein Catalog* (Jefferson, NC: McFarland, 1984), 156–240. On the proliferation of Frankenstein imagery in popular culture, see also Chris Baldick, *In Frankenstein's Shadow: Myth, Monstrosity, and Nineteenth-Century Writing* (Oxford: Clarendon, 1987); Steven Earl Forry, *Hideous Progenies: Dramatizations of Frankenstein from Mary Shelley to the Present* (Philadelphia: University of Pennsylvania Press, 1990); and Albert J. LaValley, "The Stage and Film Children of Frankenstein: A Survey," in *The Endurance of Frankenstein*, ed. George Levine and U. C. Knoepflmacher (Berkeley: University of California Press, 1979), 243–89.

2. Mary Shelley, *Frankenstein*, ed. Maurice Hindle (Harmondsworth: Penguin, 1992), 160. There is a large body of criticism on gender in the novel; for a recent assessment of this criticism, see Ellen Cronan Rose, "Custody Battles: Reproducing Knowledge about *Frankenstein*," *New Literary History* 26, no. 4 (1995): 809–32.

3. See Barbara Creed, *The Monstrous-Feminine: Film, Feminism, Psychoanalysis* (London: Routledge, 1993); and Mary Russo, *The Female Grotesque: Risk, Excess, Modernity* (New York: Routledge, 1994). For an overview of *Bride of Frankenstein*, see Alberto Manguel, *Bride of Frankenstein* (London: British Film Institute, 1997). I discuss the film at greater length in Elizabeth Young, "Here Comes the Bride: Wedding, Gender, and Race in *Bride of Frankenstein*," in *The Dread of Difference: Gender and the Horror Film*, ed. Barry Keith Grant (Austin: University of Texas Press, 1996), 309–37.

4. The director of *Frankenhooker*, Frank Henenlotter, is a historian of lowbrow horror; see "Frank Henenlotter," interview by Andrea Juno, in *Incredibly Strange Films*, Re/Search 10, ed. V. Vale and Andrea Juno (San Francisco: Re/Search, 1986), 8–17. For an analysis of *Frankenhooker*, see Mia Mazza, "Postmodern Feminism and *Frankenhooker*," *Spectator* 12, no. 1 (fall 1991): 34–43.

5. On the film in the context of gay Hollywood, see David Ehrenstein, *Open Secret: Gay Hollywood, 1928–1998* (New York: William Morrow, 1998), 57–71. On *Gods and Monsters*, see also Mark Bronski, "Gods and Monsters: The Search for the Right Whale," *Cineaste* 24, no. 4 (1999): 10–14; Joseph McBride, "The Joys of Necrophilia," *New York Review of Books*, 15 July 1999, 36–39; and Richard Porton, "*Gods and Monsters*: An Interview with Ian McKellen," *Cineaste* 24, no. 4 (1999): 15. On James Whale, see James Curtis, *James Whale: A New World of Gods and Monsters* (London: Faber and Faber, 1988) and Mark Gatiss, *James Whale: A Biography* (New York: Cassell, 1995).

6. See Vito Russo, *The Celluloid Closet: Homosexuality in the Movies* (1981; rev. ed. New York: Harper and Row, 1987), 49–52; Rhona J. Berenstein, *Attack of the Leading Ladies: Gender, Sexuality, and Spectatorship in Classic Horror Cinema* (New York: Columbia University Press, 1996), 136–47; Harry Benshoff, *Monsters in the Closet: Homosexuality and the Horror Film* (Manchester: Manchester University Press, 1997); and Bronski, "Gods and Monsters."

7. Bronski, "Gods and Monsters," 13.

23

Having Their Cake and Eating It Too

Fat Acceptance Films and the Production of Meaning

Jerry Mosher

> Here it is at last, at long last, after years and years and years: A movie
> where the smart fat kid gets the girl and humiliates the football hero.
> They say if you go to enough movies, sooner or later you will see your
> own story, and believe me, *The Natural* wasn't mine.
> —Roger Ebert, review of *Angus*, *Chicago Sun-
> Times*, September 15, 1995

BETWEEN THE SPRING of 1995 and the fall of 1996, five American
feature films portrayed a fat character's struggles with weight and social intolerance: *Heavyweights*, a Disney comedy about a group of fat
boys at a summer fitness camp; *Angus*, a bittersweet look at a fat teenager's problems in high school; *Heavy*, an indie sleeper about a shy
pizza chef that won a Special Jury Award at the 1995 Sundance Film
Festival; *The Nutty Professor* (1996), the hit remake of the 1963 Jerry
Lewis comedy starring Eddie Murphy as a bumbling college professor
morphing between fat and thin bodies; and *Thinner*, a Stephen King
story about a fat lawyer who cannot lose weight until he is cursed by
gypsies. Until this point, fat, with a few exceptions, had not been a topic
of feature films, but had been relegated to the medium of television, in
an occasional sitcom "message" episode or made-for-TV movie. While
fat actors have always been found on the big screen, a sustained, feature-length portrayal of fat experience—and, most significantly, fat sexuality—had not been produced until 1980's *Fatso*. Since then, only a few
feature films, such as *Polyester* (1981), *I Don't Buy Kisses Anymore* (1992),

Death Becomes Her (1992), and *What's Eating Gilbert Grape* (1993) had raised the issue of what it means to be fat in America.[1]

Obesity is one of the nation's leading health concerns. Estimates by the medical establishment in the mid-1990s claimed that approximately 25 percent of American adults were medically obese (20 percent above maximum healthy body weight) and 55 percent were overweight (any weight above the maximum healthy weight). Since the late 1960s, the number of overweight Americans has increased by one-third.[2] During that time, a growing fat rights movement has argued that fat is not a medical condition or a problem of public health, but rather a cultural construction and a problem of discrimination.[3] For fat rights activists, the release of *Heavyweights, Angus, Heavy, The Nutty Professor*, and *Thinner* marked the breakthrough of fat acceptance into mainstream American media. In these films, they noted, constant dieting to maintain slimness was aptly depicted as a curse worse than being fat.

The range of representations in the five films substantiate both medical and cultural perspectives on fat.[4] Several of the films mix messages of fat acceptance with jokes about body size, prompting some reviewers to accuse the filmmakers of "having their cake and eating it too." Indeed, the films' polysemic potential is made evident by the varying opinions of reviewers, whose widely divergent readings of the films often revealed more about their readership than about the films themselves.[5] In reviews, writes Chon Noriega, a film "first reveals itself as a multiple text, since each publication offers a different interpretation, one that either reflects, anticipates or attempts to influence the expectations of its readership."[6] How, then, did self-identifying members of fat groups receive these films? Did they construct meaning in ways discernibly different from reviewers for mainstream media readerships?[7]

Recognizing reception's importance to the production of meaning in these films, I will examine their publicity materials and reviews in mainstream, alternative, and fat acceptance publications and Web sites. Of particular interest will be the ideological distinctions between film reviewing that ostensibly serves to assist consumer choice and film reviewing that serves to promote identity, community, and, in this instance, a social movement. Throughout, I will analyze the ways the fat body is read as a culturally coded sign, in order to ascertain whether or not the release of the five films in 1995–96 marks a substantive change in the fat body's representation and potential for social articulation in American cinema.

FAT BY ANY OTHER NAME

Advertising tag lines, press releases, and production notes for the five films offer insight into the way studios manipulate what Hans Robert Jauss calls the "horizon of expectations," which "predisposes its audience to a very specific kind of reception by announcements, overt and covert signals, familiar characteristics, or implicit allusions."[8] What is especially revealing about the promotional material for the five films is what *isn't* said: the word "fat" is never used. Instead, the studios marketed the main characters as "lovable outsiders." For example, the production notes for *The Nutty Professor* include euphemisms like "big man on campus" to describe four hundred-pound Professor Sherman Klump. Despite the film's litany of fat jokes and obsession with flatulence, the story is posed as an outsider's noble struggle to fit in. Star Eddie Murphy declares in the production notes, "The physical stuff is superficial; what counts is who you are as a person. That's the simple truth we tried to tell."[9]

Similarly, promotional material describes *Heavyweights* as "the hilarious story of a group of underdog kids" ("they're big, loud and proud, and ready to win their way into your heart!"). The tag line for *Angus* likewise proclaims, "He doesn't fit in. He never gives up. He's something else!" That "something else," of course, is fat.

Such evasive wording neglects a fundamental issue of identity formation: the importance of naming. The National Association to Advance Fat Acceptance defends use of the word "fat": "It is an adjective, like short, tall, thin, or blonde. While society has given it a derogatory meaning, we find that identifying ourselves as 'fat' is an important step in casting off the shame we have been taught to feel about our bodies."[10] Fat protagonists and fat acceptance make these films unique. The studios' unwillingness to advertise that fact reveals their belief that the American audience will not pay to see movies about fat people, even if a majority of that audience is fat.[11] Moreover, their evasive wording undermines the very premise of the films by discursively denying "fat" as a legitimate and justifiable state of

Eddie Murphy as "the big man on campus," Sherman Klump, in *The Nutty Professor* (Universal, 1996). Fat jokes abound in the film, like this one in an aerobics studio.

being. It is thus not surprising that a growing number of fat people (myself included) have felt the need to actively "come out" as fat and thereby insist on what Eve Kosovsky Sedgwick and Michael Moon term "a renegotiation of the representational contract between one's body and one's world."[12]

Many mainstream newspaper reviews echoed the publicity materials' "lovable outsider" motif.[13] Reviews of *Angus*, for example, often reduced the film to the typical struggles of any teenager, comparing it to *The Revenge of the Nerds* (1984). The scholarly film magazine *Sight and Sound* was more philosophical about the "outsider" issue, commenting that "*Angus* argues that resistance to homogeneity causes the system to accommodate difference." *The Nutty Professor*'s over-the-top cruelty, however, prevented most reviewers from accepting Murphy's disingenuous "accept what you are" moral. The *San Francisco Chronicle* wrote, "There's a sentimental, love-the-inner-man message at the end, but it feels hypocritical after 95 minutes of fatty barbs." Many reviewers noted that such half-hearted attempts to deliver positive messages in *The Nutty Professor* and *Heavyweights* only served to undermine their comic and subversive elements. The *Washington Post* thus asked of *Heavyweights*, "Should a kids' movie be criticized for being too goody-goody and socially sensitive and correct?"[14]

FAT MASQUERADE

The specificity of fat experience was further diffused by the use of thin-bodied stars (Eddie Murphy in *The Nutty Professor*, Robert John Burke in *Thinner*), transformed by extensive make-up and computer graphics morphing to imitate fat bodies. Most mainstream reviews praised *The Nutty Professor*'s morphs, noting that such spectacular effects would enable it to compete with 1996's summer action movies. By striving for the extraordinary rather than the merely realistic, however, the special effects in *The Nutty Professor* and *Thinner* served to remind audiences that they were not watching fat men—they were watching Murphy and Burke *imitate* fat men.[15] The *Los Angeles Times* thus noted of *Thinner*,

Like Eddie Murphy in *The Nutty Professor*, Robert John Burke, the star of *Thinner* (Paramount, 1996), is a skinny guy morphed by special effects, padded costumes, and makeup to appear fat. Such special effects remind us that we're not watching fat men, we're watching actors imitate fat men.

"Burke, under a suffocating layer of Greg Cannom's special effects, does a great impression of a man drowning in his own flesh."

Further obscuring the issue of fat was *The Nutty Professor*'s reception as Eddie Murphy's return to form, a "morph" of his sagging career. Many mainstream reviews interpreted the film's Jekyll-and-Hyde plot as a deliberate allegory: the fat, cuddly professor Sherman Klump symbolized Murphy's return to likability (and bankability), and the thin, obnoxious Buddy Love exemplified the failed characters of Murphy's recent box office duds.[16] Murphy's apologetic lines near the end of the film ("Buddy's who I thought the world wanted me to be. He's who I thought I wanted to be. But I was wrong"), spoken directly to the camera, were perceived by several reviewers to be a direct reference to his recent career miscues. Mainstream reviewers were so taken with Murphy's performance, in fact, that most were willing to overlook *The Nutty Professor*'s hypocrisy. After pointing out the film's cruelty toward fat people, the *San Francisco Chronicle* wrote, "Not that moral uplift is the point here. This is a chance to see Murphy doing what he does best, and for that alone it's worth seeing."

Of the three films portraying fat adults, only one—the independent drama *Heavy*—used a fat actor (Pruitt Taylor Vince). The makers of *Heavyweights* and *Angus,* on the other hand, found it acceptable to cast fat boys. Such casting practices convey the message that children's fat is presentable because it is presumably innocent and beyond their control, whereas adult fat must be contained within the transforming effects of masquerade. The more intolerant standards of beauty to which women are held were reflected in the fact that none of these films told the story of a fat woman, which went without comment in the reviews.

Murphy's masquerade as a fat man did provoke vitriolic responses from two fat acceptance reviewers, who viewed his performance as an example of one marginalized group (African Americans) oppressing another (fat people).[17] Responding to the frequent fat jokes in *The Nutty Professor*, the reviewer "Jellyroll" commented, "People get sued over racial slurs and the like, but . . . way too many people see nothing wrong with walking up to a large person and hurling insults at them." *The Fat Person's Page* agreed and posed this question: "I wonder how amused movie audiences in the last decade of this century would be if the star of this movie was John Goodman, and he spent the first half of the movie in blackface, then his life got better when he wiped it off." The fact that the fat, African American professor decides to change his size

The fat kids at the fat camp are funny: a group shot of the portly underdogs in *Heavyweights* (Disney, 1995).

and not his color, according to *The Fat Person's Page*, suggests that "even the politically elite in Hollywood are admitting that it is now a greater social and economic liability to be fat in this country than it is to be black." While such an assertion may too easily gloss over the different historic experiences of the two oppressed groups, it astutely highlights fat's emergence as a social issue deemed worthy of big-budget motion pictures.

In publications not ostensibly focused on fat acceptance, only the alternative San Francisco *MetroActive* specifically addressed the standards of body size in the African American community. It noted, "African-American culture is one in which there was, at least once upon a time, lots of room for fat people." The reviewer thus reads the Klump family's unrestrained eating as "a vision of unassimilated funk," contrasted with the pressure on Professor Klump to "conform to a slighter —and dare we say, *whiter*?—ideal." Images of the African American professor binge eating and weeping alone in front of TV images in which he has no part, the *MetroActive* suggests, "owes as much to Ralph Ellison as it does to Jerry Lewis." In this light, the Klump family's corpulence is not a source of shame, but rather an assertion of cultural difference.

FAT RAGE AND THE TESTIMONIAL

While *Heavyweights* and *The Nutty Professor* were roundly accused of paternalistic containment of their fat characters, *Heavy*, the story of a 250-pound pizza chef who struggles to escape the control of his doting mother, was widely praised for its warts-and-all rendering of a fat man's intimate life. *Heavy* revealed the eating binges, rages, and sexual fantasies of a fat man who, according to the *Los Angeles Times*, stood as "a figure of grave dignity and vulnerability." The San Francisco *MetroActive* offered the most radical assessment of the film's unpatronizing portrayal of binge eating and rage: "This is transgressive behavior that shocks and angers all the right people. . . . And it's a gesture that will never be co-opted by corporate capitalism and the mass media." Indeed, fat jokes and fat kids have proven market appeal, but fat rage makes visible the discomforting excess that America's economy of abundance so desperately attempts to conceal. Fat rage asserts an embodied experience that refuses to be shamed into invisibility.

Rage is apparent throughout Jellyroll's review of *The Nutty Professor*, in which she exclaims, "everyone's in hysterics with the antics of this man, but I experience things like that everyday . . . every fat joke I was ever subjected to in my 36 years on this Earth were [*sic*] flashing before my eyes on the screen." The recounting of personal experience in this review is characteristic of film criticism emerging from the fat community, but this strategy is not limited to fat acceptance publications. In his sympathetic review of *Angus* quoted at the beginning of this essay, Roger Ebert—one of the most recognized film critics in America—similarly draws on the testimonial. Richard von Busack's insightful review of *Heavy* for the San Francisco *MetroActive* begins with a testimony regarding his weight: "When . . . the hero of *Heavy* got on a scale and fretted over the reading '250,' all I could think was 'Lucky.'" While personal testimony may hold film representations accountable to a standard of realism that overlooks their fictive constructs, it also inverts supposedly "universal" representations of oppression and acceptance, rendering them culturally specific and unique. Testimonials thus speak to other members of the fat community in a way that objective-based, formalist criticism cannot.

It is not surprising that mainstream reviewers tended to reduce issues of fat identity to universal stories of outsiders trying to fit in, for in most

cases the films—and the horizon of expectations studio publicity created for them—exhibited the same tendency. Even when mainstream
reviewers condemned this numbing trivialization and identified fat as
an important social issue, their condemnation tended to be blindingly
total. Few were able to recognize within these universal themes the intimate details of fat embodiment—the desire, rage, fantasy, and frustration—that contribute to the experience of being fat in America. This is
where the major distinction between publications occurs: mainstream
reviewers, serving as consumer guides, proved capable of identifying
the universal themes but failed to see how they could account for anything other than Hollywood's creative bankruptcy. Reviewers for fat
acceptance and some alternative publications, on the other hand, re-
contextualized these themes through use of testimonials and advocacy
criticism, thereby personalizing and revitalizing stories that to other reviewers seemed only formulaic. Fat acceptance reviews can thus be
seen as an effort to assert the uniqueness of fat experience and expand
the films' horizon of expectations, countering the "one-size-fits-all" lovable outsider discourses found in the films' publicity materials. These
personal testimonies demonstrate how the films' contradictory moods
of cruelty and acceptance replicate the very hypocrisy that fat people in
America face every day.

The release of the five films in 1995–96 remains historically significant as a point of emergence for fat awareness in mainstream American
film. This was duly noted by a few reviewers, who lamented the fact
that filmmakers didn't do more with the material. Of course, the same
criticism could be leveled at film reviewers. As uneven as the films
might have been, the raw material for the critical interrogation of fat
representation was there for the taking. Looking the other way to focus
only on the jokes and star performances amounts to a form of critical silence. Such silence might be more difficult to maintain as fat acceptance
continues to make headlines. Indeed, in 1998 the *New England Journal of
Medicine* published an editorial urging more fat acceptance among
medical practitioners, and in 2000 San Francisco became the third U.S.
city to enact an anti–size discrimination law.[18] Whether the five films of
1995–96 have influenced the horizon of expectations for future fat acceptance films and the representation of fat people remains to be seen.[19]
By giving voices to characters undergoing the experience of being fat in
America, the films did provide fat audiences with ample material from
which to discursively produce meaning and identity.

NOTES

I wish to thank Chon Noriega, Vivian Sobchack, and Jon Lewis for their valuable assistance with this essay.

1. Although fat experience is not the ostensible topic of his films, John Waters has probably revealed more about fat and cultural identity than any other American filmmaker. Since the late 1960s he has repeatedly cast fat actors such as Divine, Edith Massey, Jean Hill, and Ricki Lake in "underground" films such as *Pink Flamingos* (1972) and *Desperate Living* (1977), and in mainstream releases such as *Polyester* (1981) and *Hairspray* (1986).

2. Michael Fumento, *The Fat of the Land: Our Health Crisis and How Overweight Americans Can Help Themselves* (New York: Penguin, 1997), 1–55.

3. Many fat rights activists acknowledge that excessive fat can contribute to cardiovascular disease, but argue that fatness is unfairly persecuted as solely a behavioral deviation when it is actually determined by a variety of factors, among them genetic, environmental, and cultural. They maintain that moderate fatness is not necessarily unhealthy, but its stigmatization is necessary to sustain the billion-dollar diet and fitness industries. For a history of the fat rights movement in the United States and Great Britain, see Charlotte Cooper, *Fat and Proud: The Politics of Size* (London: Women's Press, 1998).

4. Kathy Bates, one of the few fat women to sustain a career as a lead actor in contemporary American cinema, appears in *Angus* as the title character's truck-driver mother, but it is an underwritten, thankless role. Bates and George C. Scott (who plays her father) appear only briefly to give pep talks to Angus and demonstrate that his size is an inherited trait.

5. The film reviews surveyed for this analysis are cited below. Because it would be cumbersome to footnote the numerous quotations from these reviews individually , please refer to this bibliography.

Heavyweights (released February 17, 1995):
L.A. Weekly, Feb. 17–23, Elizabeth Pincus; *Los Angeles Times*, Feb. 17, Peter Rainer; *New York Times*, Feb. 17, Stephen Holden; *Variety*, Feb. 20, Leonard Klady; *Washington Post*, Feb. 17, Hal Hinson.

Angus (released September 15, 1995):
Chicago Sun-Times, Sept. 15, Roger Ebert; *Fat Girl*, <http://www.fatso.com/fatgirl/fatpubs.html>; *Fat!So?* <http://www.fatso.com>; *L.A. Weekly*, Sept. 15–21, Hazel-Dawn Dumpert; *Los Angeles Times*, Sept. 15, Kevin Thomas; *MetroActive*, Don Hines, <http://www.metroactive.com/movies/capsule-a.html>; *New York Times*, Sept. 15, Janet Maslin; *San Francisco Chronicle*, Sept. 15, Peter Stack; *Sight and Sound*, April 1996, Claire Monk; *Variety*, Sept. 18, Godfrey Cheshire; *Village Voice*, Sept. 26, Georgia Brown; *Washington Post*, Sept. 15, Rita Kempley.

Heavy (released June 28, 1996):
Chicago Sun-Times, June 28, Roger Ebert; *L.A. Weekly*, June 28–July 4, Ella Taylor; *Los Angeles Times*, June 28, Kevin Thomas; *MetroActive*, July 11–17, Richard von Busack, <http://www.metroactive.com/movies/capsule-h.html>; *Nation*, June 24, Stuart Klawans; *New Yorker*, June 17, Terence Rafferty; *New York Times*, June 5, Janet Maslin; *Phoenix New Times*, June 28–July 4, M. V. Moorhead; *San Francisco Chronicle*, July 12, Edward Guthmann; *Sight and Sound*, Jan. 1996, Amanda Lipman; *Variety*, Feb. 6, 1995 (Sundance), Todd McCarthy; *Village Voice*, June 11, Amy Taubin; *Washington Post*, July 19, Hal Hinson.

The Nutty Professor (released June 28, 1996):
Chicago Sun-Times, June 28, Roger Ebert; *The Fat Person's Page*, Joe Obrin, <http://www.io.com/~joeobrin/nutty.html>; *Jellyroll home page*, Lori A. Shuler Fogg, <http://www.shulersnet.com/jellyroll/nutty.html>; *L.A. Weekly*, June 28–July 4, Ella Taylor; *Los Angeles Times*, June 28, Kenneth Turan; *MetroActive*, Richard von Busack, <http://www.metroactive.com/movies/capsule-n.html>; *New Yorker*, July 8, Anthony Lane; *New York Times*, June 28, Janet Maslin; *San Francisco Chronicle*, June 28, Edward Guthmann; *Sight and Sound*, Oct. 1996, Philip Kemp; *Variety*, June 24, Leonard Klady; *Village Voice,* July 9, Gary Dauphin; *Washington Post*, June 28, Rita Kempley.

Thinner (released October 28, 1996):
L.A. Weekly, Nov. 1–7, Paul Malcolm; *Los Angeles Times*, Oct. 28, John Anderson; *MetroActive*, Richard von Busack, <http://www.metroactive.com/movies/capsule-t.html>; *New York Times*, Oct. 26, Lawrence Van Gelder; *San Francisco Chronicle*, Oct. 26, Mick LaSalle; *Sight and Sound*, Aug. 1997, Kim Newman; *Variety*, Oct. 28, Leonard Klady.

   6. Chon A. Noriega, "Chicano Cinema and the Horizon of Expectations: A Discursive Analysis of Film Reviews in the Mainstream, Alternative and Hispanic Press, 1987–1988," *Aztlán* 19, no. 2 (fall 1988–90): 2.
   7. For years organizations like the National Association to Advance Fat Acceptance (established 1969) and its local chapters relied on newsletters to disseminate information, whereas smaller corporeal communities favored "zines" —irreverent xeroxed publications like *FatGirl* and *Fat!So?* By the early 1990s the widespread accessibility of the Internet transformed the communication and self-identifying practices of subcultural groups, whose constituents went online to form "virtual communities" in chat rooms, discussion lists, and Web pages. Many fat acceptance newsletters and zines changed to an online format; today, the *Dimensions* magazine Web page <http://www.pencomputing.com/dim/> offers links to hundreds of fat acceptance Web sites that express a wide range of voices from the institutional to the idiosyncratic. Although film criticism in

these sites remains infrequent, image analysis has emerged as a tool of social change and self-identification within corporeal communities, as groups like About-Face <http://www.about-face.org/> devote themselves to combating "negative and distorted images of women" in fashion advertising.

8. Hans Robert Jauss, *Toward an Aesthetic of Reception*, trans. Timothy Bahti (Minneapolis: University of Minnesota Press, 1982), 23.

9. *The Nutty Professor* Production Notes, <http://www.afronet.com/NUTTYPROF/nutty-prof.html>, March 1998.

10. National Association to Advance Fat Acceptance, "Why Do We Use the Word 'Fat' So Freely?" <http://naafa.org/documents/brochures/naafa-info.html#word> The NAAFA argues that "obesity" is a pathologized term of the medical industry.

11. The alternative *Phoenix New Times* articulated the film industry's position in its perceptive review of *Heavy*: "Hollywood is never too comfortable with obesity as a serious subject because fatness bumps up against one of American moviedom's few absolutes: The people with whom the audience is asked to identify must look good."

12. Eve Kosofsky Sedgwick and Michael Moon, "Divinity: A Performance Piece, A Little-Understood Emotion," in Sedgwick, *Tendencies* (Durham: Duke University Press, 1993), 230.

13. Most reviews of *Heavyweights* noted that its director, Steven Brill, wrote the first two *Mighty Ducks* films (1992–94), which employed a similar "underdog kids" formula.

14. Critical praise was strongest for the independent *Heavy*, which, like *The Nutty Professor*, was widely reviewed, although it grossed less than one-tenth as much money as the Eddie Murphy hit. The lack of reviews for *Thinner* was not surprising, as the distributor did not preview the film for critics in many cities, a sure sign of a bomb. Likewise, Disney's decision to release *Heavyweights*—a kid's summer camp movie—in February suggests that the studio had little faith in its market potential and was merely trying to minimize its losses. Some critical silence on *Heavyweights* and *Angus* was to be expected, as both films were targeted at youth audiences, upon whom reviews have little influence. According to the Internet Movie Database, the films' domestic grosses are as follows: *The Nutty Professor*, $128.8 million; *Heavyweights*, $17.7 million; *Thinner*, $15.2 million; *Angus*, $4.8 million; *Heavy*, $852, 362.

15. A variant of this phenomenon is the highly publicized real-life weight gain, most famously demonstrated by Robert DeNiro in *Raging Bull* (1980) and emulated by dozens of actors since then.

16. For example, the *Chicago Sun-Times* commented, "There is a lot of Buddy Love in the Eddie Murphy screen persona. Maybe too much. And not enough Sherman Klump." And the *Los Angeles Times* noted, "The least likable

impersonation, ironically enough, is closest to Murphy's previous onscreen roles, while the most appealing acts least of all like the ghost of Eddie past."

17. In Hollywood social problem films dealing with the "building up" of a particular ethnic or racial group, Charles Ramírez Berg has noted their similar tendency to "partake in a strange kind of Other tunnelvision, losing sight in the process of their insensitive stereotyping of any but the focused-upon ethnic or racial group." Charles Ramírez Berg, "*Bordertown*, the Assimilation Narrative, and the Chicano Social Problem Film," *Chicanos and Film: Representation and Resistance*, ed. Chon A. Noriega (Minneapolis: University of Minnesota Press, 1992), 37.

18. "Losing Weight—An Ill-Fated New Year's Resolution," *New England Journal of Medicine* 338, no. 1 (January 1, 1998): 52–54. The state of Michigan and the cities of Washington, D.C., and Santa Cruz, California, also have laws against size discrimination.

19. Two fat acceptance films were released in the summer of 2000. *The Nutty Professor II*, like its predecessor, buried its half-hearted moral under a barrage of caricatures, morphs, and gross-out humor. *The Tao of Steve*, a lightweight romantic comedy, featured a fat womanizer (tag line: "Why do women find this man irresistible?") confronted by his past and the possibility of commitment. Like *Heavy*, the film was produced cheaply and picked up for distribution after pleasing audiences at Sundance, confirming that the fresh, creative stories about fat experience (that is, fat *men's* experience) originate on the fringes of the film industry.

PART VII

INDEPENDENTS

24

A Rant

James Schamus

THE FOLLOWING IS a transcript of the keynote address I delivered at the 1999 Independent Feature Project/West Spirit Awards. Since the speech was, if I do say so myself, a bit of a bomb, I thought that, in an act of unutterable mercy, I would spare you all the lousy jokes that prefaced the substance of the talk. And, too, I thought I'd make a couple of postmortem revisions in order to underscore some of the points I hastily touched on in my rush to get off stage.

The speech was organized around a simple, perhaps tongue-in-cheek proposal: that the Independent Feature Project (IFP) as we know it, and the Spirit Awards too, should be immediately disbanded. Aside from the obvious overabundance of awards shows out there these days, the reason for the proposal was simple: the IFP has already, and fabulously, achieved its goals. It has won its battles. The war is over, and we should all at this point happily celebrate, around the pyre of our victory bonfire, the achievements that have brought the independent movement this far, and wonder, perhaps, if from the ashes something new might arise, informed by the spirit of the founding mothers and fathers of the independent movement that led to the IFP's creation twenty years ago.

Why would I argue this? Let me share some statistics with you, because statistics are objective and these statistics support my point. I did some research, and I discovered that in 1986, at the very first Spirit Awards, the total box office of the nominated films in all categories was about $20 million. Fast-forward thirteen years to this year's awards. The total box office for all nominated films, excluding foreign films, is $300 million. Now certainly there's inflation, and more films in more categories this year, but even a simple averaging out of box office would show an exponential rise in the economic heft of films considered worthy of "independent" kudos. This is a remarkable feat, all the more so when one considers the often "independent" feel—and substance—of many of the bigger-budgeted studio films.

Now back in 1986, fully 50 percent of the box office of the Spirit nominees was earned by the major studios, namely, in the form of Warner Brothers and its Martin Scorsese–helmed *After Hours*. This year, I pointed out in my speech, $299.98 million of the $300 million earned was made by either major studios, their affiliates, or distributors backed by large-scale financial institutions. Of course a key objection to this "objective" statistic is the inclusion of fiery upstart Artisan, with its enormous hit *The Blair Witch Project* (1999), in the "major corporate" category. Artisan was pulled together by a group called Bain Capital, which, in a recent press release, boasts of its more than $7 billion in capital and its record of taking "over 20 companies public with a combined current market capitalization exceeding $24 billion." But I failed to note that two of the partners in the venture had recently bought out Bain's stake in the company. In fact, it was unfair of me to lump Artisan, a marvel of entrepreneurial energy and imagination, in the same category as the studios per se. My point was simply that, for all intents and purposes, the films recognized at the Spirit Awards have succeeded overwhelmingly in entering the mainstream system of commercial exploitation and finance, and today the economics required to make oneself heard even as an "independent" are essentially studio economics. In this so-called independent arena even the "little guys" need big capital if they are to survive in any economically viable form.[1]

Sure, the IFP nominating committees have managed to make certain that a number of worthy films with little or no distribution make their way onto our ballots, and these films fulfill more than a symbolic function in reminding us of the casualties left by the side of the road in the indie rush to success. But let's face facts—the folks at the IFP are confronted with a terrible conundrum. How many of the five thousand-plus voting members will have seen these films? Does their inclusion begin to look like mere, and perhaps mildly futile, tokenism? Or is there at least some sense in which the modest "exposure" such nominations get for these films makes the gesture worthwhile?

I have no hard and fast answers to these questions, nor, I think, do most other well-meaning members of the independent community. We share simply a genuine sentiment that we like films that say something

An independent film from the likes of Viacom/Paramount? Matthew Broderick and Reese Witherspoon learn to loathe each other in Alexander Payne's terrific "independent" teen-pic, *Election* (Paramount, 1999).

to us, films that are meaningful in some way, and that such films can now be found both within the studio system, within the mini-majors and major independents, as well as "outside" the system.

But if our communal rituals like the Spirit Awards simply are little more than the expression of that sentiment, are they worth all the bother? More pressing, what if the very celebration of the success of the Independent Feature Project's "project"—the widespread acceptance of and support for a market for films with an "independent" mentality— simply reproduces the forms and rituals of judgment and exclusion that Gregory Nava and friends were fighting so hard against when, twenty years ago, they started the IFP? There is no logical reason why the towering artistic achievements of films like *Boys Don't Cry* (1999) and *Election*, brought to us by the News Corporations and Viacoms of this world, should not be celebrated, and we should be genuinely grateful that caring and savvy people who work for those corporations have cleared a path in the marketplace for these kinds of films. But this does not mean we should we go on pretending to be storming the castle when in fact "we" are well inside it. And in this best of all possible worlds, our very reasons to celebrate may in fact be portents of our eventual—perhaps imminent—extinction. The growth of independent film has occurred simultaneously with the growth of the super-transnational global media empires, and we owe much of our existence to the growth of these remarkable companies. But the next steps in those companies' evolution may mean the end of our kind of media making.

That is to say, we might want to get political, of all things, and take some cues from the people who gathered in Seattle a few months ago to find out if our current hog-heaven state might be leading us at the end of the line to a not-so-kosher termination. To understand this last point, we might consider what a new kind of IFP would look like, and articulate what its membership might be worried about.

First off, we might be worried not so much about "independent film" as about independence itself, the preservation of some form of civic space in which freedom of expression is not simply a privilege purchased with the promise of an eventual profit, but the exercise of a fundamental right.

What are the threats to freedom of expression, diversity of opinion, and open access to markets and audiences, that the astonishing growth of the horizontally integrated media giants portend?

I will mention, briefly, just a few.

First, we must simply take cognizance of the enormity of the consolidation of market share and political power that has occurred in the media industries under Clinton/Gore. A transaction like the pending AOL/Time Warner merger, perhaps the biggest economic transaction in history, has for its underpinnings some very telling logics. In particular, I would point out that the merging of the cable industry with the Internet poses crucial issues. Remember that for all the talk of free markets, cable companies in fact operate as state-sanctioned monopolies, who have the right and ability to censor and control virtually all content that goes through the coaxial cables that deliver media into your home. Once upon a time, AOL was a vigorous advocate for opening up access to those cable wires. But now, think of the extraordinary power that might come with managing, and charging for, the flow of information through the Web as it can be subsumed under the monopoly conditions that govern the cable environment. A politically informed and open study of such a merger and the regulatory regimes that govern it might

Todd Solondz's NC-17-rated *Happiness* (Good Machine/October, 1998) was so frank about the lives of its lonely misfits that the Seagram Company, which owned Universal, refused to release it, even through its subsidiary, October Films. *Happiness* then reverted to its producers, Good Machine.

just be the only hope independents—and everyone interested in a democratic civic culture—will have of surviving the new cyber era.

We might also work to understand—and repeal—key aspects of the 1996 Telecommunications Act, which has led to one of the greatest boondoggles in American history (the giveaway of over $15 billion in broadcasting spectrum), and which is one of the most important factors in the increasing consolidation of the American and global media worlds.

We also need a new mandate for aggressive antitrust enforcement. Let me give you an example of the practical consequences of how concentration in the retail video business affects us. We all know that Blockbuster, which is owned by Viacom, has a general policy of not carrying NC-17 films. Now, I had the honor of being involved in a film a couple of years back called *Happiness*, a film so morally dubious that it was sent back to Good Machine because the Seagram Company, which owns Universal, which owned what was at that time called October, didn't want anything to do with the movie. (By the way, this transfer of rights by Universal to us was a remarkably amicable and collegial transaction, but that's another story.)[2]

Fine. We released the film theatrically ourselves, unrated. But when it came time to release the video, Todd Solondz, the film's director, for some reason refused to bowdlerize and censor his movie to get an R rating, so Trimark, the film's video distributor, bravely ended up going out with an NC-17. Since, however, Blockbuster controls nearly a third of the rental market, and, in most mid- and small-size markets has vanquished its independent competition, this meant we were effectively banned throughout a great deal of the United States. That's how censorship works these days.[3]

We also need to pay attention to the WTO and WIPO intellectual property talks, and support the existence of what's left of independent media companies overseas. American independent cinema has long depended on far-thinking foreign distributors and public television stations for much of its economic subsistence. Now, with the Hollywood majors grabbing on average between 75 and 90 percent of the box office of most foreign territories, and with huge transnational satellite and cable TV companies wiping out local TV competition, the number of buyers, especially those with access to lucrative pay-TV deals, is shrinking. If those independent distributors disappear, we will be wholly at the mercy of the conglomerates, as the people who run the studio specialty divisions will be wholly at the mercy of the international TV divisions of their studios, whose deals they need to survive. By supporting independents overseas in the face of an ongoing MPAA/Jack Valenti onslaught, we also help our friends at the specialty divisions of the studios here, who need producers who can make flexible financing arrangements using the overseas markets. And we will need to find ways of achieving effective solidarity with those like the NDP in Canada and the Left Party in Sweden who are leading the fight against globalized media hegemony in their own countries.

All of the above rests on some real hope for campaign finance reform. As Robert McChesney, in his book *Rich Media, Poor Democracy*, points out, "In the United States the richest one-quarter of one percent of Americans make 80 percent of individual campaign contributions, and corporations outspend labor by a margin of ten to one." And remember, those contributions go mostly to fill the coffers of the media empires on whose airwaves the candidates spend their billions in contributions.[4]

You think I'm just being a paranoid rabble-rouser? Let's ask Gerald Levin, the head of Time Warner, and something of a real visionary in these matters. Earlier this year, on the eve of his company's historic merger with AOL, he told CNN that global media companies are "more important than government. . . . We're going to need to have these corporations redefined as instruments of public service because they have the resources, they have the reach, they have the skill base. . . . And that may be a more efficient way to deal with society's problems than bureaucratic governments."[5] On the one hand, this is the voice of a passionate and committed industry leader who I think genuinely believes that an unbridled marketplace will lead to a more "efficient" and universal democratic culture. On the other hand, you can't make this shit up. It's genuinely scary, especially when one realizes that AOL Time Warner will most likely control over half of all U.S. Internet access and a quarter of its cable market, while fighting tooth and nail to keep its systems as closed to nonpaying interlopers as is humanly possible.

The successful integration of the independent film movement into the structures of global media and finance has wrought untold benefits to American filmmakers and has resulted in the making and distribution of some of the greatest works of cinema art to come along in a long time. We should all be proud of these accomplishments, and there will be more of them to come, no doubt. But, as responsible citizens of the new global media imperium, we should take Gerald Levin up on his challenge to redefine media companies in the public service, even if that means fighting to limit their total hegemony over the marketplace of ideas. Otherwise, we may soon live in a world where we are free to say anything, but where the cost of reaching out to anyone who can afford to hear us will be beyond prohibitive.

NOTES

An earlier version of this essay appeared in the summer 2000 issue of *Filmmaker Magazine*.

1. My apologies to the Artisan team for making their daunting success at getting into this marketplace look like business as usual. The Artisans of this world, even with all the IPO lucre in the universe, are going to have a hard enough time of it in the years to come without having to have potshots taken at them by people like me.

2. See my article "The Pursuit of Happiness," *Nation*, 5 April 1999.

3. On the good news front, Blockbuster is using its enormous clout to help some excellent independent films with support for theatrical marketing campaigns. Again, my point is hardly to paint the people and companies involved in making and distributing films as intrinsically evil—far from it. Rather, I make note that the system as a whole, as it tends toward greater and greater consolidation, effectively silences alternative voices and visions when they pose political or other problems, even though no one actually need make a specific decision to do so.

4. McChesney's book is a fundamental primer on these issues. It was published by the University of Illinois Press in 1999.

5. Levin is quoted in Joel Bleifuss, "Communication Breakdown," *In These Times*, 21 February 2000.

25

The Case of Harmony Korine

Robert Sklar

ONE OF THE final images in Harmony Korine's 1997 feature film debut, *Gummo*, is of a dead and mutilated black cat, held up close to the camera by its killers for all to see. Several other cats are violently murdered in the course of the film. "It makes me want to do to Korine what his two adolescent protagonists do to the cats they sell to the local butcher for a dollar a pound," wrote Amy Taubin in her *Village Voice* review. "Shoot him, toss him in a vat of filthy water, string him up and beat him to a pulp, et cetera, et cetera." She was one of the film's and the filmmaker's strongest supporters.

"Prosthetic animals were used in some scenes," the film's rather lengthy end-credit disclaimer read in part. "Scenes depicting violence to animals were simulated." Such abjuration of the spectator's visceral experience mollified few. By critical consensus, *Gummo* was the most reviled film ever associated with the post-1990 American independent film movement. And yet, when the end-of-decade polls of critics and programmers began to appear, listing the best films, or most significant, or most underrated, et cetera, et cetera, *Gummo* not infrequently appeared, possessing more lives than its own vividly realistic, apparently suffering prosthetic cats.[1]

In the land of the blind the one-eyed man is king, goes the old saw. In the land of American independent film, with its endless array of yuppie romantic comedies and spurious neo-noirs, Harmony Korine, for all the inescapable ambivalence that even his most steadfast admirers feel about his work, stands out as the artistic equivalent of royalty. As the teenage screenwriter of *Kids* (1995) and writer-director of *Gummo* and *julien donkey-boy* (1999), Korine has created some of the most challenging and problematic works of contemporary American cinema.

Born in 1974, Korine seems anxious to be the *enfant terrible* of American film. Knowing Korine only from his self-presentation to the press, one can imagine why admirers of the work like Taubin might want to throttle the person who made it. The case of Harmony Korine is not so much about a particular individual's articulated artistic goals (which surely do exist, behind the postadolescent mendacity) as about a filmmaker's emergence under specific historical circumstances, with explicit cinematic antecedents and creative collaborations. With Korine, it's a case of older aesthetics' combining with new technologies. His work evinces the nearest thing to an avant-garde sensibility in contemporary cinema. And yet the films are distributed by companies owned by Disney and Time Warner.

There are perhaps few lessons to be learned from Korine's accomplishments so far, and surely all generalizations about their relation to cinema's future are to be rigorously eschewed. But his films are worth thinking about even if only for the attacks on them; and they are far more interesting than that.

We can get a bearing on what Korine's aesthetic aims as writer-director may be by observing what the film for which he was writer alone is not. Several astute critics hailed *Kids* as a masterpiece on its release, but one hopes that they were swayed by the film's flagrant carnality and a need to defend its controversial moral tone. Viewed a few years distant from the sensationalism that accompanied its original appearance, *Kids* has lost its novelty as a bearer of bad news about teenage sexuality and drug use, and seems no longer to possess, if it ever did, much in the way of specific cinematic value.

Kids was the first film as director for Larry Clark, a noted still photographer whose particular subject was teenage kids. (Among multiple accounts of how Clark and Korine began their collaboration, all agree that they met when Clark was photographing skateboarders in New York's Washington Square Park.) The most experienced among the principal creative personnel was cinematographer Eric Edwards, who had shot a number of feature films, including several directed by Gus Van Sant, who functioned as an executive producer on *Kids*. But nothing on Edwards's résumé, including Van Sant's *My Own Private Idaho* (1991), seems fully related to the handheld, moving-camera, faux cinema verité style chosen for the film.

Kids centers on two teen boys, Telly (Leo Fitzpatrick) and Casper (Justin Pierce), the first of whom considers himself a specialist in de-

Harmony Korine was still in his teens when he wrote *Kids* (Shining Excalibur/Miramax, 1995). The film, directed by still photographer Larry Clark, was hailed by critics as a masterpiece of cine-realism. With his more recent films as writer-director—*Gummo* and *julien donkey-boy*—Korine has laid claim to the title *enfant terrible* of American cinema.

flowering virgins. Jennie (Chloe Sevigny), one of his conquests, tests HIV-positive, and since he was her only lover, she tries to find him. They arrive separately at the same party, where Jennie walks in on Telly having sex with another girl. "Shut the fucking door!" he demands. Distraught and drunk, Jennie falls asleep on a sofa, and in that condition Casper rapes her. In recounting this story, however, the effects of spontaneity and unease for which the camera style strives are undermined by other stylistic choices. A crosscutting editing strategy, not only between shots of Jennie and Telly but also more generally between boys and girls, quickly becomes predictable. There's also a directorial penchant for telegraphing significant narrative developments, as when Jennie's HIV status is clearly announced by a nurse's gestures and expressions several shots before she actually informs the girl. *Kids* may survive as a disturbing sociological tract, but even so, director Clark has asserted—perhaps the revelation his film was aiming at—that these kids are no different, after all, from the way most of us behaved as kids.

From its first images *Gummo* introduces the spectator to a completely different realm of filmmaking. But what precisely is that realm? For commercial and promotional reasons much was made of *Gummo* as an original work of art, a forerunner and harbinger of new forms of cinema. At the same time, as if to anchor the film to familiar signposts, Korine's own publicity apparatus linked him to the work of such others as John Cassavetes, Federico Fellini, and Werner Herzog, as well as the still photographer Diane Arbus. These references cover such ground as improvisation, surreal spirituality (or spiritual surrealism), the grotesque, and, in Herzog's case, the notion of cinema as a challenge and ordeal both for filmmaker and spectator. What they leave out, to be sure, is Korine's affinities with experimental and avant-garde filmmaking. Korine's cinema seems to come from some place outside the framework of commercial narrative fiction features in which Cassavetes, Fellini, and Herzog have primarily worked.

Take, as one example, Kenneth Anger's 1963 *Scorpio Rising*. Without arguing for extensive similarities between Anger's film and Korine's *Gummo* one can see shared strategies and impulses at play. Each is an aesthetically beguiling but thematically confrontational work. Each derives its force and meaning from an accumulation and juxtaposition of disparate images, rather than from a coherent narrative progression. Each utilizes sound/image contrast, but sometimes in opposite ways. Anger's affronting images give a more deviant meaning to the otherwise harmless-seeming pop singles that compose his soundtrack. In *Gummo*, otherwise bland or simply quirky scenes take on a darker tone when accompanied by songs such as "Hellish Blasphemy" and "Demonic Evil," performed by Nifelheim. Other possible avant-garde antecedents could be proposed, and many of them, like *Scorpio Rising* and *Gummo*, possessed in their own time the power to shock and disturb. Rather than focusing on its novelty, one might regard *Gummo* as a work that brought the underground back above ground, after several decades spent beneath the radar of mainstream film criticism and culture.

A further cinematic affinity for *Gummo* lies in the transgressive fringe of the European art film, a connection already partly signaled by the publicity reference to Fellini and Herzog. Korine persuaded the French cinematographer Jean-Yves Escoffier to work as director of photography on *Gummo*. Escoffier had already by the mid-1990s made the move from European to American filmmaking, but Korine claimed to know him from his earlier work on Leos Carax's 1991 film Les *Amants du Pont-Neuf* (which received belated United States theatrical distribution in 1999 with the title *The Lovers on the Bridge*). For *Gummo*, Escoffier's shooting style and lighting technique had the capacity to impart a romantic mystery to scenes of otherwise mundane realism, and complemented Korine's collage-like use of Polaroid still images and blown-up Super-8 footage that the director himself had shot. *Gummo* opens before the credits with its most intense collage sequence, using stock footage in addition to the other visual elements (as well as music and voice-over narration) to offer a narrative pretext or preface. These purport to show the devastating emotional and physical effects that a tornado produced when it struck, some time before, the small town of Xenia, Ohio. What follows after in the film demonstrates the grotesque and untoward behavior of Xenia's residents, who, we are to understand, suffered long-lasting posttraumatic consequences that in particular affected their children. Under the main credits we see a first example of this in shots of a youth wearing only pink rabbit headgear and short pants (credited as Bunny Boy, and played by Jacob Sewell), who loiters aimlessly on a pedestrian bridge over a highway, urinating and spitting down on traffic. (For the record, on April 3, 1974, a tornado did hit Xenia, killing thirty-three people and destroying half its buildings. However, *Gummo* was shot not in Xenia but in and near Nashville, Tennessee, where Korine once lived.)

Following the credits we are immediately plunged, pardon the pun, into an episode of cat killing by the youths Solomon (Jacob Reynolds) and Tummler (Nick Sutton), who have captured a whitish cat and thrust it into a water-filled barrel, where we observe its drowning in close-up. Solomon and Tummler provide one thread through the film. So too do the bleach-haired sisters Dot (Chloe Sevigny) and Helen (Carisa Bara), with their younger sibling Darby (Darby Dougherty), whose search for their lost cat Foot-Foot offers a semblance of conventional narrative dread (is Foot-Foot the mutilated cat we see at the film's end?). Linda Manz portrays Solomon's mom, who, in one remarkable scene, shampoos the boy in a bathtub filled with black water while also feeding him a dinner of spaghetti, milk, and a candy bar. Korine himself, credited as Boy on Couch, appears as one more grotesque among the generality, nattering about family matters while also courting a black male midget.

Numerous episodes involving the principal characters, along with

a number of other peripheral figures, are capable of enthralling or of-
fending spectators, or perhaps eliciting both responses simultaneously.
If *Gummo* is a film that a number of critics have despised wholeheart-
edly, it's also proven difficult for its admirers to support it without qual-
ification. The film's pretense to sociological specificity—this is what
happens to people whose lives were devastated by a tornado—can
hardly be credited seriously. But its portrait of small-town anomie has
a precision and piquancy that many viewers will recognize. Whatever
its place in future critical assessments, for now one can appreciate
Gummo as a work of cinematic art, without condoning those aspects
that are tasteless or base.

   Gummo thrust Korine even closer to the European art cinema's self-
styled mavericks. The film caught the attention, among others, of the
Danish filmmakers who unveiled their Dogme 95 manifesto at the 1998
Cannes International Film Festival. The declaration attacked "decadent
filmmakers" who utilized computer graphics and special effects; it pro-
pounded instead a "Vow of Chastity" that required location shooting,
live recorded sound, handheld cameras, and no artificial lighting other
than a single camera-mounted lamp. The pronouncement was not
solely a publicity stunt, for it accompanied two new films that were
claimed to be made under Dogme restrictions, Thomas Vinterberg's
Festen (The Celebration) and Lars von Trier's *The Idiots*. With several
other Dogme productions already in the works, the Danes invited Korine to make the first American film to bear their seal. Korine's second
feature, *julien donkey-boy*, begins with a title card certifying that "the following motion picture has been produced in compliance with the rules
and intentions set forth in the Dogme 95 manifesto."

   Dogme gave Korine more than a certificate. It got Korine the services of the British cinematographer Anthony Dod Mantle and the Ice-
landic film editor Valdis Oskardottir, who made signal contributions to
the international success of *The Celebration*, and who also worked on the
third Danish Dogme film, *Mifunes Sidste Sang* (Mifune, 1999), directed
by Soren Kragh-Jacobsen. In particular, Mantle's shooting style utiliz-
ing handheld digital videocameras gave an immediacy and edge to *The
Celebration*, impelling the family drama. Moreover, in addition to its
principles and personnel, Korine adopted one of Dogme's dominant
narrative tropes: the effects of mental illness or retardation. Von Trier's
The Idiots concerned a group of Danes who were living communally
and feigning mental incapacity, which they called "spassing" (the film's

U.S. distributor shelved the film for two years, and cut or altered several scenes before its release in 2000). A mentally retarded character also figures significantly in *Mifune*. In like manner, the title character of *julien donkey-boy*, played by the British actor Ewen Bremner, is a schizophrenic.

Inevitably there's something phony about representing mental illness in cinema (which is perhaps one of the points Von Trier was making in *The Idiots*). The line between "authentic" portrayal and a raft of actor's vices—sentimental heart tugging, chewing the scenery, shameless self-regard—is often difficult to discern. Whatever outrageous or improbable events occur seem to have a built-in justification and an implicit appeal to spectators' understanding and sympathy. The absence of such justification or appeal was one of the most strikingly fresh aspects of *Gummo*, but *julien donkey-boy* can't entirely free itself from special pleading. However, the film doesn't completely succumb to its maudlin elements either, because it's as much a family melodrama as a portrait of an individual. And at the family's center, exerting more influence over the film's tone than a phalanx of Dogme associates, is the European rebel filmmaker named as a Korine predecessor, Werner Herzog, in the role of Father.

Herzog is the paterfamilias of a household that includes his children Julien, who works as an attendant at a school for the blind; Pearl (Chloe Sevigny), who is pregnant and won't name the father; and Chris (Evan Neumann), who is training as a wrestler. Also on hand is Grandma (Joyce Korine, Harmony Korine's own grandmother). The mother has either left the home or died, it's not clear which, and she's sorely missed. The father's patriarchal bluster now completely holds sway, and he's particularly hard on Chris, whom he's driving to become a "man" and a "winner" by trials such as spraying him with cold water from a hose ("a winner doesn't shiver"). Herzog's bizarre behavior and pugnacious self-assertion seem fully in keeping with his self-presentation in earlier documentaries by and about him, but here the thin veneer of fiction lends the character a density that mere actuality may not sufficiently possess. Herzog serves to decenter Julien's mental illness and subordinate it to the larger pathology of the family system.

Using digital video, Korine and Mantle carry their visual stylistics into more experimental modes than either had attempted, respectively, in *Gummo* or the Danish Dogme films. They utilize superimpositions, gradations of graininess in the image, out-of-focus shots, varying color tones, and still frame images to make the film far more adventurous visually than any previous Dogme-certified work (that there's an apparent contravention of the "Vows of Chastity" seems not to have disturbed anyone involved). Some aspects of the film, such as Julien's vision of a masturbating nun, have sparked expressions of outrage similar to what *Gummo* evoked. But overall *julien donkey-boy* is a more conventional film, which may be unavoidable considering that it shares an intertext with mainstream commercial films in ways that *Gummo* decisively does not. But conventional, under the circumstances, is a relative term. Harmony Korine has done more to shake up our expectations for American independent film than any other filmmaker of the 1990s.

NOTES

1. In a "Best of the Nineties" poll conducted by the Canadian film magazine *Cinema Scope* of some 180 critics and programmers primarily from North America and Europe, *Gummo* received nine votes and finished in a tie for thirty-eighth place on the list. See "Best of the Nineties Poll Results," *Cinema Scope* 2 (winter 2000): 51–58. In a "Decade Poll" conducted by the U.S. magazine *Film Comment*, some critics and filmmakers ranked their top ten and others listed "most underrated" films; although a numerical summary was not compiled, *Gummo* appears to have received one vote as an underrated film. See "Film in the Nineties: A *Film Comment* Poll," *Film Comment* 36, no. 1 (January–February 2000): 52–61.

26

Where Hollywood Fears to Tread

Autobiography and the Limits of Commercial Cinema

Kathleen McHugh

IN THE ERA of identity politics, what journalists and academics alike have dubbed the "age of the memoir," film presents a special and specialized case. While all modes (pulp, literature) and genres (novel, short story, essay, criticism, poem) of literary production have readily accommodated autobiography, in U.S. cinema the genre has been wedded solely to nonindustry modes of production. In both commercial cinema and television, autobiography is almost, if not completely, nonexistent.[1]

This representational absence might seem odd given Hollywood's relentless emphasis on the individual. But classical narrative's individuation is both abstract and imaginary. As countless essays on identification have reiterated since Laura Mulvey's "Visual Pleasure and Narrative Cinema," the coalescence of the imaginary and the ideal in Hollywood solicits a universalized identification from its audiences, efficiently combining narrative and aesthetic interests in compelling, seductive characters with the economic bottom line. In autobiography, such identification is foreclosed by the mode of narration—the author/filmmaker, usually explicitly, addresses the reader/viewer as *different* from him/herself, a narrative structure that also marks the protagonist as distinct from the narrative's audience. This marked narration and differentiation are decidedly at odds with Hollywood's invisible style. (Significantly, minority filmmakers have frequently made autobiographical films and avoided universalizing narrative discourses.)

Two early and important critical statements clearly distinguish cinematic autobiography from industry cinema. P. Adams Sitney in "Autobiography in Avant-Garde Film," defines and shapes the formal parameters of the genre by examining examples from the American avant-garde cinema.[2] Historically, the classical avant-garde (1945–75), used personal, autobiographical formats pointedly in opposition to industry cinema. Sitney abhors the oft-remarked and what he considers debased affiliation between the American avant-garde and the "personal." He articulates the principles of cinematic autobiography in completely formal, self-referential terms, contesting the presumption of extratextual reference and truth in autobiographical expression. He derives this approach from Paul de Man, who, in his reading of Rousseau, begins from the premise that all autobiography has "a referential reading-moment" and ends by arguing that such a moment is merely a "delusion," that "There can be no use of language which is not, within a certain perspective . . . radically formal."[3]

In a similar move, Sitney initially acknowledges autobiography's claims to "extra-textual veracity" but progressively displaces this feature.[4] His argument about the moment of artistic vocation, typically represented and privileged in these films, is telling. In his view, this moment always constitutes a structural meditation on the filmic apparatus and its capacities for representing a subject then and now.

Sitney's critical substitutions or displacements—from the "personal" as (extratextual) epithet to the true self-reflexive formalism of autobiography—condition his choice of filmmakers *and* his analyses of their work, his choices delimiting not only what he does see in this work but also what he cannot. Though he publishes his piece three years after Laura Mulvey's "Visual Pleasure and Narrative Cinema," in a period when feminist and ethnic filmmakers are rejuvenating the avant-garde and working in autobiographical modes, he restricts his commentary to white male filmmakers—Jerome Hill, Stan Brakhage, Hollis Frampton, George Landow, and James Broughton. Interestingly, Sitney's selections function to recuperate to the formalist project works that are more expressive of gay identities (Hill and, to a much greater extent, Broughton) and to assimilate to autobiography works that are insistently formalist and whose status as autobiography is somewhat questionable (Frampton and Landow).

Elizabeth Bruss, contributing to a 1980 collection of essays otherwise devoted to literary autobiography, takes a more general approach. In her essay "Eye for I: Making and Unmaking Autobiography in Film," Bruss commences her argument with the assertion, "[T]here is no real cinematic equivalent for autobiography." This literary genre does not translate readily to film because

> [t]he unity of subjectivity and subject matter—the implied identity of author, narrator, and protagonist on which classical autobiography depends—seems to be shattered by film; the autobiographical self decomposes, schisms, into almost mutually exclusive elements of the person filmed (entirely visible, recorded and projected) and the person filming (entirely hidden; behind the camera eye).[5]

Exploring autobiography as a particular speech act, Bruss carefully measures film's capacity to fulfill those parameters—"truth-value," "act-value," and "identity-value"—that "give classical autobiography its peculiar generic value."[6] Drawing her examples primarily from European auteurs and art cinema (again, all white men!)—Federico Fellini (*8½*, 1963; *Satyricon*, 1969; *The Clowns*, 1971; *Amarcord*, 1974), Francois Truffaut (*The 400 Blows*, 1959), Jean Cocteau (*The Testament of Orpheus*, 1960)—she determines that "Such films cannot produce the old self-knowledge (nor the old self-deceptions) of classical autobiography, but they can do something else: they can take identity beyond what one consciousness can grasp, beyond even what the unaided consciousness can encompass. . . . Film also challenges the presumed integrity of the perceiving subject."[7] Because of all the technologies (lighting, editing, etc.) mobilized to represent the autobiographical subject in film, Bruss argues that we cannot and do not understand this subject as preceding or preexisting its representation but rather as generated or invented by it. She concludes by asserting that the representational technologies of film and video apprehend, as literature cannot, the very different condition of human subjectivity as it exists today in relation to these very technologies and in complex "social interdependencies."[8]

Though these critics and other historians of the American avant-garde have consistently noted the affiliation of this mode of film production with personal and autobiographical self-expression, the character of this affiliation and of its self-expression has changed. While both Sitney and Bruss emphasize the importance of the cinematic apparatus in their formulations of filmic autobiography, Bruss insists on the importance of both social context and representational technologies as influences that alter human subjectivity and our perceptions of it.

Her essay comes closer than Sitney's to apprehending the shape of much autobiographical work done in experimental and independent American cinema in the 1990s.

In the 1970s and early 1980s, feminist, lesbian/gay, and ethnic film-makers such as Carolee Schneeman, Barbara Hammer, Jan Oxenberg, Susanna Muñoz, and Willie Varela used autobiography to represent identities unseen and unheard in industry cinema. Since then, experimental filmmakers Rea Tajiri, Guillermo Verdecchia, Janice Tanaka, Su Friedrich, Marlon Riggs, Vanalyne Green, Bill Jones, and Lise Yasui have used the inherent disunity of cinematic autobiography to question and nuance the coherence of all identities and identity categories by pointing to the aesthetic, political, cultural, and technological forces from which their subjectivities derive.

Though all these filmmakers have had extremely limited venues in which to distribute and exhibit their work, industrial and technological developments in the 1990s have begun to reshape the relationship between mainstream and experimental film, at least in terms of exhibition and reception. The globalization of media, the proliferation of cable networks and alternative cinema channels, and the rise of the Internet have all created a significant need for content that has resulted in a blurring of the boundaries between industrial and alternative cinema.

From a number of possible choices, I would like to discuss a film made within an artisanal mode of production that crossed over, briefly, into independent distribution, thereby "appearing" on Hollywood turf —Cheryl Dunye's *The Watermelon Woman* (1996). I would like to examine the ways this film, far from negating the extratextual referent, historicizes (autobiographical) subjectivity by relating it to historically variable modes of production and representation.

The Watermelon Woman is a provocative but nevertheless exemplary instance of contemporary experimental self-representation. Rather than stressing its own truth and authenticity (and the altered status of these values vis-à-vis progressive political aesthetics), Dunye's film compels an investigation of altered modes of production and self-promotion. In relating her film's autobiographical premise to its material production, we shoulder consider David James's argument that "a film's images and sounds never fail to tell the story of how and why they were produced"[9] *The Watermelon Woman* provides a telling case study of what happens when an autobiographical film made in an experimental mode is distributed as an independent.

Cheryl Dunye's *The Watermelon Woman* (1996) tells the story of a lesbian experimental filmmaker named Cheryl searching for details about an elusive African American film actress named Fae Richards. Using the conceit of fandom and star culture, Dunye collapses public and private history as they relate to media, documentation, and desire in such a way as to challenge the distinctions between fiction and nonfiction, autobiography and fantasy, actuality and invention. Her film conforms to criteria of autobiographical representation as outlined by both Sitney and Bruss, though it exceeds these criteria in each instance.

In the film's third sequence, Dunye directly addresses the camera, identifying herself as a filmmaker, then backtracking: "I'm working on being a filmmaker." She wants to make a film on black women "because our stories have never been told." Though her declaration is presented as personal and heartfelt, it also reiterates, verbatim, the stated mission of all minoritarian filmmakers. This "cliché" is matched by that of industry filmmakers—"It was my vision, my story and I had to bring it to the screen"—wherein the sense of individuation and unmarked identity can clearly be heard.

As I will discuss later, Dunye puts her cliché to very ironic use later in the film. She then decides, on camera, to make a film about a beautiful black actress she has seen, only credited as "The Watermelon Woman" in a film called *Plantation Memories*, a clip of which she then shows us.

Dunye skillfully constructs her autobiography as one in which her "moment of artistic vocation" is inseparable from her search for an obscure African American actress whom she has glimpsed in the margins of a classical industry film text. The life of the actress, Fae Richards, AKA the Watermelon Woman, uncannily turns out to mirror aspects of her own. Richards was a lesbian and had a relationship with a white film director in which she was exploited. This relationship resonates with Cheryl's on-screen relationship with Diana, played by Gwen Turner, and her offscreen partnership with Alex Juhasz, the producer of Dunye's film *The Watermelon Woman*. For example, when Cheryl discovers that Diana is "into chocolate" and not her per se, she ends the relationship, an option that Fae Richards would not necessarily have had. Though the film narrativizes issues suggested by her relationship with Juhasz, it does not present these issues as autobiographical experience.

Similarly, Dunye also self-reflexively narrativizes aspects of the film's economic production—in *The Watermelon Woman*, Cheryl works as a video store clerk and a wedding videographer in order to afford to make her film. Thus the film constitutes a meditation not only on cinematic representation, but also on its modes of production.

The beginning and end of the film mark Dunye's transformation from "working on" being a filmmaker to "being" a filmmaker. Yet she affirms her working identity in a particularly paradoxical context. At film's end, she introduces her biography of Fae Richards. As Dunye narrates Richards's life, the documentary's stills, photos, and film clips are intercut with credits that reveal that an actress has played Fae Richards and that the documentary footage, the clips, the evidence, are all invented and depict a woman who never existed. Lest the spectator miss the inference of the credits, Dunye also includes a quote, "Sometimes you have to create your own history. The Watermelon Woman is a fiction."

This sequence, structured as a palimpsest, crystallizes the brilliant interplay between history and desire cumulatively articulated by the whole film. Dunye's direct address, together with the investigatory structure of the narrative, insinuates the spectator into its protagonist's goals. By this point in the film, we *want* Fae Richards to exist. Dunye's film not only chronicles her own search, her own desire for mirroring, for a history, for origins, she also compels the spectator to experience that desire *even as* she certifies it as a fantasy. Her film thus sketches two modes of historical discourse, one of which simply documents facts and events. The second one puts desire into the picture and thereby has an elusive object that cannot be pinned down or verified. The fiction of the images does not self-reflexively explore the cinematic apparatus, but rather testifies to a history that has not been written or recorded and does not even exist. Dunye's film chronicles the social interdependencies that underlie her relationship with industrial cinema, a mode of representation she depends on to make a film about what literally isn't and wasn't there. Its insinuation of fiction within a "documentary" of black women's stories testifies to the truth of their representational absence in history, in industry cinema, in mainstream cultural narratives more forcefully than any "truthful" account could have done.

Dunye's film provides a particularly cogent example of the possibilities and pitfalls of experimental autobiographical film within independent film distribution in the 1990s. Financed by a small National

Endowment for the Arts (NEA) grant, a fundraiser, and gifts from friends, *The Watermelon Woman* was distributed by New Line Features in limited theatrical release. Though the film received rave reviews in high profile publications such as the *New York Times*, the *Los Angeles Times*, the *Los Angeles Weekly*, and the *Village Voice*, those reviews did not translate into returns at the box office, due in part to a poorly advertised and executed release by New Line.

However, *The Watermelon Woman* has certainly been seen by many more people than have ever seen any of Cheryl Dunye's short autobiographical art films. In what may offer something of an object lesson, Dunye's film has been most successful on television. Having run on the Sundance channel for a couple of years now, it has just been contracted to show on BET. Though its commercial release legitimated its placement on television, the number of people who will see it on TV will certainly be much greater than those who saw it in film theaters.

Experimental filmic autobiography has been and continues to be confined to nonindustry or artisanal modes of production, now with declining arts funding. However, in the nineties, independent film distribution and theatrical and television exhibition have become available in limited ways to these filmmakers. While this crossover between artisanal production and independent distribution provides access to alternative TV venues, it also has significant drawbacks. Experimental film directors generally have direct and substantial, if not absolute, control over their films' distribution and exhibition within the art and educational circuit, including often being present at screenings. Once their films enter the commercial arenas of distribution and exhibition, that control is lost.[10] For example, when the controversy over *The Watermelon Woman*'s NEA funding flared up in the U.S. House of Representatives in 1996 and again in 1997, politicians like Sheila Jackson Lee and celebrities like Alec Baldwin defended the film in Congress and the media. But no one ever contacted Dunye or Juhasz for input or commentary regarding the film. Their absence from the public debate and life of the film uncannily mirrored the subject of the film itself. Thus, the representational absences of black women and lesbians documented in *The Watermelon Woman* were reiterated in aspects of the film's distribution (limited bookings), exhibition (limited advertising), and reception (Dunye and Juhasz's absence within public and political discourse about the film).

NOTES

1. It bears mention here that though it is beyond the scope of this essay, the Internet is rampant with autobiographical work and new television shows like *Survivor* and *Big Brother*, along with daytime confessional shows like *Oprah,* might be said to have an autobiographical component in the "confessions" participants make to the camera. But that begs the questions and problems involved with what exactly constitutes the autobiographical within visual media.

2. P. Adams Sitney, "Autobiography in Avant-Garde Film," *Millennium Film Journal* 1, no. 1 (winter 1977): 60–106.

3. Paul de Man, "Excuses," in *Allegories of Reading* (New Haven: Yale University Press, 1979), 278, 294.

4. Sitney writes, "What makes autobiography one of the most vital developments in the cinema of the late Sixties and early Seventies is that the very making of an autobiography constitutes a reflection on the nature of cinema and often on its ambiguous association with language," 202.

5. Elizabeth Bruss, "Eye for I: Making and Unmaking Autobiography in Film," in *Autobiography: Essays Theoretical and Critical*, ed. James Olney (Princeton: Princeton University Press, 1980), 297.

6. Bruss, 299.

7. Bruss, 318–19.

8. Bruss, 320.

9. David James, *Allegories of Cinema* (Princeton: Princeton University Press, 1989), 5.

10. Dunye remarks in an interview with T. Haslett in *The Black Cultural Studies Web Site Collective*, April 12, 1997, that: "once you put work out there, especially in the sense of a theatrical release, you have no control over who is seeing it and what they are getting out of it."

27

Smoke 'til You're Blue in the Face

Murray Smith

THE HOLLYWOOD JUGGERNAUT rumbles on—reinventing itself, to be sure, to take account of new technologies, new social and demographic trends, and novel economic strategies, but in an important sense sustaining itself. The international mass media entertainment industry we know as "Hollywood" remains as committed now as it ever has been to the three S's: stories, stars, and spectacle. So in this sense at least, the cinema as we know it is not ending at all—perhaps, as Peter Greenaway has suggested, it is just beginning.

Other forms of cinematic life—like the various underground and avant-garde traditions—have emerged, flourished, declined, and revived over the years. Some of these have occupied ecological niches in the cultural environment wholly different from the Hollywood behemoth. But there is a kind of cinema, fashionable in the 1990s, that has evolved through a complex mix of antagonism toward and dependence on Hollywood, feeding it and at the same time living off it.

I'm thinking, of course, of what came to be known in the 1990s as "indie" cinema. In a way, "indie" or "independent" cinema suggests an American art cinema, much as the label "New American Cinema" did in the early 1960s. Indeed, one can now look back and see something like a continuous tradition from the late 1950s to the present. This independent cinema has had its ups and downs over this period in terms of volume of production, critical attention, and public visibility. But if we can talk about a tradition, it is a pretty accommodating one, and in this essay I want to consider some of its constituent streams, and its broader parameters, by looking at the Wayne Wang/Paul Auster "double-header," *Smoke* and *Blue in the Face*.

The two films were made back to back and released in 1995, often playing together as a double bill. *Smoke*, one might say, is a "classical" American art film—not classical in the sense that studio-era Hollywood movies are said to be classical, for art films are precisely something other than this—but classical in the sense that the film works according to some very well recognized, long-standing conventions. *Smoke* has the literary air and pedigree (from Auster's involvement), the thematic weight, and stress on character complexity long associated with the American art film, even during the studio era when such films were a minor part of studio output (think of *The Magnificent Ambersons*, 1942, for example, based on Booth Tarkington's Pulitzer Prize–winning novel). The film has a carefully crafted quality, achieved by its even, measured pacing, and five-act structure, each "act" shifting our attention to a different character. *Blue in the Face* is mostly none of these things. It is rather a self-inflicted (if playful) slap in the face of *Smoke*, the yin to its yang, the termite to *Smoke*'s white elephant. If *Smoke* is a typical American art movie, then *Blue in the Face* is at least at one further remove from Hollywood practice. (This probably explains the reaction of one disgruntled Internet Movie Data Base (IMDB) contributor, who accords the film the honor of "One of the Worst Movies of All Time.") Indeed, had it not hitched a ride with *Smoke*, it's unlikely that *Blue in the Face* would have been distributed as widely as it was, or have received as much critical coverage.

So what exactly is *Blue in the Face*, and why do I think that it is a special little film, and rather more interesting than *Smoke*? The film is in part an embellishment of *Smoke*, but just as much a "remix" of, and notebook on, its bigger, more aesthetically conservative brother. *Smoke* takes place (mostly) in Brooklyn; *Blue*, not only takes place (wholly) in Brooklyn, it is in large measure about Brooklyn. ("Welcome to the planet Brooklyn," reads the marketing tag line.)

The Brooklyn connection is clearly established in the interview segments with Lou Reed, which take place in the (set for the) Brooklyn Cigar Company, the tobacco shop that forms the hub of the action in both films. These interviews are scattered through the film, as Reed ruminates on (among other things) his—and supposedly all Brooklynites'—peculiar form of attachment to the place. "I couldn't have been unhappier in the eight years I spent growing up in Brooklyn," Reed notes, "but I say that not having realized what it would then be like on Long Island, which was infinitely worse." This opening interview segment not only establishes Brooklyn in general as the focus of

Blue in the Face, but the tobacco shop more particularly as a neighborhood in miniature. This in turn highlights the way *Blue in the Face* elaborates the narrative of *Smoke*. Four of that film's five main characters are dropped (Paul Benjamin/William Hurt, Cyrus Cole/Forest Whitaker, Ruby/Stockard Channing, and Rashid Cole/Harold Perrineau Jr). But Auggie Wren/Harvey Keitel, manager of the tobacco shop, is retained, along with a number of secondary characters whose lives, along with several new characters, now take center stage.

Along with the dramatic scenes, which move outward in various directions from the tobacco store, and the interview sequences with Reed, which take place in the store, the film moves among a variety of other modes and formats. First, there is the strand of improvised dramatic dialogue between Auggie and Bob (Jim Jarmusch) focused on Bob's decision to smoke his last cigarette with Auggie. Bob is, in a literal sense, a regular customer of the shop, just like Benjamin in *Smoke*. In a way, the scene is no different from those involving Auggie and Dot (the wife of the shop's owner, played by Roseanne), which also have the feel of improvised performance. But there is a subtle difference: Jarmusch (as Bob) seems to be just "playing" himself—independent filmmaker and *cineaste*, droll humorist, lover of "coffee and cigarettes" (the title of a series of Jarmusch shorts, alluded to in his dialogue with Auggie). Dot is certainly amply "filled out" by Roseanne's star persona, but there is still an important way Roseanne is not Dot, while Jarmusch is, well, Jarmusch.

Moving further away from the shop as both the site of the dramatic extensions of *Smoke* and the center of the most ontologically traditional dramatic fiction in the film, there are still more sequence types. There is a series of "statistical monologues," in which various figures, standing in front of the tobacco shop, deliver information about Brooklyn—the size of its constituent ethnic communities, the number of parks it contains, the number of crimes committed within it, and so forth. Periodically, other sequences are interpolated by shots of the John Lurie National Orchestra—actually a jazz trio—performing inside and outside the shop. Although the band occupies a familiar space, the performance sequences seem to occupy an ambiguous and perhaps indeterminate temporality, floating in and out of, or momentarily puncturing, other action within or around the shop. Another strand depicts Violetta, Auggie's angry but utterly besotted girlfriend, declaiming a melodramatic monologue as if rehearsing a speech she is going to deliver to him. Last but not least, the film also incorporates video footage of everyday street life in Brooklyn, as well as interviews with a variety of its residents. The film thus establishes a graduated continuum between all-out fiction and straightforward documentary in an unusually detailed way. But this is not all.

The film not only sets up an array or system of possibilities, it also short-circuits the system insofar as some scenes create connections between very different points on the fiction-faction continuum. It's very hard to construe the interview with Lou Reed as anything other than an interview with Lou Reed, in spite of the fact that he is sitting in what has been established in *Smoke* as a fictional space. The first interview segment with Reed occurs *before* Wang/Auster establish continuity between the fictional worlds of *Blue in the Face* and *Smoke*. Everything we know about Lou Reed, in terms of his background and his deadpan, ironic manner, chimes with what he "reveals" in the interview. And most literally, when discussing the flip-up lenses on his unique glasses, he talks about marketing their design with the catchphrase "Lou's Views." But a later scene depicts an interview with Jimmy Rose/Jared Harris, the simple guy who sweeps the floor of the store. Jimmy is interviewed in just the same way as Reed, thus exerting a kind of fictionalizing pull on the subsequent interview segments with the rock musician. We are led to understand Reed as a character in the fictional world of the film, not just a real person interviewed in the real space of a set for the fiction. Another example of such short-circuiting: late in the film we see video footage of a baby, accompanied by Auggie's voice-over narration telling us that he and Violetta have had a child. So the footage is directly caught up in the fictional dimension of the film. But once again, it's hard not to see the footage as part of the video documentary strand, and thus exemplifying a type of nonfiction.

The mixing of fiction and nonfiction has its precursors, not least Wayne Wang himself. Wang's wonderful first feature, *Chan Is Missing* (1982), began life as a documentary about San Francisco's Chinatown. And even as a fiction it is shot through with its documentary origins. Subsequently, Wang has moved between two types of filmmaking, which *Smoke* and *Blue in the Face*, as a pair, bring together: erratic, spontaneous movies like *Life Is Cheap . . . But Toilet Paper Is Expensive* (1990), and highly crafted, set-bound films, often literary adaptations, like *Eat a Bowl of Tea* (1989) and *The Joy Luck Club* (1993).

But let's not get ahead of ourselves: back in the late 1940s, Twenti-eth-Century Fox and a number of other studios experimented with the "semidocumentary" format—films like *The House on 92nd Street* (1945), which used extensive location shooting, and, up to a point, captured some of the texture of everyday urban life. From roughly the same mo-ment, nonstudio filmmakers began making fiction films working from a nonfiction basis. Sidney Meyers and his collaborators on *The Quiet One* (1948), for example, began by shooting documentary footage in Harlem, before evolving a story and then shooting scripted scenes. Meyers cast a young boy from Harlem with no experience of acting in the central role. Similar tactics were used by Lionel Rogosin in *On the Bowery* (1956). Rogosin cast homeless men to play "themselves" and mixed scripted and documentary footage. This is a significantly differ-ent process from the procedure whereby a scripted project is cast with professional performers in all the major roles and simply shot using real locations. Ray Carney has referred to this trend as "American neoreal-ism," and such films do parallel the aesthetics of Italian neorealism and the emerging *nouvelle vague*. By the time John Cassavetes shot *Shadows* (1957–59) in the New York locations where the fictional action of the film occurs (such as the sculpture garden of the Museum of Modern Art), such strategies were already well established.

Nowadays, while location shooting remains a live option for stu-dio filmmakers, its potential for spontaneity is rarely exploited in the way it is by filmmakers in the independent tradition. One dimension of this unpredictability derives from the real locations and events against which rehearsed performers are set. The most extreme example of this shooting strategy remains Haskell Wexler's *Medium Cool* (1969), a film that stages fictional performance amidst the demonstrations outside the 1968 Democratic Convention in Chicago.

American neo-realism feeds into *Blue in the Face* only tangentially, in the form of the video footage. But this footage remains largely segre-gated from the performed sequences. There are few scenes where one senses the film's performers acting in the midst of unforewarned pas-sersby, in the flow of everyday existence. Another "method of spon-taneity," however, informs the film much more profoundly, and this can be traced more uniquely to the work of Cassavetes. No other American director has developed a *performance*-led and -centered cinema to the degree that Cassavetes did. While Cassavetes' films always involved scripts (the nonscripted, first version of *Shadows* was almost wholly discarded and reshot by Cassavetes), his method involved development-through-improvisation with his performers, as well as a shooting style that afforded his actors maximum flexibility to develop a given moment or scene on the fly, as the cameras rolled. The lurching camera movement and unstable focus characteristic of Cassavetes' films is not—as it is so often now, in television shows like *NYPD Blue*—a primary tactic. Instead, it is a by-product of prioritizing freedom of movement and gesture on the part of performers over the "perfection" and "professionalism" of fluid camera movement and focus racking.

Blue doesn't feature much in the way of this type of seasick cinematography, opting instead—where freedom of movement is necessary, as in the scenes between Dot and Auggie—to stick with extended medium and long shots. But it clearly does feature many scenes involving improvisation, as one of the closing titles confirms: "Situations created by Paul Auster and Wayne Wang in collaboration with the actors" (a title that recalls the closing title of *Shadows*: "The film you have just seen was an improvisation"). The improvisation of *Blue in the Face* seems to have been at work both in the development of scenes and in the shooting of shots, though it is often hard, as a viewer, to know how much of this latter type of improvisation we are witnessing in a given take. One tip-off is the use of editing elisions—jump cuts in the scenes involving Dot and Auggie, dissolves in the scenes with Auggie and Bob. These cuts eliminate what presumably were considered the less successful moments of improvisation. Or perhaps instead the cuts reveal the need to maintain a rapidity of pace in the film that would be undermined by lengthy pauses and the *temps morts* beloved of a good many European art cinema directors. By contrast, *Smoke*, in a very American compromise with European tendencies, features a fair bit of dying (if not dead) time.

The brisk pace and playful editing of *Blue in the Face* are vital elements of the film, and here again the legacy of Cassavetes is relevant. I have in mind here the importance of jazz, and especially bebop and free jazz, as an analogy and model for artistic creativity in general and filmmaking in particular—a pervasive analogy in the Beat milieu that Cassavetes drew on, depicted, and critiqued. I have already noted the literal presence of John Lurie's jazz trio in the film. The band not only injects moments of modern jazz into the film, but also forms part of the film's neo-beatnik, bohemian, and emphatically male iconography (along with Jarmusch and Tommy Finelli, the hipster played by Gian-carlo Esposito). The jazz analogy is carried more widely in the film by the improvisatory acting and the capricious editing, which often moves the film in surprising directions (both in the juxtaposition of different types of footage and in the startling timing and direction of particular cuts within and between scenes). One moment brings all these elements together. In the first scene in which Dot and Auggie talk in the tobacco store, at one point Dot cries out in frustration, "I'm a fun girl!" Cut to the jazz trio playing outside the store, Lurie's saxophone squealing as if in sympathy with Dot's yelp. After a few seconds, the film cuts back inside the store to the conversation, the music lingering briefly in the background before fading out altogether. When we're inside the store, we can't see the trio sitting outside. They appear and disappear sud-denly, magically—as they will again—through the power of cinema. So if an instrument is being played here, it is not a saxophone, but an edit-ing suite, and in this respect we need to note a different aesthetic legacy. There is something Godardian in the way *Blue in the Face* delights in the possibilities of film itself—of its modes of representation, its techniques. The play with time and space and the violation of the integrity of dra-matic scenes resemble nothing so much as those moments in early Go-dard (*Une femme est une femme*, 1961; *Le mepris*, 1963) when the fabric of the diegesis mutates from moment to moment. As Manny Farber put it about his termite films, "the feeling [is] that all is expendable, that it can be chopped up and flung down in a different arrangement with-out ruin."

"Chopped up and flung down" makes for a pretty good description of the closing credit sequence of *Blue in the Face*. The sequence alternates blocks of credits scrolling up the screen with dramatic fragments repris-ing and extending familiar scenes from earlier in the film. Each time a new block of credits appears it is accompanied by a new piece of music, and almost always a piece that contrasts in style, rhythm, and ethnic identity with the previous and subsequent works. In part this empha-sizes the ethnic diversity of Brooklyn, a theme articulated through-out the film by the statistical monologues, the video interviews, and especially the ensemble scenes in the store involving Malik Yoba. Yoba plays a would-be rap singer periodically hustling the inhabitants of the store, first selling watches and then—having adopted a new Hispanic identity—Cuban cigars. In these scenes, Yoba's ability to imperson-ate a range of ethnic stereotypes is comically offset by his ideological attachment to rigid racial categories. But in addition to underlining the ethnic theme, the manic *bricolage* of musical genres accompanying the closing credits also embodies the culture of sampling and remixing that is the contemporary (musical) heir to Godard's skittish film editing of the 1960s. In this as in so many ways, *Blue in the Face* is both a film absolutely of its moment, and one drawing on a rich legacy of independent filmmaking history.

PART VIII

NOT FILMS EXACTLY

28

Pamela Anderson on the Slippery Slope

Chuck Kleinhans

IN NOVEMBER 1997 a Seattle-based business, Internet Entertainment Group (IEG), placed on its "Club Love" Web site a home video depicting genital sexual acts involving actress and model Pamela Anderson and her then husband, Tommy Lee, drummer for the rock group Mötley Crüe.[1] After a brief legal battle, IEG continued to distribute the images online and through sales as a fifty-four-minute tape. The images were widely used on other pornography Web sites, making the tape one of the most successful porn videos of all time, and the footage the most widely seen home movie since the Zapruder film of the Kennedy assassination.

The surrounding events help mark a significant change in three interrelated areas that govern celebrity and star image in the 1990s: the effects of technological change in media circulation, the law governing privacy and publication rights, and shifting social boundaries of acceptable sexual behavior.

PAMELA

Pamela Anderson (b. 1967, British Columbia, Canada) first attained fame as a busty spokesmodel for Labatt's beer in 1989. An appearance as a *Playboy* Playmate followed, and then Playmate of the Year, and TV sitcom appearances in bimbo roles (*Married . . . with Children* and *Home Improvement*). In 1992 she joined the regular cast of the lifeguard drama series *Baywatch* and remained on the show for five years. Anderson then had the title role in the Hollywood film based on an adventure comic book, *Barb Wire* (1996). An action film set in a post-nuclear-war future, it failed at the box office, but Anderson gave a credible performance in a plot lifted from *Casablanca*, with herself in the Rick role. In 1998 she produced and starred in *VIP*, a slightly campy television syndication series, based on three sexy women who operate a bodyguard/detective agency.

Repeat appearances in *Playboy* and Playboy videos in the 1990s and a steady role on *Baywatch* gave her very strong public recognition. Although generally disparaged by critics, *Baywatch* was the most successful TV series internationally in the 1990s, even playing well in countries with very socially conservative media policies. The show featured simple action-based good-versus-evil plots, lots of conventionally attractive, athletic people exhibiting their bodies in swimsuits but very little sex or even romance, or character psychology or development. Anderson fit in, wearing a standard costume of a bright red swimsuit exposing lots of thigh and cleavage (enhanced by breast augmentation). *Baywatch* episodes often showed lifeguards involved in charitable acts: the pretty people doing good for the less pretty ones.

Anderson's star image evolved in two different but complementary registers. While looking like a blonde bimbo, as a *Baywatch* lifeguard she showed she was a team player, could take action, catch the bad guys, and help the innocent and unprotected. At the same time, with repeat *Playboy* appearances, she presented a sexy and alluring body, including discreet depiction of her external genital area, somewhat obscured by immaculately groomed pubic hair. (*Playboy*'s pictorials provided a "good taste" contrast to the notorious *Hustler* photos of women exhibiting anus and open labia, with *Penthouse* occupying an in-between position on explicit display.)

Her press personality has been friendly and straightforward. Recent interviews present the persona of a smart businesswoman, cool and self-possessed about protecting her person and children, unabashed about posing nude, and willing to be frank about sex (e.g., in a recent *Playboy* interview she discusses anal sex). Her star image ranges widely enough that people who know her image from TV and mainstream publicity (e.g., *People* magazine) can be aware of her posing nude without having seen any of the nude photographs. (It is quite easy in countries with liberal media policies, for those who are interested to access these pictures.)

CELEBRITY AND SEXUAL REPRESENTATION

Modern pinups begin with nineteenth-century photo images of female performers on stage and in circuses presented as collector's cards in cigarette packages. Body display was "justified" by profession, although "respectable" society equated female performers with prostitutes. The Hollywood studio era produced a massive expansion in pinup imagery as part of its publicity machine while trying to control any scandal. An endless process of exploitation and control of star image is an inherent part of image circulation in the era of mass reproduction. Celebrity intersects with various gatekeepers in the public sphere, and the pull of star machinery works with and against the push of social forces governing sexuality. To quickly cite some familiar examples: in 1984 Vanessa Williams, the first African American Miss America, had to surrender her title when earlier photos of nude modeling became public. Williams nonetheless continued with a successful career in singing and screen acting. Similarly, after initial success, two nude photo sessions of Madonna appeared that served largely to promote her "push the limits" star image, highlighted frequently afterwards.[2] Paul Reubens, star of the popular kids' TV program *Pee-wee's Playhouse*, lost his show when he was arrested for exposing himself in an adult movie theater; but the show was rerun in the late 1990s on the Family Channel (after Rupert Murdoch purchased the channel from archconservative evangelist Pat Robertson). Rising young star Rob Lowe had his career derailed when tapes of his sexual escapades became public. Other recent star scandals surrounded arrests on sex charges for Hugh Grant (caught with a street prostitute), Eddie Murphy (caught with a transvestite street hooker), and George Michaels (caught masturbating in a public toilet), adding to the long string of star sex scandals detailed in tabloid newspapers. Yet, with time the public seems to excuse, forgive, or forget: Lowe returned as a principal in the network prime-time drama *The West Wing* in 1999. Or it remembers with amusement bordering on affection: thus former Olympic-hopeful skater Tonya Harding (costar of the *Tonya and Jeff's Wedding Night* videotape sold by her ex) becomes the butt of ongoing "trailer trash" jokes, and Charlie Sheen ends up joking on talk shows about his reputation as a frequent prostitution customer.

But the mechanisms of rejection and rehabilitation never work perfectly, and certainly not always in accord with the desires of the celebrities, especially when they do not repent publicly (the one proven path in the still-Puritan U.S. context). Repeated allegations that Michael Jackson is a pedophile seem to have taken their toll on his career, and it seems unlikely that O. J. Simpson will be accepted again in the media.

THE TAPE AND THE LAW

Pamela Anderson married Tommy Lee after a very brief courtship in 1995. They recorded some of the early days of their relationship on a small handheld video recorder. They stored the tapes in a safe at home, but later that year during remodeling and repairs the tapes were stolen. Underground copies began circulating in 1996. In April 1996, with rumors that *Penthouse* had bought the tape and was about to publish photos from it, the pair appeared on Jay Leno's *Tonight Show*. Anderson was visibly pregnant and in an apparent attempt to contain the scandal, explained that the tapes were intended to be private and had been stolen.

Of course, in the nature of publicity and celebrity, the announcement served to heighten interest. In May 1996 *Penthouse* released its June 1996 U.S. issue with photos from the video, showing Lee's erect penis, close-ups of Anderson nude with her legs spread apart, and the couple engaged in oral and genital copulation. The couple immediately sued *Penthouse* to stop further publication on the basis of invasion of privacy. However, in August a California judge denied their claim, ruling that the settings depicted were not private places. The magazine showed photos taken in their vehicle on a highway and in the outdoor area of a houseboat, apparently on Lake Mead, a large mountain reservoir. The couple filed another suit in federal court, but in March 1997 a judge dismissed it, giving three reasons: (1) the photos were taken in public places and thereby the couple had given up claim to privacy, (2) the photos were "newsworthy" because the accompanying text included the couple's reactions to earlier French and Dutch versions of the pictures, and (3) the couple had revealed details of their private life.[3]

In two appearances by the couple on the Howard Stern radio show in October 1997, the host apparently played parts of the tape in the studio and commented on it, particularly about their physical attributes and activities. *Penthouse* sold the tape to Internet Entertainment Group (IEG), a leading purveyor of pornography on the World Wide Web, and in November 1997 IEG put the tape on its "Club Love" Internet site as a free digital movie. Immediately confronted with a suit, IEG stopped

Webcasting and the parties agreed to binding arbitration. A settlement was arranged in December. Apparently the couple thought the (still private) agreement amounted to a total "cease and desist," but IEG put the tape back on its site and began selling VHS video copies immediately. Again the couple sought relief in the courts, but in December 1998 a federal judge ruled that the couple had waived their rights in the 1997 agreement with IEG.

Some elaboration of the core legal issues may be helpful here. In general, U.S. courts have held that a certain threshold of celebrity (even when unintended—the lottery winner, or a witness to a news event) makes someone newsworthy and that freedom of the press and the public's interest in knowing override privacy. At the same time the press is not allowed to invade private property. (Acts that could be witnessed by the public in public places, or cameras in public places—looking in an open window—are okay; pushing aside curtains to peer inside or placing surveillance cameras in bathroom stalls are not.)

Stars, as celebrities who create and maintain an image, have the right to profit from their notoriety. Certain images can be regarded as intellectual property.[4] The particular problems that Anderson and Lee faced were first, that the original *Penthouse* photos were published abroad, outside U.S. jurisdiction. The publication of the photos and the existing celebrity of the pair made subsequent publication "newsworthy." Second, *Penthouse* published images that were technically in public places (although common sense—not law—would regard them as private places). Third, by going along with Howard Stern's bawdy radio commentary on the tape, Anderson and Lee allowed the images to be part of their publicity (that is, information about them that serves to promote their star image, which is part of their intangible celebrity value). Thus the publicist's commonplace: there's no such thing as bad publicity (since all notoriety increases public awareness). Fourth, the court also found that they had been forthcoming about intimate details of their life before, for example, that her name is tatooed on his penis. Thus, Anderson and Lee could not easily claim that the tape was stolen intellectual property to which they had the sole rights. Privacy claims were compromised because under current American law, disclosure of a part for a limited purpose cancels claims of privacy over the whole.

(IEG's publication of the full tape leaves intact all of the bedroom scenes. But images from the set of *Barb Wire* are digitally blurred. A sequence at a Mötley Crüe studio rehearsal includes audio of instruments, but no recognizable music because their songs are protected by copyright).

A plausible case could be made that although the couple had the obligation to sue to prevent distribution of the tape, the resulting publicity in fact was beneficial to their careers. A few years later, Anderson threw Lee out of the house, sued for divorce, and got a restraining order after he kicked her during a quarrel. She divorced him, appeared on Leno again as a woman standing against wife abuse—as a woman solely interested in protecting her children. Later, after Lee went through rehabilitation and anger management counseling, she allowed him back (with a strongly implied "he's my kids' father" excuse). Then it happened again, and she ended the relationship. These last events, the threatened appearance of another sex tape with another ex, rocker Brett Michaels of Poison, distributed by IEG, and the reduction of her breast implants rolled into the ongoing promotion of her show *VIP*. Another *Playboy* cover followed.

TECHNOLOGY

Pamela Anderson's image developed through the diversity of media technology in the 1990s. She was celebrated in newspapers at birth because she was the first child born on the Canadian centennial. Her modeling career began at a football game she attended, when her busty image wearing a Labatt's beer shirt was put on the stadium's Jumbotron display and the crowd cheered wildly. *Playboy* images in print and Playboy videos extended her visibility, as did *Baywatch* and the many print swimsuit images connected with that show (advertising, entertainment press, pinup posters, etc.). In the 1990s the expansion of the Internet and the proliferation of cable/satellite television channels multiplied image outlets. Computer and software development made it easier for fans to generate their own sites with prominent use of images from many sources, including corporate sites or scanned copies of print images. Large media corporations such as Disney and Playboy extensively and intensively policed the Internet for copyright infringement. But this was complicated by the difficulty of tracking down site operators, the ease of setting up new sites, and the international nature of the traffic and complications of intellectual property law and enforcement. Anderson, for example, appears prominently on official and amateur sites for *Baywatch*, and now *VIP*, as well as hosting her own "official" fan site (payment required for access). Her image can be found represented in news and publicity photos on commercial celebrity and entertainment news sites (free, supported by banner advertising), and on "friendly" fan sites (which present her in a positive light and present legal—and generally modest—images of her) as well as fan sites that use pirated (occasionally explicit) images.

The expansion of commercial pornography sites compounded policing problems. As with other new media technologies (e.g., the home video player, c. 1980), pornographers pioneered the field, moving farther and faster than legitimate product providers. Thus after *Penthouse* successfully exploited still images from the Anderson/Lee home video in its medium, IEG purchased the tape for its medium, the Internet.

By 1997 "streaming" technology and more advanced consumer computers allowed (relatively coarse) motion images to be broadcast over the Internet, bypassing established print/broadcast/video gatekeepers and control systems. IEG claimed it was the leader in Internet porn and its presentation of the Anderson/Lee images certainly catapulted its site to prominence. At the same time, competing porn sites pirated the material for their own use. In practical terms, for consumers, explicit images, including moving image highlights, of the stolen home video were widely available. At the time of writing this essay (summer of 2000) any standard Internet browser accessing any of the standard Internet search engines would produce thousands of "hits" (Web pages) that featured the material, including many that displayed it as a come-on to invite more detailed viewing available with a credit card (the industry standard for "adult verification"). Thus anyone, of any age, able to operate a Web-accessible computer could easily view some of the images. A postage-stamp-sized animation of Anderson fellating her husband seems to be the most common image used in these promos.[5]

HOME MOVIES

The tape that IEG circulates as *Pam and Tommy Lee: Hardcore and Uncensored* (1998) is an edited version of about three hours of stolen home video. It is selective: segments are divided by intertitles; digital blurs obscure people who appear other than the principals; and there is audio distortion of others' voices, and music added (possibly to cover ambient commercial music originally on radio or CD and legitimately copyrighted). For all its notoriety, only a fraction (about eight minutes) of the fifty-four minute tape contains explicit sexual imagery.

The tape begins without titles in a dressing trailer on the set of *Barb Wire*, followed by Anderson's birthday morning in a bedroom, then a visit to a luxurious powered yacht (apparently a rental) where Anderson opens gifts. On open water, the couple sunbathe. She pulls his shorts, exposing him, flashes a breast to the camera, accompanied by kissing and proclamations by both, "I love you. I love you, baby." Especially at the start, the camera work is quite shaky and sometimes the lens is dirty. One twenty-two-second shot shows a blow job from his point of view. After a few shots of a band rehearsal, at about fifteen minutes into the tape, their Malibu residence is shown with Anderson operating the camera. Outdoors with their three dogs, among more declarations of love, she asks, "When you going to get me preggos?" She encourages him to flash his penis, but one of the dogs bumps her at the crucial moment.

At eighteen minutes they head out for their "first holiday" in a Chevy Suburban with a boat in tow. On the road she tapes his erect penis sticking out of his shorts while he drives. She fellates him. He exclaims, "Fuck, I'm so fucking horny!" Video taping his penis on display, she says to the viewer, "I get this for the rest of my life, kids! Yes! Mom is a lucky camper! . . . Oh, we're not going to show our kids this tape." They finally pull over to the side of the highway to finish the activities.

At Lake Mead the couple travels about most of the time in a houseboat. Shots of each other mix with the scenery. Pam shows Tommy fishing and catching a small fish, naked with an erection preparing a breakfast plate, driving, diving nude off the boat, calling out in a canyon, which produces an echo, toasting marshmallows over a campfire, and so forth. He shows her swimming nude, sunning (he asks her to spread her legs), plays with an orange filter to produce a "sunset" scene, and shoots her strumming a guitar at the campfire. Sex alternates with other mundane vacation moments in this section. In several cases they seem to trade the camera back and forth while lovemaking proceeds.

In the late 1980s, and continuing into the 1990s, the commercial porn videotape business witnessed a remarkable expansion of tapes shot with high-quality consumer-format cameras. Often the maker worked solo and was both performer and cameraman hiring "amateur" talent (who often seemed to be sex industry workers and were "ama-

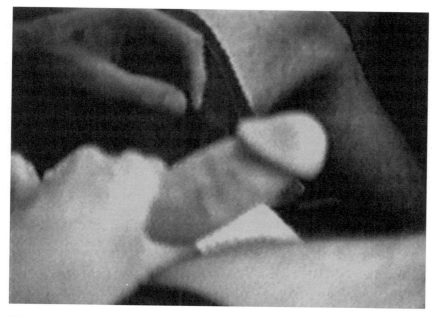

"I get this for the rest of my life, kids! Yes! Mom's a lucky camper . . . Oh we're not going to show our kids this tape." Anderson and Lee, 1995 home video; subsequently pirated.

teur" only in the sense they were not familiar actors). This "gonzo" subgenre foregrounds the personality of the maker, such as John "Buttman" Stagliano, who traveled to Europe and Brazil looking for his fetish, and Ed Powers, who did over a hundred of his "Dirty Debutantes" series in ten years. Over time Powers often used additional camerapeople, which allowed for more variety in camera angles and cutting.

The Anderson/Lee tape fits the familiar style of gonzo porn in the sex scenes when Lee holds the camera and his POV predominates. However, when Anderson controls the camera the POV shifts out of the dominant norm of heterosexual pornography. We get a relatively unusual shot of his face while he operates in the missionary position, as well as her view of him performing cunnilingus. In one episode, after fucking he withdraws and masturbates to ejaculation. Why he does this is not stated, but the effect is to re-create the traditional porn "money shot" of ejaculation outside the partner's body.[6] This raises questions about the difference between the articulated goal of getting

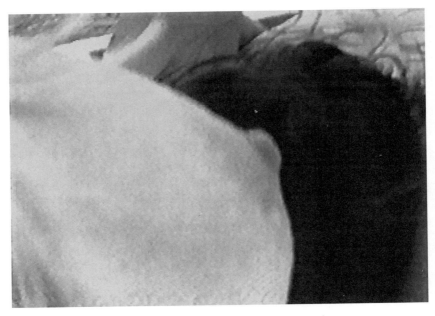

Gonzo porn? The most widely seen home "movie" since the Zapruder film. Anderson and Lee, 1995 home video; subsequently pirated.

her pregnant and the conventions of porn (showing ejaculation), or perhaps he can climax, or climax better, by finishing with his own hand rather than inside her. Since the POV is hers, the shot functions as well as a way for her to study him, capturing the image of his face in orgasm as well as the sight of his penis ejaculating—not so unusual for new lovers since the exploratory process involves much more than carnal knowledge.

In the later 1990s external male ejaculation also became a popular topic of public discourse, ranging from the presidential stain on Monica Lewinsky's dress to the "hair gel" joke in *There's Something about Mary* (1998). In the Anderson/Lee tape such sexual moments provide the voyeuristic allure of documentary "authenticity." Since celebrities and stars are usually experienced and talented in performing their personas, the press and public are always fascinated with the unguarded moment (such as public drunkenness or press access to otherwise private space). The Anderson/Lee tape promises precisely such "authenticity." Although on-camera, the space is considered private by the performers, and the performance is simply for each other (although the couple refer to an upcoming visit to his parents where they might show an edited version of the tape as vacation footage). But, as is often remarked about "private" diaries—that they are written with the knowledge that they will be read by others at some point—Pamela's exclamation about Tommy's penis states and then erases the idea of viewers other than the couple themselves. But this is precisely what makes the tape seem especially interesting to celebrity watchers. In viewing the tape we assume that we are seeing the "real" Pamela and Tommy, not their media images.

SLIPPERY SLOPES

The Right, in particular, makes policing sexual images a full-time obsession, often with the stated or implied worry of slippery slopes: any and every change from the norm in the direction of liberalization leads us all to worsening social decay. Our only protection is to stand fast against change, with the moral panics about movie and TV violence, rap music, and Internet pornography in the 1990s providing visible examples, and the ludicrous Ken Starr investigation and presidential impeachment proceeding another prime example of "slippery slope" rhetoric and politics. The Left too can fall into this mode of punditry, especially about popular TV. But for serious historically situated analysis, the description of gradual accumulated changes is tricky. No one step is totally decisive, and in fact may be reversed, but the general trend is clear. How to make a case without overstating it along the way?

Does Pamela Anderson's representation in the stolen home videotape significantly change her star image? Have we reached a new limit point in having access to a popular female star in explicit sexual activity while also having her appear as a delightful mom on network TV? Yes and no. That the tape was stolen provides an excuse. That she was having sex with her husband is also a pardon. In fact, the overall effect of the entire tape is—counterintuitively—not a highlighting of the sensational parts, but a placing of explicit newlywed sex in the context of love, affection, enthusiasm, mutual playfulness, and exploration. Two healthy people in a healthy relationship. Tommy and Pamela are endlessly professing their love, clearly passionate, and devoted—exactly what is left out of pornography.

NOTES

For helpful discussion, thanks to Julia Lesage, Kate Kane, Rick Morris, Jon Lewis, Lars Hubrich, the students in my spring 2000 Contemporary Documentary class who showed up for the optional screening/discussion, participants in the Eighth Visible Evidence documentary conference in Utrecht, August 2000, and seminar participants at Northern Illinois University, November 2000.

Many of the conclusions here are based on familiarity with Anderson's image for over a decade: e.g., different appearances on *The Tonight Show with Jay Leno*. Complete documentation and reviewing are probably possible, but for my purposes here would simply be pedantic and beside the point.

1. IEG originally netcast about thirty minutes of the tape on the Web. It released an X-rated version (*Pam and Tommy Lee: Hardcore and Uncensored*) for retail sale of about $100, and also an R-rated version (as *Pam and Tommy Lee: Stolen Honeymoon*). In late 1999 it advertised a version that included more footage, including the Anderson/Lee wedding. Pirate versions of the tape were also available (e.g., *The Honeymooners*). I have worked from a pirate version labeled *Uncensored and Untamed: Pamela and Tommy Lee*, which has removed initial titles and credits from the IEG tape, but it does have commercials at the end for the "Club Love" Web site.

2. MTV balked at showing one of Madonna's videos because it appeared she was wearing only an open mesh outfit. Assured that she was wearing a bodystocking underneath, they chose to program it. Later it was revealed that she was indeed exposing her skin in the video.

3. I am not trained as a lawyer and my discussion comes largely from press reports and Web sites for legal affairs (e.g., courttv.com, lawstreet.com, findlaw.com, hollywoodnetwork.com/Law/) and celebrity/fan sites (e.g., mrshowbiz.go.com, pamwatch.com, bestcelebritysites.com, etc.). Given a grant that would provide me access to Lexis/Nexis for legal research and pay me at standard-rate billable hours for legal research, I'd be delighted to provide full-bore traditional scholarly documentation of all this material.

4. For an excellent explanation in terms of case studies, see Jane Gaines, *Contested Culture: The Image, the Voice, and the Law* (Chapel Hill: University of North Carolina Press, 1991).

5. IEG founder and CEO Seth Warshavsky rose quickly as a *wunderkind* in Internet porn. An exposé in *Rolling Stone* by a former staffer contains many allegations of shady and sleazy business deals by Warshavsky, including the claim that he has cheated many other pornographers, which may be why they

freely bootleg "his" tape. Evan Wright, "Porn.com?" *RS*, no. 846 (August 3, 2000): 40–44, 46–48.

6. Linda Williams's well-known analysis of this obligatory shot, at variance from typical sexual practice, describes the necessity for "proof" of the male orgasm, which is precisely what the moving image cannot provide in relation to the female. Williams, *Hard Core: Power, Pleasure, and the Frenzy of the Visible* (Berkeley: University of California Press, 1989).

29

King Rodney

The Rodney King Video and Textual Analysis

Hamid Naficy

GEORGE HOLLIDAY'S VIDEO of the beating of Rodney King by Los Angeles police officers and the way it was deployed in court by both defense and prosecution attorneys highlight yet again some serious problems besetting film and television studies, problems that have remained largely dormant. These problems have to do with overreliance on vision as a marker of truth. One of the most often heard public responses to the acquittal of the officers in the case was disbelief, the realization that compelling visual evidence had failed to deliver the truth in the court of law. This realization flies in the face of certain branches of textual analysis, or close reading of images, which for over two decades has placed its emphasis on the primacy of the text and of vision as arbiters of truth. According to this theory, that which is visible is knowable, that which is visible is real.

The purpose of the defense in the King case, however, was exactly the opposite: to argue that "the video was something of an illusion." In presenting this tape to the one Asian, one Hispanic, and ten white jurors, an attorney for officer Theodore Briseno—who five years earlier had been suspended for two months for using excessive force—claimed that despite appearances, Briseno was not attacking King, he was merely holding him down with his foot on the neck to prevent him from being shot by angry fellow officers. Now, what factors worked to transform this documentary footage into fiction, the text into an illusion?

Although textual analysis problematizes "normal" vision, it ultimately places its trust in the truthfulness of "dissected" vision. Textual analysts in both film-TV studies and sports broadcasting have been

What factors worked to transform this documentary footage into fiction? A still from George Holliday's Rodney King video.

telling us that by repeatedly dissecting an image, slowing it down, and showing it in single frames and freeze-frames, we somehow can gain access to the truth hidden behind the images. However, the repeated screening of dissected images turns them into abstractions, into images without referent, into simulacrum. The spatial and temporal integrity that informed the images is vitiated. What further reduces the "reality effect" of these abstracted images is the total absence of sound.

The decision of King's attorneys to bar him from the court fed into this abstraction by erasing his presence and voice from the proceedings. Through abstraction, absence, and voicelessness, the subject of both the video and the court, in effect, disappeared. In a postmodern sleight of hand, the absent and voiceless referent could now be replaced by other intertextual images, chiefly racist stereotypes of African Americans from the popular culture, particularly the movies. Rodney King was thus turned into a sort of monster that could not be kept down: two jolts of Taser darts, each carrying 50,000 volts of electricity, had proven insufficient, thus necessitating nearly sixty baton strikes by four officers.

Rodney King: victim of police brutality or monstrous brute restrained by officers of law and order? A still frame from George Holliday's Rodney King video.

This prompted Tim Singer, a highway patrol officer, to testify that the scene reminded him of a movie "where the monster gets shot and still is coming at you."

Likewise, the Pulitzer Prize–winning *Los Angeles Times* TV critic, Howard Rosenberg, made a faux pas in a TV interview by saying that TV coverage of the "riots" after the verdict "affirmed" the inaccurate and unfair "Gorillas in the Mist" image that many people believed motivated the King beating. He later apologized, replacing the word "affirm" with "reinforce," but his slip of the tongue points to the way the absence of the referent—celebrated so much by proponents of postmodernism—can produce politically reactionary and destructive outcomes even in seasoned observers by filling the absence with stereotypical images widely circulated in the mass media. This accounts for how Rodney King, the TV image, was replaced by something like the movie image, King Kong. The civilizing mission that subjugated Kong now justified the violence used on King.

This is why when one day later, Rodney King himself appeared on TV for the first time since the beginning of the trial, so many viewers were shocked. First, they heard his voice making conciliatory remarks: "Can we get along? Can we get along?" Second, he criticized the image projected by his dissected video: "I'm not like they're making me out to be." Third, countering his video image of a brute that would not go down, he appeared to be meek, frightened, and vulnerable—an appearance reinforced by his halting speech. By this brief appearance, the absent referent had been brought to life, the real King had broken through the image of Kong. Hence the shock of recognition.

Postmodern theorists pride themselves on replacing texts with intertextuality. The problem, however, is that emphasis on texts or the intertext without context encourages the kind of readings that are regressive and hegemonic—they tend to tap into the dominant intertextual views that are readily available in mass media. This is disempowering and it plays into racist, ethnic, and sexist stereotypes. In the light of the Rodney King video and the use of textual analysis in courts of law, as film and TV studies scholars we need to rethink the liberatory social

The shock of recognition. Rodney King, beating victim.

power of video outside the context of mainstream television—which is related precisely to the video's referentiality—and to reexamine the politics and the political ramifications of our discourses.

NOTE

An earlier version of this essay, under the title "King Rodney: The Rodney King Video and Film and TV Studies" appeared in *High Performance,* summer 1992, 66–67.

30

Live Video

Laura U. Marks

YOU ARE IN a dim room in a Toronto gallery, lying on a sprawling beanbag chair that must be two meters long, gazing up at a screen. A strange little character, emitting wordless cries, stumbles across a sort of brightly colored postapocalyptic landscape. It must be a science fiction movie! But wait: every time the forms on screen shift, the music hums and twitters in sympathy: it's a melodrama!

The answer to what kind of movie you are watching lies in a studio in Brooklyn, where a collection of food wrappers, twine, labels, and styrofoam peanuts is blowing around on a huge round table. With no human present, computer-driven cameras switch among views of the trash, and simple software analyzes its movement to generate sounds that seem to correspond to the images. The same software, programmed by the invisible artists of this piece, edits in shot–reverse shot rhythms that seem to come straight out of a daytime soap opera. A live Internet feed streams the images and sounds to where you are lounging in Toronto, and it is you who are projecting characters, motivations, and genre styles on these innocent bits of refuse.

The piece, called the Appearance Machine, is the work of longtime collaborators Willy Le Maitre and Eric Rosenzweig, a.k.a. Screen. It is one of the exciting manifestations of a recent development in low-tech digital media, in which artists take advantage of commercial platforms, pro-sumer mixing boards, and developments in digital cinema to mix video live. Live video performances draw variously on DJ- and VJ-style mixing, free jazz, vaudeville, and avant-garde performance art.

Production has skyrocketed in recent months, as digital mixing equipment becomes more affordable and artist-programmers develop software. Among the numerous fascinating experiments in this

The Appearance Machine is streamed to the gallery where viewers recline on a huge beanbag pad and watch the live audio/video transmission projection (Appearance Machine, 2000).

burgeoning medium, the five artist teams I will look at in this essay are Screen (Le Maitre and Rosenzweig); Stackable Thumb (Naval Cassidy and Valued Cu$tomer); the RK Corral (Kristin Lemberg, Rajendra Serber, Bulk Foodveyor, Cheryl Leonard, and Scott "Scooter" Wilson); Jennifer and Kevin McCoy (no alias); and Animal Charm (Rich Bott and Jim Fetterley). Their low-end extravaganzas make use of sampling, improvisation, homemade platforms, trash props, and the artists' own bodies to produce unique audiovisual "concerts." Image feeds are synthesized live and projected, or translated in real time into other sorts of information that affect the multisensory spectacle. Live video is an interesting intervention in the virtual or simulacral quality of digital cinema, for it can only exist live; live-to-tape video documents are just that. The "content" of these works is obsolescence and cultural detritus: they recycle cast-off images from commercial culture, as well as real trash.

Live video is an offshoot of the general resurgence of performance video. If you take a look at the output of M.F.A. programs in recent years, you'll see many works that look like they could have been produced in 1972, except for that giveaway digital shimmer: single-shot sight gags for camera; intimate, improvised performances; feedback experiments that take advantage of machine randomness. Paradoxically, now that digital cameras, editing, and effects are giving almost unlimited control to artists, it seems that many are choosing to give up their control and allow the live event, or the whims of the medium (whims that must be assiduously programmed back in to control-freak editing software), to determine the look and feel of their final project. While commercial and high-end art applications use digital technology to increase the filmmaker's control of the spectacle, live video uses computers to emphasize the role of chance. This is a hands-off aesthetic.

FIRST-WAVE LIVE VIDEO

Many live video artists consciously seek their roots in the analog experiments of the knob-twiddling early 1970s. Benton Bainbridge (Valued Cu$tomer) of Stackable Thumb writes,

> When I and my cohorts leaped into the live video thing as the '90s kicked off, we had the same conviction that cinema was a performable medium, but little knowledge of our predecessors. In the Postmodern '80s, the abstract qualities of the medium, a fundamental issue to wrestle with when trying to "play" video in concert with others, was not really up for discussion.

But when video was young, many artist-scientists ignored the event in front of the camera in favor of the loopy effects that could be achieved by manipulating the electronic signal. The Paik-Abe Synthesizer may be one of the best remembered, but artists speak fondly of (and still use) other analog synthesizers like the Jones Colorizer, the Rutt-Etra Video Synthesizer, and the Sandin Image Processor. The Experimental Television Center in Owego, New York is home to many of these "obsolete" computers, and video artists who have done residencies there take advantage of the equipment's rich and varied effects to make idiosyncratic and complex works. Peer Bode, a former director of the ETC, and

Andrew Deutsch now oversee analog-digital miscegenations at Alfred University's Institute of Electronic Arts.

Pioneer live video artists Carol Goss and William Wright, interviewed in 1998 by Bainbridge, describe their experiments in the early 1970s that share many concerns of contemporary live video. (The fascinating full text of the interview is on the Pulsating OKAY! Web site, www.p-o-k.com.) Goss describes the intuitive leap into the void that is live improvisation: "The sense of form of a piece was something that everybody was breathing together." They speak especially fondly of the Jones Colorizer, which mixed signals from four black and white Portapak cameras with separate red, blue, and green color controls.

It must be noted that analog synthesis is cumbersome—Goss and Wright admitted that it took "about 18 hours" to set up the equipment —and that these experiments with live generation and synthesis are harder to carry out with sound than image. Naval Cassidy (Jonathan Giles) of Stackable Thumb notes that, short of using turntables, he could not mix sound live without a digital audio sampler. "I would have to create all the sound on 1/4-inch reel to reel, and cut it and paste it by hand; not suited for fast-paced live work."

Like their analog predecessors, live video artists tip their hats not to film or video art but to improvised music. Eric Rosenzweig comes to live video from free improvised music. Jonathan Giles, although he has an experimental filmmaking background, is the music-generating half of Stackable Thumb. Cheryl E. Leonard (a.k.a. the Black Box) of the RK Corral, a composer, improvises acoustic and electronic music in a triple interaction with actors and video images. The McCoys perform with musicians, from the "art" side, like Pauline Oliveros, Steina Vasulka, and Peter Bode, as well as experimental electronica DJs like Soundlab, DJ Spooky, Nerve, and DJ Anna Lee (with whom they mixed at the New York Underground Film Festival). The basic principles that structure improvised music allow musicians to generate new sounds and rhythms in the freedom of the moment. Kevin McCoy writes similarly of the live video event: "a flow of images and/or sounds the sequence and structure of which emerge 'immanently' and instantly." Live video gives up tight control of image and sound editing and content in favor of the surprising relationships that result from chance encounters. As with improvised music, it's the responsibility of listeners or viewers to create meanings, if they want to, or to enjoy the image/sound flow and groove on how the artists handle their instruments.

AGAINST VIRTUALITY

By popular accounts, digitization is taking audiovisual media (at least for us in the wealthy countries) from the physical, substantial stages of movie theaters and television sets to the seemingly weightless, immaterial space of so-called virtuality. The myth of virtuality, the search for the seamless human-computer interface, is of course in the interests of global corporations. Microsoft, Adobe, Sony, et al. encourage computer users continually to upgrade hardware and software and rudely abandon us when instead we make do with obsolete platforms. Many makers of digital media fall into the upgrade trap. But the live video artists embrace an aesthetics of appropriate, rather than high, technology. By appropriate technology, I mean technology that's no more sophisticated than necessary to do the job: a twig for eating ants (if you're a primate), a bicycle for getting around the city (if you're a human), an obsolete Amiga for generating video effects live (if you're Stackable Thumb). Live video artists can thus be seen in light of the materialist politics that media theorist Sean Cubitt calls "digital aesthetics."[1]

Cubitt believes that global corporations are infinitely capable of incorporating resistance, and that their conquest of everyday life is aided by digital technologies. If it can be digitized, it can be assimilated, is the essence of his argument. He calls for social alternatives grounded in the materiality of specific human-machine interfaces. Physical materiality —the analog side of digital life—is hard to assimilate.

Live video performances are chock-full of digital aesthetic values, because they do not try to hide their material construction, the social relationships that produced their technology, the economics of their low-tech platforms, and the quirkiness of their human-computer interfaces. Like all software, their applications are developed/pirated from military and commercial uses. Yet while the latter attempt to hide their technology behind a smoothly functioning interface, artists' live mixing platforms make the interface tangible, always reminding viewers of how the images and sounds are actually produced. Software is available for live image and sound mixing (for example, the Dutch company Steim develops software for electronic musicians and sponsors artists to experiment with its products: see www.steim.nl/products.html), but a number of artists cobble together their own homemade hardware-software platforms. Stackable Thumb's video is a combination of analog and low-end digital technology: security cameras, camcorders, VCRs, and video switchers designed for wedding videography. They do not rely on digital video effects or any heavily processed computer imagery, and have largely shunned the more recent platforms and software. Bainbridge writes, "We like the old stuff, particularly Amigas [the extinct Commodore computer], because Amigas remain much more responsive and reliable than Macs and Wintel machines running 10–50 times faster!"

Other live video artists use homemade software to produce their own platforms. Homemade software is the digital equivalent to processing film in the bathtub instead of sending it to a lab: if you are willing to make do with a less seamless final product, you can bend the rules on how to create it. Jennifer and Kevin McCoy's video installations and performances produce a live mix of prerecorded and appropriated images with Kevin McCoy's program Whirlygig, a sampling and mixing program for the Mac. The software functions "like a giant flip book," allowing the mix artist to access a database of hundreds of frames. McCoy stresses the musical, rather than cinematic, basis of the platform: "Whirlygig is a tool for doing live mixes with musicians and DJs. I've tried to match the formal language of electronic, mix-based music with my software: scratching, sampling, layering, looping, speed control, etc."

The most sophisticated variant of homemade programming belongs to those interactive media artists who are developing or adapting translation platforms, which digitize information in order to convert it from one modality to another: to generate sound from image, for example, or images from words. One of the most popular is The Very Nervous System developed by Toronto artist David Rokeby to analyze video frames and convert light patterns into a database of information. The user can then translate that information into another modality. (For more on the VNS, see www.interlog.com/~drokeby.) In their ongoing project called Fleabotics, Le Maitre and Rosenzweig use the VNS to generate sound from the live-video image. Using Max MIDI-based live music software, they program sounds to respond to the image's rhythms and shifts in brightness.

SO HOW DOES LIVE VIDEO LOOK, SOUND, AND FEEL?

Le Maitre and Rosenzweig recently completed the newest iteration of Fleabotics in the Appearance Machine, the hands-off moviemaking engine described above. This massive Lautréamont-like installation of video cameras, motors, discarded medical equipment, and trash produces video in a huge feedback loop so the artists need not intervene once it is set up. Fleabotics itself is a series of "nonintentional dramas" in which settings and characters are constituted entirely of trash-food wrappers, product packaging, and other refuse from the world of low-end commerce. The resulting movies are entrancing and can be experienced for hours.

The Appearance Machine is its own metteur-en-scène as well as its own editor. The artists use the Very Nervous System to convert the video images into instructions to fans, vibrators, and other motors that move the trash around to create a new setting. The image of a "character," a machine-generated spew of small bits of trash, is keyed into the "landscape" image at regular intervals. Scene changes are elicited by a feed from network television. Such cinematic conventions keep this work looking eerily like a real movie, but the crux of its movielikeness is atmospheric music worthy of Douglas Sirk. Visual rhythms and intensities generate audible rhythms and pitches that seem to be emitted by the objects themselves: they seem to squeal, hum, converse, and be accompanied by mood music and sound effects.

Yet it is all structured by chance. When I first saw Fleabotics I was sure it was a blurry version of a nature documentary on pollination I was seeing, and the artists tell of one performance in which a spectator, who had heard a detailed explanation of the random generation of the images, nevertheless remarked at the end, "It was very interesting, but why did you make the woman in the last scene Asian?"

In earlier versions, such as a show at the Kitchen in New York in 1999, the Machine was present in the same room as the images it produced, so viewers could see Fleabotics in both live and mediated versions. More recently, the artists have decided to heighten the mystery of the image source by stabling the Appearance Machine in a Brooklyn studio and streaming the images it produces in real time over the Internet. They are reembodied by a live feed to a faraway monitor—recently at the artist-run center InterAccess in Toronto and the Wexner Center in Ohio. Le Maitre and Rosenzweig kindly acknowledge the difference between virtual and physical space by letting viewers have an enormous beanbag pad to lounge on while they take in the work.

Jennifer and Kevin McCoy do VJ-style live mixes of prerecorded and plundered video. The musical format of their Whirlygig software results in images that are painterly and abstract, their mass-media content almost obscured. Interestingly, their work for the Web is also live mix. Their Web site Airworld.net is stylishly ambiguous, like many of those mysterious e-commerce sites that give you no idea what they're actually selling. Airworld is programmed to search the Web on buzzwords and download images and text from corporate Web sites into their own, changing all company names to Airworld, so indeed it looks like you could join the Airworld company, invest in Airworld stock, fly Airworld airlines, and purchase Airworld hair products. In a recent performance, Airworld Tonight, they keyed their own newscasters over live feeds from Bloomberg financial news, with their own economic analysis, then resent the mix as a low-power pirate TV signal. While Web work is beyond the scope of this essay, the potential to mix live feeds and resend the processed information makes the Web a live video engine par excellence.

Animal Charm, the Chicago-based duo of Rich Bott and Jim Fetterley, makes "scratch" videos (again the term refers to DJ techniques) of the trashiest of trashy images. In performance, Animal Charm invites guests to bring tapes to "video kitchens," which they mix up on the spot: in Surrealist fashion, the emerging content is the unanticipated meetings between unknown objects. Many of their live-mixed works are also distributed as single-channel tapes. Their content includes QVC ads for jewelry and desk accessories, infomercials for easy-install tennis courts (*Family Court*) and insurance (*Preserve Your Estate*), an early-1980s TV documentary on a San Diego city administrator (*Mark Roth*). Animal Charm's uncanny works give new, zombie life to images meant to disappear in the amnesia of commercial culture: I think of these images as the kind that, beaming into space, will first give news of life on Earth to creatures on other planets.

The most exuberantly live of all live video works are those by Stackable Thumb. Their events are more like concerts, or as they say, vaudeville shows, than video projections. Perhaps this reflects these artists' relative analog bias. In performance, Valued Cu$tomer and Naval Cassidy perform manic actions, such as burning small objects or destroying them on a grinding machine. At the same time they use tiny Internet cameras to shoot close-ups of these actions, their own bodies, and a dizzying array of trash props. (Like Rosenzweig and Le Maitre, they jealously guard their garbage collection and bring it to each performance; this can create problems at international borders.) The performance is already quite heady even before images are projected, and even includes an olfactory dimension when they burn plastic or grind dessicated citrus fruit. The resulting images are synthesized and mixed live using the aforementioned low-end synthesizers and wedding video switchers. At the same time music is mixed and performed live using a digital audio sampler. Images are projected behind the performers, so the audience has the choice whether to watch the artists producing them (for example, with a camera millimeters away from a melting honey bear or inside someone's mouth) or to gaze at the bear's curvy pastel silhouette, mixed on-screen with an exercise video, while hearing a feedback loop of polkas.

Live video, as well as grafting performance onto image mediation, can be used to insert mediation into liveness. The use of video mixing to amplify the effect of live performance is probably most familiar from rock concerts and football games, where video projections offer close-ups of the distant performers. As Phillip Auslander argues, "liveness" is nigh on impossible in an age when the authentic, or at least originary, media artifact is the recorded one: for example, live concerts attempt to replicate the band's music videos with which audiences are familiar.[2] Hovering between live theater, dance, and video, the Los Angeles–based RK Corral creates elaborate productions that test the relative interest of two "live" performances, that of the physically present actor and that of the electronically mediated image. Their performance "Enie Macy" at San Francisco's Lab Theater in November 1999 interwove the stories of its hapless eponymous protagonist and other characters with, projected behind them, live-mixed images of the actors and animated tableaux. A roving videographer records the actors, sometimes obscuring them from the audience so we have no choice but to look at their on-screen images. In this work, the relationship between liveness and mediation is as much a narrative as a formal concern. By way of introduction, dancer Kristin Lemberg pauses to explain that since the "Big Deal," space and time have been fragmented into an infinite series of steady states; the tinsel-crowned "Future Boy" appears intermittently to explain why he is refraining from living in the present, effectively mediating himself: "Sex will be better in the future (what with the eradication of AIDS, genetic on/off switches to enable pregnancy, and genetically engineered orgasms). That is why I am not having sex now." Mixed with the performers' images on-screen are live shots of weird dollhouse-scale sets and fetishlike animatronic puppets, which offer a kind of melodramatic complement to the action onstage. These are the products of Bulk Foodveyor (Philip R. Bonner), a former collaborator with Screen, who clearly shares their awareness of the anthropomorphic qualities of found objects. What I find to be the most interesting aspect of RK Corral's performances is the different reactions elicited by a performer's live body and his or her mediated image. The "Placid Couple" may be quarreling onstage, or Enie may be absorbedly twisting her skirt up around her waist, but it's just when the screen behind them affords a simultaneous close-up of outraged faces or neurotic gestures that the audience laughs.

All these live video teams critically recontextualize mass-cultural detritus, with approaches that vary from a "cool" machine aesthetic (Fleabotics) to a punk sensibility (Stackable Thumb, RK Corral) to a mocking/melancholy remix of trash corporate culture (McCoys and Animal Charm). Animal Charm remixes QVC in sharp comment on commodity culture; the McCoys poke fun at corporate jargon; Fleabotics and Stackable Thumb revel in the materiality of trash itself, recreating it in a sort of digital Merzbau; RK Corral invites found objects to share the action with the goofball improvisations of real bodies, themselves found objects of a sort.

In live performance, live video's hardware and software reveal themselves as mutable and fragile. It thus invites participants to experience our own corporeality, by reminding us that we live in nonvirtual space. While the military and commercial applications from which they were developed attempt to conceal the platforms on which they were built, effectively making the interface opaque, artists' live mixing platforms make the interface physical and transparent. Live video explores society's refuse, prying into the cracks in virtual culture, in order to reveal its underlying material and economic structures. Yet these low-tech digital works also re-enchant the world and our material and transient love affair with it.

NOTES

My warm thanks to all the artists who are quoted in this essay from live and electronic interviews. Additional sources:

Airworld, http://www.airworld.net
Animal Charm, http://www.animalcharm.com

Appearance Machine, http://appearancemachine.com/
Jennifer and Kevin McCoy, http://home.earthlink.net/~mccoy/
RK Corral, http://www.Rkcorral.com
Screen, http://www.interport.net/~er/
Stackable Thumb, http://www.stackable.com/
Video Data Bank, distributor of Animal Charm, http://www.vbd.com

An earlier version of this essay appeared in *The Independent*, July 2000.
    1. Sean Cubitt, *Digital Aesthetics* (London: Sage, 1998).
    2. Phillip Auslander, "Is It Live or . . . ?" in *Liveness: Performance in a Mediatized Culture* (New York: Routledge, 1999), 23–38.

PART IX

ENDGAMES

31

End of Story

The Collapse of Myth in Postmodern Narrative Film

Christopher Sharrett

POSTMODERN CULTURE IS representative of the exhaustion of late capitalist civilization. Adjacent to this exhaustion is an epoch of hyperinflation, where overproduction of cultural commodities and the consoling narratives they generate make transparent, by the endless repetition of narrative formulas, the wasteland of the commercial entertainment industry.[1] In this, commercial culture reflects late capital's insistent engendering of false needs and consoling narratives even as all parties acknowledge fraudulence.

The cinema of postmodernity suggests a society no longer able to believe fully its received myths (the law of the father, the essential goodness of capitalism, the state, religious authority, the family). Yet it is also unable to break with these myths in favor of a historical materialist view of reality. Large sectors of the media industry, including cable television's Nick at Nite and TV Land channels, are involved in this endgame, with "classic" sitcoms of the 1950s and 1960s (*Leave It to Beaver, The Andy Griffith Show*) presented with a nudge and wink that nevertheless project a yearning for stable, white, middle-class suburban life at a time when "family values" form a leitmotif of the major political parties. The cinema shares this general ideological project. Robin Wood has noted that films as seemingly different as *Blue Velvet* (1986) and *E.T.* (1982) convey the essential dynamic of postmodern thought: the need to affirm what is manifestly risible, to continue, with a knowing cynicism, to support bankrupt institutions.[2] To be sure, a number of celebrated works of the neoconservative canon (*Forrest Gump* [1994], *Saving Private Ryan* [1998]) dispense with postmodern irony and cynicism, opting for a tad of reflexivity and plenty of techno-wizardry to sell films that evoke a yearning for a pastoral, unified, pre-1960s America.

Self-reflexivity has become the order of the day in commercial cinema. This sensibility was fully in place in the 1980s, with films like Walter Hill's *Streets of Fire* (1984), a remake of *The Searchers* (1956) in a foreboding urban backdrop. Hill's *The Long Riders* (1980) and *Extreme Prejudice* (1987) both contain extended homage to Peckinpah. These films and Clint Eastwood's *Pale Rider* (1985), a scene-by-scene remake of *Shane* (1952), all attempt to resurrect through allusion a sense of the mythic, archetypal and portentous dimension of traditional narrative, and the past ability of genre conventions to reflect (often bogus) social consensus. Such strategies continue, sometimes modified by attempts at genre revision, as in Eastwood's *Unforgiven* (1993).

The 1990s saw a panicked predicament for narrative, as traditional notions of storytelling disappeared in the hyperactive montage of a new cinema that is essentially visual entertainment, the eye candy of image culture where the referent vanishes amid a whirlwind of spectacular editing. The visual hysteria of the new Hollywood product suggests an unraveling of any social consensus toward received notions of order.

APOCALYPTICISM AND THE ELEGY FOR THE MALE

In the last decades of the twentieth century, the apocalyptic continued to hold a powerful fascination within dominant ideology and commercial entertainment culture, particularly with the hype surrounding the approaching millennium. As a perpetual wish-dream within dominant culture, the apocalyptic prefers conflagration and self-immolation to radical transformation.

Apocalypticism's basic thematic was furthered by the rise of religious fundamentalism since the rightist backlash of the Reagan era. The apocalyptic became associated with the rise of male hysteria reacting against gender equality, gay liberation, and the supplanting of male authority by various phenomena, including the cybernetic revolution.

David Fincher's *Seven* (1995) is an unremittingly bleak *policier* that takes place in a dark, generic city of eternal rain (this is one of many postmodern films owing a great deal to *Blade Runner*, 1982). The search for the serial killer suggests a careening world, evident from its jagged, neoprimitive opening credits to a conclusion that allows the audience little consolation. While the unsettling *mise-en-scène* of the film makes it appear the kin of 1970s horror, its conservative ethic is manifest in its notion of reason and knowledge, as well as the fate of the male group. Two detectives, Somerset (Morgan Freeman) and Mills (Brad Pitt), represent an archetypal mainstay of the action cinema—the older man and his young acolyte, who together embody the passing down of wisdom and professionalism from one male generation to the next. In *Seven* the construct fails, and its failure is basic to the film's apocalypse. The famous denouement, with Mills's wife decapitated by John Doe, her head delivered in a cardboard box, is the film's underscoring of a basic failure within the male group—the pupil will not learn, and the teacher is exhausted, with nothing left to teach. The perspective of the film is evident in the beginning of the investigation, with Somerset going to a large, deserted public library, Bach playing on a radio, while Mills attempts to decipher crime scene pictures. Somerset's perusal of Dante, Chaucer, and Milton (Mills eventually glances at the Cliff Notes versions) is less about finding clues to the killer's logic than it is about valorizing pre-Enlightenment thought and recovering a philosophy that will restore stability to the off-kilter world. The film insists on the notion that crime is rooted in an unknowable "evil" rather than social causes, and is therefore beyond the remedy of science and reason as marshaled by modern institutions.

David Fincher continues this discourse in the far more challenging *Fight Club* (1999), the postmodern cinema's most compelling film on male hysteria and late capitalist culture. *Fight Club* is among the most self-reflexive of commercial films, making use of direct address to the audience, obvious "subliminal" edits, and simulated "breaks" in the film that make it appear to vibrate in the projector, exposing its sprocket holes. The film's style supports a far-ranging set of concerns—the emasculated male, consumer capital as cannibalistic, the female as specter haunting the remains of male privilege. The film's conclusion is an imaginary apocalypse of exploding office buildings, witnessed by Jack/Tyler as he at last comes to terms with the vampish Marla (Helena Bonham Carter). *Fight Club* seems to be a satiric response to works like Mel Gibson's *Braveheart* (1995), films that yearn for the restoration of male authority by reference to legendary triumphs of primeval patriarchal heroes.[3] But *Fight Club*, with its doom-laden, apocalyptic city (shot almost entirely at night), cannot conceive of a humane social vision, yet its catastrophe isn't total and absolute. Its focus is entirely on the male's attempt to prove he is still sentient by pain and self-destruction, making the film collude with the apocalyptic environment it posits. Its very disjunctive style seems suitable for the film's free-for-all survey of neurotic postmodern consumer/media society. The film's kick is the roller coaster through this illness, not a critical exposition of it. (The last "subliminal" shot as the credits roll is of the male genitals.)

Films of more straitlaced genres evidence a similar nostalgia—with little satire—for the fading cult of the male group. Michael Mann's *Heat* (1995) is noteworthy. Photographed with melancholy amber or blue lighting, Mann's "Los Angeles crime saga" (as the poster states) constantly frames its protagonists, policeman Vincent Hanna (Al Pacino) and his prey, gangster Neil McCauley (Robert De Niro), against the icy backdrop of Mike Davis's city of quartz, the thoroughly corporatized cityscape of the new Los Angeles downtown, whose hyperalienation has become a key exemplar of postmodernism.[4] While *Heat* seems to accept Davis's critique of Los Angeles, it does so from a rightist perspective, bemoaning capitalism's emasculating effects. Mann's compositions are reminiscent of the paintings of David Hockney and Eric Fischl (figures framed against lonely urban and suburban vistas). Mann emphasizes the torpor of the male, with stasis becoming the dominant tone as the characters only occasionally rupture the landscape's glacial mood with desperate actions. The exposition in the film, with its constant *longeurs*, owes as much to Visconti as to Wellman, Hawks, or Walsh, its operatics centered on a liturgy for the male, suffocated at one end (Hanna) by domesticity, at the other (McCauley) by the impossibility of men of action in the postmodern environment. At one point detective Hanna complains about having to live in his wife's "dead-tech bullshit postmodern house," conflating the postmodern scene itself with domestic strangulation. An elaborately staged bank robbery recapitulates the Last Stands of Peckinpah and earlier male action directors, as the gang decides (in the words of Neil's sidekick Michael), "Fuck it, let's do it!"

The often extraordinary films of Abel Ferrara offer a similar liturgy for the enervated male, especially *King of New York* (1990), *Bad Lieutenant* (1992), *The Funeral* (1997), and *New Rose Hotel* (1998), three of which feature the remarkably iconic presence of Christopher Walken, an emblem of the postmodern male as schizoid, enervated ghoul. Ferrara's films are apocalyptic in their sense of the dissolution of narrative, their often impossibly elliptical style (very much so in *New Rose Hotel*), and their

Al Pacino and Robert De Niro face off in Michael Mann's gorgeous gangster picture, *Heat* (Warner Brothers, 1995).

notion of the utter unraveling of the social contract. In *King of New York*, a crime lord named Frank White (Walken) is the city's last social conscience. White funnels drug money into ghetto hospitals and hires only minorities—the logic here is deliberately absurd, since he fills the hospitals with his victims, and uses his young black acolytes as cannon fodder. Most interesting is White's moribund, vampiric countenance, often caught mournfully scanning the cityscape while a symphonic composition fills the soundtrack. The essence of *King of New York* is the notion that the white liberal conscience—what's left of it—is actually predatory. The male and the story that contains him are ineffectual, decadent, depleted. It makes sense that several of Ferrara's films have strong elements of the Christian morality play (especially *The Addiction* and *Bad Lieutenant*), since their most extraordinary feature is the sense of lethargy and defeat encompassing the male protagonist. At the end of *New Rose Hotel*, Fox (Walken) commits suicide in an offhand, cavalier way while the unnamed Willem Dafoe character retreats to a hotel where he dreams about their failed schemes (as corporate raiders), fantasizes about lost love, and masturbates. The world itself implodes as the male characters evanesce.

Christopher Walken, emblem of the postmodern male as schizoid, enervated ghoul. As crime boss Frank White in *King of New York* (New Line, 1990), Walken plays an end-of-the-century Robin Hood, a white liberal capitalist drug lord who gives generously to good causes and hires people of color to do his often dangerous dirty work.

Abel Ferrara directing Lili Taylor in his contemporary Christian morality play,
The Addiction (October, 1995).

This trope of male self-absorption appears in pedestrian end-of-the-world films like the Schwarzenegger vehicle *End of Days* (1999). In the prerelease hype for this film, its star referred to the work of Susan Faludi, the backlash against feminism and the failure of the male to get "in touch," as the cause of the calamity of male culture. Both *End of Days* and the far superior *Fight Club* disingenuously appropriate popular and academic discourses about the postmodern situation, but only to serve the hoariest ideological agenda. The *locus classicus* of this neoconservative apocalypticism is no doubt *The Matrix* (1997), which uses a well-worn and incomprehensible messiah narrative to carry a jumble of special effects pretending to comment on the culture of the simulacra (as Baudrillard pops up in several gratuitous allusions).

NEW HORROR AND THE OBSOLETE HUMAN

Another cultural requiem surrounds the presentation of the body in postmodern horror sci-fi. While "evisceration cinema" was a term often applied to films such as *The Texas Chainsaw Massacre* (1973) and *Dawn of the Dead* (1978), the destruction of the body in those films constituted an assault on the family, bourgeois normality, and the consolation of narrative closure. The new horror film occasionally preserves the notion of the monster as scapegoat, but in so doing offers an image of the body as Other that makes these works decidedly incoherent.[5] The neoconservatism of new horror cuts across national borders, and finds its way even into fringe cinema that previously critiqued the mainstream. Take, for example, *Strangeland* (1998), a project of heavy metal star Dee Snider. *Strangeland* concerns a sadistic "modern primitive" named Captain Howdy (a nod to *The Exorcist*) who rapes and tortures young girls he meets through computer chat rooms. Captain Howdy extols the modern primitive lifestyle of tattooing, body piercing, genital torture, and body scarification as the pathway to the restoration of a pure, tribalistic community in the face of cybernetics and postindustrialism. Howdy's neoprimitivism is embodied in his "hacking away at the roots of evil," his destruction of the children of cyberculture. While at one point the film poses Captain Howdy as a scapegoat of a neurotic, repressed community, the film cannot part with the notion of the monster as evil aberration, along with the modern primitive counterculture, portrayed as crazed and degenerate. Similar sentiments pervade Shinya Tsuka-

Former heavy metal icon Dee Snider (left) as Captain Howdy, a modern primitive on a mission to silence the children of the dawning cyberculture (right).
Snider's *Strangeland* (Artisan, 1998) is one of many neoconservative horror
picture released in the last years of the century.

moto's far more sophisticated *Tetsuo* films. Both *Tetsuo: Iron Man* (1988)
and *Tetsuo II: Body Hammer* (1992) (which essentially rethinks the first
film) share with *Strangeland*, Clive Barker's *Hellraiser* films, and the
Alien, Predator, Terminator, and *Species* cycles a sense of the human subject's disastrous fate in postindustrialism, the age of AIDS, and the end
of the social contract in neoconservative political culture. All these films
reflect a reactionary culture's new anxieties about the body.

It has been argued that David Cronenberg is the prophet of the new
cinema of body horror, especially in the wake of his adaptation of J. G.
Ballard's *Crash* (1996), a film about a car crash cult that generates community out of a shared fixation on technology, celebrity, and death.
There is perhaps no irony in the fixation of the ideologically denuded
belief system of the crash cult on commodity fetishism, itself linked to
compulsive behavior, self-mutilation, and suicide. *Crash* might be Cronenberg's *Discreet Charm of the Bourgeoisie*, were it not for the film's
many morbid arias, particularly its operatic conclusion. Ballard (James

Spader) and wife Catherine (Deborah Kara Unger) copulate on a road-bank overlooking an industrial wasteland after their (deliberate) near-fatal crash. With *Fight Club, Crash* poses the notion that the bourgeoisie must cause itself pain to prove it can still feel something.

ALLUSIONISM AND THE BANKRUPTCY OF CODES

Allusionism continues to be a central strategy by which the commercial entertainment industry conceals its exhaustion and attempts to protect its legitimacy. Suggesting to the spectator that we are all in on the joke, that the cinema apparatus needs to be exposed, that genre conventions need to be ripped apart is central to rebuilding enlightened false consciousness.[6] The emphasis on allusionism is also crucial to furthering the conservative agenda of the new cinema.

That allusionism has a privileged place in the current cinema is made plain enough by the centrality of Quentin Tarantino. His films, especially *Pulp Fiction* (1994), are fixated and abound with pop products and references to the very recent (mostly 1970s, suggesting the narrowness of Tarantino's sensibility) past of the commercial entertainment industry. The much-ballyhooed "parallel narrative" of this film is an incidental, indulgent conceit that provides the vehicle for endless nods at cultural fads and the image industry. *Pulp Fiction* is one of the quintessential postmodern works for its assertion—beginning with its title—that there is little of worth or concern outside the realm of cheap commercial representation.

An instructive moment of the new cinema of allusion is George Cosmatos's *Tombstone* (1993), yet another rendering of the Wyatt Earp / Doc Holliday / OK Corral story. The hard times of the western since the 1960s have been well documented, and it is useful to note that *Tombstone* does not attempt to continue the genre in its revisionist mode, for example, *Unforgiven* or the earlier, more pivotal *The Wild Bunch* (1969). Instead, *Tombstone*, like another Earp film of the same year, Lawrence Kasdan's *Wyatt Earp*, is something of a throwback, a neoconservative work that gains legitimacy precisely by acknowledging its incredible story and narrative lineage. The film's black and white prologue, narrated by Robert Mitchum, introduces images of the Old West in silent footage mainly from *The Great Train Robbery* (1903). This bogus documentary establishes the film's bona fides by adding reflexivity and acknowledging the roots of this most conservative genre. The film's credentials are established also by the inclusion of Mitchum and other actors long associated with the western (and the old Hollywood) like Harry Carey Jr. and Charlton Heston. More claims to artistic sophistication are attempted by emphasis on "realism" (a Tombstone somewhat closer to the historical record, a gritty and small-scale OK Corral gunfight). Of greater importance to the film's legitimacy as a new take on the western is its acknowledgment of Wyatt Earp (Kurt Russell) as something less than Henry Fonda's town tamer. He is a post-Reagan businessman and cynical pragmatist, thus incorporating some of the historical record on the real Earp, but more importantly acknowledging the public's dismissal in the post-Vietnam years of the traditional western's objective good and evil. The Earp brothers and the reprobate Doc Holliday (a wonderful turn by Val Kilmer) are less than sterling. But they are the heroes of the day nonetheless, with this western ultimately extolling vigilantism basic to the most reactionary examples of the action cinema.

The later horror films of Wes Craven are perhaps more straightforward emblems of the commercial cinema's exhaustion under the guise of provocative, risk-taking works. Craven took a first step into self-reflexive cinema with *Wes Craven's New Nightmare* (1994), the last installment (or postscript) to his *Nightmare on Elm Street* series. The film showcases the actors in all the previous Freddy Krueger films in a film-within-a-film, as the series' female lead (Heather Langencamp) suffers nightmares shared with her young son about a new Freddy project. The film centers on the Freddy Krueger phenomenon (at one point Freddy —or the actor, Robert Englund, who incarnates him—cavorts on a talk show and shouts, "You're all my children now") and the need to find a form of catharsis to end these obsessions.

Craven's *Scream* films seem less about that project than a grab bag of allusions and conventions of the stalker film, which the young audience, like the characters of these films, is supposed to know by heart, yet respond to anyway. There is no irony in the series' stalker wearing a dark shroud and an elongated mask mimicking Edvard Munch's painting *The Scream*, a kind of cultural touchstone for critics like Fredric Jameson who differentiate anxiety-laden modernism from vacant postmodernism. The collection of tropes that is *Scream* and its sequels is nothing so much as the cinema disclosing its frustrations, its desire, in

Robin Wood's sense, to have it both ways by drawing in the teen crowd while admitting that it has nothing more to say.

Among the most intelligent responses to the bankruptcy of the commercial cinema is Gregg Araki's *The Doom Generation* (1995), one of a series of marginal, independent films by Araki that comment intelligently on the postmodern predicament.[7] The film acknowledges the garish, decayed circumstances of postindustrial society, its capitalistic framework, image culture, and renewed reactionary political climate. But instead of valorizing alienation, savoring pop culture detritus, or dabbling in angst about the lost centrality of the male, it offers a humorous bisexual triad, three young Generation Xers who share a vital if unfocused contempt for the standing order of things. Their revolt evolves from anarchical antics to the construction of a nascent bisexual family, destroyed in the film's savage conclusion. *The Doom Generation* contains the grim assertions of much of the apocalyptic cinema, but does not see them as givens of human destiny, and has the temerity to suggest an adversarial culture. Unlike Tarantino, Araki views with sarcastic contempt the commodity culture, including representational cinema (the gory convenience store robbery is completely presentational, the portrayal of violence fully supporting the film's sense of the devaluation of life, a theme most palpable when the trio accidentally kill a dog). For all its chaotic atmosphere, embodying the hyperactivity and extreme disaffection of contemporary youth, the film is among the few to suggest that humanity can survive the postmodern condition.

Films such as *The Doom Generation* seem few and far between, and the prospects for a genuine alternative cinema rather bleak. Films such as Todd Solondz's *Happiness* (1998), Alexander Payne's *Election* (1999), and Sam Mendes' much-overrated *American Beauty* (1999) show the current bourgeois order as fragile, but treat it with snide contempt, the controlling sensibility being that sympathy is for suckers, the current world composed of "losers" deserving of each other.

The contemporary collapse of Hollywood representational narrative and the myths it supports may seem a consolation in the sense that it suggests the slow coming-apart of a political/social order that has defied progressive values and the advancement of democratic society. It is difficult to take heart in this, however, since in the absence of progressive politics the collapse is itself implicated in furthering an inhumane vision, a worldview that prefers the cynicism and self-absorbed death fantasies that have always been the hallmark of capitalist civilization.

NOTES

1. The notion of the exhaustion of film genres is discussed in David Sanjek, "Same As It Ever Was: Innovation and Exhaustion in Horror and Science Fiction Films of the 1990s," in *Film Genre 2000: New Critical Essays,* ed. Wheeler Winston Dixon (Albany: State University of New York Press, 2000), 111–25. While I disagree with any number of his assertions about art, economy, and postmodernity, Charles Newman offers interesting remarks about overproduction, inflation, and culture in *The Post-Modern Aura: The Act of Fiction in the Age of Inflation* (Evanston, IL: Northwestern University Press, 1985).

2. Robin Wood, *"Rally 'round the Flag, Boys,* or, Give It Back to the Indians," *Cineaction* 9 (1987): 8.

3. An important analysis of this topic is William Luhr, "Mutilating Mel: Martyrdom and Masculinity in *Braveheart,"* in *Mythologies of Violence in Postmodern Media,* ed. Christopher Sharrett (Detroit: Wayne State University Press, 1999), 227–41.

4. Davis has produced a canonical work in *City of Quartz: Excavating the Future in Los Angeles* (London: Verso, 1990). Davis extends his work on alienation and the postmodern city in *Ecology of Fear: Los Angeles and the Imagination of Disaster* (New York: Metropolitan/Henry Holt, 1998).

5. I borrow the idea of the "incoherent text" from Robin Wood, who in his discussion of seventies and early eighties films such as *Taxi Driver, Raging Bull,* and *Cruising,* remarked that these works are incoherent not because they are unreadable but because their ideological agendas are unresolved. The incoherence of the new horror film is based less on a tension between ideological arguments than a failure to recognize any adversarial culture. See Wood, *Hollywood from Vietnam to Reagan* (New York: Columbia University Press, 1986), 46–70.

6. The idea is developed in Peter Sloterdijk, *Critique of Cynical Reason,* trans. Michael Eldred (Minneapolis: University of Minnesota Press, 1987), 6, passim.

7. The most eloquent analysis of this neglected film is in Robin Wood's invaluable *Sexual Politics and Narrative Film: Hollywood and Beyond* (New York: Columbia University Press, 1998), 336–45.

32

Waiting for the End of the World

Christian Apocalyptic Media at the Turn of the Millennium

Heather Hendershot

IN THE FINAL months of 1999, Y2K anxiety reached a frenzied peak in America. The world might end, do you have plenty of batteries and bottled water? The nightly news gave regular updates on how to safeguard personal computers, and the Sunday *New York Times* featured articles on how the rich were stocking up on canned goods to prepare gourmet dishes that did not require refrigeration. Meanwhile in movie theaters, a few films tried to tap into the zeitgeist. The Arnold Schwarzenegger apocalyptic thriller *End of Days*, for example, told the story of a cop who hit the bottle after his family was gunned down. An atheist, he finds redemption by helping a damsel in distress, a virgin whom Satan intends to impregnate on New Year's Eve. If the Prince of Darkness succeeds, the world will end. The film is tedious, but Gabriel Byrne plays Lucifer with panache. He engages in a ménage à trois with his henchman's wife and daughter and blows stuff up by setting his own thick black urine on fire. He is, in short, a bad ass.

Cut to another apocalyptic flick, also released just before the dawn of the new millennium. This one stars Michael York as the Antichrist, "a fictional cross between . . . Romano Prodi, current president of the European Commission, and Rupert Murdoch."[1] He has brought about global peace, and the world is ready to worship him as the new Messiah. Our hero, who feebly attempts to stop York, is a motivational speaker who rejected God after his mother was killed by a drunk driver. He hides biblical decoder disks from the Antichrist and is ultimately redeemed when he asks Jesus to save him. Nobody in this film is a bad ass. The film is called *The Omega Code*, and it was the first feature-length evangelical Christian film to receive a national theatrical release.

The Omega Code is an odd piece of the jigsaw puzzle that is American popular culture. On the one hand, it is a typical Hollywood film, with lots of action and a lost-yet-redeemable hero. And films about the devil and the end of the world are certainly nothing new. On the other hand, the film offers a "family values"–type Satan who could only (maybe) frighten a born-again Christian already well versed in end of the world eschatology. The film is ostensibly designed to win souls, although, as a number of dubious Christian viewers have pointed out, there is only one overt mention of Jesus in the whole film.[2] If you weren't already "saved," you probably wouldn't get that the hero's "Save me Jesus"—shouted as computer-generated demons swirl around him—is supposed to represent a born-again experience. In sum, the film seems to be preaching to the choir.

The Omega Code was made for just over $7 million. It took in more than $2 million its first weekend, ranking number ten in per-screen box office gross. With $7,869 per screen, *The Omega Code* surpassed *Fight Club*'s per-screen box office average. *Fight Club* opened on two thousand screens. *The Omega Code* was on three hundred, mostly in Bible Belt cities, but also in a number of large midwestern cities and on the East Coast.[3] Advance tickets were sold through the national Family Christian Bookstore chain.[4] Churches in Jacksonville, Phoenix, and Oklahoma City bought out whole theaters for weekend screenings.[5] In Portland, Oregon, a thousand advance tickets were sold, the most advance tickets sold in local history, with the exception of *The Phantom Menace*.[6] As of December 1999, *The Omega Code* had grossed $11.5 million, and revenue will continue to roll in with TV broadcasts and video sales.

Why did this film succeed? One obvious answer is that there are millions of evangelicals in America, so there was an untapped market for the film.[7] Eamonn Bowles, president of distribution for Manhattan's Shooting Gallery, compared the film's audience to that of Robert Duvall's 1997 film *The Apostle*, which Duvall promoted by appearing on Christian talk shows and by inviting ministers to preview the film.[8] Jimmy Daddabbo, a secular producer, even compared evangelicals to black women and the success of *The Omega Code* to the success of *Waiting to Exhale*.[9] Both films filled vacuums of underserved audiences. Yet there is more to *The Omega Code*'s success. To really understand the *The*

Omega Code phenomenon, one must situate it on the map of American apocalyptic media.

The Omega Code was financed by the Trinity Broadcasting Network, the nation's largest Christian television broadcaster. TBN, which is geared toward a charismatic and Pentecostal audience, was founded in 1973 by Paul and Jan Crouch. Paul Crouch was *The Omega Code*'s executive producer and is the father of Matt Crouch, the film's producer. As a not-for-profit ministry, TBN cannot sell ads, but viewers donate an estimated $80 million to the network each year. TBN is a privately owned network with twelve full-power and more than three hundred low-power stations nationwide.[10] TBN also has five thousand cable outlets accessible to over seventy million households.[11] TBN will get the initial exclusive rights to air *The Omega Code* on television, as well as an undisclosed chunk of the theatrical revenue.

TBN has turned to filmmaking to counter the sex, violence, and secular messages of mainstream movies and to redeem media as a salvation tool. As Paul Crouch explains, "two thousand years ago, Jesus told His followers vivid stories and parables about life. Today we use film and television. Millions of people see Hollywood films filled with violence and sex, yet we offer an exciting movie filled with hope."[12] Like his father, Matt Crouch believes that film is not inherently sinful. *The Omega Code*, he explains, taps into "a market of people who for years had wanted to embrace Hollywood but couldn't."[13]

This picture of modern evangelicals flies in the face of the image of the old-fashioned fundamentalist, who withdrew from the world and unambivalently rejected cigarettes, liquor, movies, and dancing. There's no liquor, dancing, or cigarettes in Crouch's film—not to mention sex or profanity (unless you count "Balderdash!")—but the film earned a PG-13 rating for violence. The scriptwriter retorts, "violent things happened in the Book of Revelations. There's no way to get around that."[14] (Skeptics note that the Bible also includes plenty of illicit sex.)

The Omega Code had an initial marketing budget of only $600,000, low by Hollywood standards. The secular press credits the film's success to TBN's "grassroots" strategy of soliciting volunteers to publicize the film by sending e-mails, putting up posters, and spreading word of mouth. The official *The Omega Code* Web site received twelve thousand hits a day in the weeks following the film's release, and according to the distributor, Providence Entertainment, one day the site got 500,000 hits, and 150,000 posters were downloaded.[15] Providence distributed "Marketing 101 kits" that included "a sample sales pitch to turn church-goers into movie-goers."[16] Interestingly, *The Omega Code* has been widely compared to *The Blair Witch Project* (1999), as this independent film was also publicized in large part via the Internet. A Tulsa, Oklahoma, religious film production company, Impact Productions, also helped market *The Omega Code* by contacting 2,400 pastors around the country,[17] and Matt Crouch himself showed two-minute promotional clips of the film during worship services in Houston, Texas, five days before the national release on October 15.[18] *The Omega Code* certainly owes much of its success to these tactics, but the film also received many hours of free publicity on TBN; unlike most low-budget independent films, this film was massively promoted on television.

While many journalists have noted that evangelical Christians constitute a large, often untapped market segment, they have nonetheless tended to position this film as something *outside* popular culture that has *intruded into* the so-called secular mainstream. Conservative Christians are thus nodded to, but still dismissed as weird cultural outsiders. While end of the world eschatology may seem bizarre to non–born-agains, it is quite problematic to conceive of Christian apocalyptic belief as marginal to American culture. For one thing, there are millions of born-again Christians in America.[19]

Widespread interest (if not universal belief) in prophecy is a fact of American popular culture. Millions of apocalyptic books have been sold here in the United States. One of the classic texts of twentieth-century apocalypticism, Hal Lindsey's 1970 *The Late Great Planet Earth*, is still in print and has sold well over fifteen million copies in the United States alone.[20] The *New York Times* declared Lindsey the best-selling author of the seventies.[21] Lindsey remains active, and he was officially billed as *The Omega Code*'s "prophecy consultant." Today, prophecy books once again top the best-seller lists, although these books are now officially classified as fiction rather than nonfiction. Tim LaHaye and Jerry Jenkins's "Left Behind" series has included eight books since 1995, and they have sold more than a million copies each. Like most prophecy novelists, LaHaye and Jenkins tell the same basic story of the Rapture (when saved people are suddenly removed from the earth), the rise of the Antichrist, and the martyrdom of the saints (Christians converted after the Rapture). The difference is that instead of doing all of this in one book, the authors spread it out, thereby spreading out the profits. The authors have also produced a film and are developing a TV series.[22] *The Omega Code* must be understood in this context; American popular culture is comprised of both evangelicals and nonevangelicals, and, if the best-seller lists offer any indication, millions from both groups are apparently fascinated by apocalyptic narratives.

While Christian apocalyptic books are recognized as best-sellers only after they expand beyond Christian bookstores to the secular marketplace, Christian films are usually distributed exclusively through alternative means, shown in churches or sold on video in Christian bookstores. These films rarely make a blip on the secular culture's radar screen, but they are widely known among born-agains. The most famous prophecy films are a series of four movies that began with *Thief in the Night* in 1973 and concluded with *The Prodigal Planet* in 1983. Like LaHaye and Jenkins's book series, *Thief in the Night* and its sequels depict the Rapture, the Antichrist, and God's final triumph over Satan. Never released in conventional theaters, "*A Thief in the Night* has been translated into three foreign languages, subtitled in countless others, and its international distribution continues strongly . . . six or seven hundred prints now circulate, in addition to videocassettes."[23] Religious studies scholar Randall Balmer reports that

> In the United States, where distribution is limited to church groups, camps, youth organizations, and the like, it is difficult to quantify the number of people who have seen the film. When I pressed [the film's co-producer] for a figure, he reluctantly estimated that one hundred million people had seen *A Thief in the Night* in the United States, a figure, he hastened to add, that would include those who had seen it more than once. Even if you slash that number in half to account for hyperbole, fifty million is still a staggering figure, a viewership that would be the envy of many Hollywood producers.[24]

Hollywood producers would hardly approve of the usual ticket price, however: an optional donation.

In addition to the dramatic fictional format of the "Left Behind" series and of films like *The Omega Code* and *Thief in the Night*, there is a second apocalyptic subgenre, which I call the post-Rapture video. These videos vary, some focusing on a pastor explaining what will happen after the Rapture and explaining how to accept Jesus into your heart, and some mixing the pastor's explanation with dramatized post-Rapture events, such as CNN-style newscasts showing the rise of the Antichrist. With or without dramatic elements, all these videos address the viewer as someone who has been "left behind" after the Rapture.[25] The pastors who narrate post-Rapture videos emphasize that they will be gone when "you," the unraptured viewer, watch the video. Viewers are admonished to accept Christ, reject the Antichrist, and die a martyr's death.

It is unclear how unraptured people are expected to find the videos. In *Left Behind*, the first book in the Jenkins and LaHaye series, a newly born-again person offers a video to the book's hero, explaining that the pastor of his church had recorded the tape and put it in the church library with instructions to "play it if most everyone seemed to have disappeared."[26] In reality, these tapes are widely distributed via Christian book clubs and bookstores. Many small Christian stores with virtually no videos for sale will have at least one post-Rapture video and at least one video from the *Thief in the Night* series. *Left Behind*, a post-Rapture video produced by prophecy ministers Peter and Paul Lalonde, has sold over 200,000 copies. The front of the box bills the video as "the *original* video produced especially for those who will be left behind," presumably in response to the LaHaye and Jenkins video—*Have You Been Left Behind?*—released in 1995, concurrently with their *Left Behind* book.

The cover of the Jenkins and LaHaye video tells viewers, "If you find this tape, play it immediately. Your future depends on it!" The video is more or less an exact rendition of the video used in the book. As *Left Behind*'s hero, Rayford Steele, watches the tape, he periodically pushes the pause button to think things over. Convinced by the tape, Steele finally concludes that "It was time to move beyond being a critic, an analyst never satisfied with the evidence. The proof was before him: the empty chairs, the lonely bed, the hole in his heart. There was only one course of action. He punched the play button."[27] A few moments later, the hero kneels in worship for the first time. No longer a doubter, he loses the need to use the pause button to allow time for reflection. "He pushed the play button and tossed the remote control aside."[28]

All these different apocalyptic media—the books, the dramatic films, the post-Rapture videos—emphasize the need for conversion. All of them, that is, except for *The Omega Code*. *The Omega Code* does not even include the Rapture, the opening event of virtually all prophecy media. The fear of being "left behind" is a key dramatic and evangelistic tactic, the idea being that one must be born again *immediately*, since the Rapture could happen at any second.[29] Could it be that the film's low-key evangelism actually explains its success in secular theaters?

Interestingly, this "first crossover Christian film" has been rejected by many Christian viewers as not Christian enough.[30] A subtle or absent salvation message seems to be the hallmark of much of the media that find financial success beyond the Christian market.[31] The Christian music industry is a case in point. Since the early eighties, contemporary Christian music (commonly called CCM) has been rapidly growing. Like small independent film distributors, who have been bought up by the majors over the past few years, the once small CCM companies have been bought up by larger entertainment conglomerates. Christian musicians who have had crossover hits in the secular market have tended to do so with "wholesome love songs and not the 'confessional' lyrics that originally qualified as contemporary Christian music."[32] As disgruntled CCM musician Steve Camp has argued, much of the Christian music on the market is "Christ-less, watered-down . . . God-as-my-girlfriend kind of thing."[33] There is, of course, plenty of hard-core evangelistic music, but the softer stuff is the only thing that has a chance of getting played on big radio stations and becoming a hit. "'It's frustrating,' sighs Toby McKeehan, songwriter and mouthpiece for dc Talk, an indie band now backed by Virgin Records, whose execs have told them flatly that their explicit Christian content is limiting their crossover success. 'It feels like you sneak into the mainstream, [radio] figures out you're Christian, and then they shut you down.'"[34]

The LaHaye and Jenkins books are filled with evangelical fervor. But in terms of financial success beyond the Christian bookstore circuit, that makes them more the exception than the rule. *The Omega Code*, conversely, is more like successful crossover CCM tunes: clean, upbeat, and Christian only by virtue of not being anti-Christian, not promoting premarital sex, swearing, drinking, rebellion against parents, and so on. If you don't already understand the evangelical interpretation of the Book of Revelations, *The Omega Code* only seems Christian because it is square.

The *Variety* review described *The Omega Code* as "a ham-handed, flat-footed B-movie that makes *The Omen* look like *Citizen Kane*."[35] On the surface this assessment doesn't seem very complex: *Kane* is a classic, *The Omen* is crap, and *The Omega Code* is even crappier. But those who have simply dismissed *The Omega Code* as a fluke, a kooky Christian action picture with an indecipherable plot, might learn something by reading between the lines of the *Variety* critic's barb. *Variety* references a schlocky horror film about a young boy who, it turns out, is the Antichrist. *The Omen*'s story is better, and it is much scarier, but the movie depends on the same premises that *The Omega Code* does, that moviegoers are fascinated by evil, and that they are sufficiently acquainted with biblical prophecy to be drawn to a film about the Antichrist. Evangelical and nonevangelical audiences may not all agree that the end is genuinely near, but we are all happy to see the end played out over and over again at the movies.

NOTES

1. Phil Miller, "Christian Thriller Has Fans Flocking to Cinema Aisles," *Scotsman*, 27 Oct. 1999, 11.

2. Viewer cited in Scott Martelle and Megan Garvey, "A Film Christians Believe In," *Los Angeles Times*, 22 Oct. 1999, A1. A more enthusiastic viewer conceded that "the movie gives us something a little more pro-family, more uplifting and at least points us toward hope and faith, if not God personally." David Germain, "Church Moves into Mega-Plex," *Ottawa Citizen*, 21 Oct. 1999, A16.

3. This is an interesting inversion. Usually small independent films with a limited market open only in a few select big cities such as New York, Chicago, and Los Angeles. But these cities are not where the most born-agains are found, so *The Omega Code* opened in the southern and midwestern cities that are usually *least* likely to screen independent films.

4. Martelle and Garvey.

5. Germain.

6. Richard Vara, "Box Office Bonanza: Unorthodox Marketing Promotes Movie," *Houston Chronicle*, 23 Oct. 1999, religion sec., 1.

7. Sociologist Christian Smith contends that there are "20 million Americans who identify themselves with the evangelical movement." *American Evangelicalism: Embattled and Thriving* (Chicago: University of Chicago Press, 1998), 1.

8. The film opened weakly but ended up grossing $20 million, drawing mostly Christian audiences in Middle America. Martelle and Garvey.

9. Martelle and Garvey.

10. Scott Collins, "TBN Turns to Film to Spread Faith," *Los Angeles Times*, 16 Sept. 1999, C1.

11. Vara.

12. "God's Big Break," *Guardian*, 19 Oct. 1999, 17. Crouch also says, "I see these megaplex theaters filled up on weekends. For young people, it's the place

to be, and the church parking lots are empty. . . . Why not utilize the influence of these huge theaters? I think they're the new street corner churches of the new millennium." Germain.

13. Rick Lyman, "A Sleeper Movie Awakened by a Hungry Audience," *New York Times*, 25 Oct. 1999, E1.

14. Michael H. Kleinschrodt, "Anti-Catholic Heavy Hand Breaks Code," *Times-Picayune*, 28 Oct. 1999, E9.

15. Lyman.

16. Germain. Providence was founded in 1998 by Norm Miller, chairman of Interstate Battery System of America, in Dallas, Texas. Martelle and Garvey.

17. Germain.

18. Vara.

19. That does not mean, of course, that all evangelicals see apocalyptic films, novels, and nonfiction books such as Pat Robertson's *New York Times* best-seller *The New World Order* (Dallas: Word Publishing, 1991) as accurate biblical interpretations, or that they will be moved to act politically based on the dystopic predictions made in these books and films. One fundamentalist Baptist interviewed in Christian Smith's study, for example, says, "I'm not a radical activist at all . . . I have no interest in blowing up Satan's ammunition depot" (147). The image is striking, as it is exactly what happens in dramatic prophecy films.

20. Lindsey's book has also been translated into over fifty languages and sold millions of copies internationally. Tapping into Cold War fears of nuclear annihilation, in his book Lindsey "systematically went through the apocalyptic scriptures mechanically transcribing every phrase and image into the vocabulary of Pentagon strategists." Paul Boyer, *When Time Shall Be No More: Prophesy Belief in Modern American Culture* (Cambridge: Harvard University Press, 1992), 127.

21. Randall Balmer, *Blessed Assurance: A History of Evangelicalism in America* (Boston: Beacon, 1999), 53.

22. *Entertainment Weekly*, 3 Dec. 1999, 55–64. The film, starring Kirk Cameron, is scheduled for release on February 2, 2001. See Gillian Flynn, "Deliverance," *Entertainment Weekly*, 22 Sept. 2000, 18–19.

23. Randall Balmer, *Mine Eyes Have Seen the Glory: A Journey into the Evangelical Subculture in America* (New York: Oxford University Press, 1993), 61.

24. Balmer, *Mine Eyes*, 61–62.

25. "Left Behind" is the title of a sixties song by Larry Norman, considered by many to be the father of contemporary Christian music. Norman's song tells the tragic story of loved ones disappearing suddenly. "There's no time to change your mind, the son has come, and you've been left behind." This is the opening song of *Thief in the Night*, and clearly the reference point for the first book in the Jenkins and LaHaye series.

26. LaHaye and Jenkins, *Left Behind* (Wheaton: Tyndale House, 1995), 194.

27. LaHaye and Jenkins, 214.

28. LaHaye and Jenkins, 216. The book transcribes the video but does not include the text at the end of the real video, which says, "Every Christian needs to keep a copy of this video accessible in his or her home for those left behind." If it's not clear how the unraptured would run across this tape, it is at least clear that Jenkins and LaHaye have hit upon a clever marketing tactic.

29. There are complex theological disputes among evangelicals about details of the Rapture, and some, like Pat Robertson, do not believe it will happen. Unfortunately, space does not allow me to unpack much of the complexity of prophecy theology. For a historical introduction, see George M. Marsden's classic *Fundamentalism and American Culture: The Shaping of Twentieth-Century Evangelicalism, 1870–1925* (New York: Oxford University Press, 1980). See also Boyer.

30. See www.hollywoodjesus.com, a site offering "pop culture from a spiritual point of view" for an archive of negative Christian responses to the film. One viewer writes, "I was very surprised to think that someone would come to the Church because of *The Omega Code*. When did it say anything about the story of Christ at all? That's what Christianity is about, isn't it? Isn't it?" Another viewer observes that "What little scripture that was quoted was quoted out of context and applied to the wrong persons. Even someone knowing their Bible would have a problem following this film and finding Jesus in it. To bill it as a tool for salvation is a joke."

31. See Heather Hendershot, "Onward Christian Soldiers? A Review Essay," *Velvet Light Trap* 46 (fall 2000).

32. William D. Romanowski, "Evangelicals and Popular Music: The Contemporary Christian Music Industry," in *Religion and Popular Culture in America*, ed. Bruce David Forbes and Jeffrey H. Mahan (Berkeley: University of California Press, 2000), 108–9.

33. Cited in Romanowski, 115.

34. *Entertainment Weekly*, 3 Dec. 1999. The article continues,

"It's a real tension—if you cross over, is it Christian anymore?" says Greg Ham, president of ForeFront Records, which handles dc Talk for the Christian market and was bought by EMI in '96. "The motto we tell our artists to live by is: Don't cross over unless you plan to take the cross over." . . . But for major labels, success among Christians may not be enough. "Atlantic doesn't want me spending their hard-earned cash on some crusade," says Atlantic Records VP of Christian-music marketing Mark Lusk.

35. Joe Leyden cited in Alan Chadwick, "Keep Taking the Tablets," *Scotsman*, 14 Nov. 1999, 8.

33

The Four Last Things

History, Technology, Hollywood, Apocalypse

Paul Arthur

Eternity is in Love with the productions of time.
—William Blake, "The Marriage of
Heaven and Hell"

When they said: Repent, Repent / I wonder what they meant.
—Leonard Cohen, "The Future," from the
soundtrack of *Natural Born Killers*

OF LATE HOLLYWOOD has been haunted—at times quite profitably so—by the specter of its own demise. Symptoms of a historically grounded, industry-specific eschatological anxiety reverberate across the landscape of nineties movies. At once transgeneric and bolstered by particular narrative motifs (e.g., time travel) and formal options (e.g., temporal dislocation), this anxiety is virtually endemic to the dooms-day formulas of contemporary disaster films.[1] Nonetheless, perhaps the most resonant and deeply ambivalent expressions of the studio sys-tem's looming obsolescence, the eclipse of its material bases of image production, are found in a cluster of films reviving the venerable, now terminal, struggle between advanced technology and human agency. Inscribing what amounts to an Armageddon of "good" versus "evil" machines, they surround heroic figures with resources linked symboli-cally to our waning industrial age. Staring back across the technological divide that threatens collective as well as individual survival is an in-formation-age avatar of uncontrollable, autonomous, inscrutable dread emanating from one or another version of the Beyond: either the future, an alien planet, a foreign adversary, or even prehistory.

The type of thematic opposition at issue here is of course hardly unique to the nineties. What are unusual, however, in recent allegories of endangered technologies and their embattled guardians are thinly veiled analogies between menacing creatures and salient physical or ontological properties—scale, ubiquity, ability to change shape—of an electronic regime that in reality is poised to supplant the dynamics of traditional movie production. Thus in blockbusters as otherwise distinct as *Terminator 2: Judgment Day* (1991) and *Jurassic Park* (1993), the attributes of a malevolent Other may be viewed as paradoxically the product and iconographic emblem of the same computer-driven effects currently propping up the mass appeal of these spectacles.[2] In narrative terms, the failure or defeat of a misguided or downright sinister technocratic initiative acts as decoy for the industry's technical mastery. Obeying a time-honored imperative, movies dependent on cutting-edge techniques of necessity celebrate what they pretend to disavow, exonerating by proxy the evil machinery with which they are ultimately complicit.[3] Consequently, a form of techno-nostalgia is generated around "extinct" orders of visuality—embodied by dinosaurs, androids, or similar beings—marked by a double-edged ideological slippage: mechanical aspects of an antiquated system are valorized and naturalized in and through the promotion of a DGI wave of the future. Extending the coded reflexivity already evident in *Star Wars'* (1977) cuddly robots, personifications of a humanizing, Dream Factory mechanical order are portrayed as benign, user-friendly, and because prone to the ravages of time, redeemably mortal.

The moral imperatives lodged in the representation of antithetical technologies are readily apparent in *Virtuosity* (1995), *The Net* (1995), *Johnny Mnemonic* (1995), *Strange Days* (1995), and other dystopic thrillers. Here the deployment of digital screens, video footage, or hardwired "brain movies" almost inevitably signals a weakening of personal identity and vulnerability to concealed networks of domination. Not simply a harbinger of physical danger or increasing social isolation, the domain of cyberspace is imagined as inimical to the conditions of motion picture production and reception; that is, the digital enforces a level of privatization and centralized control that obviates the social function of movies. In order to defeat a corporate scheme to monopolize the cure for a deadly epidemic, *Johnny Mnemonic*'s info-courier hero joins forces with a retro gang of Luddites dubbed "Lowtechs," media guerrillas whose operations recall the heyday of sixties counterculture. Similarly, *The Net*'s protagonist resorts to predigital devices such as a still camera as she struggles to reclaim an identity erased by computers. For both films, the permeable, frangible storage of digital "memory" is finally resisted with less advanced but socially affirmative "weapons" supplied by older media. In slightly different ways, contradictory efforts to contain the supposedly dehumanizing, destabilizing implications of electronic imagery are immersed within reassuring conventions of genre, morality, and visual syntax.

The clash between adjacent image technologies has a less judgmental spin in *Natural Born Killers* (1994). For Oliver Stone, the categorical threat to cinematic sovereignty is not replacement by newly minted gadgetry but rampant dispersion, in which prerogatives of the movie image—including its narrative armature—have already metastasized into an entropic web of TV sitcoms, video *verité*, comic books, computer animation, and music videos. Willfully shattering the seamless coherence of Hollywood storytelling and visual design, *Natural Born Killers* nonetheless embeds a rosy prospectus for cinema as *the* medium capable of co-opting, or merely reformatting, the technical options of every competitor.

Regardless of the variety of stylistic approaches and messages limned by the industry's internal dialogue with encroaching technologies, the tendency needs to be understood in the context of broader strands of recent American culture. Most obvious is the media fascination with millennial nightmares of cataclysmic dissolution: ecological and geopolitical as well as religious.[4] In a different vein, the motion picture centenary of 1995 served as catalyst for various grim meditations on the closure of film history, as if revisiting the medium's birth lent substance to its imminent passing.[5] A third factor has been the alternately dire or optimistic forecasts for the industry's accelerating digitalization, a *fin de siècle* staple of both newspaper journalism and infotainment news. Typical of the near-biblical pitch of many prognosticators, sound engineer Walter Murch declares that film's reigning apparatus—"a digital sandwich between slices of analogue bread"— will within a decade "telescope in upon itself with great suddenness."[6] Needless to say, it is entirely in the self-interest of commercial movies to capitalize on public fears of imminent catastrophe, to anathematize the spread of emerging technologies, and simultaneously to paint for itself a continuing role in a brave new world of image production. If, as Jonathan Edwards famously announced, "The Millennium shall begin in America,"[7] Hollywood films of the nineties seemed intent on offering up sneak previews of coming attractions.

APOCALYPSE NOW?

Envisioning the death of cinema via stories of individual and/or collective obliteration provided a sort of talisman for nineties cinema, a nod to the uncanny to ward off onrushing technological change. The necessity of couching such trepidations in fantasies of historical collapse and renewal, accompanied by longing for a "prelapsarian" modernity in the form of commodity production, is nowhere more tellingly amplified than in three of the decade's landmark productions: *Terminator 2, Jurassic Park,* and *Schindler's List* (1993). As with the filmic representation of death in general, the threat posed by techno-apocalypse is one of disappearance, loss, and absence, the disavowal of which functions as a confirmation of presence and mastery.[8] In this we can locate a convergence in the mature careers of James Cameron and Steven Spielberg, two titans of contemporary cinema whose work has, in somewhat different regards, been dedicated to ideas of time travel and historical retrieval as undergirded by a desire to resuscitate Hollywood's faded entertainment empire of the thirties and forties. Cameron has characterized the *Terminator* series as "all about trying to change history, and the importance of the individual in the grand scheme of things,"[9] while Spielberg, whose films are clogged with dramatic instances of resurrection, imagines himself as "basically a reincarnated director from the 1930s."[10] In their remarkably successful and ambitious productions, millennial pessimism is made to share center stage with troubled yet vainglorious affirmations of the studio system.[11]

The *Terminator* (1984) introduced an android sent back in time to kill the mother of a future commander in "the war against the machines." As the film meticulously details, the humanoid is an amalgam of two distinct material orders, industrial-mechanical and cybernetic: an infrastructure of stainless steel rods and levers, electrical wiring, and camera-like optics (with the capacity to zoom, change speeds, etc.) controlled by a microprocessor.[12] As Doran Larson has proposed, "He is thus in body and cultural mythos our perfect champion against postmodern, postindustrial society."[13] An emissary of a semiautonomous electronic state, Terminator was built by an "automated factory" and at the film's climax is in essence disassembled on a factory production line by a resourceful female "worker."

In the sequel, this iconic blend of past and future is already obsolete. It has been replaced by a prototype made from a "mimetic polyalloy" whose ontogeny and material structure are deliberately obscure. Its creepy mixture of phallic projections and soft flowing outlines short-circuits familiar gender associations while casting into relief the immutably masculine image of its nemesis and robot antecedent.[14] The new Terminator has no anatomy or organ-ization; it does not bleed, wear down, or exhibit humanoid affective functions.[15] Significantly, and in contrast to the earlier model, the "T-1000" is given no subjective point of view. What is at stake then in *T2*'s battle for human survival against an elusive future technocracy is a clash between two hostile systems of production. Eulogizing the moral superiority of the mechanical and the iconically stable "in the grand scheme of things," Cameron validates endangered institutions by conflating the Hollywood factory with vestiges of patriarchy and the nuclear family; the film's warrior-mom insists that given a choice of potential fathers for her child, "this machine was the only one who measured up."[16]

Bracketed by an inverted social and historical trajectory, *T2* advances from an initial action sequence set in a suburban shopping mall, our culture's paradigmatic locus of consumption, to a rousing climax in a steel mill, the very crucible of modern production and a sort of primal scene for the development of cinema technology. At a narrative midpoint between these sites lies the sterile information-age headquarters of "Cyberdyne" (like the hapless corporate functionary "Dyson," the name is rife with "dying"). The humans' ultimate mission is to blow up the skyscraper containing plans for the development of the original cyborg, and thus alter history *avant la lettre*. However, as an arch-villain in *Blade Runner* (1982) once stated, "It is not so easy to meet your maker." In the final scene, the T-1000 is extinguished in a vat of molten steel, followed shortly by the self-immolation of the now-humanized retro cyborg, his plaintive image reverting to the status of raw material.[17] While ensuring that the human species will survive, *T2* is none too sanguine about the afterlife of its totemic commodity: the movie star as figurehead of studio production. Despite the recent promise of a third *Terminator*, Schwarzenegger's ubiquitous publicity line, "I'll be back," has a

"Hasta la vista, baby." Arnold Schwarzenegger's last stand in James Cameron's mostly gleeful millennial nightmare, *Terminator 2* (Universal, 1993).

hollow ring.[18] The well-oiled machinery of Hollywood spectacle—including the well-oiled acting machine—is nearing an end. Unacknowledged in the film's signal pronouncement, "No fate but what we make for ourselves," is the dramatized wisdom that machines we construct can annihilate their makers.

The fiery ending in *T2* finds a strange echo in *Alien*[3] (1992) where a seemingly invulnerable otherworldy monster is consumed, along with her human host, in a dilapidated blast furnace. To be sure, the allegorical charge in the latter film is directed more toward the modern city than the modern movie studio, yet it is sufficient to note the wider confluence of recent sci-fi cataclysm of useful remnants of Fordist manufacture. It is possible that despite Hollywood's long-standing aversion to narratives devoted to industrial labor, the description of any work site involving processes of fabrication—from Dr. Frankenstein's laboratory to *Darkman's* abandoned chemical plant (producing yet another mimetic technology)—nurtures allusions to the Dream Factory.[19]

Not surprisingly, given the director's previous films, the genetic manufacturing facility in *Jurassic Park* is geared to the reproduction of "nature" rather than mechanized devices. Spielberg, the man who "saved Hollywood," has spent much of his career traveling Back to the Future (a series he helped produce), not just to Hollywood's golden age of genre formula, to *1941* (1979) and *Always* (1989), but to luminous zones of childhood anamnesis. As has been argued by critics at some length, what transpires in these journeys is usually the defeat of rationality by belief, the displacement of culture by imagination.[20] Lacking the signature tropes of time travel and magical rebirth, *Jurassic Park* makes a leap into prehistory, conjuring the Garden as theme park or, more accurately, a "universal" studio tour gone woefully astray. The main body of the narrative is introduced by a second, shorter and nonviolent behind-the-scenes excursion—complete with theatrical trailer, science displays, and animatronics—detailing the creation of the park and its genetically cloned inhabitants.

This preview is informed by a debate between two flawed voices of authority, in effect directorial surrogates: an elderly billionaire entrepreneur who conceived the park as the realization of a childhood dream ("I wanted to show them something that wasn't an illusion, something that was *real*") and a cynical mathematician specializing in chaos theory. Although neither has a crucial role in the subsequent adventures, they argue the conflicting imperatives of nature versus artifice. The benevolent patriarch-showman spouts a populist rhetoric about making his zootopia accessible to the masses; in doing so he downplays his own, and by implication the film's, overweening commercial motives.[21] This character clearly smacks of Walt Disney, Spielberg's self-professed "parental conscience,"[22] by encoding sentimental ideas about artistic creation and the social benefits of reanimating history as child's spectacle. The scientist, speaking for the uncontrollable forces of nature, is convinced that "what you study"—or indeed create—"will eventually eat you."

The preprogrammed but quickly derailed journey through the park is, at first, graphically mapped on a video screen in the administrative offices and intermittently "narrated" by safely distanced characters. Unable to recontain the anarchic animal energies set loose during the tour—sprung in part by the rapacious designs of a maverick computer guru—the island paradise is in the end wordlessly abandoned by its producer and inaugural "spectators." Even sophisticated technological safeguards cannot secure the untroubled passage from Imaginary to Real. It is perhaps the only Spielberg film in which a childlike character's faith in illusion fails to save the day. If as the mathematician complains, our human privilege makes us insufficiently humble before the power of nature, even the endless computerized cloning of movie dinosaurs is unlikely to assuage our appetite for something beyond, or maybe *before*, the image was the (last) word.

According to W. J. T. Mitchell, dino-mania in the nineties can be read as a "cultural allegory of monopoly capitalism."[23] It is a measure of *Jurassic Park*'s ideological confusion that while it is eager to bash the greed or shortsightedness of lawyers and technicians—the first two characters devoured—it lays blame for the collapse of this tropical Magic Kingdom not on the hubris of the entrepreneur's creative vision but on a tiny design flaw. The problem is surely not that simple. Spielberg's artificial Eden, an etiolated inheritor of Emerson's "nature's nation," is coextensively pre- and postcinematic, a world with no place for image makers.

Jurassic Park is the pet project of the reigning monarch of a generation of directors promising a "second coming" of the studio system. Unlike sci-fi dystopias, its idea of the future is best served by voiding technology altogether, or as the now-chastened entrepreneur intones in *The Lost World: Jurassic Park* (1997), "These creatures require our absence to survive." The baleful aspiration of the original adventure is belied of course by its sequel: *"Après moi le raptor."*[24] In rather different terms, Spielberg's Darwinian struggle between technology and nature is prime evidence of Guy Debord's well-known dictum: "The spectacle, as present social organization of the paralysis of history and memory . . . is the false consciousness of time."[25]

The prophecy of historical extinction issued by *Jurassic Park* is symbolically retracted in virtually the same creative breath in *Schindler's List*, which along with its celebrated agenda attempts nothing less than the salvation of the image factory's cultural mythology. The historical primal scene revisited here is Year Zero, the universal trauma of the Holocaust. Once again a thematic of production and/as annihilation is hinged by the philosophical dialogue of two authority figures *cum* creative directors, this time in management positions. Once again debate centers on the relationship between artifice and reality, the continuation or annulment of history. In a crucial exchange that encapsulates much of *Schindler's* allegorical undertow, the commandant of a Nazi labor camp, who has previously proclaimed the desire to cancel three hundred years of European history, asserts that "Power is the ability to kill arbitrarily." Schindler responds that "Power is the ability *not* to kill."

In other words, while Amon Goeth operates his factory as a simulation of productive labor concealing its true commodity, Death, Oskar Schindler commands his factory workers to manufacture faulty military supplies and ordnance as a masquerade for sustaining Life. Indeed it is not only individual lives that are redeemed—primarily, it seems, the lives of intellectuals and artists—but a Jewish culture nearly extinguished but literally rekindled on the shop floor through Sabbath observances. Entering gates that look suspiciously like those at Paramount, a woman disguised as a gentile pleads with "Herr Director" to admit her parents: "They say no one dies here, they say your factory is heaven." What greater tribute to the Spielberg ethos and oeuvre: no (central, childlike, freedom-loving) character ever dies in his celluloid factory.[26]

For Leon Wieseltier, *"Schindler's List* proves again that, for Spielberg, there is a power in the world that is greater than good and greater than evil, and it is the movies."[27] Wieseltier refers to this posture as a "cineaste's theodicy," and as such it may be regarded as an implicit rebuke to the millennial pessimism—however superficial or self-contradictory— in *Jurassic Park, T2* and other films. Tempting as it is, however, to frame *Schindler's List* as a vehicle for rescuing commercial cinema *tout court*, it is clear that the apotheosized factory in the film, in both its dramatized social organization and symbolic hierarchy of roles (stars and bit players, patriarchal boss and secondary "collaborators"), is a mawkish throwback, a version of the studio system not as it currently exists but as it functioned during the so-called classical period. This rewriting of history does not merely repress cinema's social meaning, it fetishizes an industry stuck in an eternal present, a state of suspended animation.

Or perhaps not. In a work crammed with improbable occurrences and a multitude of potential endings, no event is more confounding than the return of a trainload of female detainees from Auschwitz.[28] For Spielberg, the power of cinema is its ability to reverse time and existence, to make the dead rise from their graves. Yet despite what might be called his visionary myopia, he is only one in a throng of fellow passengers on the platform of recent history waving repeated and half-hearted farewells as the Lumières' train, that "invention without a future," backs slowly and unsteadily out of the station.

NOTES

1. An odd mixture of commercial practices employed time-warping strategies during the nineties, from the shopworn futurism of *Timecop* (1994) and *Stargate* (1994) to more provocative exercises like *Twelve Monkeys* (1995) to the metaphysical screwball of *Groundhog Day* (1993) and *Back to the Future Part III* (1990). While an interesting phenomenon, it is somewhat peripheral to my main argument. It is worth noting, however, that a (post)modernist interest in the fragmentation of linear narrative also made a surprising comeback in American independent and low-budget European production: for example, *Go* (1999), *Run Lola Run* (1998), and *After the Rain* (1999). For a reading of industry-reflexive subtexts in nineties disaster epics, see Paul Arthur, "Un-Natural Disasters," *Film Comment*, July–August 1998, 72–76.

2. The template for this form of invidious technological competition is clearly Hollywood's demonization of TV, a trope that extends from fifties melodrama (e.g., *All That Heaven Allows*, 1955) to eighties sci-fi (*Looker*, 1981). In a related trajectory, it is perhaps no accident that Hollywood's last three disaster cycles correspond historically to the explosion of broadcast television in the fifties, the rapid spread of videotape and VCRs in the seventies, and the saturation of cable TV and advent of new systems of image production and transmission (including the Internet) in the nineties. In different ways, then, our familiar movie catastrophes may be seen as symbolically mediating technological incursions, real or imagined, on the film industry's business-as-usual practices.

3. Dan Rubey, following the lead of Adorno and Horkheimer, analyzes the techno-duplicity of *Star Wars* in much the same fashion, and I am indebted to his prescient comments: "Not So Long Ago, Not So Far Away," *Jump Cut* 18 (1978); reprinted in *Jump Cut* 41 (1997): 2–12. As Rubey asserts, "practically every frame is a hymn to the technology which made the film possible" (11). The same can be said of films under consideration here. Peter Biskind makes a similar argument by relating *Star Wars'* fears of the technocratic state to the shadow problem of excessive control exerted by studio executives: "Blockbuster: The Last Crusade," in *Seeing through Movies*, ed. Mark Crispin Miller (New York: Pantheon, 1990), 113–14.

4. Computers, the primary object of Hollywood's new technophobia, are crucial in the millennial literature of Christian fundamentalists, deemed the instrument of the Antichrist, whose machinations were to culminate in a Y2K chaos of technological and social breakdown. On the other hand, it was widely reported that Heaven's Gate cultists were avid fans of *Star Wars*, *Star Trek*, and other outer space adventures. For more on technophobic currents in prophetic thought, see Paul Boyer, *When Time Shall Be No More* (Cambridge: Harvard University Press, 1995). There has been a veritable flood of books on the sacralization of computers in American society: two useful studies are David Noble, *The Religion of Technology* (New York: Knopf, 1997) and Erik Davis, *Techgnosis: Myth, Magic, and Mysticism in the Age of Information* (New York: Harmony, 1998).

5. Frank Kermode reminds us that the idea of Apocalypse is founded in a "concordance" of past and future, beginning and ending, birth and death: *The Sense of an Ending* (New York: Oxford University Press, 1967), 5. With all but a few pioneers of silent cinema now deceased, the notion that film has assumed the shape of a single attenuated life span gained rhetorical prominence in centenary observances. Along with a spate of feature films set in the immediate aftermath of 1895 and making reference to the emergence of cinema—*Bram Stoker's Dracula* (1992), *Wilde* (1997), and *The Portrait of a Lady* (1996), among others—several productions explicitly addressed the limits of film history: Godard's *2 Times 50 Years of Cinema* is exemplary; Sarah Moon's omnibus collaboration, *Lumière and Company* (1995) interviews directors about a future for cinema and contains dramatic sequences that relate the moment of inception to Hiroshima and the Holocaust, potent signifiers of historical declension.

6. Walter Murch, "A Digital Cinema of the Mind? By 2099, It's Possible," *New York Times*, 2 May 1999, sec. 2, p. 1. In the course of his optimistic predictions for a more democratic, infinitely malleable form of electronic cinema, he refers to the "final capitulation of the two last holdouts of film's nineteenth-century, analog-mechanical legacy [camera recording and projection]." From 1997 to 1999, newspapers and mass market magazines, to say nothing of industry organs such as *Premiere*, devoted extensive coverage to the emerging technical "revolution" in movies.

7. Cited in Sacvan Bercovitch, *The American Jeremiad* (Madison: University of Wisconsin Press, 1978), 94.

8. Catherine Russell, *Narrative Mortality: Death, Closure, and New Wave Cinemas* (Minneapolis: University of Minnesota Press, 1995), 7.

9. Cameron, in production notes to *Terminator 2*, undated.

10. Cited in Philip M. Taylor, *Steven Spielberg: The Man, His Movies, and Their Meaning* (New York: Continuum, 1992), 105. The resurrection motif is blatant across Spielberg's entire corpus, from *Jaws* (1975) to *Raiders of the Lost Ark* (1981) to *Schindler's List*.

11. For an analysis of the studio allegory in *Titanic*, see Arthur, "Un-Natural Disasters," 73.

12. *Terminator*'s opening sequence, in which the android is "born" into the present and acquires clothing, weaponry, and a motorcycle, tosses off allusions to Frankenstein, Marlon Brando in *The Wild One* (1954), and John Wayne westerns. Fred Pfeil makes an interesting case for Arnold Schwarzenegger's conflation of Star and Studio in "Home Fires Burning: Family *Noir* in *Blue Velvet* and *Terminator 2*," in *Shades of Noir*, ed. Joan Copjec (New York: Verso, 1993), 246–47.

13. Doran Larson, "Machine As Messiah: Cyborgs, Morphs, and the American Body Politic," *Cinema Journal* 36, no. 4 (summer 1997), 62.

14. Discussion of the Terminators' gendered associations has been quite extensive: see, for example, Scott Bukatman, *Terminal Identity* (Durham: Duke University Press, 1993), 304; also Yvonne Tasker, *Spectacular Bodies: Gender, Genre, and the Action Film* (New York: Routledge, 1993), 83.

15. See Larson, "Machine As Messiah," 63–64.

16. On *T2*'s recuperation of patriarchy, see Susan Jeffords, *Hard Bodies: Hollywood Masculinity in the Reagan Era* (New Brunswick: Rutgers University Press, 1994), 156–70.

17. It is useful to recall that nineteenth-century Romantics William Blake and the painter J. M. W. Turner both identified the foundry as a gaping maw to the underworld. Harold Bloom unpacks the apocalyptic associations of fire and molten metal in various religious orthodoxies in *Omens of Millennium* (New York: Riverhead, 1996), passim.

18. Hollow though it might be in allegorical terms, the line was nonetheless cited in a recent *USA Today* survey as the most popular "favorite film phrase" of all time, just in front of "Frankly my dear, I don't give a damn." *USA Today*, 11 August 2000, sec. E, p. 1.

19. Fredric Jameson briefly examines the thematization of work in fifties sci-fi and its role in suppressing traces of filmic manufacture in *Marxism and Form* (Princeton: Princeton University Press, 1971), 405–8.

20. A single, particularly useful example of this line of inquiry is Ilsa J. Bick, "The Look Back in *E.T.*," *Cinema Journal* 31, no. 4 (summer 1992): 25–41.

21. Charles B. Strozier makes the interesting observation that "End time

theory is democratic, accessible, and imaginable in its literalism, while also being highly evocative in its mysticism. . . . These are not the concerns of erudite theologians but the narratives of popular culture." *Apocalypse: On the Psychology of Fundamentalism in America* (Boston: Beacon, 1994), 88. The currents of a Christian, antinomian faith in Spielberg's work have to date not been adequately explored; however Tony Williams offers an interesting starting point in: "Close Encounters of the Authoritarian Kind," *Wide Angle* 5, no. 4 (1983): 22–29. And am I the only person to note the facial resemblance between the young Spielberg and cult leader David Koresh?

22. Cited in Taylor, *Steven Spielberg*, 52. Michael Crichton's source novel, *Jurassic Park* (New York: Ballantine, 1990), treats this figure in far less benign fashion. Although explicit comparison is made to Disney (42), John Hammond is portrayed as a ruthless, nasty profiteer. After rehearsing for an underling the obstreperous governmental controls on the development and marketing of new drugs, he proclaims, "think how different it is when you're making entertainment. . . . That's not a matter for government intervention. If I charge five thousand dollars a day for my park, who is going to stop me?" (200).

23. W. J. T. Mitchell, *The Last Dinosaur Book* (Chicago: University of Chicago Press, 1998), 26.

24. There is likely an impulse in each of us to equate the end of our biological, or for that matter creative, lives with the end of history itself. It is perhaps especially salient for a middle-aged Hollywood director who in today's economic climate is already within sight of his/her last production. Film has never been an old person's art form, and the unbroken succession of films by, say, Alan Dwan is no longer possible, even for as protean and supremely powerful a presence as Spielberg's. By symbolically instating the end of film history, by giving it final closure, he is able to fix his creative contribution to "the grand scheme of things."

25. Guy Debord, *The Society of the Spectacle*, trans. Donald Nicholson-Smith (New York: Zone Books, 1995), 14.

26. Spielberg's work is notoriously queasy about giving death its on-screen due. Minor characters, and minority characters, tend to expire in quick painless fashion, and *Schindler's List* was criticized in some quarters for avoiding the Holocaust subject of mass-produced death: see, for example, Omer Bartov, "Spielberg's Oskar: Hollywood Tries Evil," in *Spielberg's Holocaust: Critical Perspectives on Schindler's List*, ed. Yosefa Loshitzky (Bloomington: Indiana University Press, 1997), 46. It is not until *Saving Private Ryan* that Spielberg positions his camera for a long painful look at the face of human death (specifically, the sequence in which a medic instructs soldiers on treating his wound as he expires).

27. Quoted in David Thomson, "Presenting Enamelware," *Film Comment* 30, no. 2 (March–April 1994): 33. Thomson's commentary sees a connection to cinematic production that runs parallel to the one offered here.

28. Although the almost endlessly deferred finale is a point too intricate to argue here at any length, there are by my count seven consecutive scenes offering conventional cues for dramatic closure, starting with Schindler's male workers watching in awe as the women return and ending with the documentary coda in which actual survivors place stones at Schindler's grave site.

34

Twenty-five Reasons Why It's All Over

Wheeler Winston Dixon

"It's the end of cinema."
"No, I believe that the cinema will last forever."
—Godard's *Le mépris* (1963)

EVEN AS EARLY as 1963, Godard was positing "the end of cinema," while simultaneously insisting on its inevitable survival. Now, in the first years of the second century of cinema, we are faced with the inescapable fact that, at the very least, "film" has become an altogether different medium from that imagined and practiced by its pioneers and classicists. A few key points immediately emerge:

1. *Theatrical distribution is no longer a certainty.* This factor alone accounts for a dramatic shift in cinema practice over the past forty years. In the 1960s, and as late as the early 1980s, each 35mm film was virtually guaranteed a shot at the theatrical marketplace, if only because this was the only way that producers could earn back their costs. Television was a "second run" medium; pay-per-view, videotapes, DVDs, cable, the Web, and the Internet did not exist. Now films can be disseminated in a variety of ways, and many wind up going straight to tape because the costs of distribution and advertising are so high.

2. *Movies cost too much to make, and there's too much to merchandise.* In the 1960s, Godard could make a film like *Masculine/Feminine* (1966) for $150,000, and a "blockbuster" like *Contempt* for a mere $1 million; today a modest picture costs between $14 and $15 million, and the average big-screen spectacle between $40 and $80 million. Add to that the costs

356

of prints and advertising, and it's no wonder that only safe, "bankable" projects get made.

3. *Contemporary films are relentlessly teen-driven.* From *The Matrix* (1999) to *American Beauty* (1999), the target audience of contemporary mainstream cinema is aged twelve to twenty-four. Kevin Spacey smokes marijuana and regresses into his supposedly idyllic teenhood in *American Beauty*. *Sleepy Hollow* (1999), *The General's Daughter* (1999), *Scream 3* (2000), *The Beach* (2000) . . . it doesn't matter what genre. All films are calculated to appeal to a teenage audience above and beyond any other considerations. Substance, depth, and characterization are ruthlessly stripped down in favor of a succession of instantly readable icons.

4. *Conglomerates have imposed institutionalized mediocrity on the films they produce.* In view of the enormous cost of production and distribution, this only makes financial, if not artistic, sense. Even a relative "failure" like *Godzilla* (1998) will still outperform such modest films as *Next Stop, Wonderland* (1998), *Go!* (1999) or *The Winslow Boy* (1999). Why not throw your production and advertising dollars behind a sure bet, like *Viva Rock Vegas* (2000), the Flintstones sequel? Why risk your resources on a small, offbeat project?

5. *Foreign films no longer get international theatrical distribution.* Once upon a time, *La Dolce Vita* (1960) or *L'Avventura* (1960) could count on significant returns on the U.S. "art house circuit"; now, that circuit has shrunk to a few theaters in a few major metropolitan centers. With cable, DVD, and straight-to-tape available as viable distribution markets, there is no need to launch a foreign-language film in theatrical situations. The buffs will wait until it comes out on videotape or DVD. Gone are the days when films such as *The Discreet Charm of the Bourgeoisie* (1972) could win an Oscar as the best foreign film; such projects are too cerebral, too challenging. Instead, the award goes to something safely sentimental, like *Life Is Beautiful* (1998), dubbed into English after the fact. With the collapse of international distribution of foreign films, European filmmakers, in particular, are increasingly shooting their films in English, and using Hollywood stars to ensure box office. Often the original film is simply "remade" by Hollywood to become more accessible to mainstream audiences. Thus, *Wings of Desire* (1987) "becomes" *City of Angels* (1998).

6. *Movies must be in color, not black and white, for sale to television, and to please viewers who simply refuse to watch black and white films.* There are, of course, exceptions. Woody Allen still occasionally shoots in black and white (and suffers at the box office as a consequence). Tim Burton's *Ed Wood* (1994) was a mainstream black and white success, but for the most part, black and white cinematography is used in contemporary film-making as an *effect*, rather than as a medium. When Gus Van Sant re-made *Psycho* in 1999 in a virtual shot-for-shot copy of the original, one of the reasons that the project was so fervently embraced by producers was that it potentially opened up the door for a series of exact copies of classic films, rephotographed in color, with contemporary stars (in this case Vince Vaughan and Anne Heche). The box office and critical failure of the 1999 *Psycho* put an end to this strategy, but as any academic who regularly teaches film history knows, present-day audiences have an aversion to black and white films, almost on a par with their dislike of films with subtitles.

7. *The majors have an international lock on distribution and production, which is only intensifying as new markets open up.* The major studios all have extensive acquisition, promotion, and exhibition mechanisms. Distribution is the key to all film production, for only effective and widespread dissemination of a film can guarantee any sort of social, artistic, or financial impact. Benôit Jacquot, Amos Gitai, Tom Twyker, and Pedro Almodovar, to name just a few possible auteurs, were all making brilliant and challenging films in 1999, but almost no one got to see them. As the conglomerate parents of the major studios extend their reach through the portals of cyberspace, they seek to find a wider audience for films devoid of risk, talent, or originality, rather than giving voice to the new.

8. *We (the audience) no longer believe in images, since computer-generated images make any effect possible.* If one posits that film has its origins in spectacle (Méliès) and reality (Lumière, Guy), then reality (with the ex-ception of the recent Dogme 95 films) has lost out decisively, in favor of the utterly synthetic images of such blockbusters as *Titanic* (1997) and *The Matrix*. Mundanely perfect, these computer-engineered images conjure up the mechanical perfection of Maxfield Parrish illustrations, while simultaneously banishing the real to a phantom zone of nonexis-tence. And yet, as one eye-popping scene of spectacle and destruction

TWENTY-FIVE REASONS WHY IT'S ALL OVER 359

after another fills the screen, audiences are bored, unsatisfied. What have they truly seen? Just plotted points on a computer graph. The veracity of the moving image has been hopelessly compromised; the demarcation line between the real and the engineered (both aurally and visually) has been obliterated. All is construction and fabulation. All is predetermined; nothing natural remains.

9. *Digital production and distribution save money and time, thus making it easier and cheaper to produce films. Still, there's no guaranteed access to distribution.* The best example of this is the recent digital film *The Last Broadcast* (1998), which was produced for a total of $900, shown via satellite download at Cannes, and screened at various international film festivals to great acclaim. For all the attention, however, the film still failed to secure a distributor, while the similarly themed *Blair Witch Project* (1999, and actually not a digital feature at all, but rather a mixture of analog video and 16mm film) got picked up by Artisan Releasing and, thanks to a shrewd Internet and word-of-mouth ad campaign, made a fortune. (George Lucas has already announced that the final two segments of the *Star Wars* series will be created entirely digitally in both production and exhibition, but Lucas will have no trouble finding a distributor for his efforts.) Distribution via the Web is in its infancy, and picture and sound quality will no doubt improve. While there is a plethora of moving image sites on the Web, all of them deliver an image that is technically inferior, and in no way competes with the immersion of the theatrical presentation experience. In addition, the thousands of Web sites that offer moving image downloads are often lost in an avalanche of competing Web media, and search engines often produce a bewildering array of results that fail to provide direct access to the consumer.

10. *All films are now "composed" for TV screens rather than cinema screens, leading to a barrage of flat, uninvolving visuals.* Yes, films are made for theatrical distribution, but they all end up on television. Letterboxing is still not popular with general audiences, and so the use of "pan and scan" cropping to blow up the image to full screen size is still widely used. HDTV's new wide-screen format may alter this situation somewhat, but even a casual glance at contemporary cinema reveals that nearly all CinemaScope (and related process) films are now composed with the characters in the middle of the frame, while the left and right

portions of the frame are relegated to background details. The adventurous compositions of 1960s wide-screen cinema, particularly in the films of the French and British New Wave (*The 400 Blows*, 1958; *Jules and Jim*, 1961; *The Innocents*, 1961; *2 or 3 Things I Know about Her*, 1967; and others) have been abandoned in favor of a simplistic visual style that translates easily to the standard television aspect ratio.

11. Sitcom editorial styles have become sacrosanct in comedies. Here comes the joke, this is the joke, that was the joke. *Dumb and Dumber* (1994), *Liar, Liar* (1997), *Deuce Bigalow: Male Gigolo* (1999) . . . this editorial rule of thumb has become almost axiomatic to make sure that no member of a film's puerile audience fails to grasp the (however feeble) punch line.

12. MTV hyperedited "shot fragment" editing has become the rule for dramas and action films. An entire new generation of viewers became visually hooked on the assaultive grabbing power of MTV's rapid cutting, which thrusts new images—*any* image—at the viewer to prevent her/him from becoming even momentarily bored. Meaningless switches from black and white to color, different film stocks and grains, manipulation of film speed and density make the trick films of an earlier era (*Paris qui dort*, 1924; *The Knack*, 1965; *Performance*, 1970) seem positively restrained when compared to the hysterical blenderization of visuals in *Nixon* (1995) or *Leaving Las Vegas* (1995). As with all other aspects of the new commercial and semicommercial cinema, excess is the dominant characteristic.

13. Films have become solely driven by marketing and linear narrative concerns. Who can "open" a movie in today's market? Harrison Ford, Julia Roberts, Jim Carrey, Bruce Willis, and a few other actors—the list is short. Any one of these "marketable" actors can instantly green light any mainstream project they wish to appear in. This, in itself, is no different from the Hollywood star system of the 1920s–50s, but during the classical studio era, the major stars were all, for the most part, contract players. Now, as free agents, they can reasonably command up to $20 million to star in a film, simply because their track records have proven that audiences will come to the theaters to see them (so long as the projects they appear in do not appreciably differ from their past efforts). The cost of talent having risen, the need for a simple (not to say simplistic) narrative that all audience members can follow becomes paramount.

14. "Alternative" festivals such as Sundance, Slamdance, and the like are simply mainstream spawning grounds; Cannes has become solely a market. At a recent Independent Spirit Awards show, emcee Jennifer Tilly attempted desperately to pump some life into the proceedings, while an audience of nearly a thousand participants watched glumly as one predictable project after another walked off with awards. No matter what their first projects may be, contemporary directors see their initial features as springboards to "major" productions.

15. We need to acknowledge the malign influence of Steven Spielberg and George Lucas. Spielberg is a superb action filmmaker; *Duel* and the *Indiana Jones* series proved this. When he ventures into more thoughtful territory, as in *Schindler's List* (1993), or *Amistad* (1997), the results reveal a distressing lack of depth that one might expect to find in a filmmaker whose favorite graphic artist is Norman Rockwell. In another time, Spielberg would have been quite at home at Republic Pictures, making Saturday morning serials. If *Saving Private Ryan* (1998) proves anything, it is that one can cobble together a stunning opening sequence by duplicating (or replicating) actual battle footage, and then graft it on to a thoroughly sentimental and ordinary combat narrative, with Tom Hanks standing in for Jimmy Stewart. As for Lucas, is he really a director? Or is he more accurately a salesman and entrepreneur of toys and ancillary marketing gimmicks, someone who is absolutely up to date on technical effects, but woefully out of touch with humanist concerns? But the emptiness of Lucas and Spielberg has been embraced by the public, and their films have thus become emblematic of late-twentieth- and early-twenty-first-century cinema; visuals over content, excess before restraint, spectacle rather than insight.

16. We are experiencing the "Oprahfication" of contemporary consumer culture, and the hegemony of false consensus. Oprah Winfrey's "Book Club" deals solely in the most maudlin, simplistic narratives in which loss and adversity are inevitably countered by triumph and hope. The public, in turn, is drawn to the certainty of expectation these prepackaged constructs offer them, and so the cycle perpetuates itself. Coupled with this is the absence of dissent, if only because communication conglomerates now control nearly all the major film, television, and Internet broadcast outlets. As always, genuine innovation is marginalized. By the time any issues raised by alternative media have reached mainstream discourse, they have become hopelessly compromised through distortion or reinterpretation, or packaged as disruptive cultural artifacts that can be effectively ridiculed, and thus used to further strengthen the dominion of the dominant culture.

17. *The demise of film itself in favor of digital video production and distribution is imminent.* As we say goodbye to the twentieth century, we can also say goodbye to film as a production and distribution medium. Already, films such as *Star Wars: Episode I—The Phantom Menace* (1999), *The Mummy* (1999), and even *An Ideal Husband* (1999) have been screened in major cities in digital video format with great success—the average audience member doesn't even know that the film projector has been replaced with a video "light valve" projection device. The demise of the 35mm format is eagerly anticipated by the major studios and distributors, who according to one industry estimate will save $1.2 billion a year in prints, shipping, and storage by converting to digital video satellite downloads. Traditional film lighting, the depth of image possible with film, and a host of other aesthetic qualities unique to the film medium will be abandoned, in favor of a clearer, more "stripped down" image. Film will reside only in the domain of archives, museums, and specialized revival houses.

18. *The canon is increasingly rigid, and noncanonical films are disappearing.* Increasingly, certain groups of "canonically approved" films, such as the American Film Institute and British Film Institute lists of "best films," have transubstantiated the entire history of cinema. *Stagecoach* (1939), *Citizen Kane* (1941), *Casablanca* (1942), *North by Northwest* (1959) —these are touchstones that even the most casual filmgoer knows, but as critics and historians, we know that these films represent only an infinitesimal fraction of the films produced in the last hundred years. Further, women, especially Alice Guy, Dorothy Arzner, Dorothy Davenport Reid, Lois Weber, straight up through Chantal Akerman and other contemporary feminist filmmakers, are routinely left off such lists. In addition, the AFI and BFI lists are shamelessly Eurocentric; entire continents (the works of thousands of talented filmmakers in Africa, New Zealand, and elsewhere) are ignored. Turner Classic Movies and the related "classic movie" networks on cable television present an extremely tight play list of canonical classics, about five thousand films in all, which still

represent only the smallest sample of cinema history. But as long as these films continue to sell videocassettes and DVDs (the real purpose behind the compilation of all "greatest films" lists—"you too can *own* the classics!"), the canon will continue to be perpetuated. It represents convenience, a limited base of knowledge that one person can easily absorb, and a retreat from an engagement with the vastness of international cinematic practice. Future generations will not be aware of the existence of such films as *Les dames du Bois de Boulogne* (1945), *Born to Kill* (1947), *The Belles of St. Trinian's* (1954), *The Chelsea Girls* (1967), and numerous other shorts, features, and narrative and nonnarrative films that have been excised from the cinematic canon.

19. Contemporary cinema "strip-mines" its past with feverish ferocity. Movie remakes are as old as the medium itself, but in the past few years, presold remakes have come to dominate the market in an unprecedented fashion. Old television shows are recycled for feature films: *Dragnet* (1987), *The Brady Bunch Movie* (1995), *Mission Impossible* (1996), *Sgt. Bilko* (1996), *McHale's Navy* (1997), *The Avengers* (1998), *Lost in Space* (1998), and *The Adventures of Rocky and Bullwinkle* (2000) are just a few examples of this recent trend. As F. Scott Fitzgerald correctly observed in *The Great Gatsby*, "you can't repeat the past," but Hollywood, now run solely by accountants, agents, and marketing experts, devoid of creativity or passion, seems simplemindedly intent on doing just that, at the expense of creating anything new.

20. We now witness the collapse of narrative and the demise of audience consciousness. Plots are reduced to the simplest possible linear graphs: here's the good guy, here's the bad guy, here's the conflict, the good guy wins. The audience is confronted with one violent spectacle after another, devoid of any context or explanation. The human has been reduced to the level of mere agency in these mechanistic spectacles, which have been created to cater to the ever-diminishing attention spans of image-saturated viewers. Contemporary audiences don't want complexity, they want hand-holding simplicity, in which every step of the narrative construction is heavily foreshadowed and plays out in a nondisruptive manner. Because of the wide variety of new and competing media, more has become less. We no longer have the *time* to become intensely engrossed in a complex narrative structure, or the desire to be surprised or challenged. Escape is everything, delivered in small doses, never leaving the viewer truly satisfied.

21. *Classical film production methodology has collapsed.* One of my favorite films is François Truffaut's *Day for Night*, which won the Academy Award for best foreign film in 1974. It's a light piece of work, but it nevertheless gives the viewer some idea of how studio films were made before the digital revolution. Seen today, nearly every one of its technical production methods is obsolete. Workprints, magnetic film sound transfers, Steenbeck editing machines, Chapman cranes (human-controlled rather than robotically activated), Mitchell BNC cameras, the film stock itself—all of this has disappeared. Optical effects, such as fades and dissolves, which once required extensive laboratory work, are accomplished with the flick of a switch. Smaller cameras, digital videotape, and smaller crews mean it's easier to light, shoot, edit, and post-produce one's film—indeed, we're on the edge of an onslaught of digital cinema. While the "star system" remains as pernicious as ever, the style and polish with which contemporary mainstream films are made seem entirely synthetic, the result of tweaking video monitors.

22. *The Internet and the Web have become important alternative visual/information mediums.* In the 1940s, there were only movie theaters, radio, newspapers, magazines, and the telephone. Television was added in the early 1950s. Gradually faxes, e-mail, cell phones, and the vastness of the Web have been added to the mix, until there are so many potential avenues of exploration that one is hard pressed to commit to any one image stream for more than a few minutes. Films, almost as a defense mechanism, it seems, have become longer and louder in a desperate attempt to *compel* our attention. But can we afford to ignore the ever increasing flood of data that engulfs us? Is it even possible? In a typically prescient essay entitled *Pessimism*, written in 1980, Luis Buñuel noted that

> the glut of information has . . . brought about a serious deterioration in human consciousness today. If the pope dies, if a chief of staff is assassinated, television is there. What good does it do one to be present everywhere? Today man can never be alone with himself, as he could in the Middle Ages. The result of all this is that anguish is absolute and confusion total.

Thus, we can no longer willingly surrender to the image on the screen, even for a few hours; too many alternative sounds and images are constantly vying for our attention.

23. *Film theaters are no longer the social gathering places they were from 1900 to the late 1960s.* With the rise of television, families began to stay home. Whatever sense of community that had existed within the darkened space of the cinema auditorium was abolished. With the advent of DVDs and videotapes, one can now control the length and intensity of the viewing experience through the medium of the remote control. Is this section moving slowly? No need to wait; fast-forward to the next car crash. Would you like to repeat a particular segment? It's as simple as pushing a button.

24. *We no longer believe in the images we see on the screen, if we ever did; now their syntheticity is a demonstrated fact.* The classical shot structure employed by four generations of filmmakers has been abandoned for a scattershot explosion of images, with arbitrarily shifting colors, frame sizes, film stocks, video and film images intermixed, rapid cutting— anything to keep the viewer momentarily dazzled. The courage to hold on to a close-up of an actor's face, the patience to build up a mood through a lengthy establishing sequence (as in Clouzot's *Wages of Fear*, 1953), the faith that classical directors had in the audience's ability and willingness to follow them through a slowly developing and complex narrative—all these qualities are things of the past. Instant audience capture with a violent opening, regular doses of violence and brutality thereafter (or ruthless sentimentality), and a cutting style that resembles nothing so much as a bored insomniac maniacally channel-surfing at 3 A.M., desperately searching for *some* image to hang on to—these are the hallmarks of the new cinema, where the viewer cannot be left unattended for a second.

25. *And yet, despite all this, the cinema will live forever.* What I'm really talking about here is a technology shift, albeit a profound one, one that will end "movies as we know them," but not the cinema itself. It may be that 35mm film will be consigned to the scrap heap of memory. All-digital production and exhibition will offer us an entirely different sort of theatrical viewing experience. Audiences keep getting younger and more impatient, and yet the classics of the past will continue to haunt

us, informing our collective consciousness of mid-to-late-twentieth-century culture. It is entirely appropriate that we should witness this seismic adjustment in the first few years of the new century; seen from this perspective, one might just as easily argue that far from dying, the movies are reinventing themselves for the patrons of a new era. No, we'll never see the like of *Casablanca* again, or *Pillow Talk* (1959), or *Psycho* (1960), but then again, the late-twentieth-century novel is an altogether different affair from the days when F. Scott Fitzgerald commanded the public's attention, and drama has moved a long way from *Waiting for Lefty* and *Death of a Salesman*. When Antonin Artaud declares in *The Theatre and Its Double* that "the masterpieces of the past are no good for us," he is partly right. They do not speak to our present condition, but they reveal much about ourselves as members of a global imagistic tribe; they tell us tales of our ancestors, they serve as totemic emblems of our earlier age. Film "as we know it" has always been dying and is always being reborn. What we are witnessing now is nothing more nor less than the dawn of a new grammar, a new technological delivery and production system, with a new series of plots, tropes, iconic conventions, and stars. What happens next is a matter for future historians to document, but for the moment, we must be content to speculate, and realize that no matter how the cinematic medium transforms itself in the coming decades, it will always continue to build on, and carry forward, the past.

Contributors

PAUL ARTHUR is a Professor of film and literature at Montclair State University. He is a regular contributor to *Film Comment* and *Cineaste* and is coeditor of *Millennium Film Journal*.

WHEELER WINSTON DIXON is the Ryan Professor of Film Studies, chairperson of the film studies program, professor of English at the University of Nebraska, Lincoln, and the editor-in-chief of the *Quarterly Review of Film and Video*. His newest books are *The Second Century of Cinema: The Past and Future of the Moving Image*; *Film Genre 2000: New Critical Essays*; and *Disaster and Memory: Celebrity Culture and the Crisis of Hollywood*.

THOMAS DOHERTY is an associate professor of American studies and chair of the film studies program at Brandeis University. He serves on the editorial board of the film magazine *Cineaste* and is the author of *Teenagers and Teenpics: The Juvenilization of American Movies in the 1950s*; *Projections of War: Hollywood, American Culture, and World War II*; and *Pre-Code Hollywood: Immorality and Insurrection in American Cinema, 1930–1934*.

THOMAS ELSAESSER is a professor in the department of art and culture at the University of Amsterdam and chair of film and television studies. His writings on film theory, national cinema, and film history are frequently featured in collections and anthologies. His books as author and editor include *New German Cinema: A History*; *Early Cinema: Space, Frame, Narrative*; *Writing for the Medium: Television in Transition*; *A Second Life: German Cinema's First Decades*; *Fassbinder's Germany: History, Identity, Subject*; *Cinema Futures: Cain, Abel or Cable*; *Weimar Cinema and After*, and *Metropolis*.

KRIN GABBARD is a professor of comparative literature at the State University of New York at Stony Brook. He is the author of *Jammin' at the Margins: Jazz and the American Cinema* and *Psychiatry and the Cinema*.

HENRY A. GIROUX is a writer and professor at the Pennsylvania State University. His most recent books include *Stealing Innocence; Impure Acts; Beyond the Corporate University;* and *Public Spaces, Private Lives: Beyond the Culture of Cynicism.*

HEATHER HENDERSHOT is an assistant professor of media studies at Queens College/CUNY. She is the author of *Saturday Morning Censors: Television Regulation before the V-Chip,* and she is currently completing a book on conservative evangelical Christian culture.

JAN-CHRISTOPHER HORAK is curator at the Hollywood Entertainment Museum. He was founding director of archives and collections at Universal Studios; director of the Munich Filmmuseum; and senior curator of film at George Eastman House. He is a visiting professor in critical studies at UCLA, and has published books on film and photography, avant-garde cinema, the Hollywood studio system, German exiles in Hollywood, and Dr. Arnold Fanck.

ALEXANDRA JUHASZ is an associate professor of media studies at Pitzer College. In the 1990s she wrote books about activist AIDS video (*AIDS TV*) and feminist media history (*Women of Vision*), and produced the feature film *The Watermelon Woman* as well as other feminist/activist media.

CHARLIE KEIL is an associate professor of history and cinema studies at the University of Toronto. He is the author of *Early American Cinema in Transition: Story, Style and Filmmaking, 1907–1913* and has published extensively on early cinema.

CHUCK KLEINHANS coedits *Jump Cut: A Review of Contemporary Media* and is director of graduate studies, radio/television/film at Northwestern University. His current research develops a sociological aesthetics of U.S. experimental film/video.

JON LEWIS is a professor of English at Oregon State University, where he has taught film and cultural studies since 1983. His books include: *The Road to Romance and Ruin: Teen Films and Youth Culture; Whom God Wishes to Destroy . . . Francis Coppola and the New Hollywood; Hollywood v.*

Hard Core: How the Struggle over Censorship Saved the Modern Film Industry; and (as editor) *The New American Cinema*.

ERIC S. MALLIN is an associate professor of English at the University of Texas at Austin, where he specializes in Shakespeare and early modern literature. His essay here is part of his forthcoming study on the transformations of Shakespearean texts and subtexts in popular cinema.

LAURA U. MARKS, a critic, theorist, and curator of independent media, is an assistant professor of film studies at Carleton University. She is the author of *The Skin of the Film: Intercultural Cinema, Embodiment, and the Senses*.

KATHLEEN McHUGH, an associate professor of comparative literature and film, teaches in the film and visual culture program at the University of California, Riverside. She is the author of *American Domesticity: From How-To Manual to Hollywood Melodrama*. She has published articles on domesticity, feminism, and film theory, the avant-garde, and autobiography in such journals as *Cultural Studies, Jump Cut, Screen, South Atlantic Quarterly*, and *Velvet Light Trap*. She is currently working on a book-length study of experimental filmic autobiography.

PAT MELLENCAMP is a distinguished professor of art history at the University of Wisconsin-Milwaukee. She is the author of *A Fine Romance . . . Five Ages of Film Feminism; High Anxiety: Catastrophe, Scandal, Age and Comedy; Indiscretions: Avant-Garde Film and Video*, and editor of *Cinema Histories/Cinema Practices; Re-Vision: Essays in Feminist Film Criticism; The Logics of Television*; and *Essays in Cultural Criticism*.

JERRY MOSHER teaches film and new media studies in the department of communication studies at California State University, Los Angeles. He is a doctoral candidate in the department of film and television at the University of California, Los Angeles. His dissertation examines how the American film industry has historically figured the fat body.

HAMID NAFICY, an associate professor of film and media studies at Rice University, Houston, has published extensively about theories of exile and displacement; exilic and diasporic cultures, films, and media;

and Iranian, Middle Eastern, and Third World cinemas. His latest books are *Home, Exile, Homeland: Film, Media, and the Politics of Place* and *An Accented Cinema: Exilic and Diaspora Filmmaking.*

CHON A. NORIEGA is an associate professor in the UCLA department of film and television. He is the author of *Shot in America: Television, the State, and the Rise of Chicano Cinema* and editor of eight books, including *I, Carmelita Tropicana: Performing between Cultures* and *Visible Nations: Latin American Cinema and Video.* Since 1996 he has been the editor of *Aztlán: A Journal of Chicano Studies.* He recently curated the art exhibition *East of the River: Chicano Art Collectors Anonymous* at the Santa Monica Museum of Art.

DANA POLAN is a professor of critical studies in the School of Cinema-TV at the University of Southern California. He is the author of five books on film, including *Pulp Fiction* and *Power and Paranoia: History, Narrative and the American Cinema, 1940–1950.*

MURRAY POMERANCE is the chair of the department of sociology at Ryerson Polytechnic University and the author of *Magia d'Amore*; *Ludwig Bemelmans: A Bibliography*; and *The Complete Parititas.* He has edited a number of collections, including *Pictures of a Generation on Hold: Selected Papers* and *Bang Bang, Shoot Shoot! Essays on Guns and Popular Culture.* He is at work on a volume of essays about Alfred Hitchcock.

HILARY RADNER is an associate professor in the department of film, television, and theater at the University of Notre Dame. She is author of *Shopping Around: Feminine Culture and the Pursuit of Pleasure,* and coeditor of *Film Theory Goes to the Movies*; *Constructing the New Consumer Society*; and *Swinging Single: Representing Sexuality in the 1960s.*

RALPH E. RODRIGUEZ is an assistant professor of English and comparative literature at the Pennsylvania State University. He has published and presented papers on varying aspects of Latina/o culture and politics.

R. L. RUTSKY teaches film studies at the University of California, Irvine. His work has recently appeared in *Film Quarterly, Discourse,* and

Style, and he is the author of *High TechnË: Art and Technology from the Machine Aesthetic to the Posthuman*.

JAMES SCHAMUS is copresident of the New York–based independent film production company Good Machine and an associate professor of film history and theory at Columbia University. He has served as screenwriter and producer on such films as *The Ice Storm* and *Crouching Tiger, Hidden Dragon*.

CHRISTOPHER SHARRETT is a professor of communication at Seton Hall University. He is the author of the recent book *Mythologies of Violence in Postmodern Media* as well as numerous essays published in *Cineaste*, *Film Quarterly*, and *Journal of Popular Film and Television*.

DAVID R. SHUMWAY is a professor of English and literary and cultural studies, and director of the Center for Cultural Analysis, Carnegie Mellon University, where he teaches film, cultural theory, and American literature. He is the author of *Michel Foucault* and *Creating American Civilization: A Genealogy of American Literature as an Academic Discipline*. He has recently completed a book on romance and intimacy in film and other texts.

ROBERT SKLAR is a professor of cinema in the *Tisch School of the Arts*, New York University. His book, *Film: An International History of the Medium*, won a Kroszna-Krausz award. From 1996–1999 he was a member of the selection committee for the New York Film Festival. He is a member of the National Society of Film Critics.

MURRAY SMITH is the chair of film studies at the University of Kent at Canterbury. He is the author of *Engaging Characters: Fiction, Emotion, and the Cinema*, and coeditor of *Film Theory and Philosophy* and *Contemporary Hollywood Cinema*.

MARITA STURKEN is an associate professor at the Annenberg School for Communication at the University of Southern California. She is the author of *Tangled Memories: The Vietnam War, the AIDS Epidemic, and the Politics of Remembering*; *Thelma and Louise*; and, with Lisa Cartwright, *Practices of Looking: An Introduction to Visual Culture*.

IMRE SZEMAN is an assistant professor of English and cultural studies and associate director of the Institute on Globalization at McMaster University. He is coeditor of *Pierre Bourdieu: Fieldwork in Literature* and author of *Zones of Instability: Literature, Postcolonialism and the Nation*.

FRANK P. TOMASULO teaches film history and theory at Georgia State University in Atlanta and is the editor of *Cinema Journal*. Tomasulo has published over fifty articles and essays on film and television topics, including several on Steven Spielberg.

MAUREEN TURIM is a professor of English and film studies at the University of Florida. She is the author of *Abstraction in Avant-Garde Films*; *Flashbacks in Film: Memory and History*; and *The Films of Oshima Nagisa: Images of a Japanese Iconoclast*. She has published over sixty essays in anthologies and journals on a wide range of theoretical, historical, and aesthetic issues in cinema and video, art, cultural studies, feminist and psychoanalytic theory, and comparative literature.

JUSTIN WYATT is a senior research analyst at Frank N. Magid Associates, a marketing research and consulting firm working in the areas of entertainment, new media, and the Internet. He holds a Ph.D. in critical studies from UCLA and has taught at the University of Arizona and the University of North Texas.

ELIZABETH YOUNG is an associate professor of English at Mount Holyoke College. She has published essays on the horror film in *Camera Obscura* and *Feminist Studies* and is the author of *Disarming the Nation: Women's Writing and the American Civil War*.

Index

Kaufman, Philip, 24
Kazan, Elia, 76, 77, 141, 142, 145, 146
Keaton, Diane, 196
Keep It for Yourself, 63
Keitel, Harvey, 145, 279
Kennedy, Beth, 35
Kennedy, John F., 154, 155
Kermode, Frank, 352n. 5
Kidman, Nicole, 25
Kids, 261–263
Killers, The, 153
Kilmer, Val, 329
King of New York, 322–324
King, Rodney, 7, 300–303
King, Stephen, 237
Klein, Naomi, 56
Knack, The, 360
Koresh, David, 354n. 21
Korine, Harmony, 7, 261–268
Korine, Joyce, 267
Kragh-Jacobsen, Soren, 266
Kubrick, Stanley, 23–27, 31n. 1, 152

La Cava, Gregory, 152
La Dolce Vita, 357
La Gran Carpa de los Rasquachis, 180
Lacan, Jacques, 161, 162
Laemmle, Carl, 35
Lake, Ricki, 246n. 1
Lalonde, Paul, 37
Lalonde, Peter, 337
Lambert, Phyllis, 36
Lanchester, Elsa, 226–228, 232–235
Landau, George, 270
Lang, Fritz, 85
Larson, Doran, 345
Last Broadcast, The, 359
Late Great Planet Earth, The, 335, 340n. 20
L'Avventura, 357
Lawless, The, 176
Lawrence of Arabia, 34
Le Mepris, 283, 356
Leave It to Beaver, 319
Leaving Las Vegas, 360
Lee, Ang, 61, 63, 65–69
Lee, Sheila Jackson, 275
Lee, Tommy, 7, 287, 290–296, 298n. 1
Leeson, Lynn Hershman, 165
Left Behind (film series), 337, 340n. 28
Left Behind (novel), 335, 337, 340n. 28

LeHaye, Tim, 335–338, 340n. 25
LeMaitre, Willy, 305, 306, 310–312
Lemberg, Kristin, 306, 313
Leno, Jay, 290
Leonard, Cheryl, 306, 308
Leonard, Josh, 105, 110–113
Les dames du Bois de Boulogne, 363
Levey, William, 225
Levin, Gerald, 259
Levy, Daniel, 63
Lewinsky, Monica, 296
Lewis, Jerry, 221n. 1, 237, 243
Lewis, Juliette, 198, 199
Liar, 360
Life Is Beautiful, 357
Life Is Cheap . . . But Toilet Paper Is Expensive, 280
Lincoln, Abraham, 123, 136, 150, 151
Lindsey, Hal, 335, 340n. 20
Lion King, The, 11, 21
Lions Gate, 205, 230
Lipsitz, George, 176
Little Buddha, 192
Little, Dwight, 155
Littleton (Colorado school shootings), 164
Long Gray Line, The, 151
Long Riders, The, 320
Looker, 351n. 2
Los Angeles Film Critics Association, 28, 31
Lost in Space, 363
Lost World: Jurassic Park, The, 349, 350
Love Affair (1939), 145,
Love Affair (1994), 144–148
Lovers on the Bridge (*Les Amants du Pont-Neuf*), 265
Lowe, Rob, 289
Lucas, George, 359, 361, 362
Lumiere and Company, 352n. 5
Lumiere, August, 351, 358
Lumiere, Louis, 351, 358
Lurie, John, 279, 282
Lusk, Mark, 341n. 34
Lyotard, Jean-Francois, 158

Macbeth, 105, 106, 108–113, 114n. 4
Macho Dancer, 69
Madonna, 298n. 2
Magnificent Ambersons, The, 278
Magritte, Rene, 158